HOUNDED

Volume 3

D1235722

CHECKER BOOK PUBLISHING GROUP

HOUNDED

NEGATION

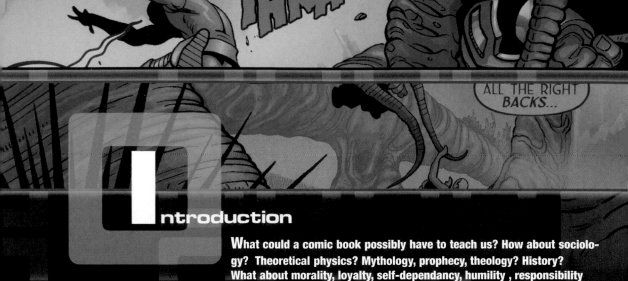

ALL THE RIGHT BACKS...

Introduction

What could a comic book possibly have to teach us? How about sociology? Theoretical physics? Mythology, prophecy, theology? History? What about morality, loyalty, self-dependancy, humility , responsibility and honor? Sorry, is this too much heavy stuff to think about? Too much critical thinking? Well, good news, Negation® will teach you aspects of all of these, and you won't even realize it...

In Tony Bedard (X-Men, Retro Rocket) and penciler Paul Pelletier's (Exiles, Green Lantern) story, there are few left of the human race on the planet Earth. Was there a war or a pestilence or famine? Even the Atlanteans that stayed behind to assist the eventual human transition to a higher plain did not awake from stasis in time. The landscape is one of desolation and ruin. What was the cause of the apocalypse? Only a small number of survivors in Australia have the answer - human arrogance.

The "Mad God" Charon of the Negation Universe and his Lawbringers turn their sights toward the bright universe - our universe - as their next conquest, kidnapping a group of its inhabitants for testing. Led by human tactician Obregon Kaine, the prisoners, some bearing Sigils, have staged a daring escape and allied with the mysterious and powerful Australians to rescue the baby Memi and the Atlantean Gammid from the Negation Throneworld.

Back to the deep stuff for a minute:

As the philosopher George Santiana said, "Those who forget the past are doomed to repeat it." A tired, old over-worked quote designed to get school-kids to study, you're thinking. Maybe, but oh, so apropos. After all, Negation® is set in the future. You're thinking, *but its only a story*. The Orwellian-like Negation police-state only exists Bedard's imagination, doesn't it? *Homeland Security* ring a bell? While you're at it, think about the ramifications of a disposable workforce in a capitalist society. Has that happened yet? Hmmm. Many times the story speaks of the Earth's past, which, of course, is our present and not-so-distant future. The characters are desperate to know just what event or events set these occurences in motion. Maybe if they can find out how Charon came to be, then they can defeat him.

Will the different races in the group be able to harness their new powers and set aside their differences to focus on a single goal? Will emotion override wisdom? How long can this gang of outlaws possibly withstand the Negation armies? What will they learn about the past that may give them the power to change the future - a proverbial coin to pay the ferryman?

See you around the bright universe,

Cammie C. Ledbetter
Editor, Checker Books

printed in china

NEGATION
KEY ISSUE
NEGATION
NEGATION
NEGATION
NEGATION
NEGATION

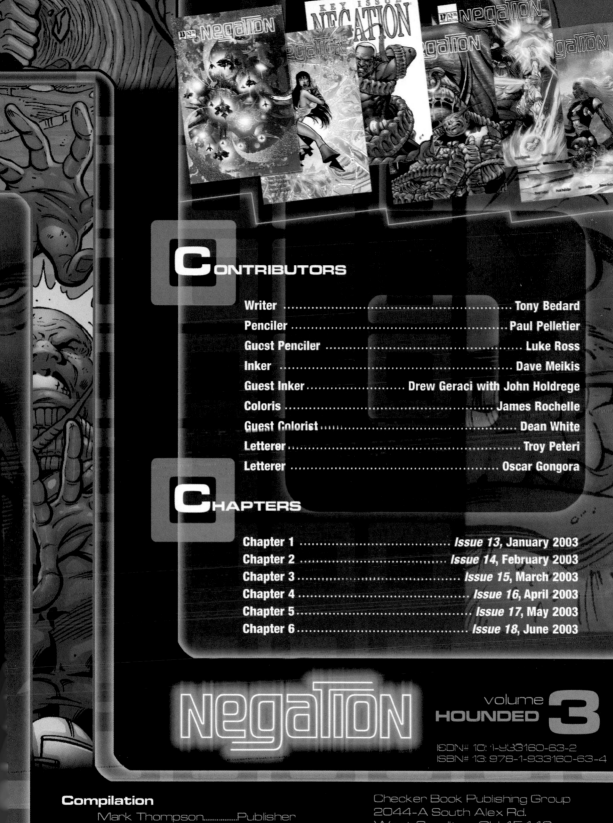

CONTRIBUTORS

Writer	Tony Bedard
Penciler	Paul Pelletier
Guest Penciler	Luke Ross
Inker	Dave Meikis
Guest Inker	Drew Geraci with John Holdrege
Coloris	James Rochelle
Guest Colorist	Dean White
Letterer	Troy Peteri
Letterer	Oscar Gongora

CHAPTERS

NEGATION

volume 3
HOUNDED

ISBN# 10: 1-933160-63-2
ISBN# 13: 978-1-933160-63-4

Compilation

Mark Thompson........Publisher
Stani Butler........Controller
Andrew Paavola........Graphic Design
Cammie Ledbetter........Graphic Design / Editorial
Trevor Goodman........Graphic Design
Susan Koller........Publicity Director

Checker Book Publishing Group
2044-A South Alex Rd.
West Carollton, OH 45449

Visit us at www.checkerbpg.com

No Solicitations Accepted

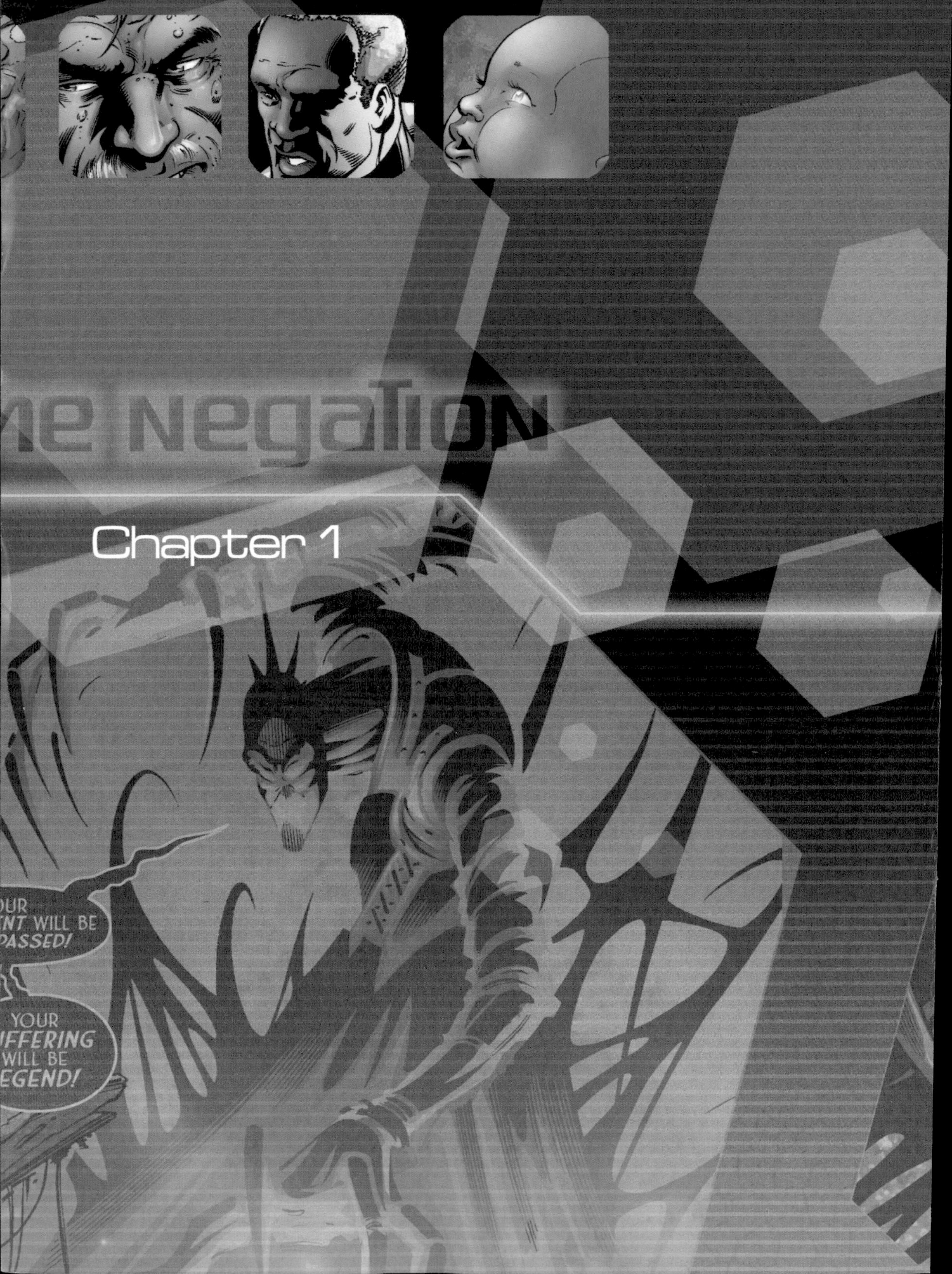
NEGATION

Chapter 1

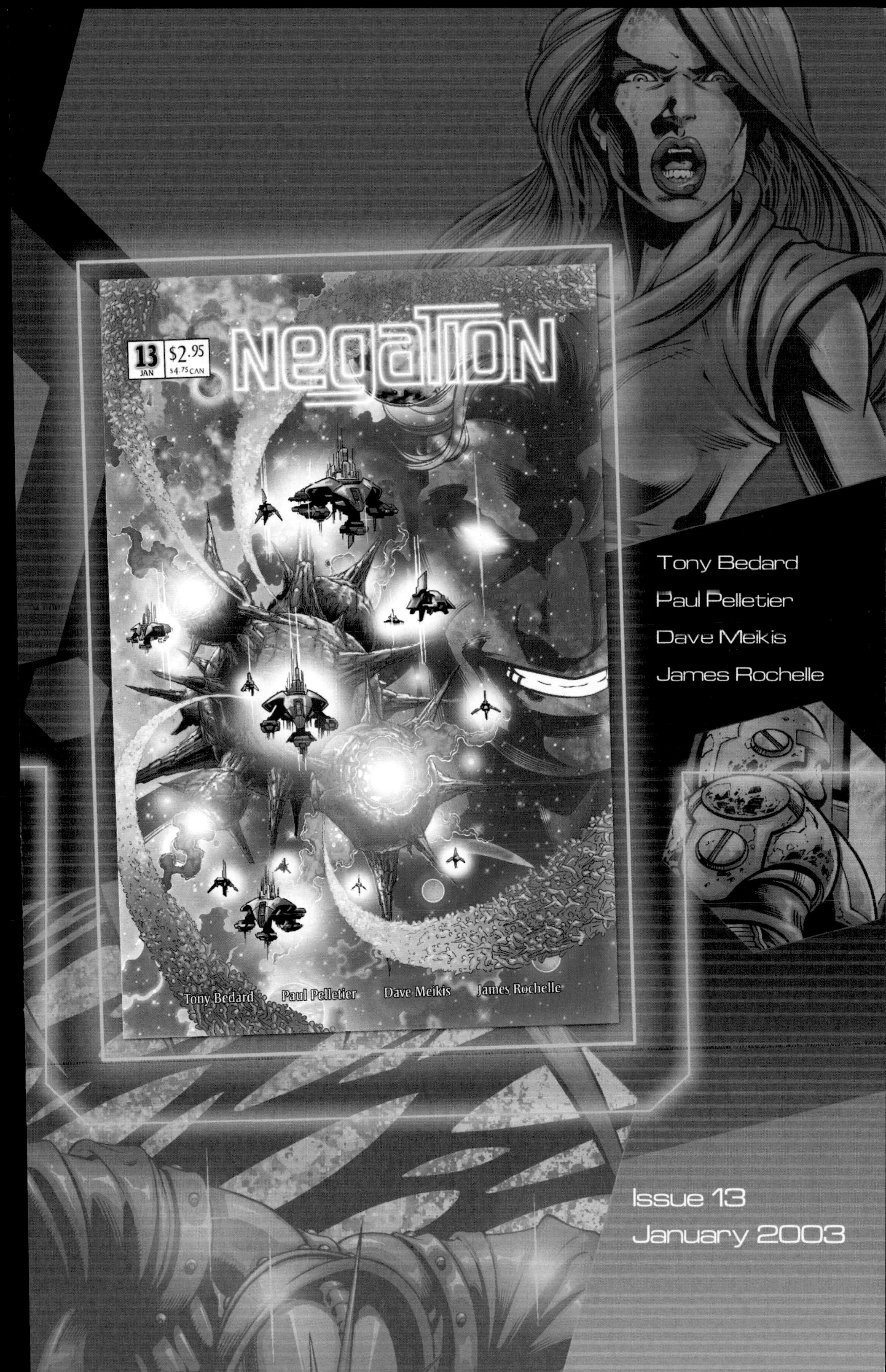
13 JAN
$2.95 $4.75 CAN
Negation
Tony Bedard Paul Pelletier Dave Meikis James Rochelle
Tony Bedard
Paul Pelletier
Dave Meikis
James Rochelle
Issue 13
January 2003

The God-Emperor CHARON conquered His chaotic universe and forged an intergalactic empire known as:

the NEGATION

Charon now casts His baleful eye across the gulf between realities and covets the bright and thriving worlds in *our* cosmos.

On His orders, one hundred strangers were abducted from our universe and brought to His dark realm to be studied and tested on a harsh prison-world. Some captives bore a mysterious mark known as the Sigil, granting them astonishing abilities. Others were inherently powerful. Most, however, were simple, ordinary humans.

One such human named Obregon Kaine led a bloody uprising against the Negation prison warden, Komptin. The few captives who escaped along with Kaine wander the hostile stars, seeking a way home.

Kaine and company have joined forces with a group of superhuman Australians led by a woman called Samakar. Kaine's group seeks to rescue baby Memi. Samakar's people are searching for their Atlantean ally, Gammid. Both of their lost comrades are being held captive on the Negation Throneworld by Charon and his enforcer, Lawbringer Qztr. Now the fugitives and the Australians launch a daring raid on the heart of the evil empire...

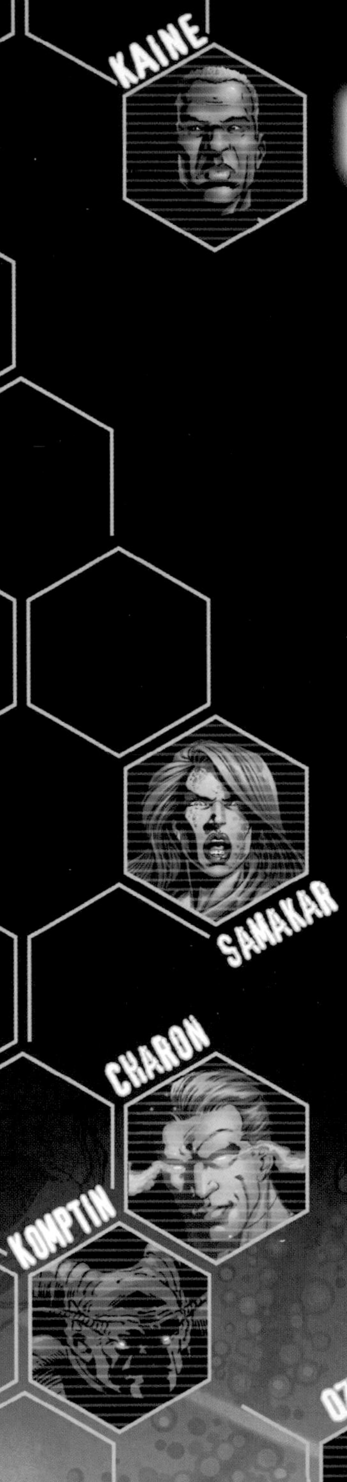
KAINE
SAMAKAR
CHARON
KOMPTIN

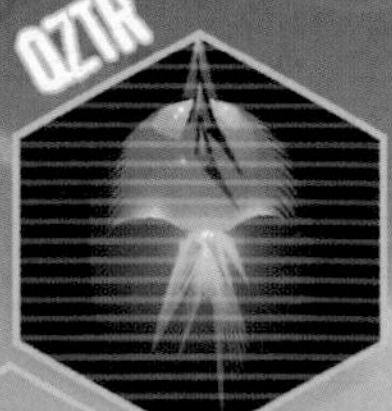
QZTR

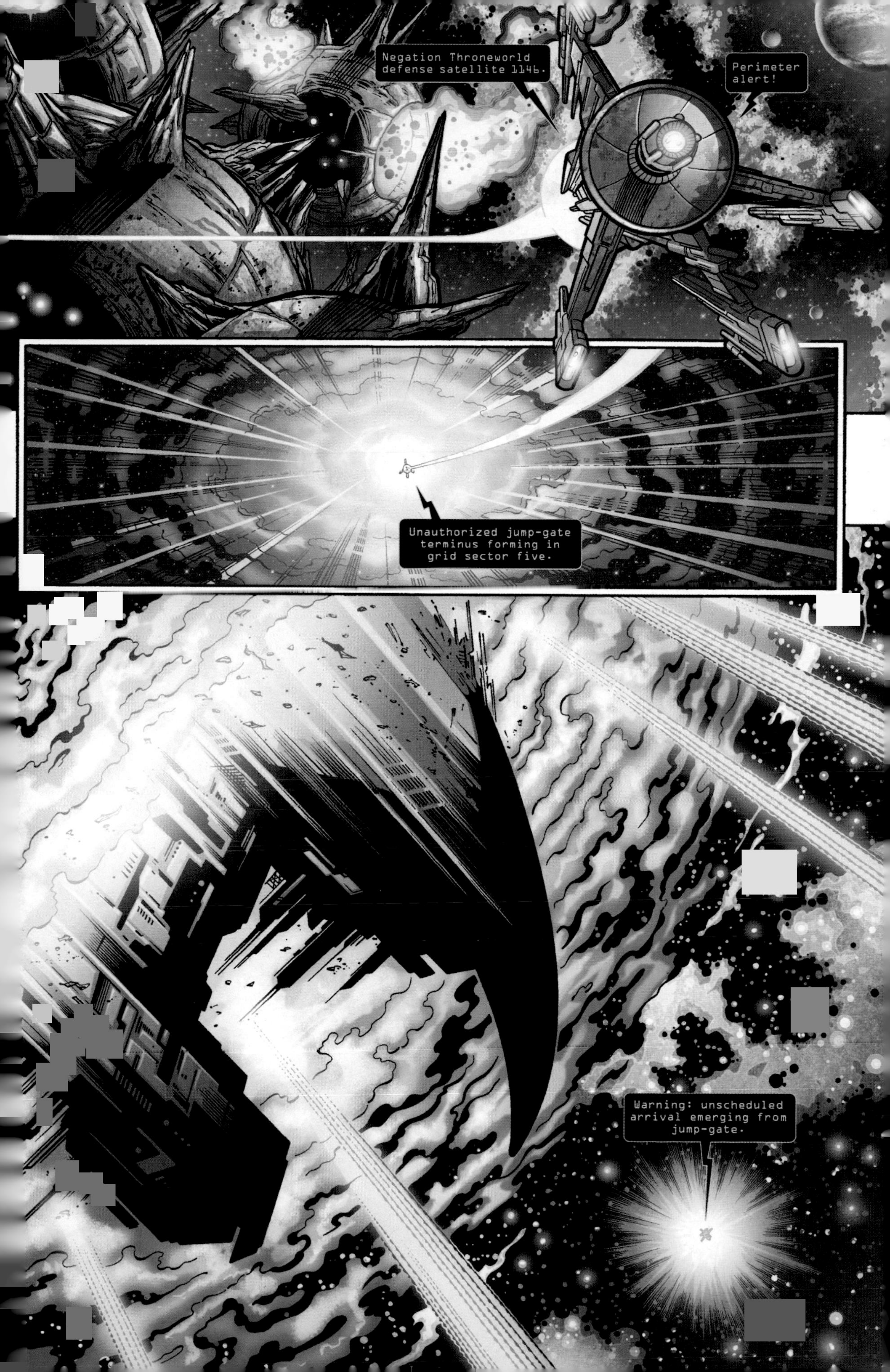
Negation Throneworld defense satellite 1146.
Perimeter alert!
Unauthorized jump-gate terminus forming in grid sector five.
Warning: unscheduled arrival emerging from jump-gate.

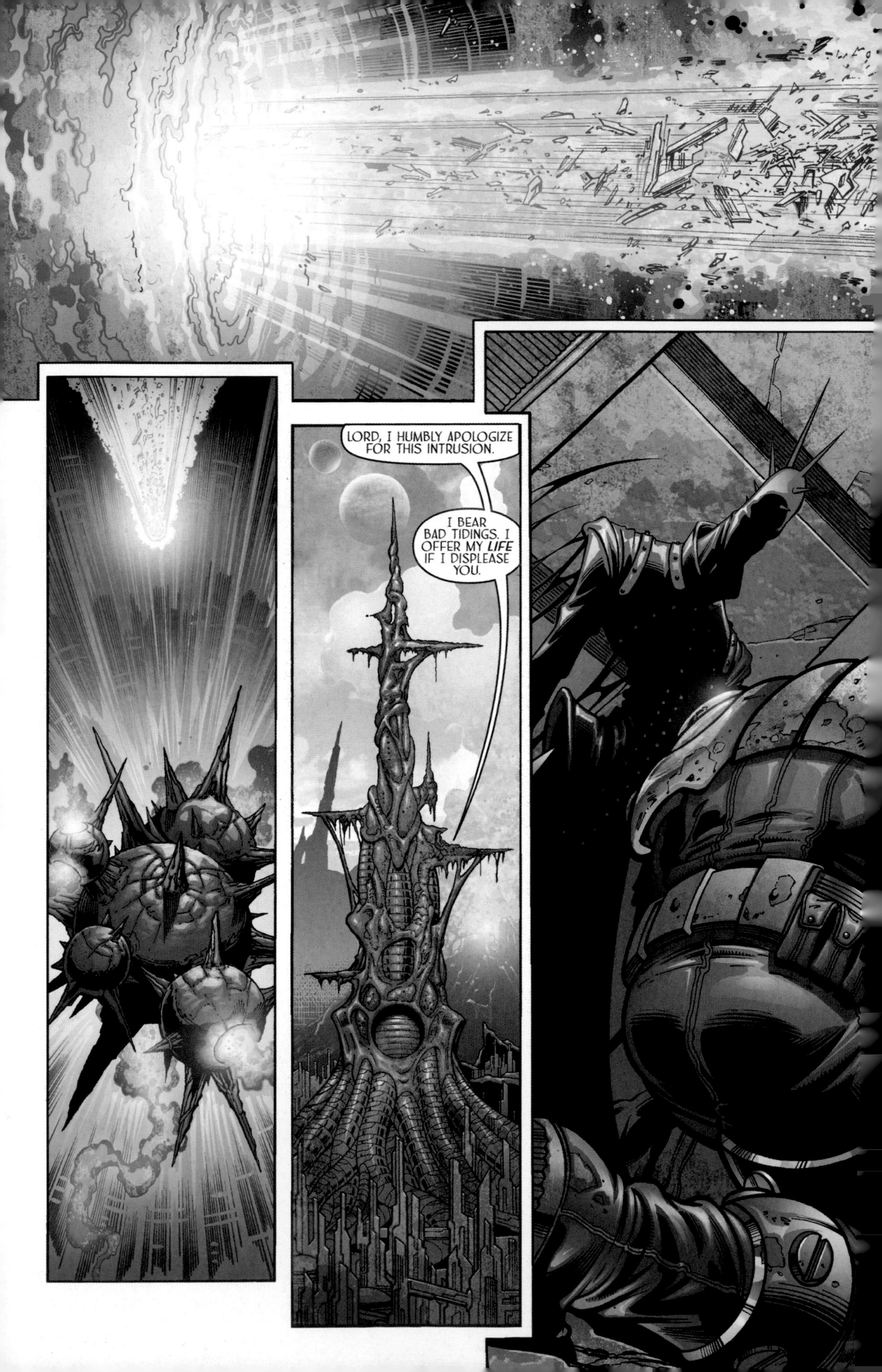
LORD, I HUMBLY APOLOGIZE FOR THIS INTRUSION.
I BEAR BAD TIDINGS. I OFFER MY *LIFE* IF I DISPLEASE YOU.

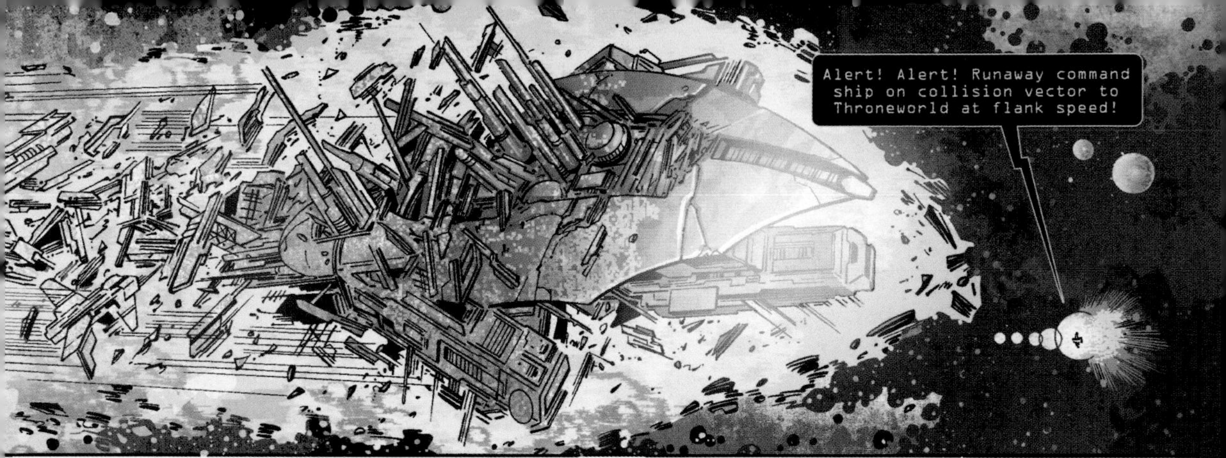
Alert! Alert! Runaway command ship on collision vector to Throneworld at flank speed!

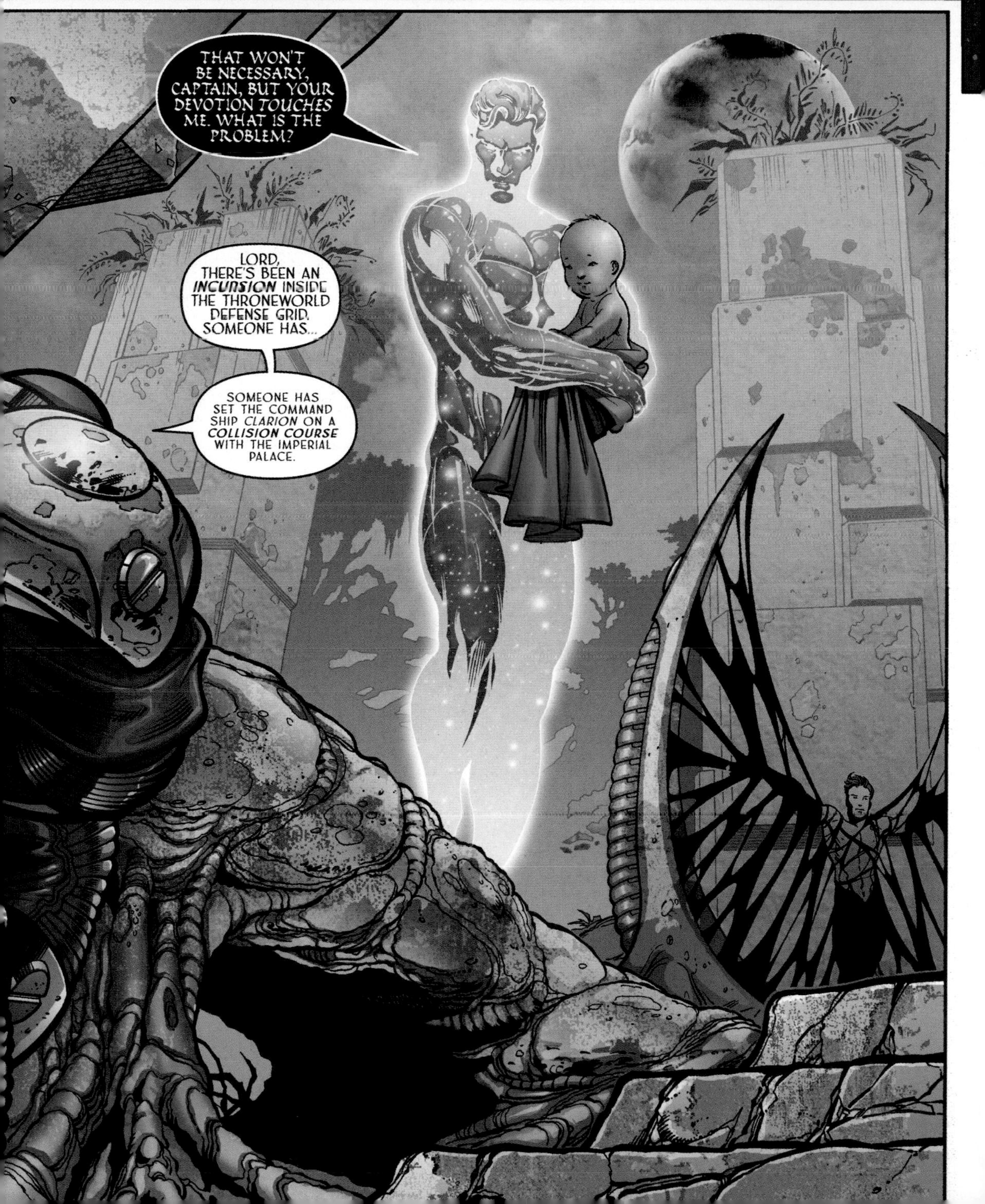
THAT WON'T BE NECESSARY, CAPTAIN, BUT YOUR DEVOTION *TOUCHES* ME. WHAT IS THE PROBLEM?
LORD, THERE'S BEEN AN *INCURSION* INSIDE THE THRONEWORLD DEFENSE GRID. SOMEONE HAS...
SOMEONE HAS SET THE COMMAND SHIP *CLARION* ON A *COLLISION COURSE* WITH THE IMPERIAL PALACE.

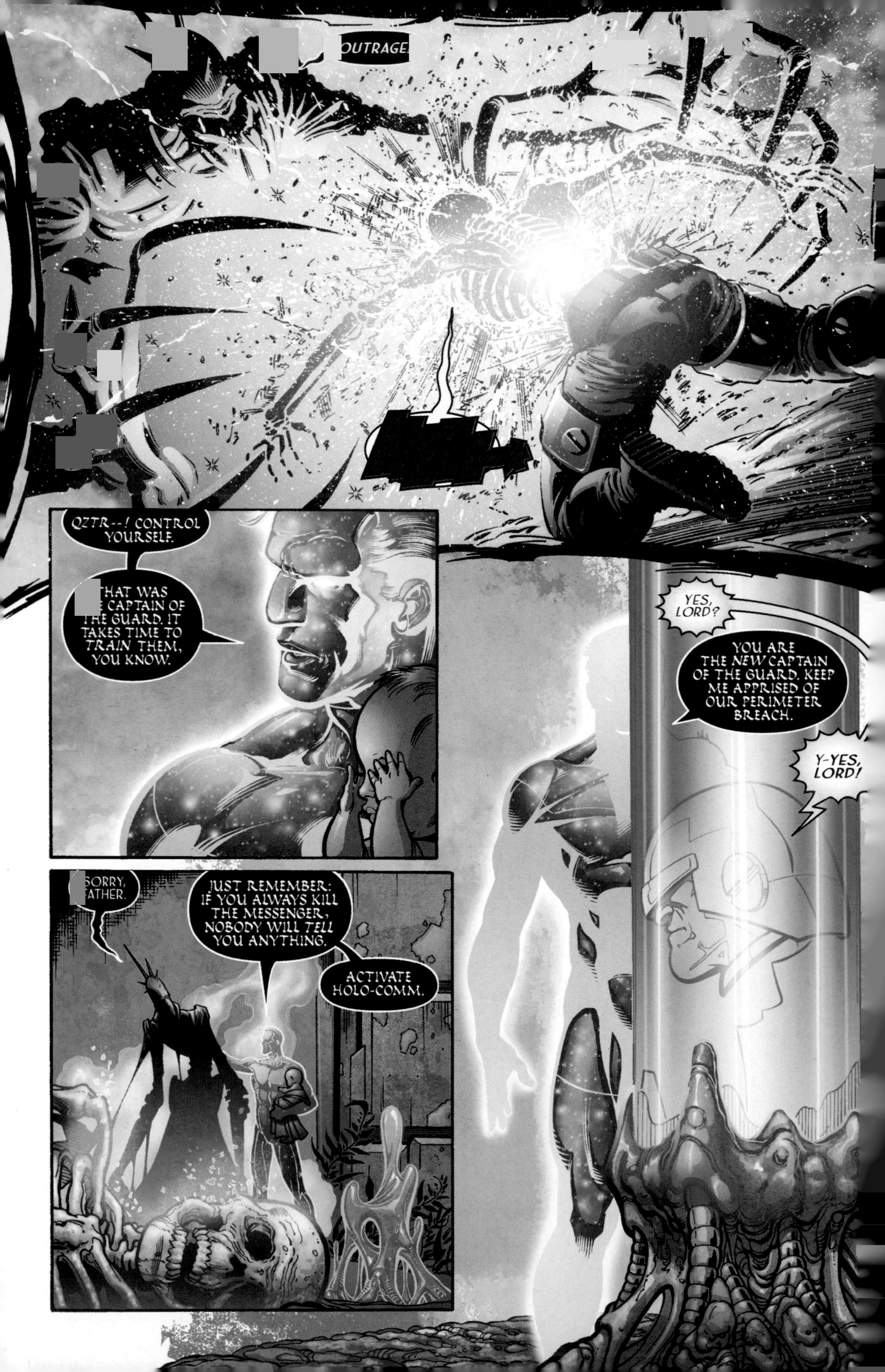

OUTRAGE.
[redacted]
QZTR--! CONTROL YOURSELF.
THAT WAS E CAPTAIN OF THE GUARD. IT TAKES TIME TO *TRAIN* THEM, YOU KNOW.
SORRY, ATHER.
JUST REMEMBER: IF YOU ALWAYS KILL THE MESSENGER, NOBODY WILL *TELL* YOU ANYTHING.
ACTIVATE HOLO-COMM.
YES, LORD?
YOU ARE THE *NEW* CAPTAIN OF THE GUARD. KEEP ME APPRISED OF OUR PERIMETER BREACH.
Y-YES, LORD!

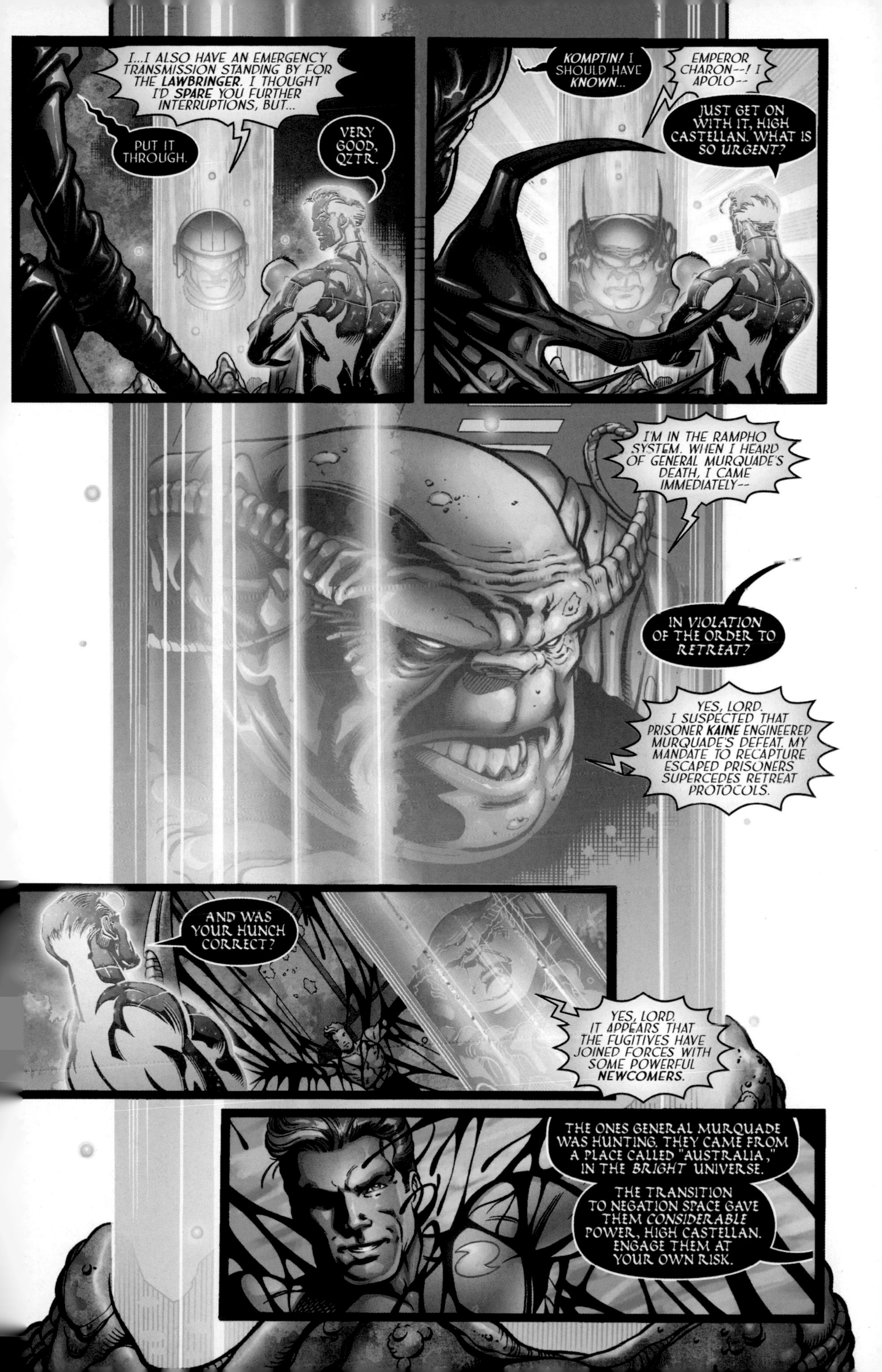
I...I ALSO HAVE AN EMERGENCY TRANSMISSION STANDING BY FOR THE LAWBRINGER. I THOUGHT I'D SPARE YOU FURTHER INTERRUPTIONS, BUT...
PUT IT THROUGH.
VERY GOOD, QZTR.
KOMPTIN! I SHOULD HAVE KNOWN...
EMPEROR CHARON--! I APOLO--
JUST GET ON WITH IT, HIGH CASTELLAN. WHAT IS SO URGENT?
I'M IN THE RAMPHO SYSTEM. WHEN I HEARD OF GENERAL MURQUADE'S DEATH, I CAME IMMEDIATELY--
IN VIOLATION OF THE ORDER TO RETREAT?
YES, LORD. I SUSPECTED THAT PRISONER KAINE ENGINEERED MURQUADE'S DEFEAT. MY MANDATE TO RECAPTURE ESCAPED PRISONERS SUPERCEDES RETREAT PROTOCOLS.
AND WAS YOUR HUNCH CORRECT?
YES, LORD. IT APPEARS THAT THE FUGITIVES HAVE JOINED FORCES WITH SOME POWERFUL NEWCOMERS.
THE ONES GENERAL MURQUADE WAS HUNTING. THEY CAME FROM A PLACE CALLED "AUSTRALIA," IN THE BRIGHT UNIVERSE.
THE TRANSITION TO NEGATION SPACE GAVE THEM CONSIDERABLE POWER, HIGH CASTELLAN. ENGAGE THEM AT YOUR OWN RISK.

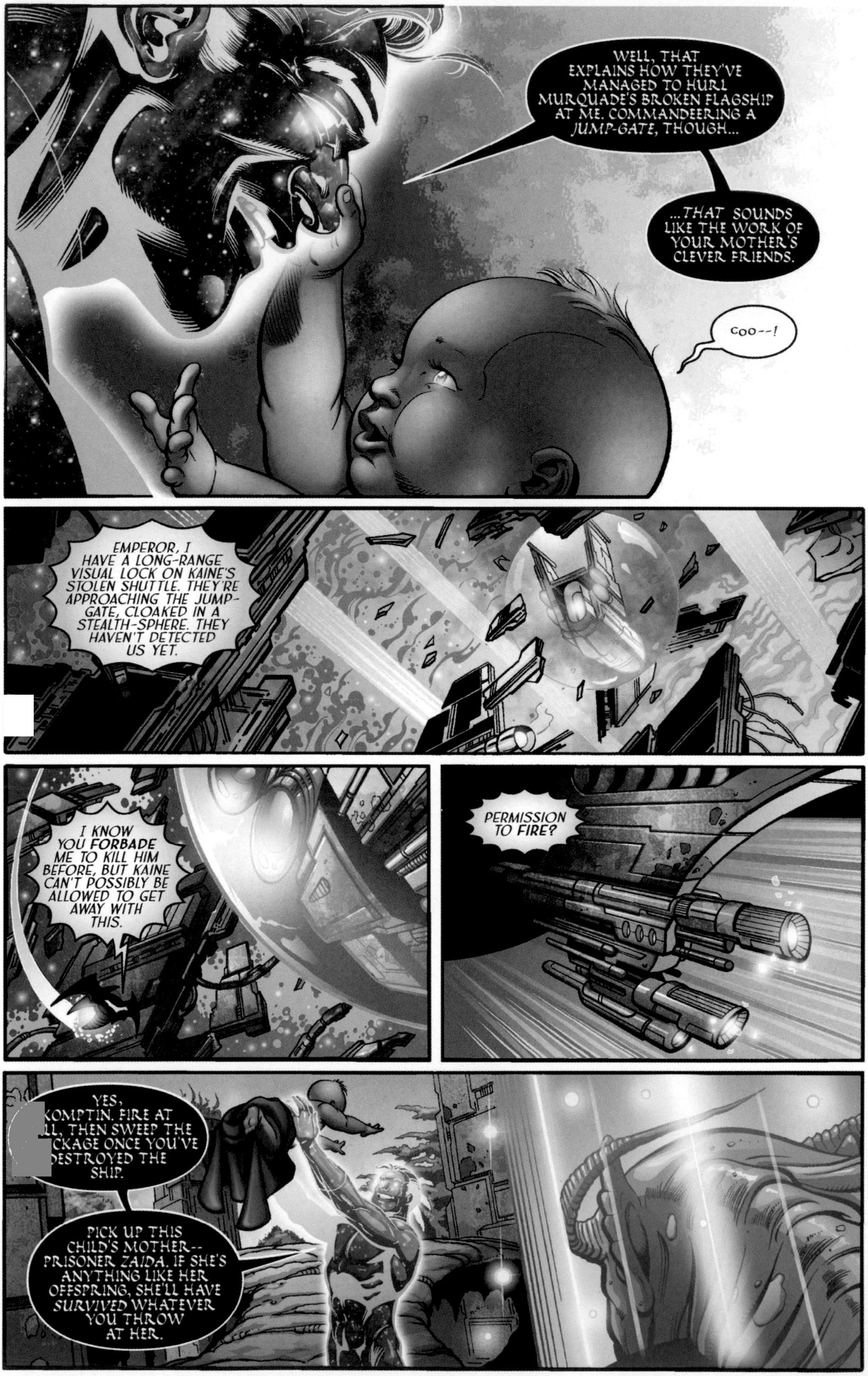
WELL, THAT EXPLAINS HOW THEY'VE MANAGED TO HURL MURQUADE'S BROKEN FLAGSHIP AT ME. COMMANDEERING A JUMP-GATE, THOUGH...
...THAT SOUNDS LIKE THE WORK OF YOUR MOTHER'S CLEVER FRIENDS.
COO--!
EMPEROR, I HAVE A LONG-RANGE VISUAL LOCK ON KAINE'S STOLEN SHUTTLE. THEY'RE APPROACHING THE JUMP-GATE, CLOAKED IN A STEALTH-SPHERE. THEY HAVEN'T DETECTED US YET.
I KNOW YOU FORBADE ME TO KILL HIM BEFORE, BUT KAINE CAN'T POSSIBLY BE ALLOWED TO GET AWAY WITH THIS.
PERMISSION TO FIRE?
YES, KOMPTIN. FIRE AT LL, THEN SWEEP THE CKAGE ONCE YOU'VE DESTROYED THE SHIP.
PICK UP THIS CHILD'S MOTHER-- PRISONER ZAIDA. IF SHE'S ANYTHING LIKE HER OFFSPRING, SHE'LL HAVE SURVIVED WHATEVER YOU THROW AT HER.

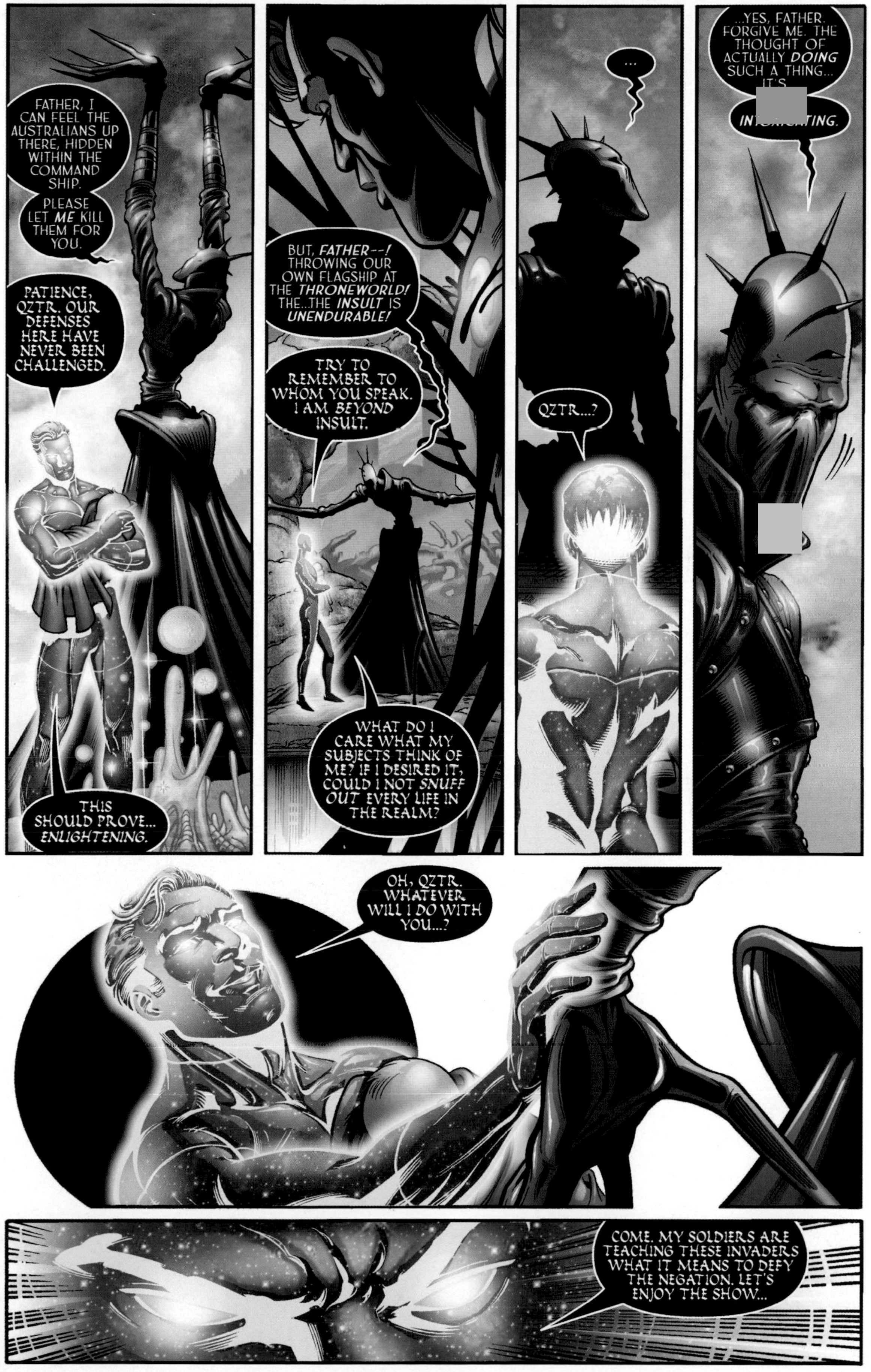
FATHER, I CAN FEEL THE AUSTRALIANS UP THERE, HIDDEN WITHIN THE COMMAND SHIP.
PLEASE LET ME KILL THEM FOR YOU.
PATIENCE, QZTR. OUR DEFENSES HERE HAVE NEVER BEEN CHALLENGED.
THIS SHOULD PROVE... ENLIGHTENING.
BUT, FATHER--! THROWING OUR OWN FLAGSHIP AT THE THRONEWORLD! THE...THE INSULT IS UNENDURABLE!
TRY TO REMEMBER TO WHOM YOU SPEAK. I AM BEYOND INSULT.
WHAT DO I CARE WHAT MY SUBJECTS THINK OF ME? IF I DESIRED IT, COULD I NOT SNUFF OUT EVERY LIFE IN THE REALM?
...
QZTR...?
...YES, FATHER. FORGIVE ME. THE THOUGHT OF ACTUALLY DOING SUCH A THING... IT'S...
INTOXICATING.
OH, QZTR. WHATEVER WILL I DO WITH YOU...?
COME. MY SOLDIERS ARE TEACHING THESE INVADERS WHAT IT MEANS TO DEFY THE NEGATION. LET'S ENJOY THE SHOW...

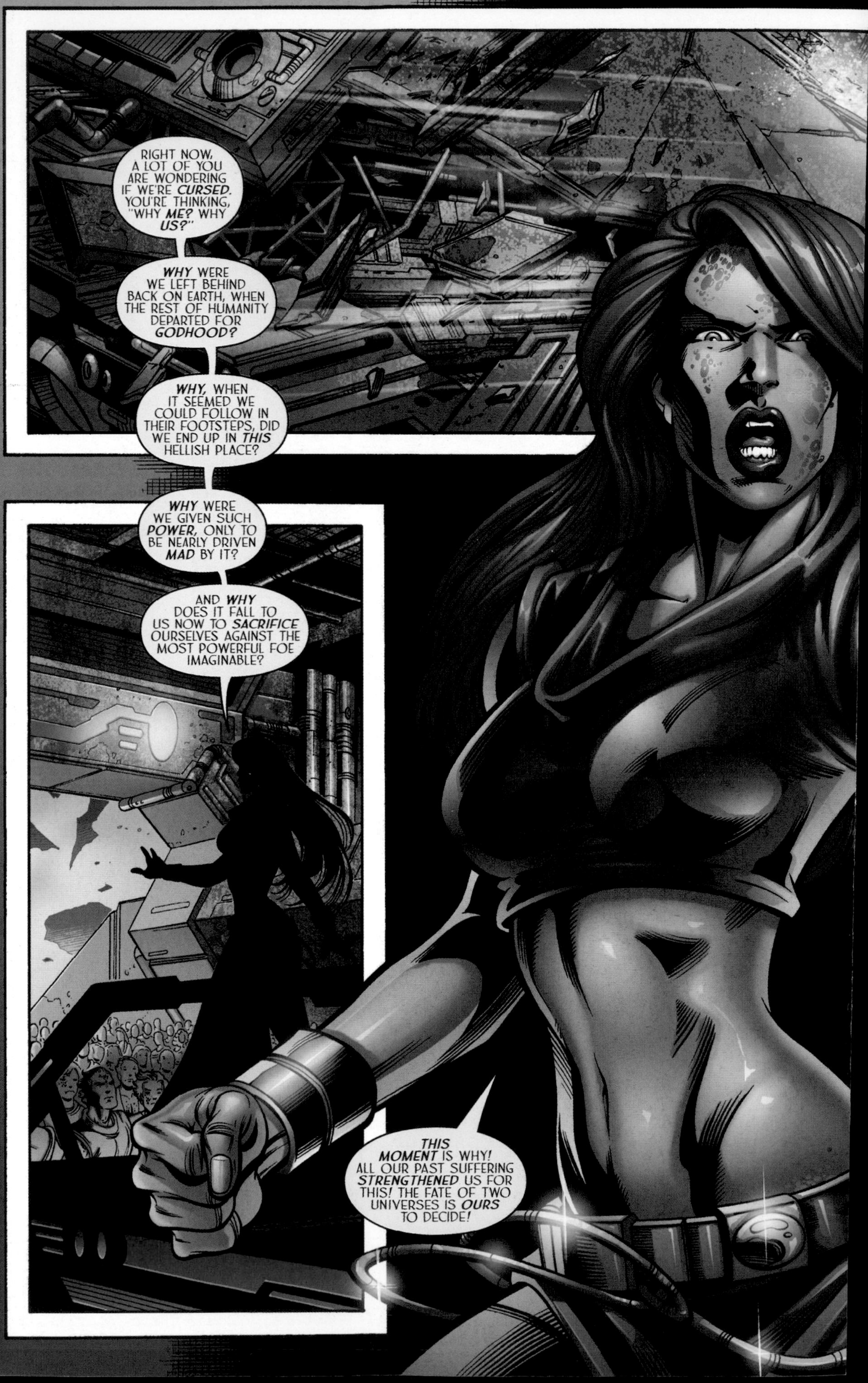
RIGHT NOW, A LOT OF YOU ARE WONDERING IF WE'RE *CURSED.* YOU'RE THINKING, "WHY *ME?* WHY *US?*"
WHY WERE WE LEFT BEHIND BACK ON EARTH, WHEN THE REST OF HUMANITY DEPARTED FOR *GODHOOD?*
WHY, WHEN IT SEEMED WE COULD FOLLOW IN THEIR FOOTSTEPS, DID WE END UP IN *THIS* HELLISH PLACE?
WHY WERE WE GIVEN SUCH *POWER,* ONLY TO BE NEARLY DRIVEN *MAD* BY IT?
AND *WHY* DOES IT FALL TO US NOW TO *SACRIFICE* OURSELVES AGAINST THE MOST POWERFUL FOE IMAGINABLE?
THIS MOMENT IS WHY! ALL OUR PAST SUFFERING *STRENGTHENED* US FOR THIS! THE FATE OF TWO UNIVERSES IS *OURS* TO DECIDE!

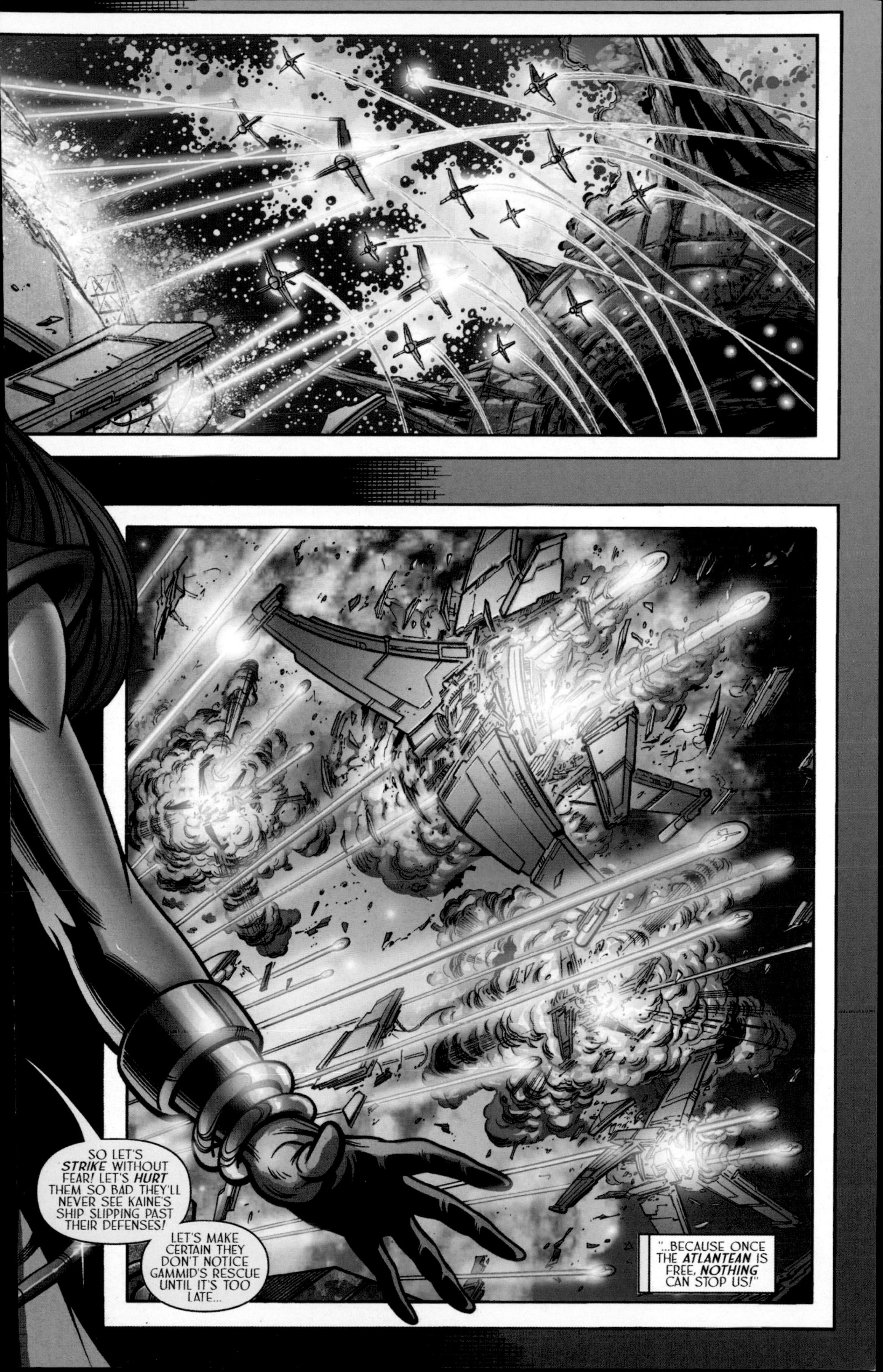
SO LET'S *STRIKE* WITHOUT FEAR! LET'S *HURT* THEM SO BAD THEY'LL NEVER SEE KAINE'S SHIP SLIPPING PAST THEIR DEFENSES!
LET'S MAKE CERTAIN THEY DON'T NOTICE GAMMID'S RESCUE UNTIL IT'S TOO LATE...
"...BECAUSE ONCE THE *ATLANTEAN* IS FREE, *NOTHING* CAN STOP US!"

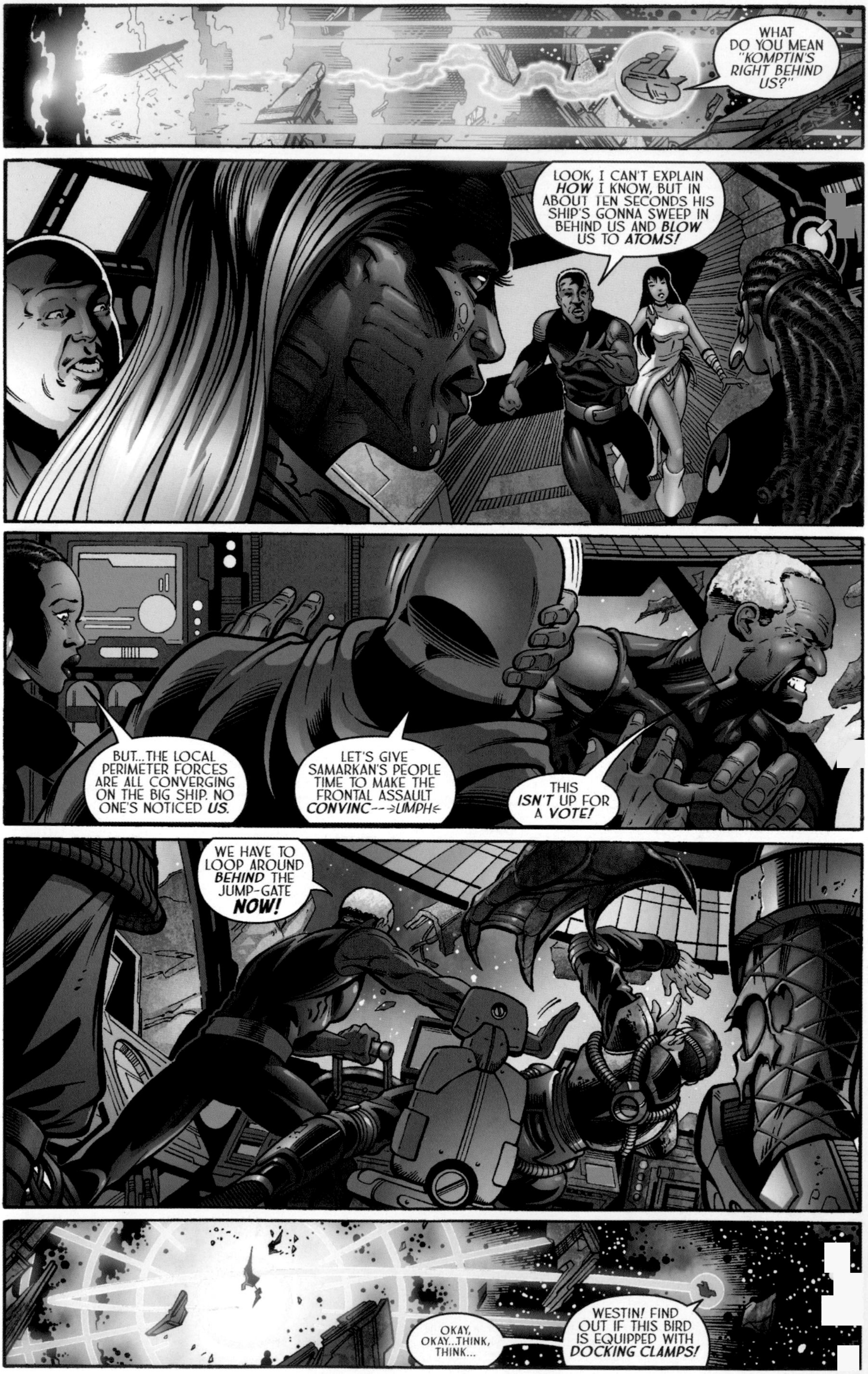
WHAT DO YOU MEAN "KOMPTIN'S RIGHT BEHIND US?"
LOOK, I CAN'T EXPLAIN HOW I KNOW, BUT IN ABOUT TEN SECONDS HIS SHIP'S GONNA SWEEP IN BEHIND US AND BLOW US TO ATOMS!
BUT...THE LOCAL PERIMETER FORCES ARE ALL CONVERGING ON THE BIG SHIP. NO ONE'S NOTICED US.
LET'S GIVE SAMARKAN'S PEOPLE TIME TO MAKE THE FRONTAL ASSAULT CONVINC-- UMPH
THIS ISN'T UP FOR A VOTE!
WE HAVE TO LOOP AROUND BEHIND THE JUMP-GATE NOW!
WESTIN! FIND OUT IF THIS BIRD IS EQUIPPED WITH DOCKING CLAMPS!
OKAY, OKAY...THINK, THINK...

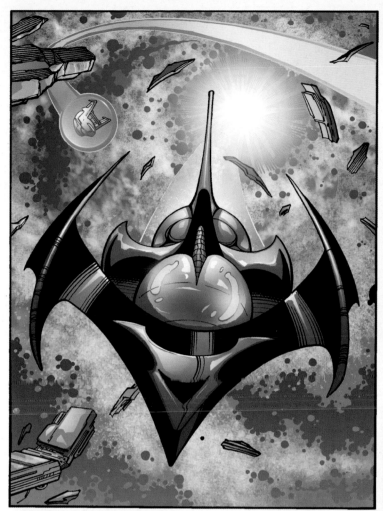

HOW DID YOU KNOW...?

I'LL EXPLAIN LATER. WE'LL ALL HAVE SOME EXPLAINING TO DO LATER.

RIGHT NOW WE'VE GOT TO HIT KOMPTIN HARD BEFORE HE KNOWS--

--WHAT'S HAPPENING?! THEY WERE RIGHT IN FRONT OF US!

I DON'T KNOW, SIR!

OF COURSE, YOU DON'T! AS LONG AS THEIR STEALTH-SPHERE'S ENGAGED, OUR ONLY CHANCE IS A VISUAL--

KANGG

WHAT IN THE--?

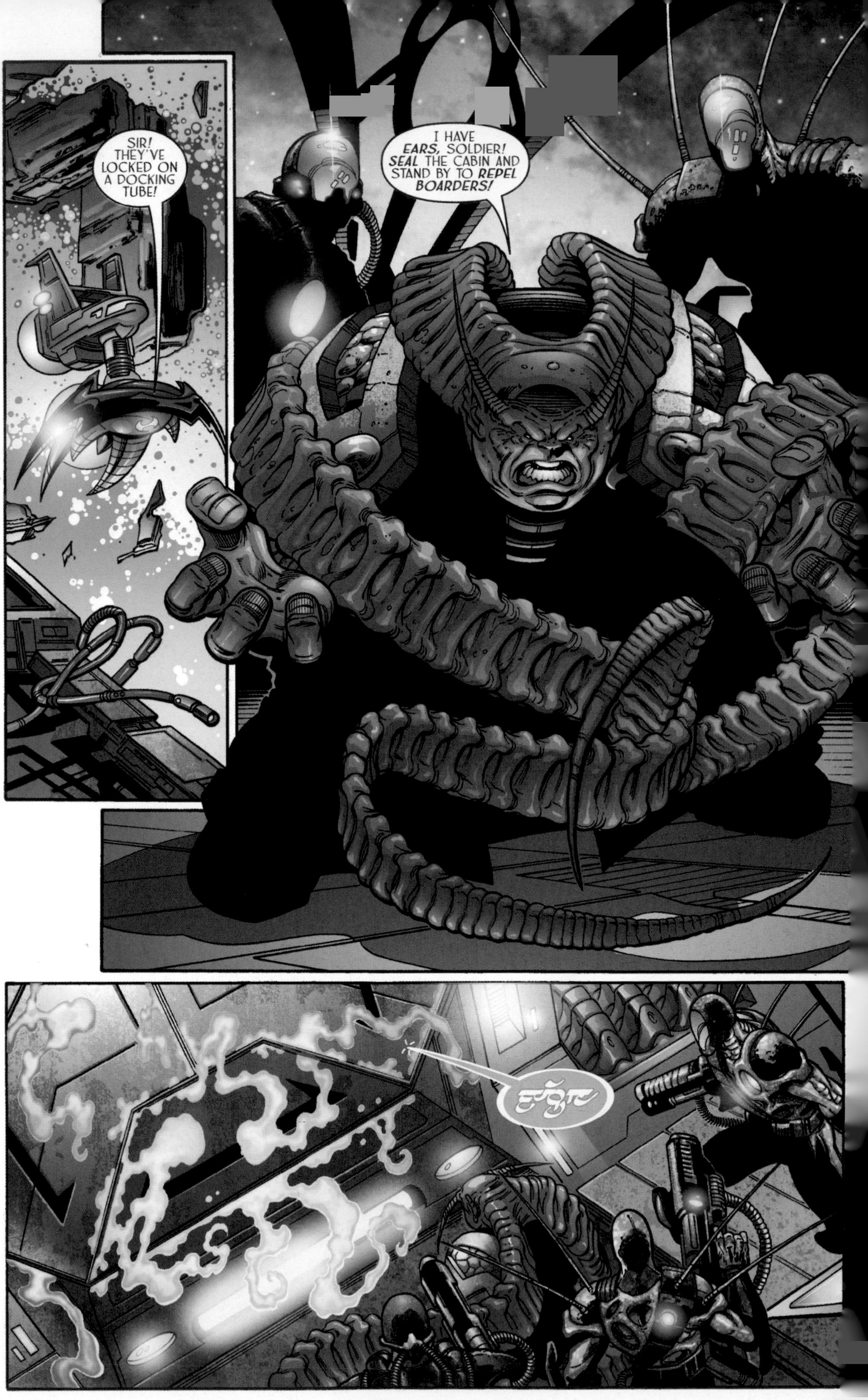
SIR! THEY'VE LOCKED ON A DOCKING TUBE!
I HAVE EARS, SOLDIER! SEAL THE CABIN AND STAND BY TO REPEL BOARDERS!

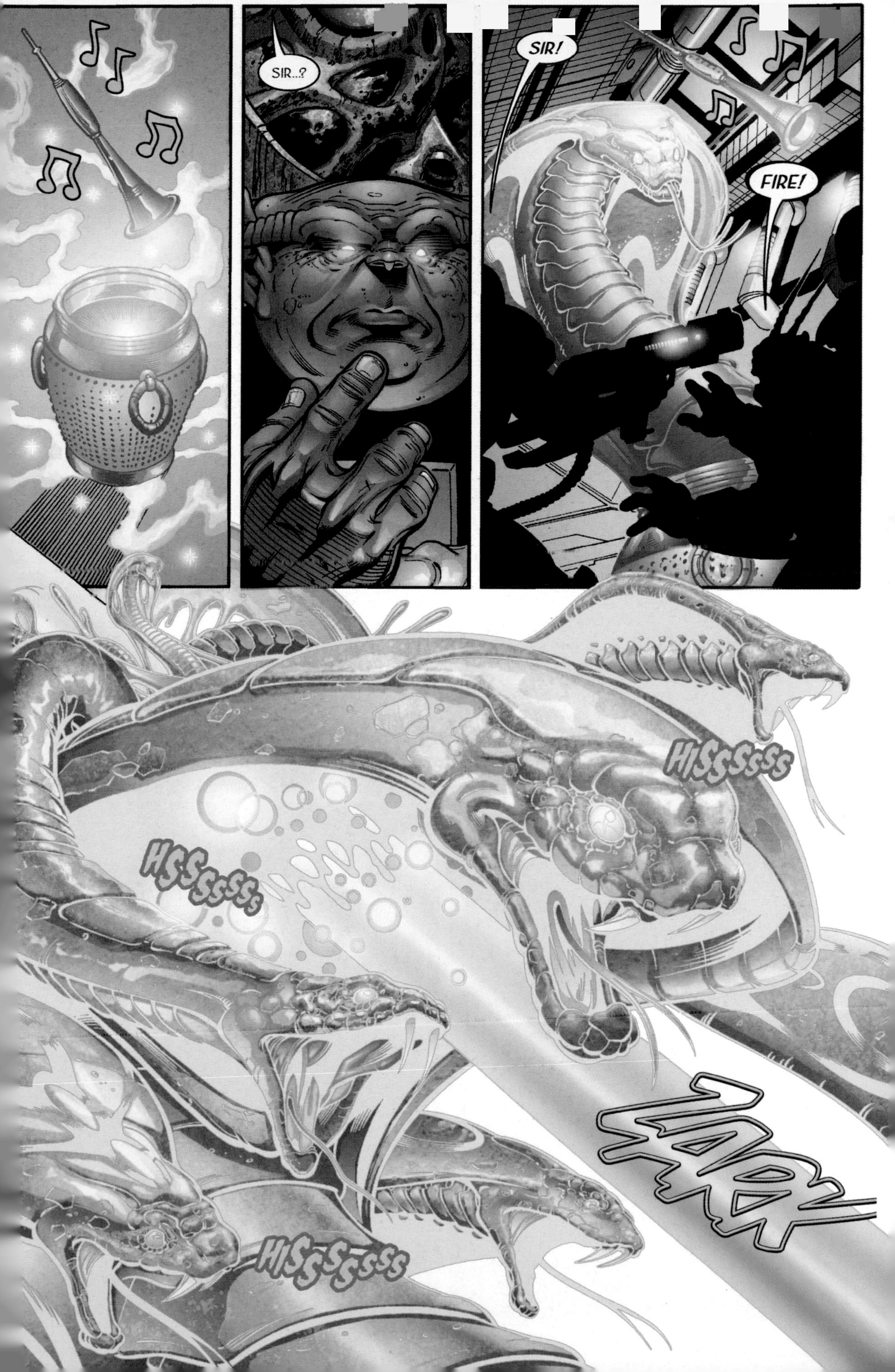
SIR...?
SIR!
FIRE!
HISSSSSS
HISSSSSS
HISSSSSSS
ZARK

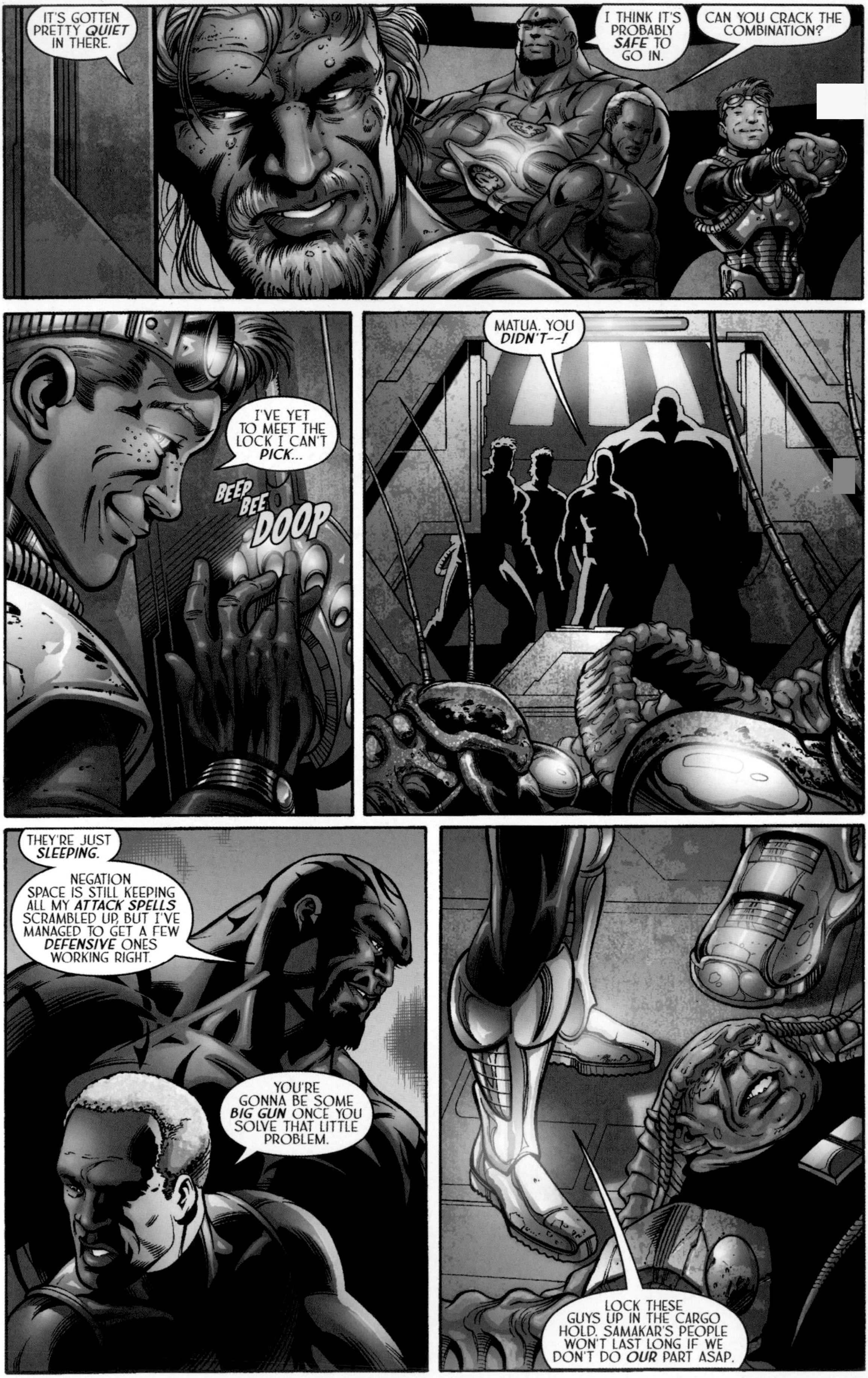
IT'S GOTTEN PRETTY QUIET IN THERE.
I THINK IT'S PROBABLY SAFE TO GO IN.
CAN YOU CRACK THE COMBINATION?
I'VE YET TO MEET THE LOCK I CAN'T PICK...
BEEP BEE DOOP
MATUA. YOU DIDN'T--!
THEY'RE JUST SLEEPING.
NEGATION SPACE IS STILL KEEPING ALL MY ATTACK SPELLS SCRAMBLED UP, BUT I'VE MANAGED TO GET A FEW DEFENSIVE ONES WORKING RIGHT.
YOU'RE GONNA BE SOME BIG GUN ONCE YOU SOLVE THAT LITTLE PROBLEM.
LOCK THESE GUYS UP IN THE CARGO HOLD. SAMAKAR'S PEOPLE WON'T LAST LONG IF WE DON'T DO OUR PART ASAP.

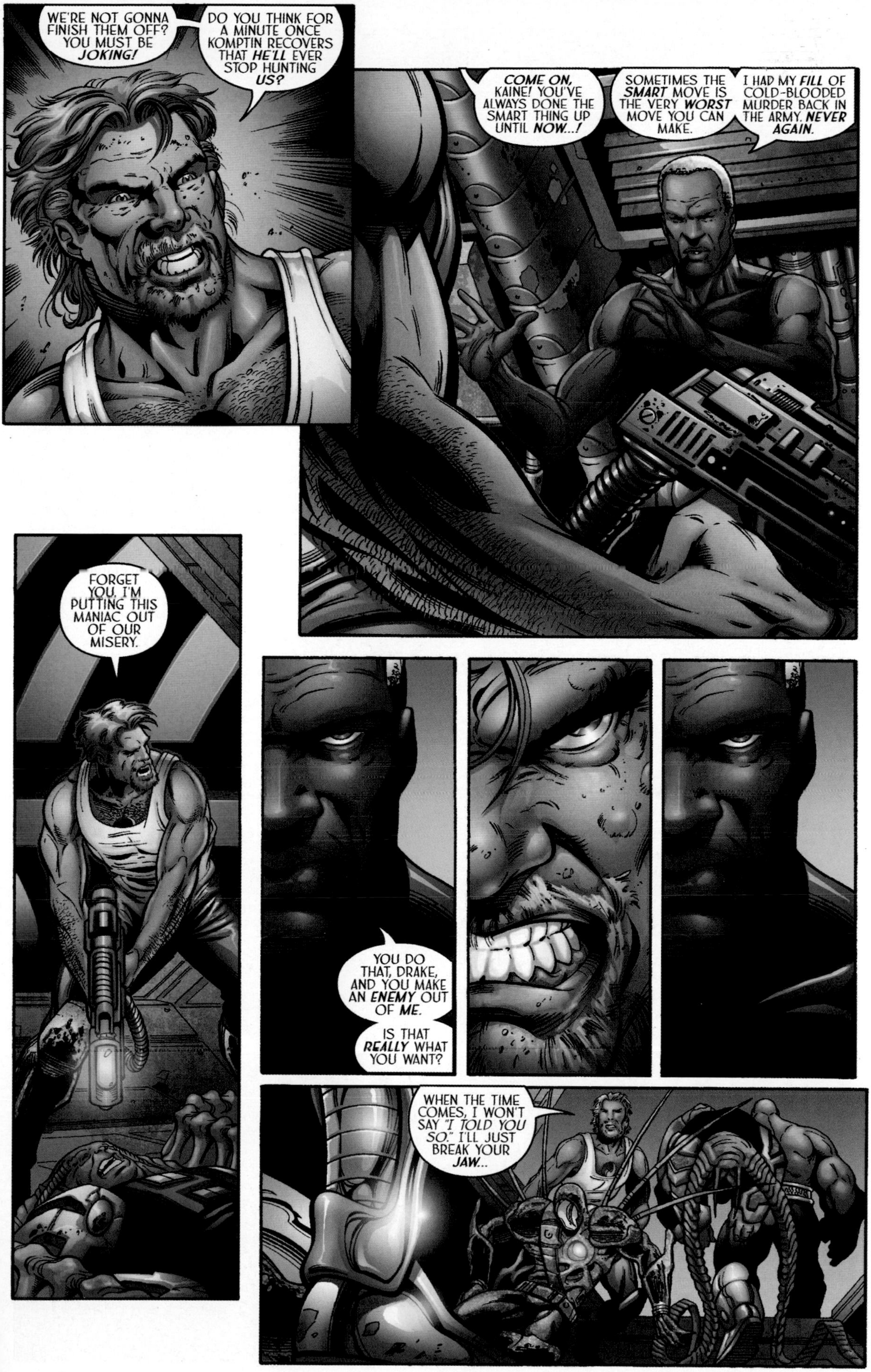
WE'RE NOT GONNA FINISH THEM OFF? YOU MUST BE *JOKING!*
DO YOU THINK FOR A MINUTE ONCE KOMPTIN RECOVERS THAT *HE'LL* EVER STOP HUNTING *US?*
COME ON, KAINE! YOU'VE ALWAYS DONE THE SMART THING UP UNTIL *NOW...!*
SOMETIMES THE *SMART* MOVE IS THE VERY *WORST* MOVE YOU CAN MAKE.
I HAD MY *FILL* OF COLD-BLOODED MURDER BACK IN THE ARMY. *NEVER AGAIN.*
FORGET YOU, I'M PUTTING THIS MANIAC OUT OF OUR MISERY.
YOU DO THAT, DRAKE, AND YOU MAKE AN *ENEMY* OUT OF *ME.*
IS THAT *REALLY* WHAT YOU WANT?
WHEN THE TIME COMES, I WON'T SAY *"I TOLD YOU SO."* I'LL JUST BREAK YOUR *JAW...*

IF THIS CARGO HOLD'S *FULL,* WE TOSS THEM OUT THE AIRLOCK.

NOW, NOW...

WHAT IN THE WORLDS...?

O-KAY...

NO REACTION AT ALL. MAYBE IT'S *SLEEPING.*

MAYBE WE'LL GET LUCKY AND IT'LL *EAT* THESE GUYS.

AND BITE THE HAND THAT FEEDS IT...?

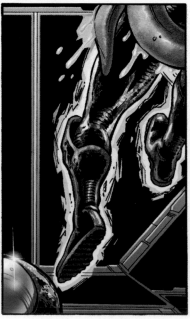

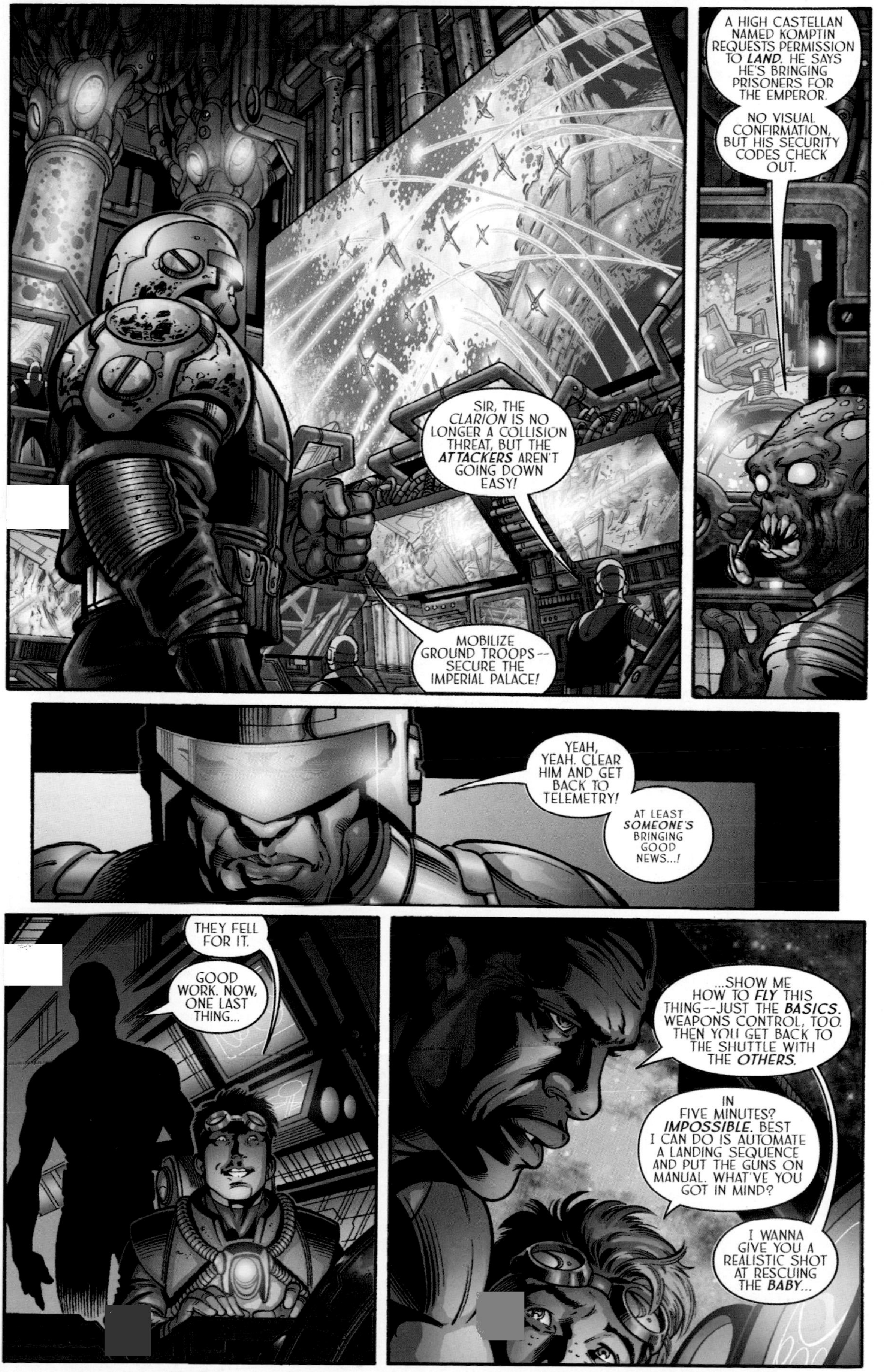
SIR, THE CLARION IS NO LONGER A COLLISION THREAT, BUT THE ATTACKERS AREN'T GOING DOWN EASY!
MOBILIZE GROUND TROOPS-- SECURE THE IMPERIAL PALACE!
A HIGH CASTELLAN NAMED KOMPTIN REQUESTS PERMISSION TO LAND. HE SAYS HE'S BRINGING PRISONERS FOR THE EMPEROR.
NO VISUAL CONFIRMATION, BUT HIS SECURITY CODES CHECK OUT.
YEAH, YEAH. CLEAR HIM AND GET BACK TO TELEMETRY!
AT LEAST SOMEONE'S BRINGING GOOD NEWS...!
THEY FELL FOR IT.
GOOD WORK. NOW, ONE LAST THING...
...SHOW ME HOW TO FLY THIS THING--JUST THE BASICS. WEAPONS CONTROL, TOO. THEN YOU GET BACK TO THE SHUTTLE WITH THE OTHERS.
IN FIVE MINUTES? IMPOSSIBLE. BEST I CAN DO IS AUTOMATE A LANDING SEQUENCE AND PUT THE GUNS ON MANUAL. WHAT'VE YOU GOT IN MIND?
I WANNA GIVE YOU A REALISTIC SHOT AT RESCUING THE BABY...

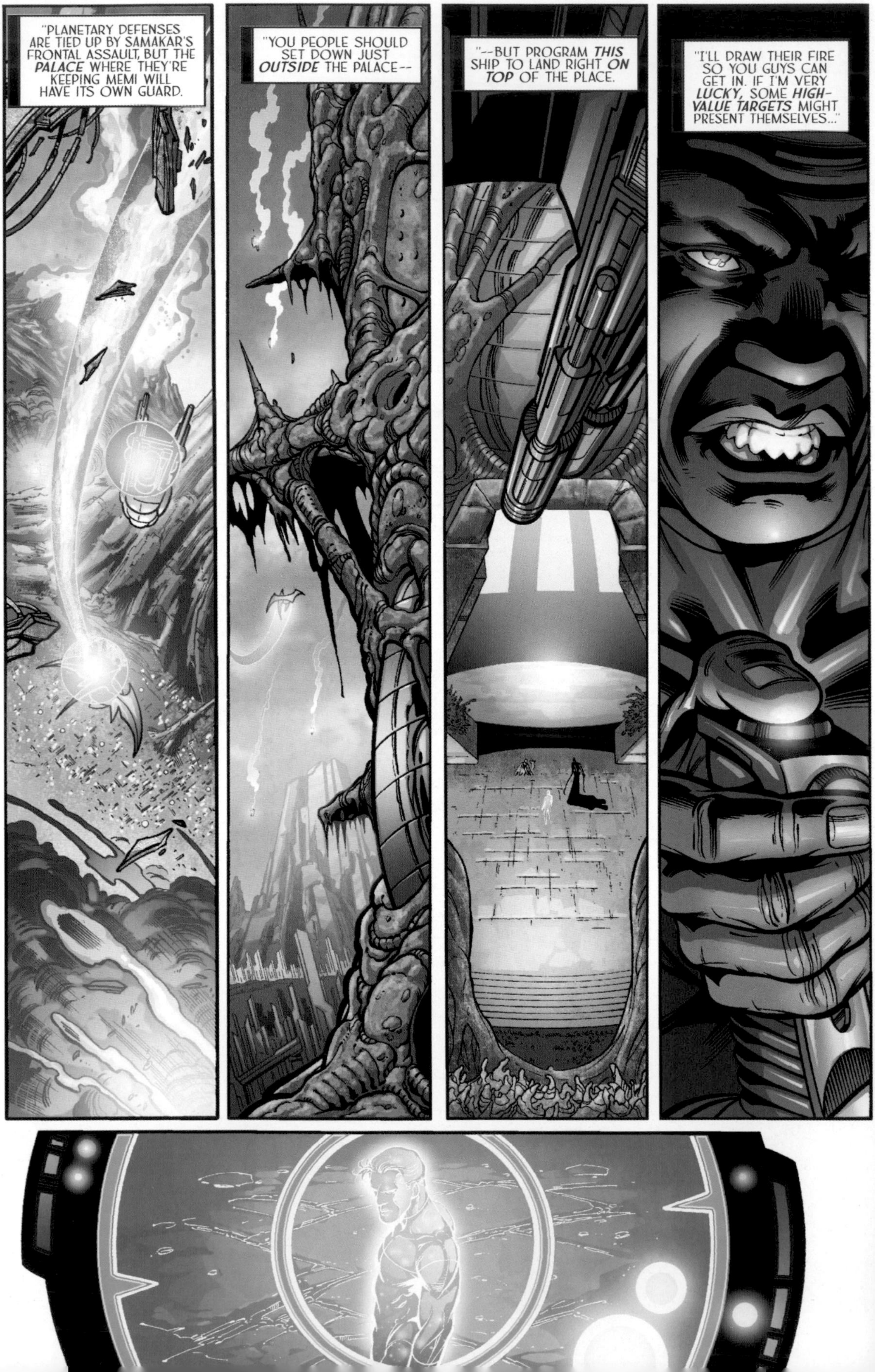
"PLANETARY DEFENSES ARE TIED UP BY SAMAKAR'S FRONTAL ASSAULT, BUT THE PALACE WHERE THEY'RE KEEPING MEMI WILL HAVE ITS OWN GUARD.
"YOU PEOPLE SHOULD SET DOWN JUST OUTSIDE THE PALACE--
"--BUT PROGRAM THIS SHIP TO LAND RIGHT ON TOP OF THE PLACE.
"I'LL DRAW THEIR FIRE SO YOU GUYS CAN GET IN. IF I'M VERY LUCKY, SOME HIGH-VALUE TARGETS MIGHT PRESENT THEMSELVES..."

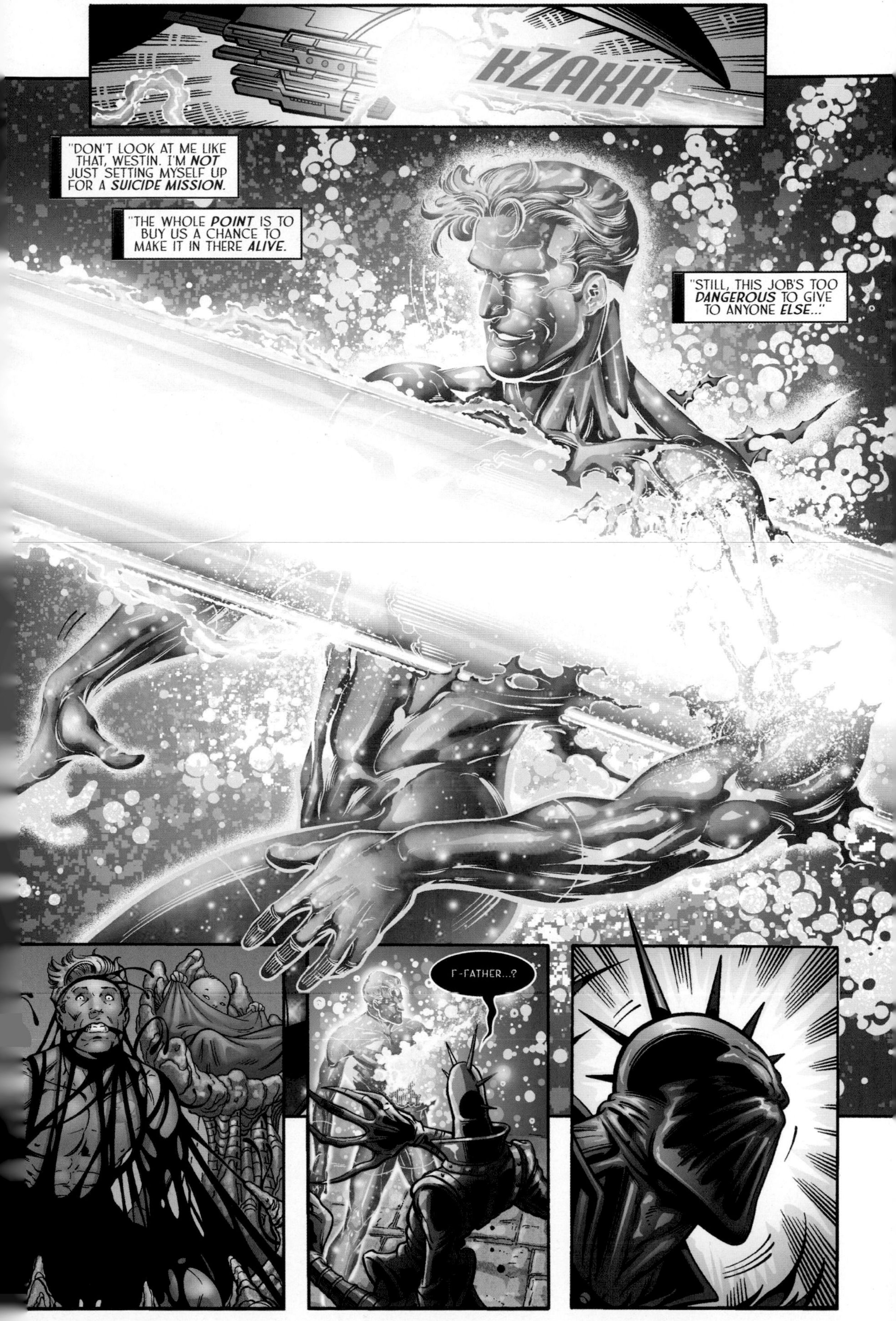
KZAKK
"DON'T LOOK AT ME LIKE THAT, WESTIN. I'M NOT JUST SETTING MYSELF UP FOR A SUICIDE MISSION.
"THE WHOLE POINT IS TO BUY US A CHANCE TO MAKE IT IN THERE ALIVE.
"STILL, THIS JOB'S TOO DANGEROUS TO GIVE TO ANYONE ELSE..."
F-FATHER...?

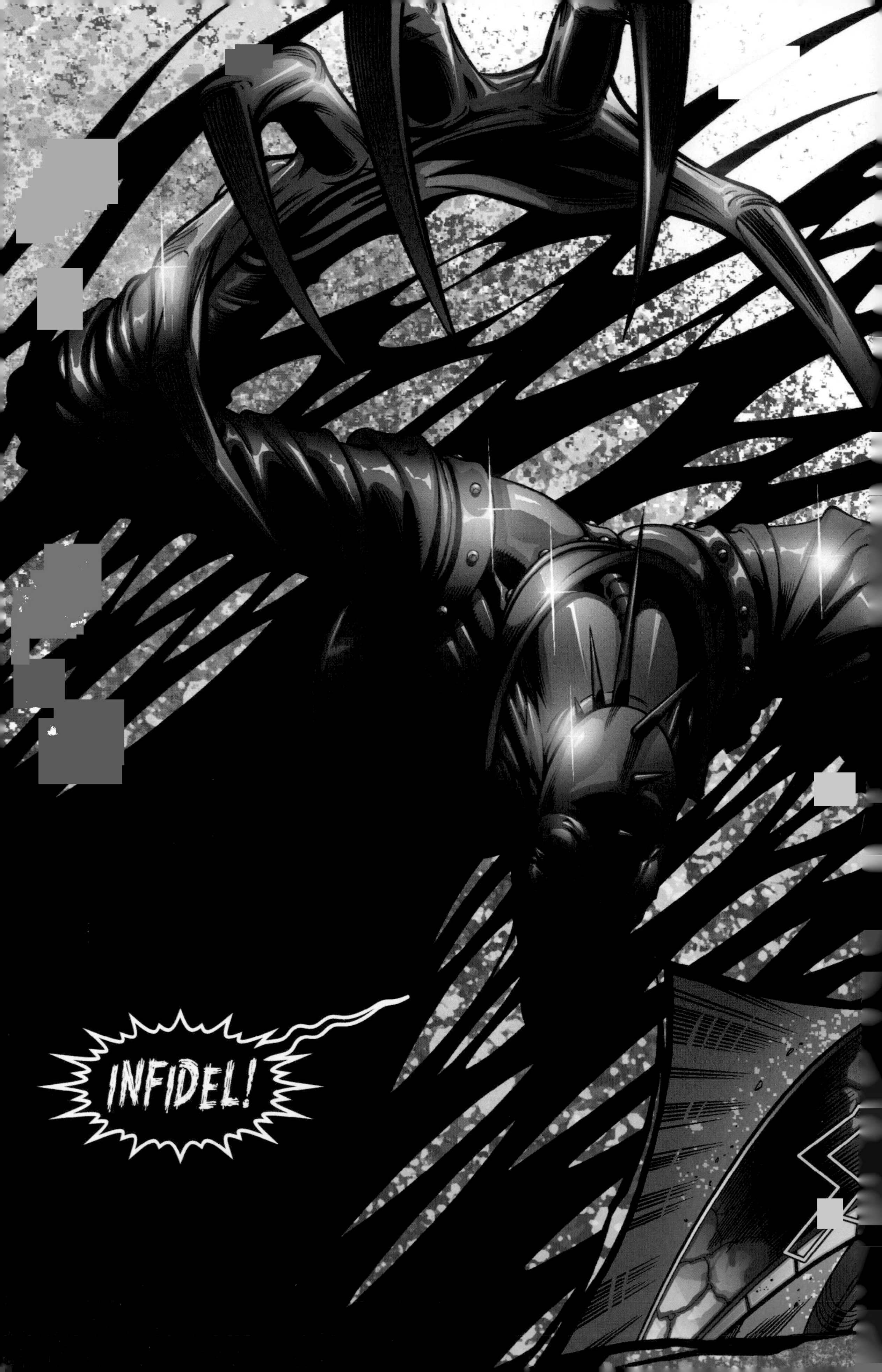
INFIDEL!

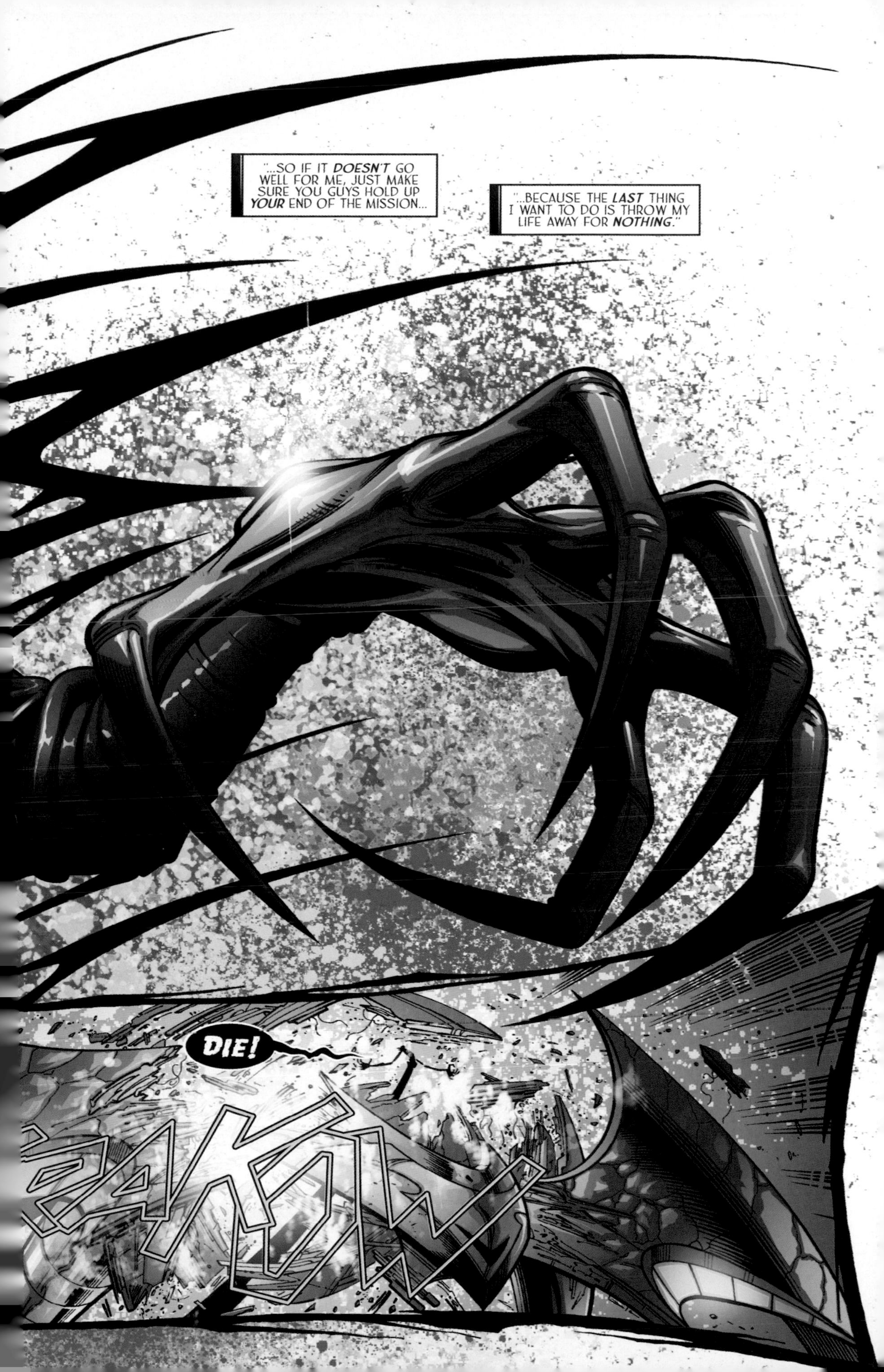
"...SO IF IT DOESN'T GO WELL FOR ME, JUST MAKE SURE YOU GUYS HOLD UP YOUR END OF THE MISSION...
"...BECAUSE THE LAST THING I WANT TO DO IS THROW MY LIFE AWAY FOR NOTHING."
DIE!

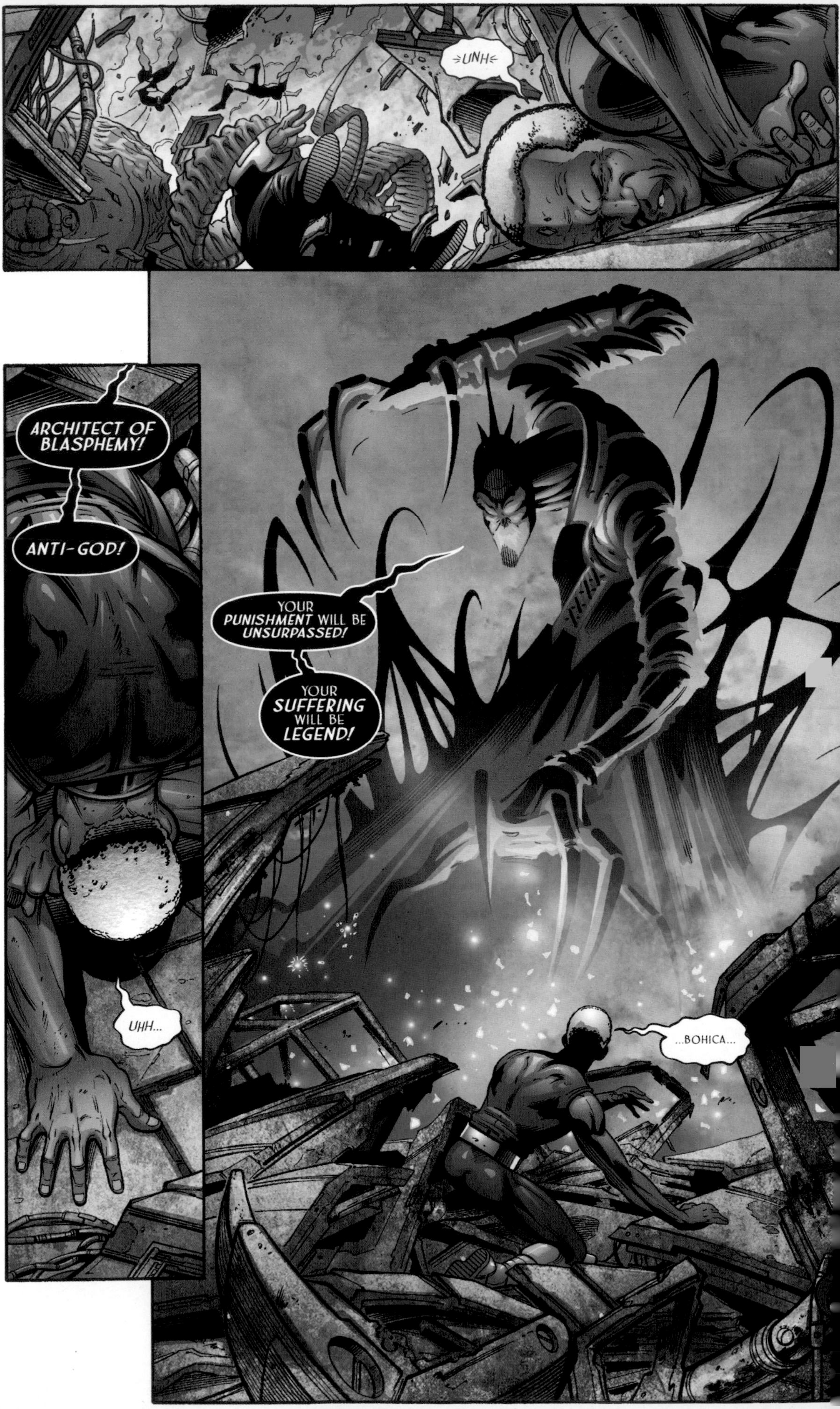
UNH
ARCHITECT OF BLASPHEMY!
ANTI-GOD!
YOUR PUNISHMENT WILL BE UNSURPASSED!
YOUR SUFFERING WILL BE LEGEND!
UHH...
...BOHICA...

STORYTELLERS

TONY BEDARD
WRITER

PAUL PELLETIER
PENCILER

DAVE MEIKIS
INKER

JAMES ROCHELLE
COLORIST

TROY PETERI
LETTERER

The
CrossGen
Universe
created by
Mark Alessi &
Gina M. Villa

MARK ALESSI Publisher & Chief Executive Officer * GINA M. VILLA Chief Operating Officer
MICHAEL A. BEATTIE Chief Financial Officer * JENNIFER HERNANDEZ General Counsel
TONY PANACCIO Vice President Product Development * CHRIS OARR Vice President Sales & Marketing
JAMES BREITBEIL Director Marketing & Distribution * IAN M. FELLER Director Corporate Communications
COURTLAND WHITED MIS Director * GABO MENDOZA Internet Services Director
CHARLES DECKER Director Production Control * BRIAN M. SOLTIS Controller
BRANDON PETERSON Vice President Special Projects * BARBARA KESEL Head Writer
BART SEARS Art Director * PAM DAVIES Vice President Production
SYLVIA BRETZ Production Supervisor Advertising/Web * ERIN FLANAGAN Web Designer
JANET BECHTLE Production Supervisor Books * RANDY MARTIN Production Designer
MICHELLE PUGLIESE Freelance Coordinator

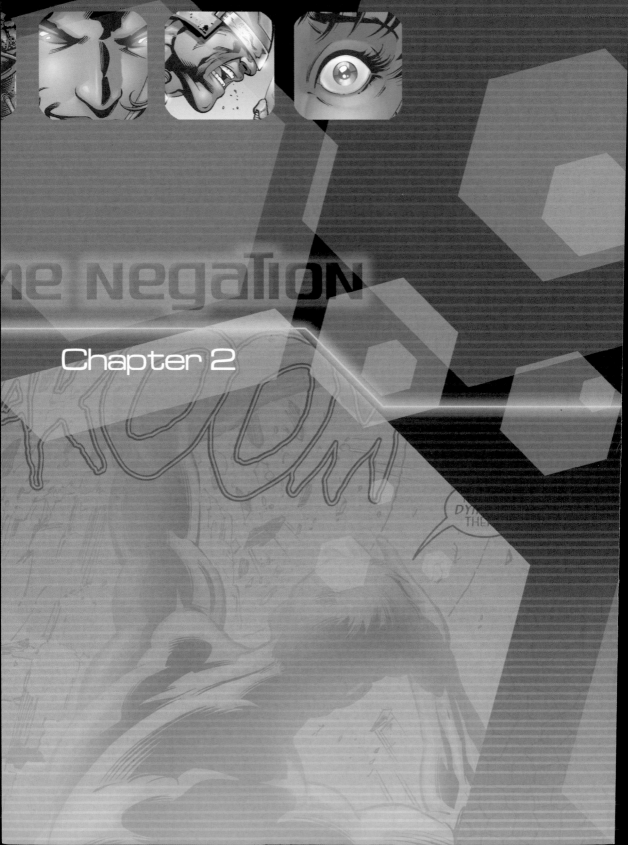

me negaTion

Chapter 2

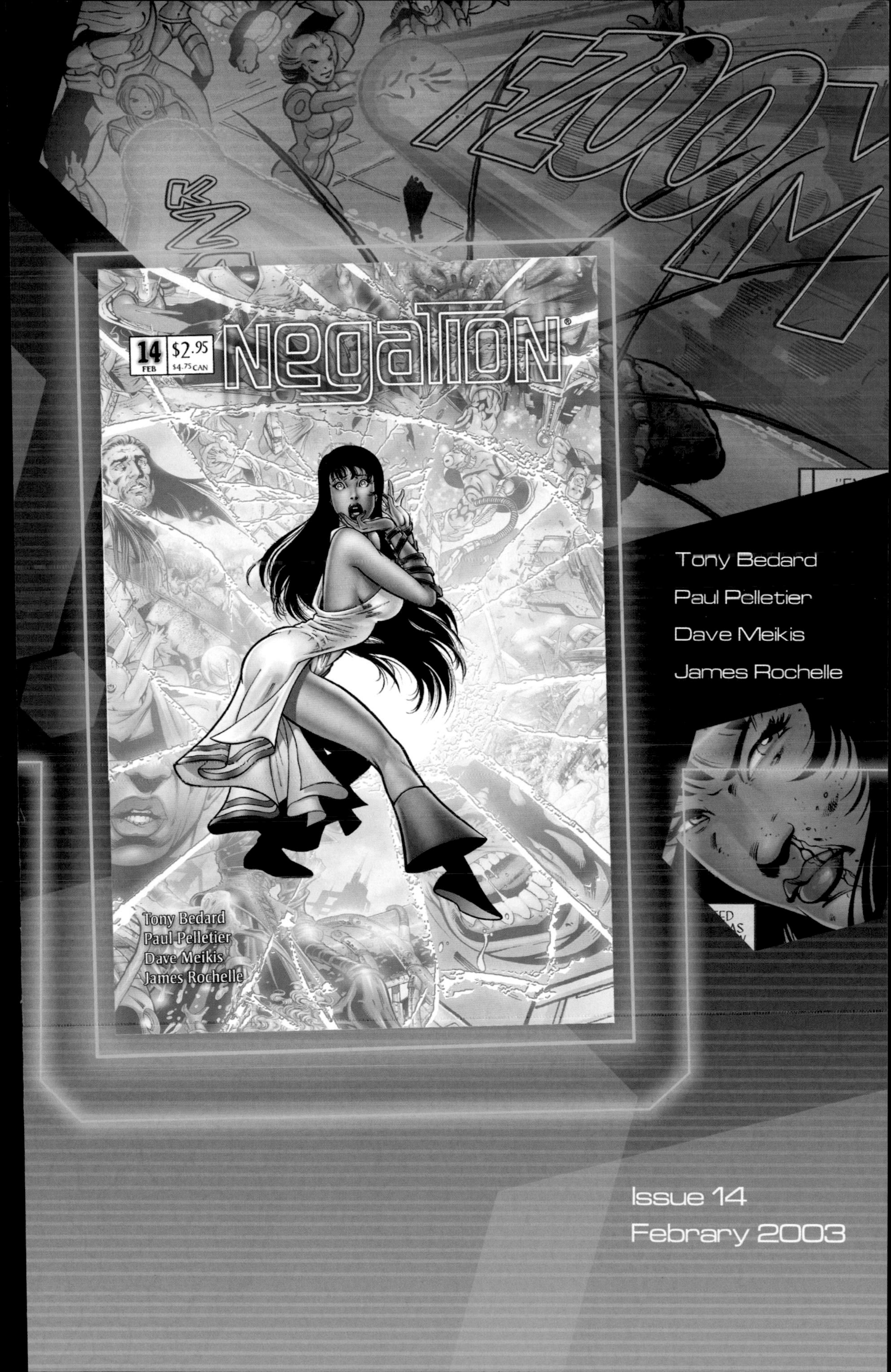
14
FEB
$2.95
$4.75 CAN
Negation
Tony Bedard
Paul Pelletier
Dave Meikis
James Rochelle
Tony Bedard
Paul Pelletier
Dave Meikis
James Rochelle
Issue 14
Febrary 2003

The God-Emperor CHARON conquered His chaotic universe and forged an intergalactic empire known as:

the Negation

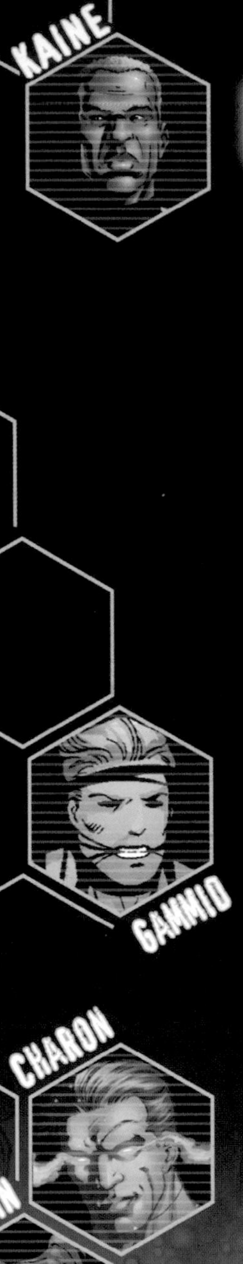
KAINE
GAMMID
CHARON

Charon now casts His baleful eye across the gulf between realities and covets the bright and thriving worlds in *our* cosmos.

On His orders, one hundred strangers were abducted from our universe and brought to His dark realm to be studied and tested on a harsh prison-world. Some captives were inherently powerful. Most, however, were simple, ordinary humans.

One such human named Obregon Kaine led a bloody uprising against the Negation prison warden, Komptin. The few prisoners who escaped along with Kaine wander the hostile stars, seeking a way home.

With a group of superhuman allies leading the charge, Kaine and company launched a daring raid on the Negation Throneworld. In order to rescue Charon's hostages, baby Memi and the Atlantean called Gammid, the fugitives landed their shuttlecraft near the Imperial Palace. Kaine, however, stayed aboard the warship they captured from Komptin and attacked the palace directly. Kaine's diversion proved costly as he was struck down by Charon's enforcer, Lawbringer Qztr, and the chances are slim his comrades will reach him in time for a rescue...

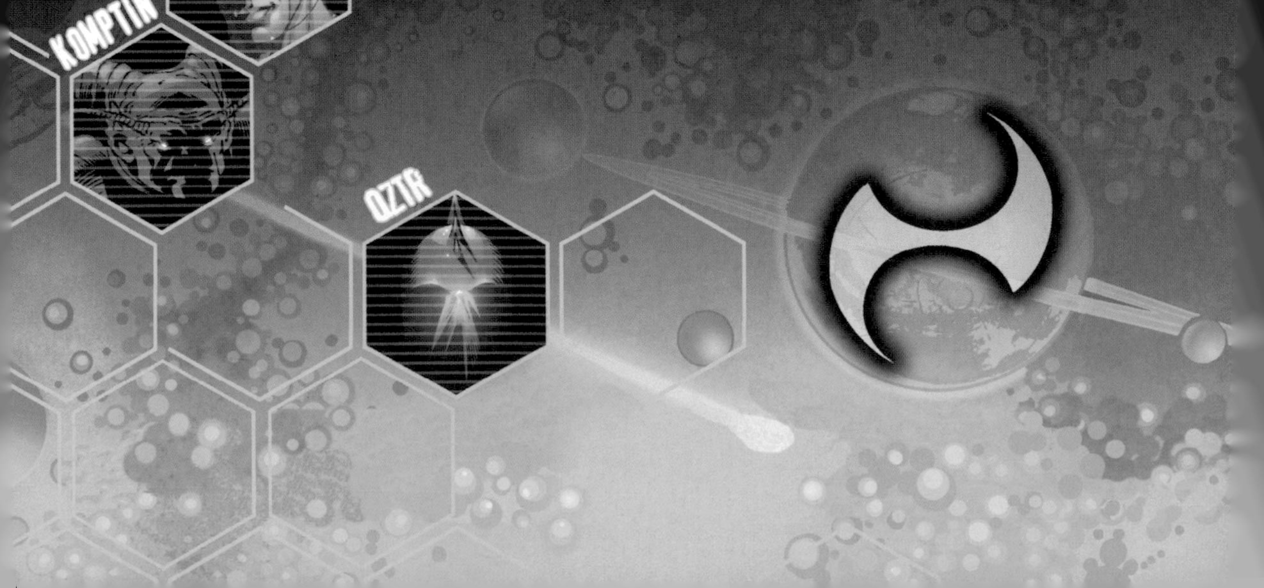
KOMPTIN
QZTR

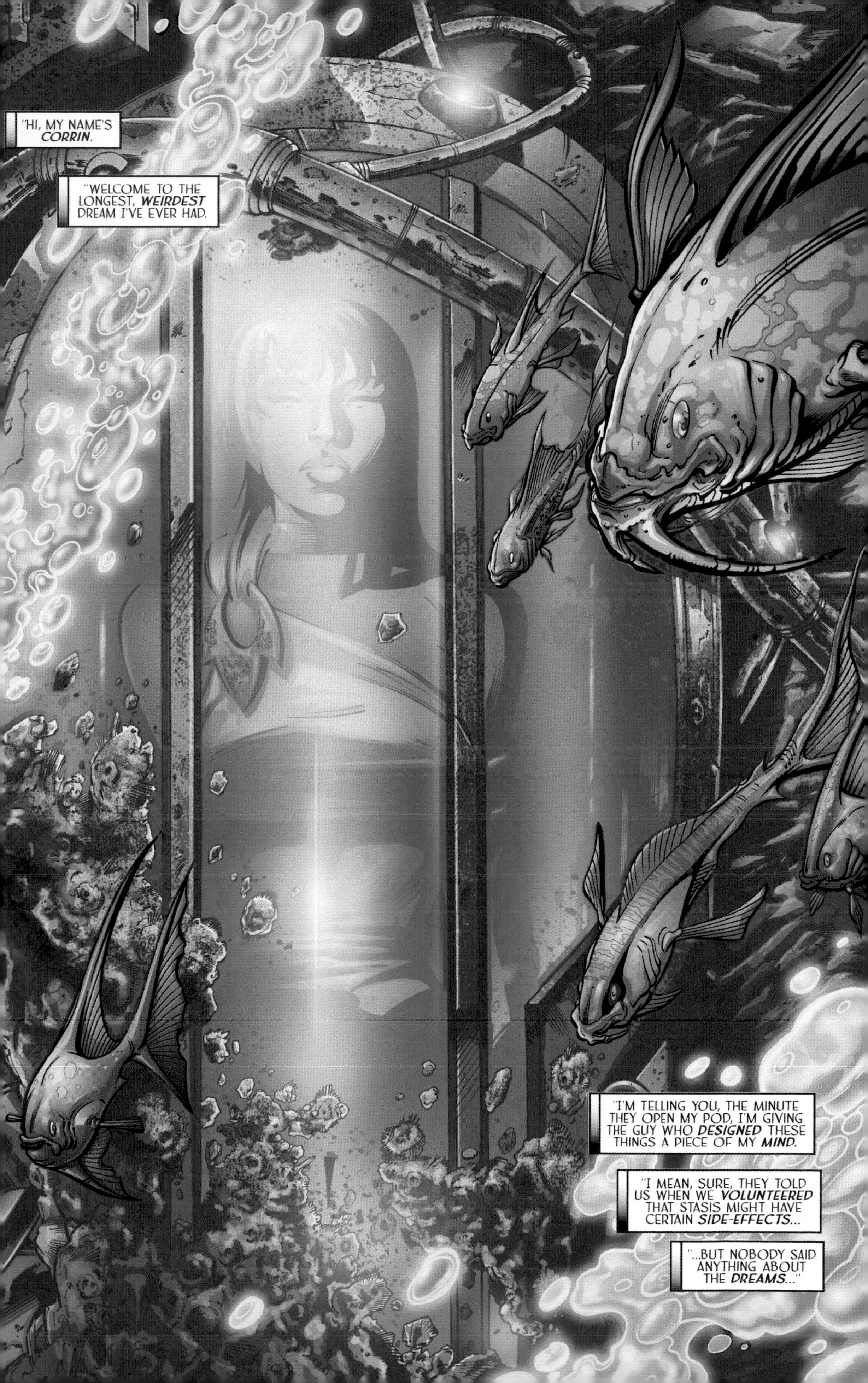
"HI, MY NAME'S CORRIN.
"WELCOME TO THE LONGEST, WEIRDEST DREAM I'VE EVER HAD.
"I'M TELLING YOU, THE MINUTE THEY OPEN MY POD, I'M GIVING THE GUY WHO DESIGNED THESE THINGS A PIECE OF MY MIND.
"I MEAN, SURE, THEY TOLD US WHEN WE VOLUNTEERED THAT STASIS MIGHT HAVE CERTAIN SIDE-EFFECTS...
"...BUT NOBODY SAID ANYTHING ABOUT THE DREAMS..."

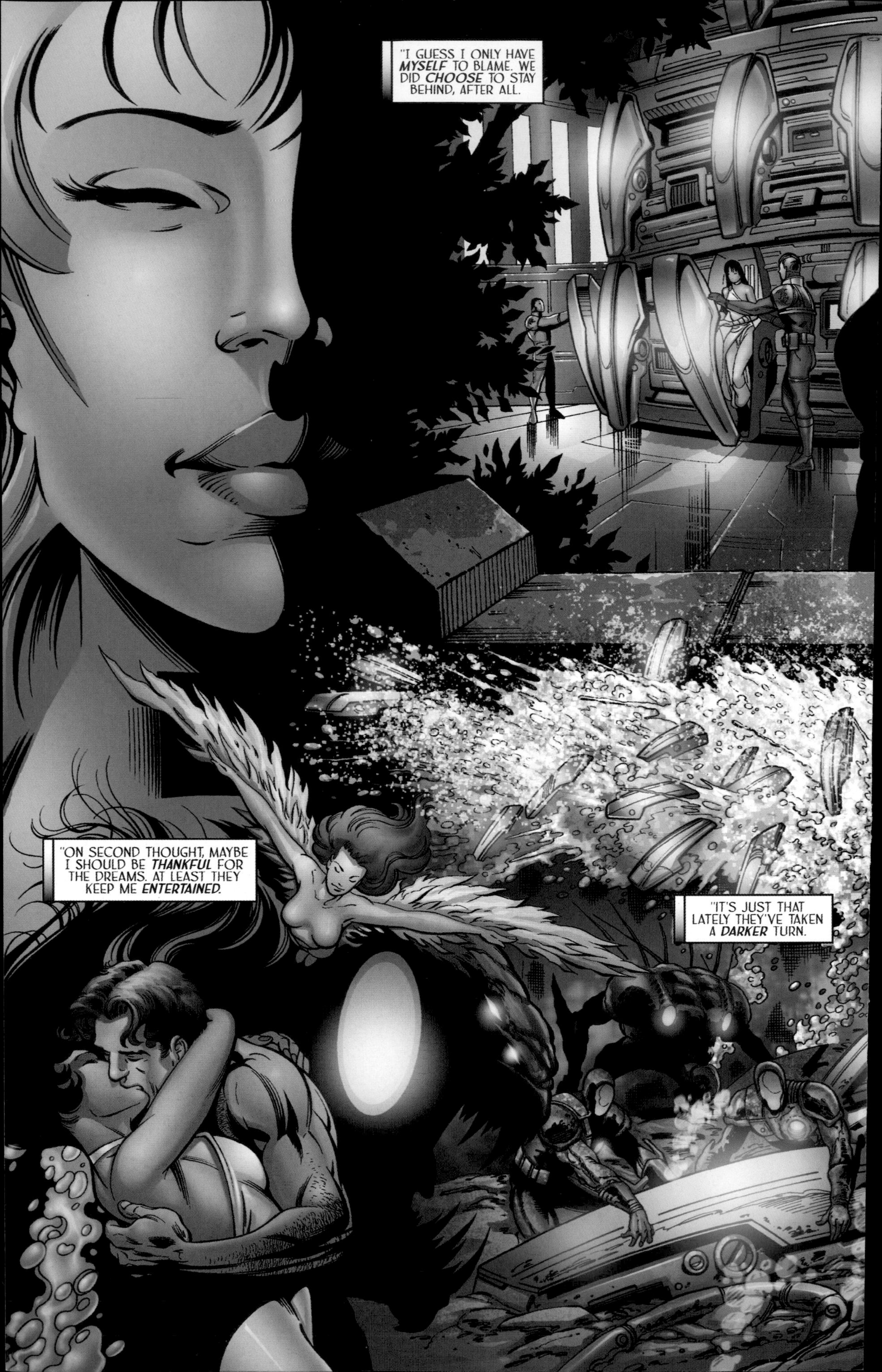
"I GUESS I ONLY HAVE MYSELF TO BLAME. WE DID CHOOSE TO STAY BEHIND, AFTER ALL.
"ON SECOND THOUGHT, MAYBE I SHOULD BE THANKFUL FOR THE DREAMS. AT LEAST THEY KEEP ME ENTERTAINED.
"IT'S JUST THAT LATELY THEY'VE TAKEN A DARKER TURN.

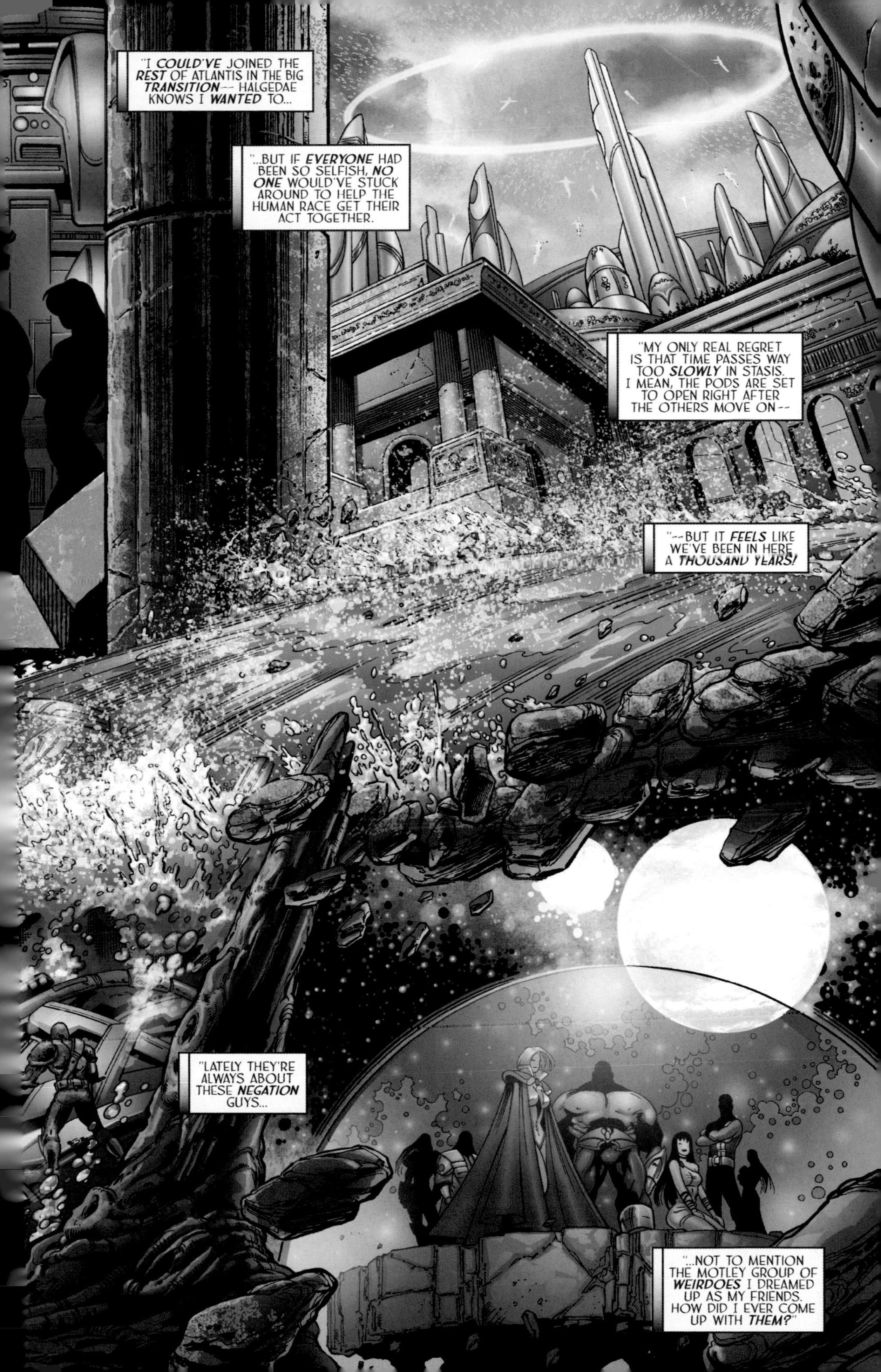
"I COULD'VE JOINED THE REST OF ATLANTIS IN THE BIG TRANSITION-- HALGEDAE KNOWS I WANTED TO...
"...BUT IF EVERYONE HAD BEEN SO SELFISH, NO ONE WOULD'VE STUCK AROUND TO HELP THE HUMAN RACE GET THEIR ACT TOGETHER.
"MY ONLY REAL REGRET IS THAT TIME PASSES WAY TOO SLOWLY IN STASIS. I MEAN, THE PODS ARE SET TO OPEN RIGHT AFTER THE OTHERS MOVE ON--
"--BUT IT FEELS LIKE WE'VE BEEN IN HERE A THOUSAND YEARS!
"LATELY THEY'RE ALWAYS ABOUT THESE NEGATION GUYS...
"...NOT TO MENTION THE MOTLEY GROUP OF WEIRDOES I DREAMED UP AS MY FRIENDS. HOW DID I EVER COME UP WITH THEM?"

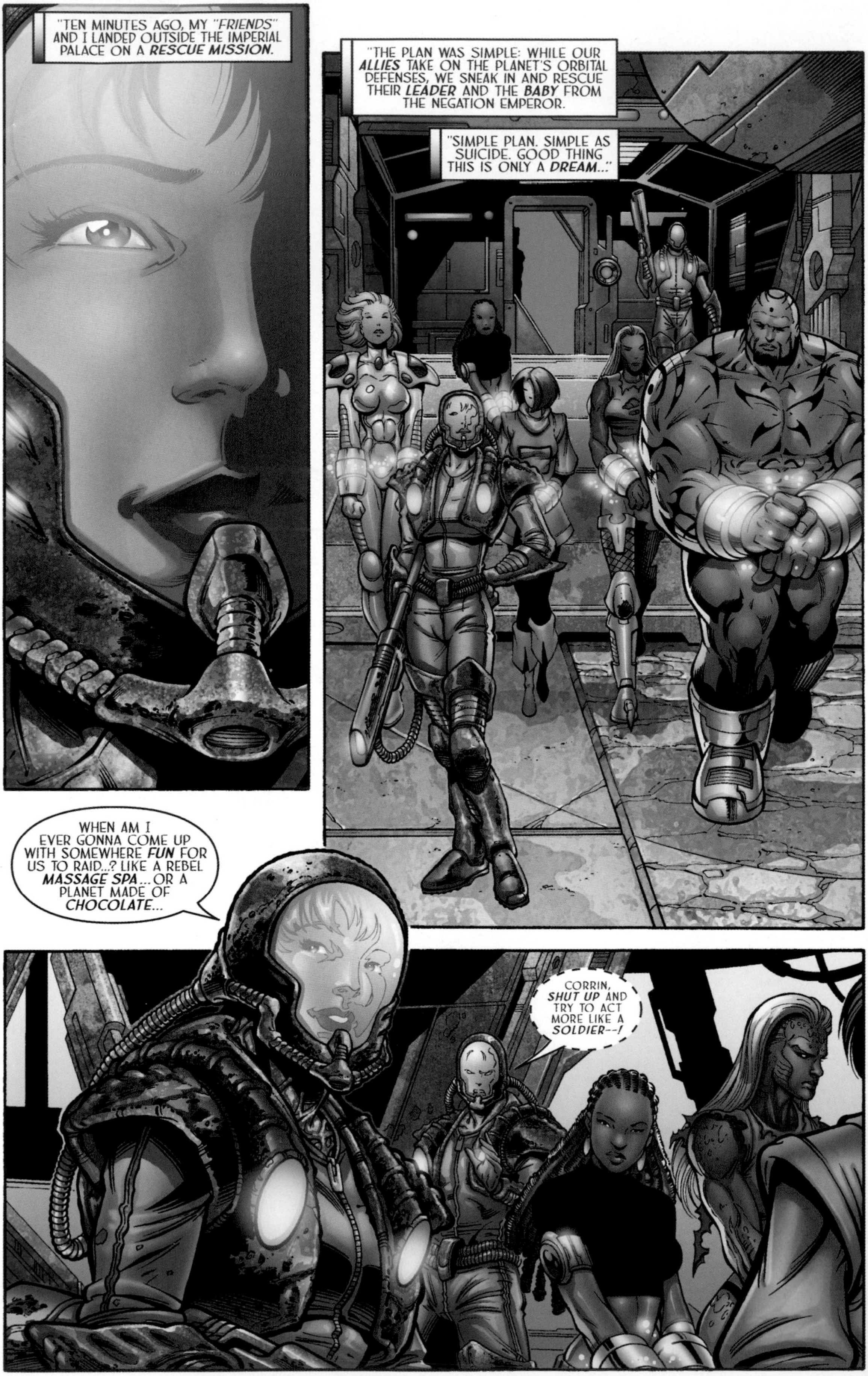
"TEN MINUTES AGO, MY "FRIENDS" AND I LANDED OUTSIDE THE IMPERIAL PALACE ON A RESCUE MISSION.
"THE PLAN WAS SIMPLE: WHILE OUR ALLIES TAKE ON THE PLANET'S ORBITAL DEFENSES, WE SNEAK IN AND RESCUE THEIR LEADER AND THE BABY FROM THE NEGATION EMPEROR.
"SIMPLE PLAN. SIMPLE AS SUICIDE. GOOD THING THIS IS ONLY A DREAM..."
WHEN AM I EVER GONNA COME UP WITH SOMEWHERE FUN FOR US TO RAID...? LIKE A REBEL MASSAGE SPA... OR A PLANET MADE OF CHOCOLATE...
CORRIN, SHUT UP AND TRY TO ACT MORE LIKE A SOLDIER--!

YOU SURE YOU DON'T WANT TO LEAVE THE QUEEN OF DENIAL WITH *US*?

SHE'S *STRONGER* THAN SHE LOOKS, WESTIN. *REAL* STRONG. PLUS, THE ARMOR *FIT* HER.

JUST WAIT HERE, AND DON'T OPEN THE DOOR FOR ANYONE BUT US.

DON'T BE LONG. I GOTTA LISTEN TO *HIM* THE WHOLE TIME YOU'RE GONE.

DID I EVER TELL YOU ABOUT THE TIME I LED A RAID ON THE NEGATION WASTE REFINERY ON RIOPAN MINUS...?

MONCHITO, MONCHITO!

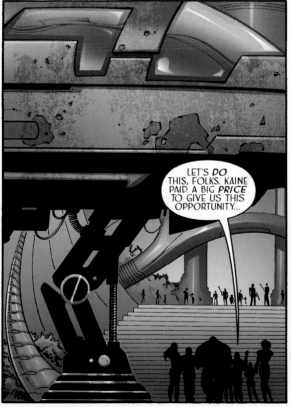

LET'S *DO* THIS, FOLKS. KAINE PAID A BIG *PRICE* TO GIVE US THIS OPPORTUNITY...

...I ONLY HOPE HE DIDN'T PAY WITH HIS *LIFE*...

BOOM

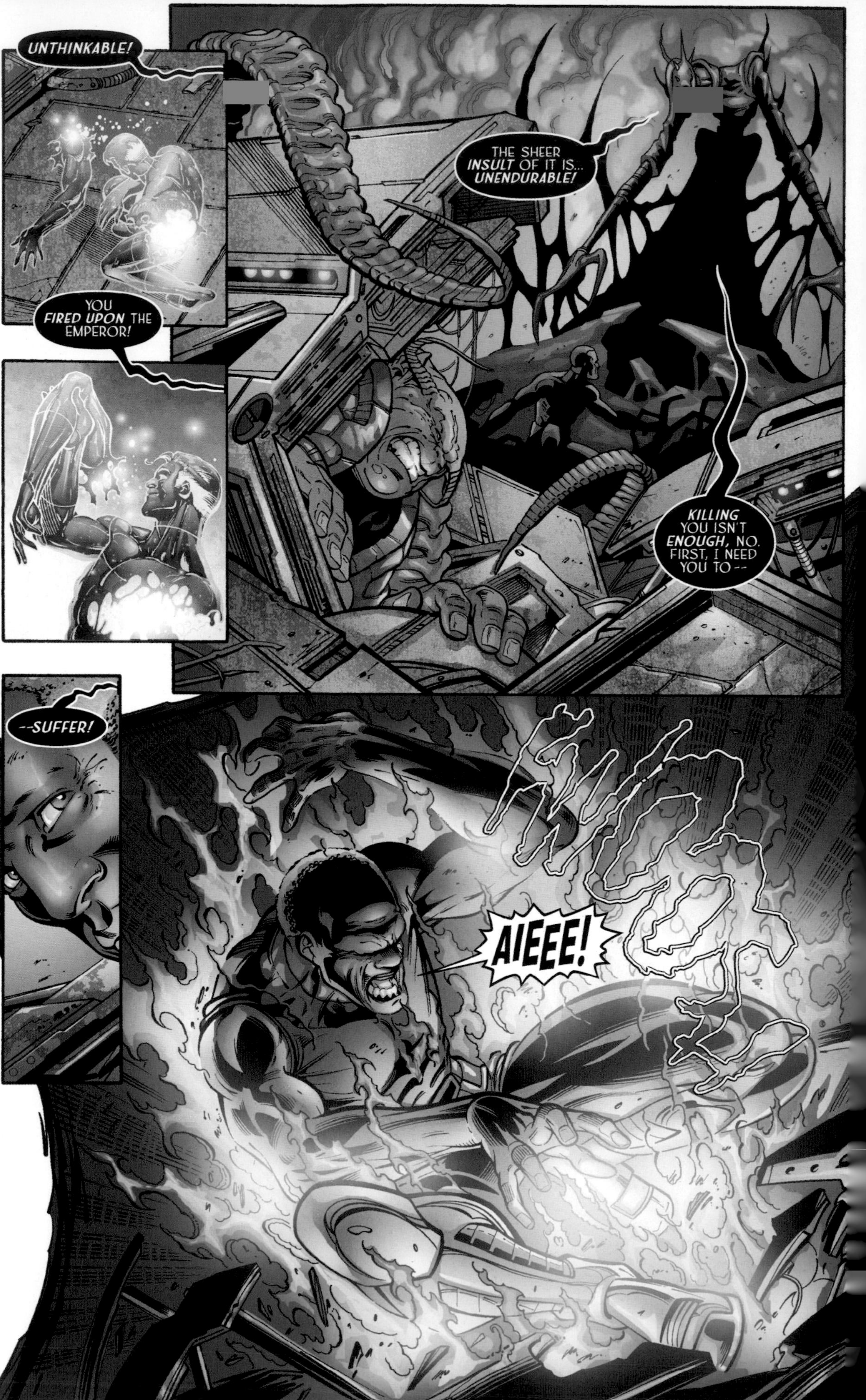
UNTHINKABLE!
THE SHEER INSULT OF IT IS... UNENDURABLE!
YOU FIRED UPON THE EMPEROR!
KILLING YOU ISN'T ENOUGH, NO. FIRST, I NEED YOU TO --
--SUFFER!
AIEEE!

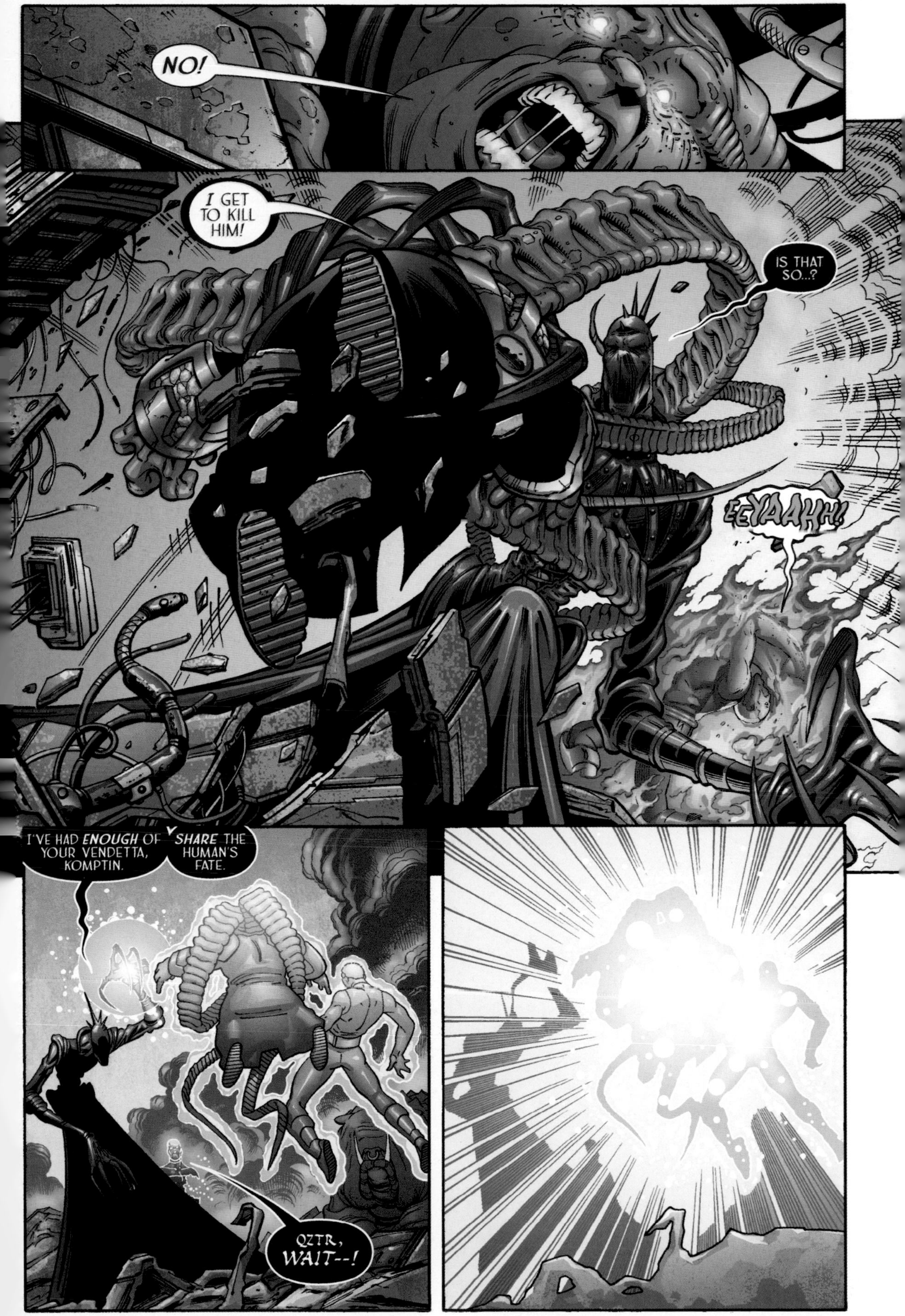
NO!
I GET TO KILL HIM!
IS THAT SO..?
EEYAAHH!!
I'VE HAD ENOUGH OF YOUR VENDETTA, KOMPTIN.
SHARE THE HUMAN'S FATE.
QZTR, WAIT--!

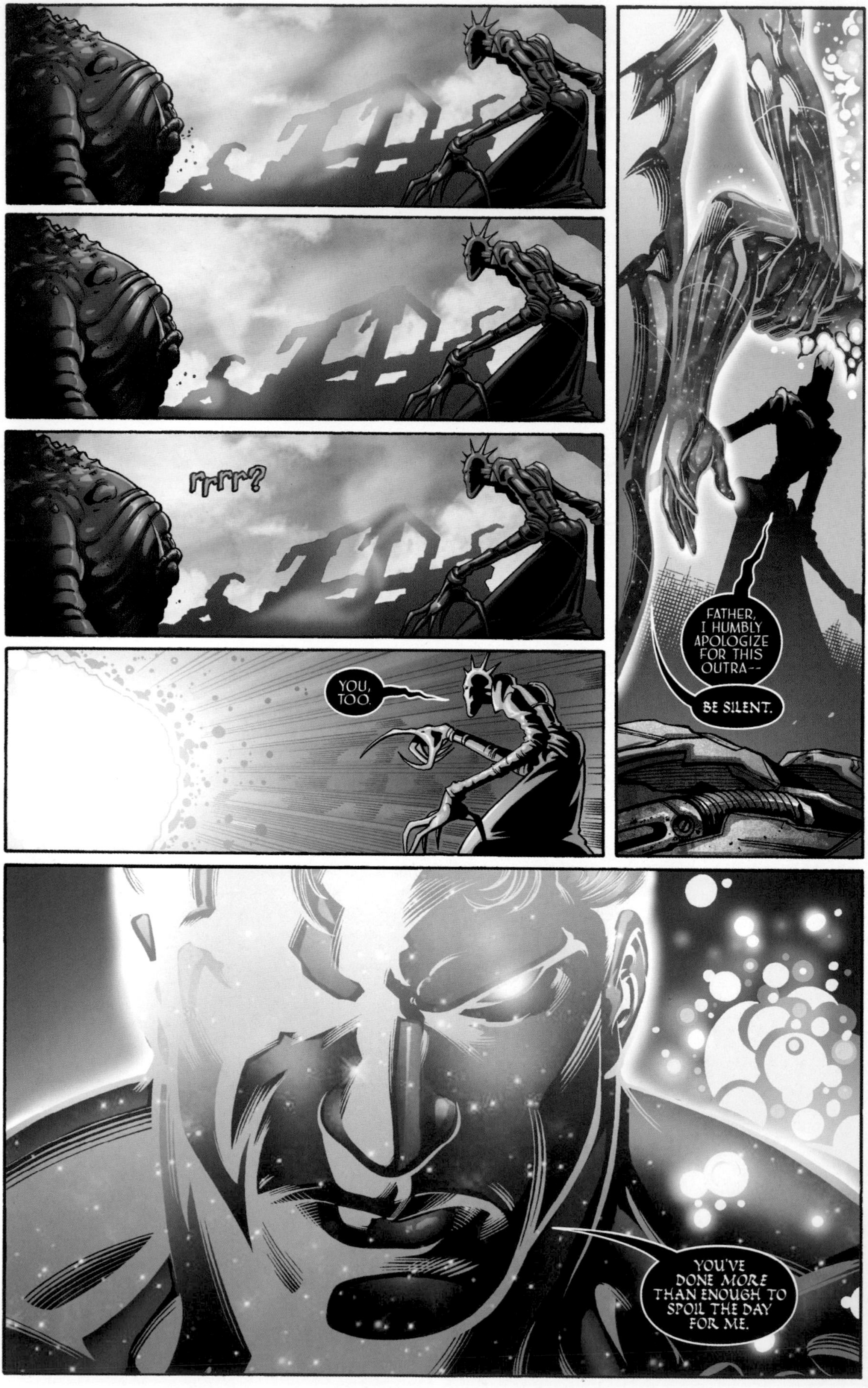
rrrr?
YOU, TOO.
FATHER, I HUMBLY APOLOGIZE FOR THIS OUTRA--
BE SILENT.
YOU'VE DONE MORE THAN ENOUGH TO SPOIL THE DAY FOR ME.

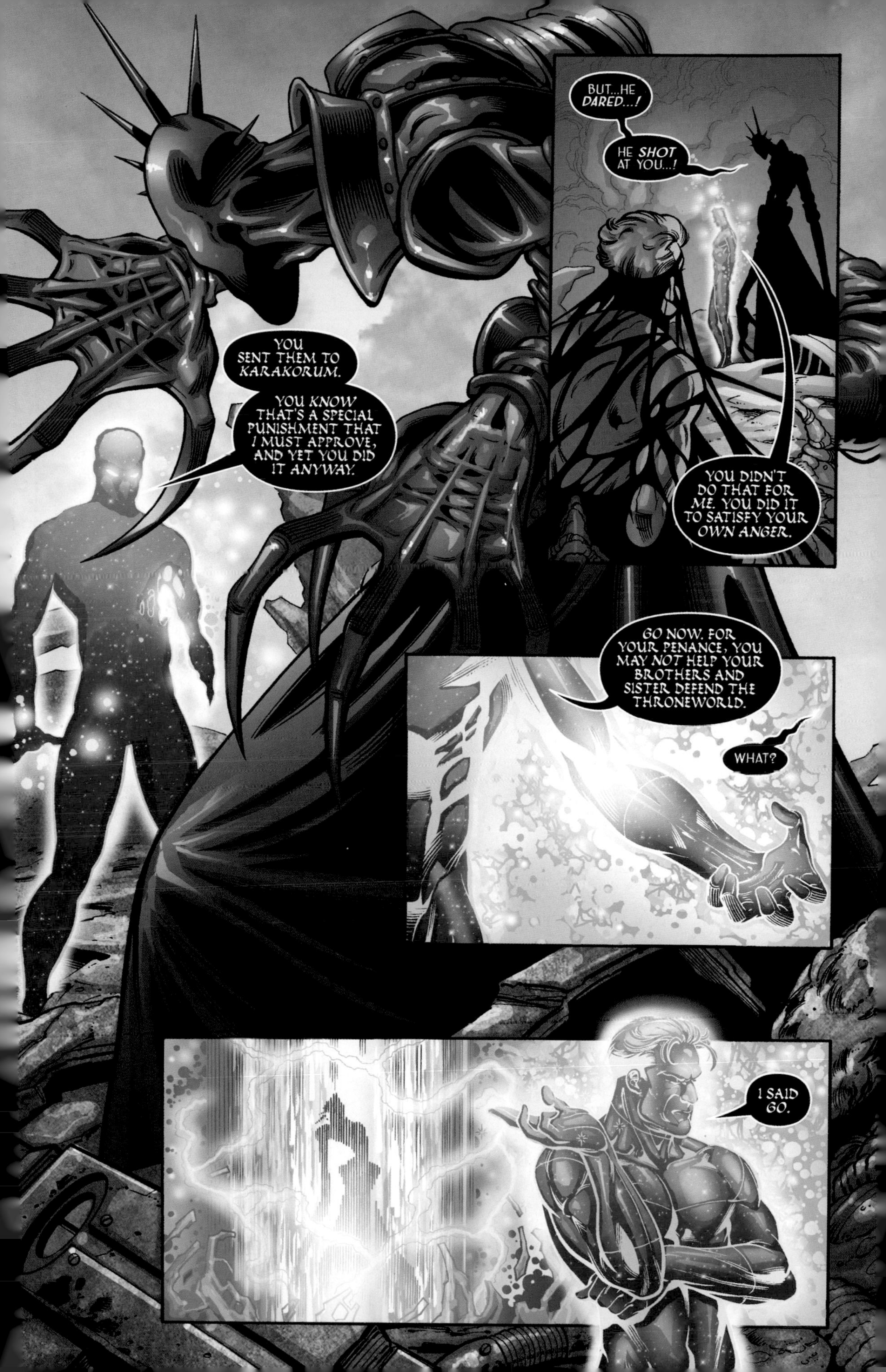

YOU SENT THEM TO KARAKORUM.
YOU KNOW THAT'S A SPECIAL PUNISHMENT THAT I MUST APPROVE, AND YET YOU DID IT ANYWAY.
BUT...HE DARED...!
HE SHOT AT YOU...!
YOU DIDN'T DO THAT FOR ME. YOU DID IT TO SATISFY YOUR OWN ANGER.
GO NOW. FOR YOUR PENANCE, YOU MAY NOT HELP YOUR BROTHERS AND SISTER DEFEND THE THRONEWORLD.
WHAT?
I SAID GO.

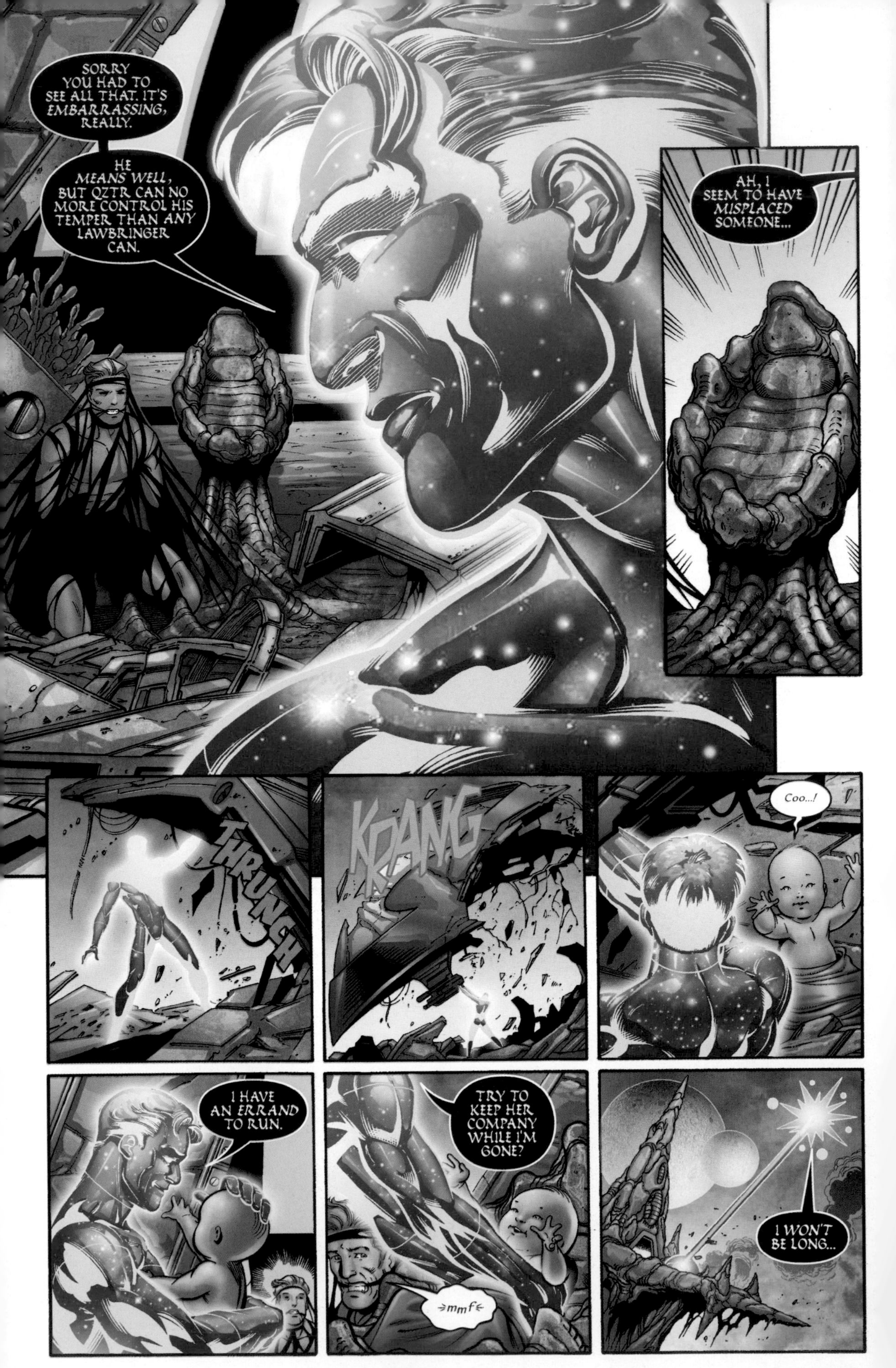
SORRY YOU HAD TO SEE ALL THAT. IT'S EMBARRASSING, REALLY.
HE MEANS WELL, BUT QZTR CAN NO MORE CONTROL HIS TEMPER THAN ANY LAWBRINGER CAN.
AH, I SEEM TO HAVE MISPLACED SOMEONE...
THRUNCH
KRANG
Coo...!
I HAVE AN ERRAND TO RUN.
TRY TO KEEP HER COMPANY WHILE I'M GONE?
mmf
I WON'T BE LONG...

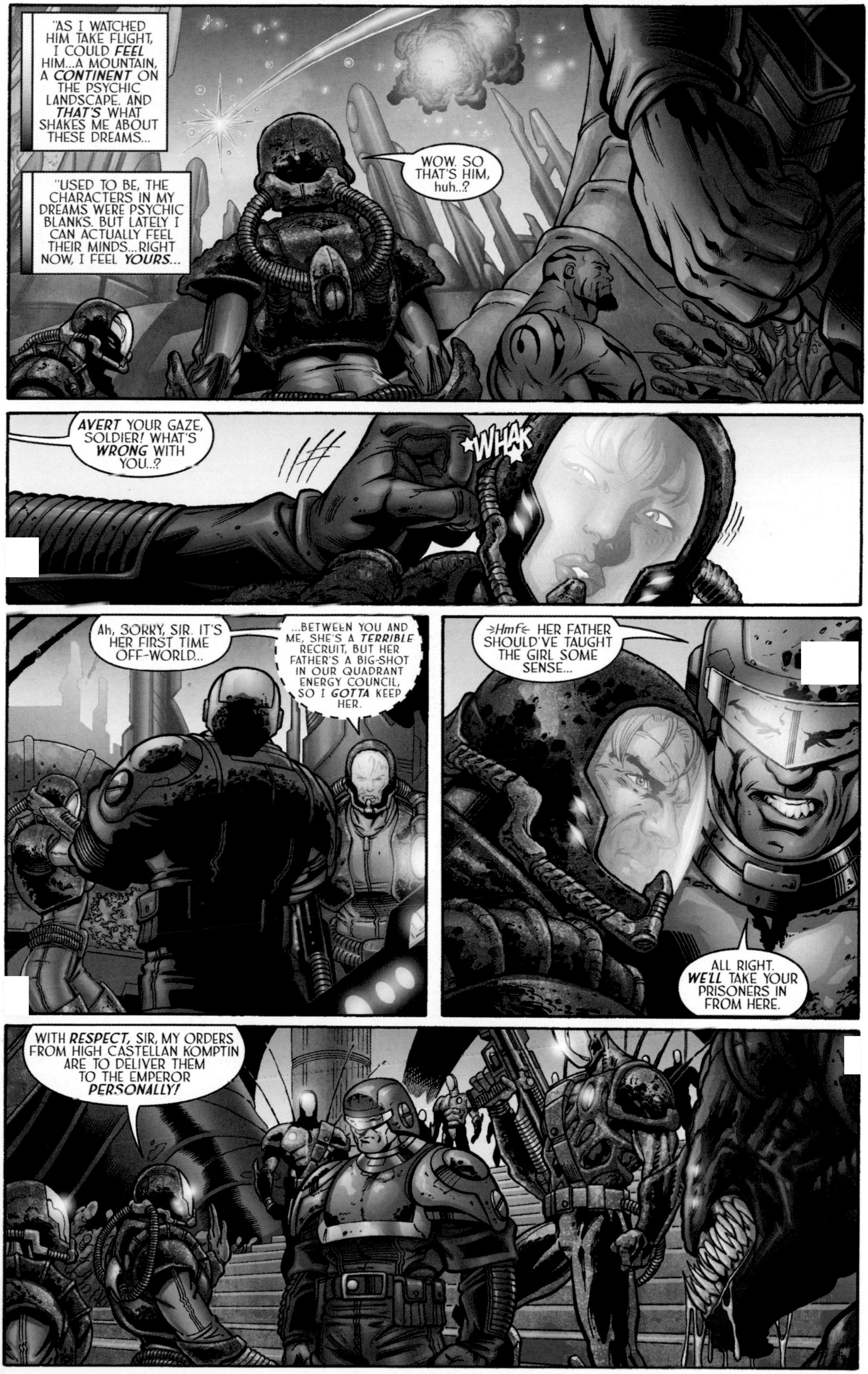

"AS I WATCHED HIM TAKE FLIGHT, I COULD FEEL HIM...A MOUNTAIN, A CONTINENT ON THE PSYCHIC LANDSCAPE. AND THAT'S WHAT SHAKES ME ABOUT THESE DREAMS...
"USED TO BE, THE CHARACTERS IN MY DREAMS WERE PSYCHIC BLANKS. BUT LATELY I CAN ACTUALLY FEEL THEIR MINDS...RIGHT NOW, I FEEL YOURS...
WOW. SO THAT'S HIM, huh..?
AVERT YOUR GAZE, SOLDIER! WHAT'S WRONG WITH YOU..?
WHAK
Ah, SORRY, SIR. IT'S HER FIRST TIME OFF-WORLD...
...BETWEEN YOU AND ME, SHE'S A TERRIBLE RECRUIT, BUT HER FATHER'S A BIG-SHOT IN OUR QUADRANT ENERGY COUNCIL, SO I GOTTA KEEP HER.
Hmf HER FATHER SHOULD'VE TAUGHT THE GIRL SOME SENSE...
ALL RIGHT. WE'LL TAKE YOUR PRISONERS IN FROM HERE.
WITH RESPECT, SIR, MY ORDERS FROM HIGH CASTELLAN KOMPTIN ARE TO DELIVER THEM TO THE EMPEROR PERSONALLY!

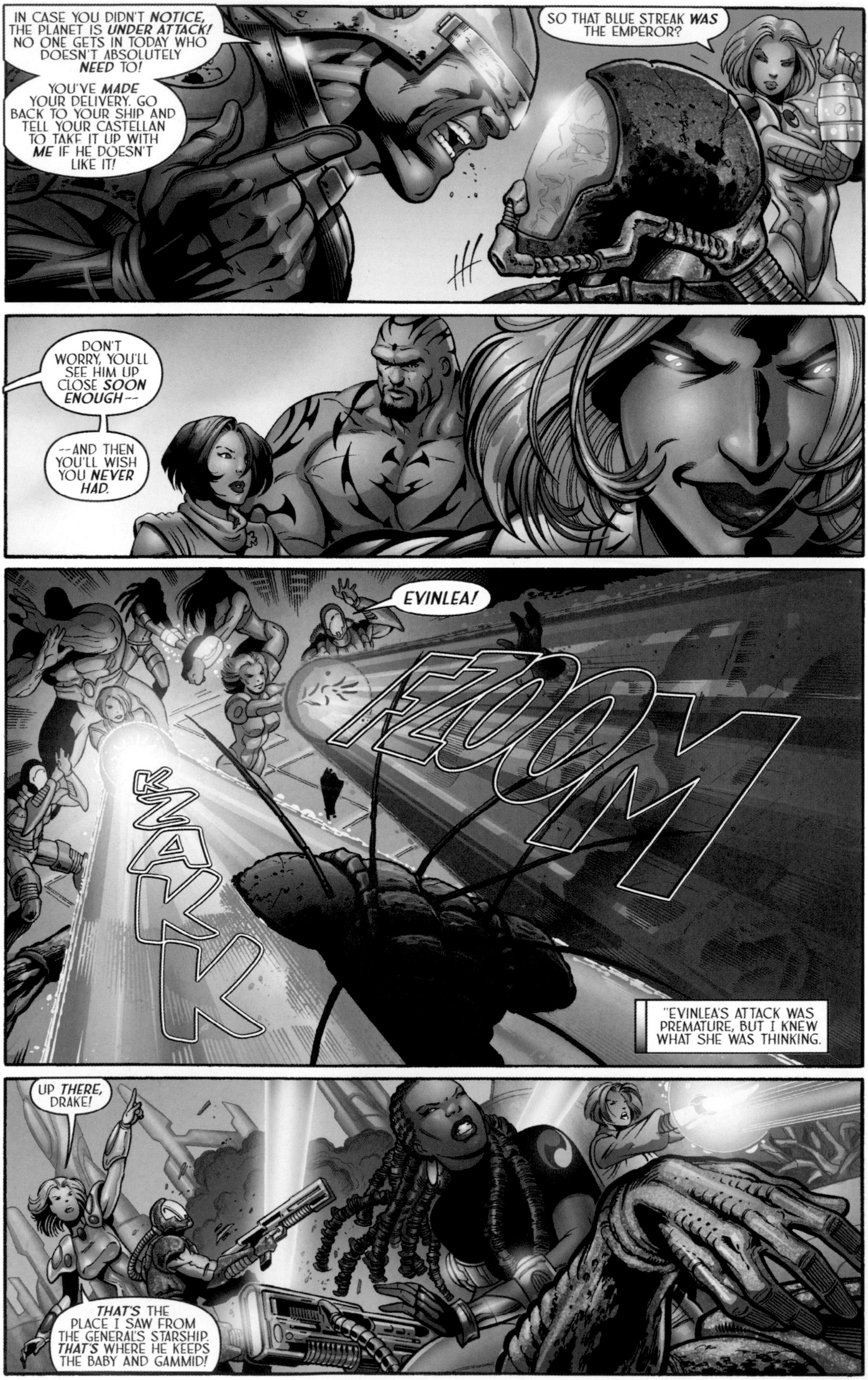
IN CASE YOU DIDN'T NOTICE, THE PLANET IS UNDER ATTACK! NO ONE GETS IN TODAY WHO DOESN'T ABSOLUTELY NEED TO!
YOU'VE MADE YOUR DELIVERY. GO BACK TO YOUR SHIP AND TELL YOUR CASTELLAN TO TAKE IT UP WITH ME IF HE DOESN'T LIKE IT!
SO THAT BLUE STREAK WAS THE EMPEROR?
DON'T WORRY, YOU'LL SEE HIM UP CLOSE SOON ENOUGH--
--AND THEN YOU'LL WISH YOU NEVER HAD.
EVINLEA!
FZOOM
KZAKK
"EVINLEA'S ATTACK WAS PREMATURE, BUT I KNEW WHAT SHE WAS THINKING.
UP THERE, DRAKE!
THAT'S THE PLACE I SAW FROM THE GENERAL'S STARSHIP. THAT'S WHERE HE KEEPS THE BABY AND GAMMID!

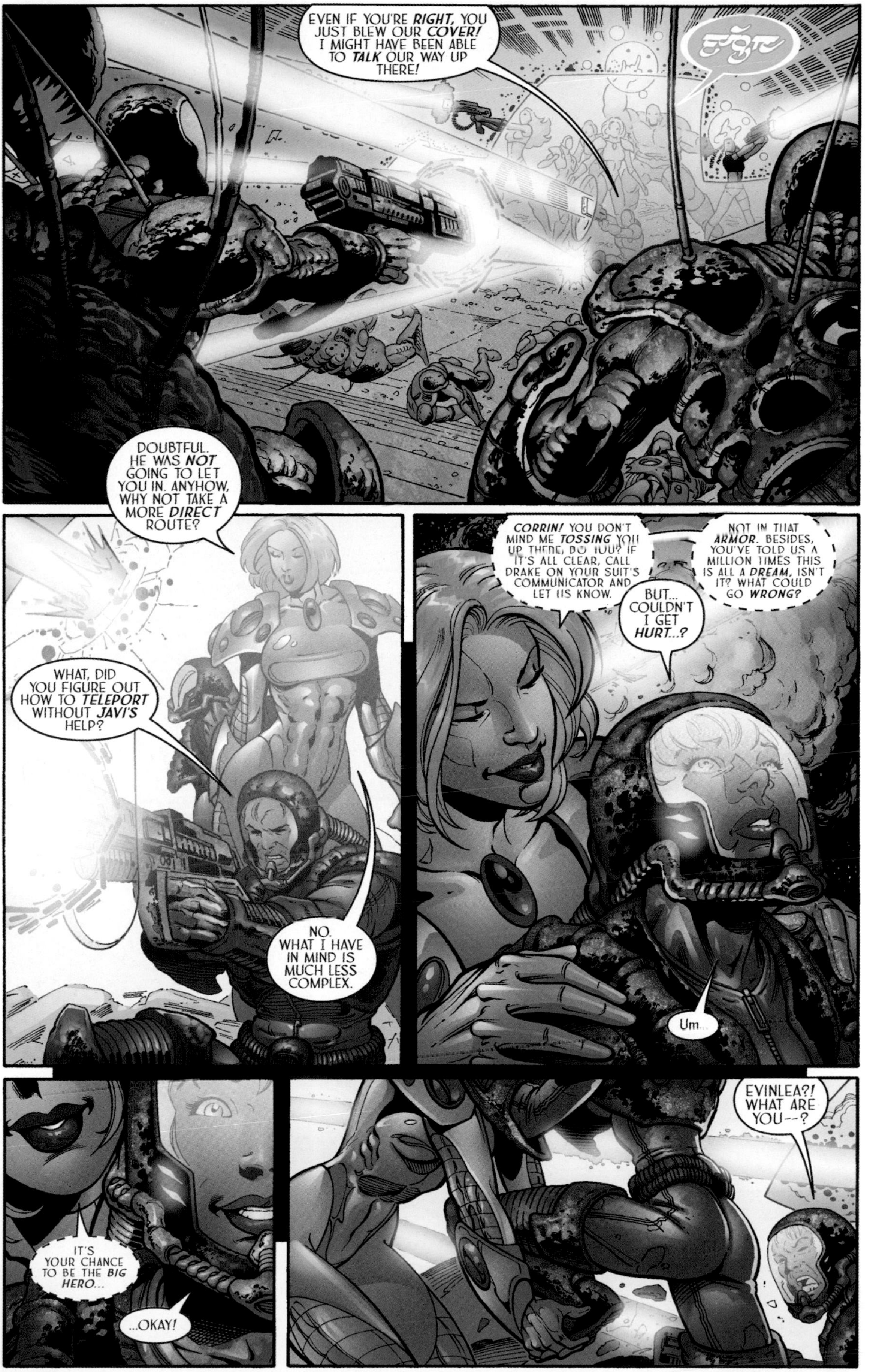
EVEN IF YOU'RE RIGHT, YOU JUST BLEW OUR COVER! I MIGHT HAVE BEEN ABLE TO TALK OUR WAY UP THERE!
DOUBTFUL. HE WAS NOT GOING TO LET YOU IN. ANYHOW, WHY NOT TAKE A MORE DIRECT ROUTE?
WHAT, DID YOU FIGURE OUT HOW TO TELEPORT WITHOUT JAVI'S HELP?
NO. WHAT I HAVE IN MIND IS MUCH LESS COMPLEX.
CORRIN! YOU DON'T MIND ME TOSSING YOU UP THERE, DO YOU? IF IT'S ALL CLEAR, CALL DRAKE ON YOUR SUIT'S COMMUNICATOR AND LET US KNOW.
BUT... COULDN'T I GET HURT...?
NOT IN THAT ARMOR. BESIDES, YOU'VE TOLD US A MILLION TIMES THIS IS ALL A DREAM, ISN'T IT? WHAT COULD GO WRONG?
Um...
IT'S YOUR CHANCE TO BE THE BIG HERO...
...OKAY!
EVINLEA?! WHAT ARE YOU--?

"IT SEEMED LIKE GOOD DREAM-LOGIC TO ME. AND IT *WAS* FUN..."

"BUT EVINLEA WAS *WRONG* ABOUT ONE THING..."

"...IT *DID* HURT."

→whung←

KRAH

unh...

...MEMI...?!

AM I GLAD TO SEE *YOU,* LITTLE GIRL!

?

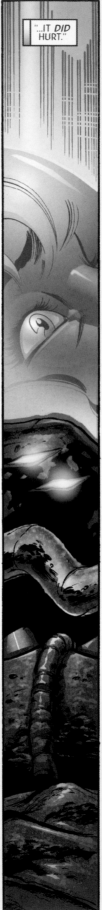

Um...HI. YOU'RE *GAMMID*, RIGHT? I'M HERE TO *RESCUE* YOU...

ZARK

"ACTUALLY, *ALL* OF THIS HURT QUITE A BIT.

"AND I BEGAN TO WONDER IF MY DREAMS HAD BECOME SO REALISTIC THAT I COULD BE *KILLED* HERE.

"FINE...

"I'D MOSTLY FLOATED THROUGH THIS DREAM AS AN *OBSERVER* UNTIL NOW.

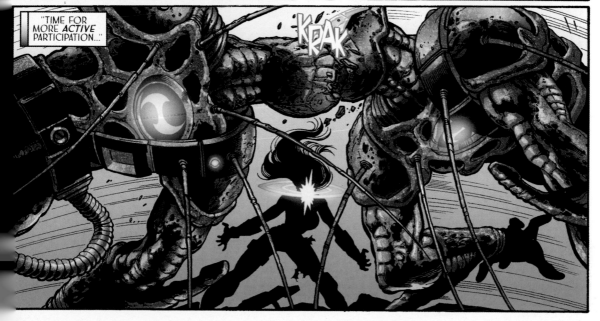

"TIME FOR MORE *ACTIVE* PARTICIPATION...

KRAK

"I FIGURED THESE PEOPLE HAD NEVER FACED SOMEONE FROM *ATLANTIS* BEFORE..."

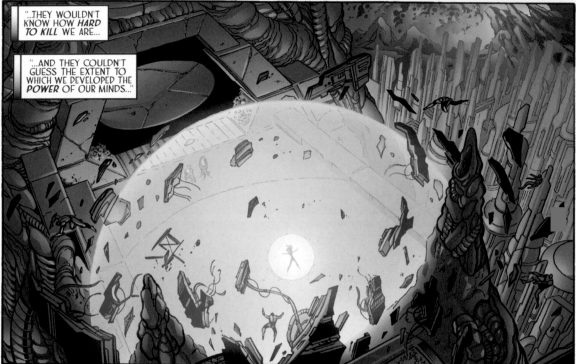

"...THEY WOULDN'T KNOW HOW *HARD TO KILL* WE ARE..."

"...AND THEY COULDN'T GUESS THE EXTENT TO WHICH WE DEVELOPED THE *POWER* OF OUR MINDS..."

mm-MMMFF!

SORRY. I KIND OF LOST MY *TEMPER* THERE...

THAT *TELEKINETIC* FLASH AROUND YOUR HEAD--I *RECOGNIZE* IT!

SHRPP

YOU... YOU'RE *ATLANTEAN,* LIKE ME--?!

YOU, *TOO...?*

EXCELLENT! YOU'RE THE FIRST ATLANTEAN I'VE DREAMED OF SINCE--

WHOA, *BACK UP* A SECOND. DID *CAPRICIA* SEND YOU? HAVE THEY AWOKEN ANY *OTHERS?*

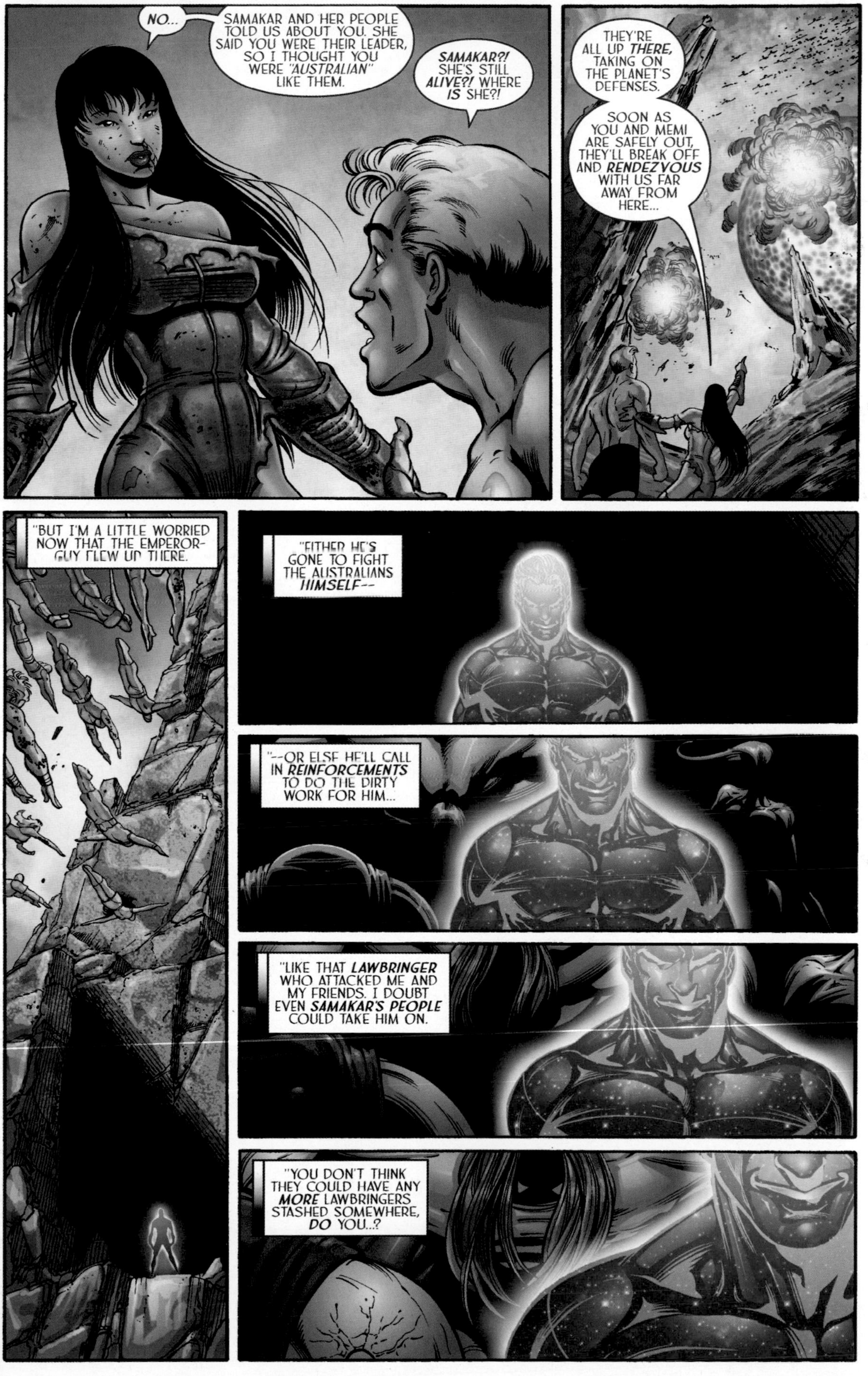
NO...
SAMAKAR AND HER PEOPLE TOLD US ABOUT YOU. SHE SAID YOU WERE THEIR LEADER, SO I THOUGHT YOU WERE "AUSTRALIAN" LIKE THEM.
SAMAKAR?! SHE'S STILL ALIVE?! WHERE IS SHE?!
THEY'RE ALL UP THERE, TAKING ON THE PLANET'S DEFENSES.
SOON AS YOU AND MEMI ARE SAFELY OUT, THEY'LL BREAK OFF AND RENDEZVOUS WITH US FAR AWAY FROM HERE...
"BUT I'M A LITTLE WORRIED NOW THAT THE EMPEROR-GUY FLEW UP THERE.
"EITHER HE'S GONE TO FIGHT THE AUSTRALIANS HIMSELF--
"--OR ELSE HE'LL CALL IN REINFORCEMENTS TO DO THE DIRTY WORK FOR HIM...
"LIKE THAT LAWBRINGER WHO ATTACKED ME AND MY FRIENDS. I DOUBT EVEN SAMAKAR'S PEOPLE COULD TAKE HIM ON.
"YOU DON'T THINK THEY COULD HAVE ANY MORE LAWBRINGERS STASHED SOMEWHERE, DO YOU..?

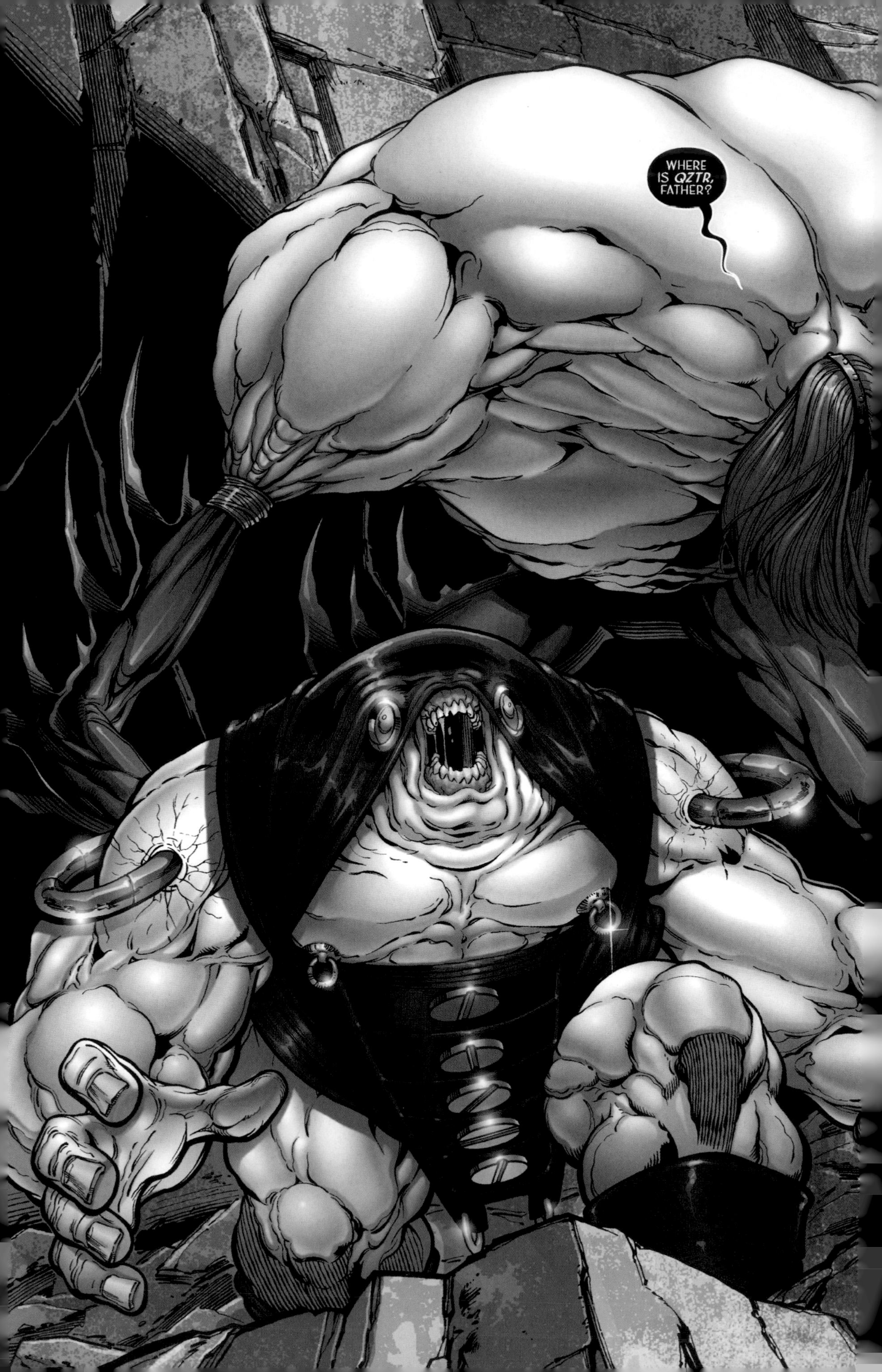
WHERE IS QZTR, FATHER?

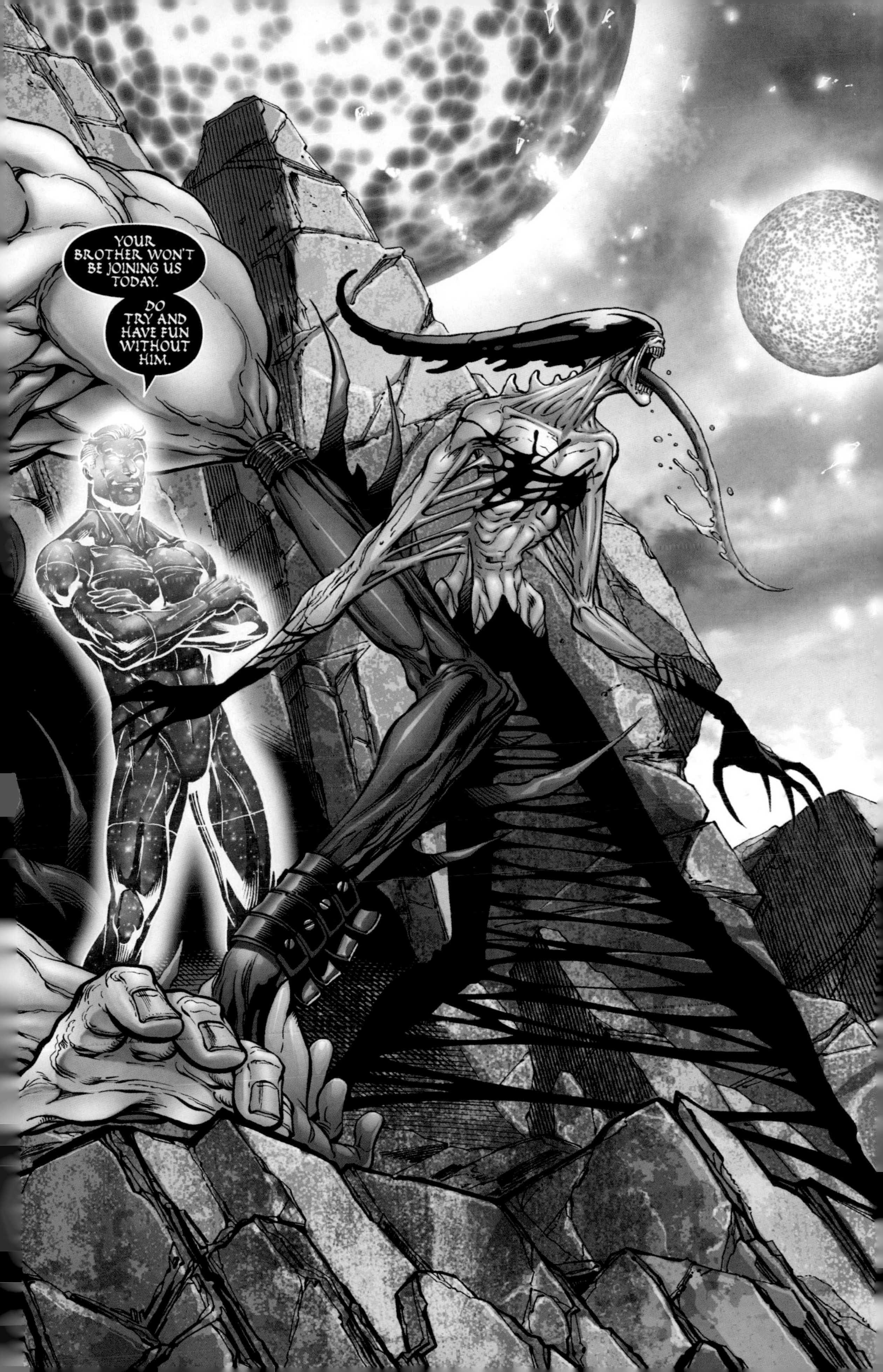
YOUR BROTHER WON'T BE JOINING US TODAY.
DO TRY AND HAVE FUN WITHOUT HIM.

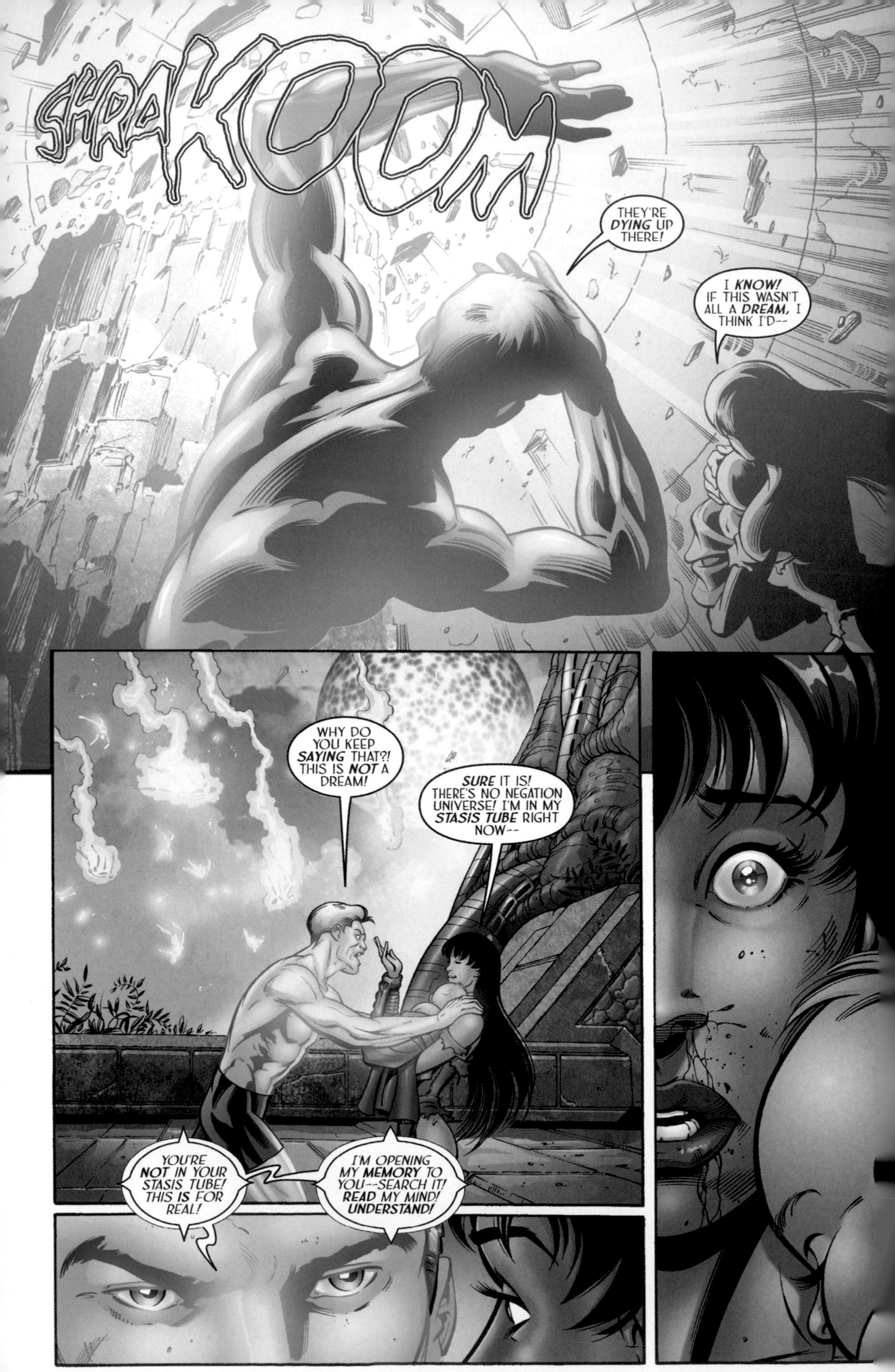
SHRAKOOM
THEY'RE DYING UP THERE!
I KNOW! IF THIS WASN'T ALL A DREAM, I THINK I'D--
WHY DO YOU KEEP SAYING THAT?! THIS IS NOT A DREAM!
SURE IT IS! THERE'S NO NEGATION UNIVERSE! I'M IN MY STASIS TUBE RIGHT NOW--
YOU'RE NOT IN YOUR STASIS TUBE! THIS IS FOR REAL!
I'M OPENING MY MEMORY TO YOU--SEARCH IT! READ MY MIND! UNDERSTAND!

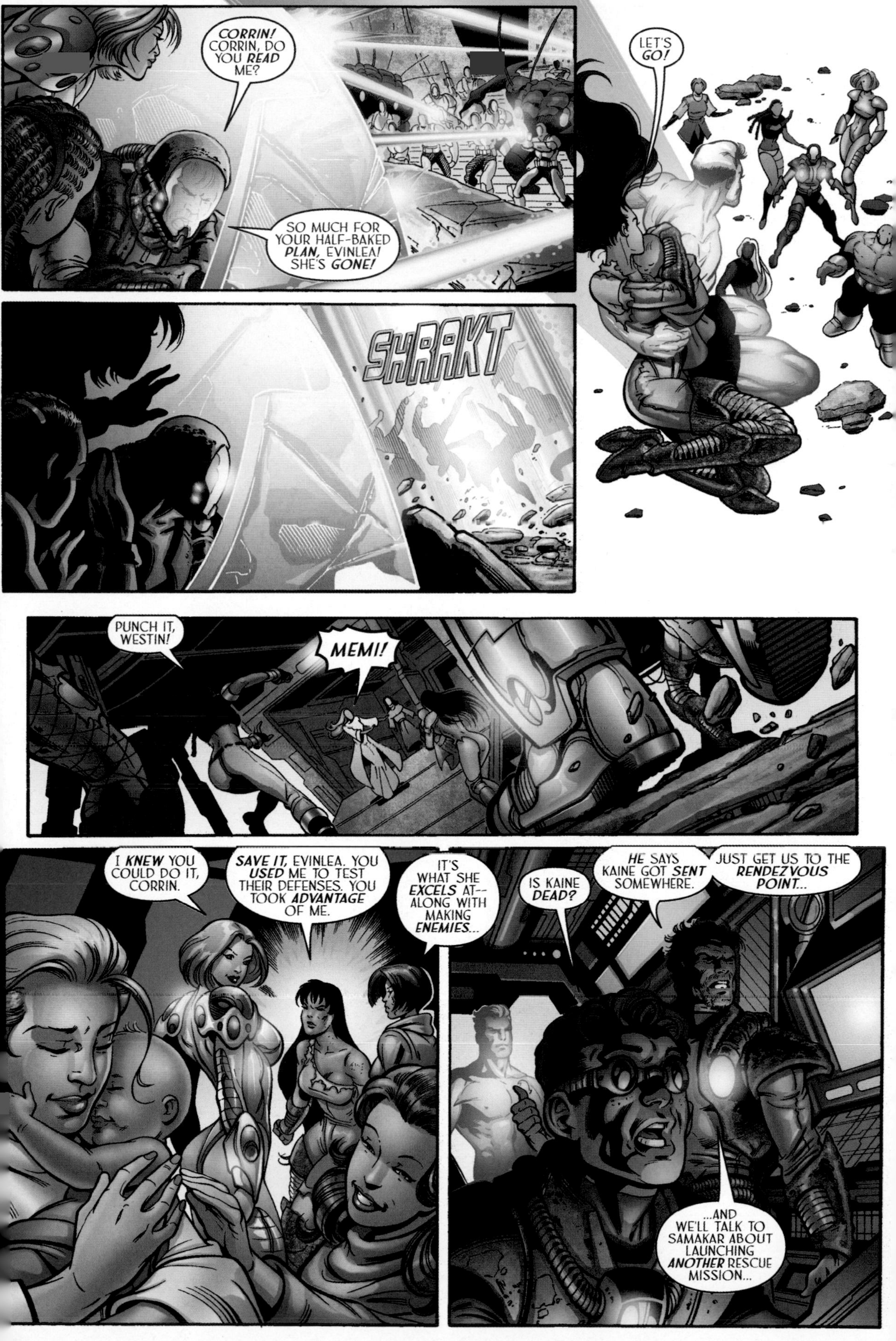
CORRIN! CORRIN, DO YOU READ ME?
SO MUCH FOR YOUR HALF-BAKED PLAN, EVINLEA! SHE'S GONE!
LET'S GO!
SHRAKT
PUNCH IT, WESTIN!
MEMI!
I KNEW YOU COULD DO IT, CORRIN.
SAVE IT, EVINLEA. YOU USED ME TO TEST THEIR DEFENSES. YOU TOOK ADVANTAGE OF ME.
IT'S WHAT SHE EXCELS AT-- ALONG WITH MAKING ENEMIES...
IS KAINE DEAD?
HE SAYS KAINE GOT SENT SOMEWHERE.
JUST GET US TO THE RENDEZVOUS POINT...
...AND WE'LL TALK TO SAMAKAR ABOUT LAUNCHING ANOTHER RESCUE MISSION...

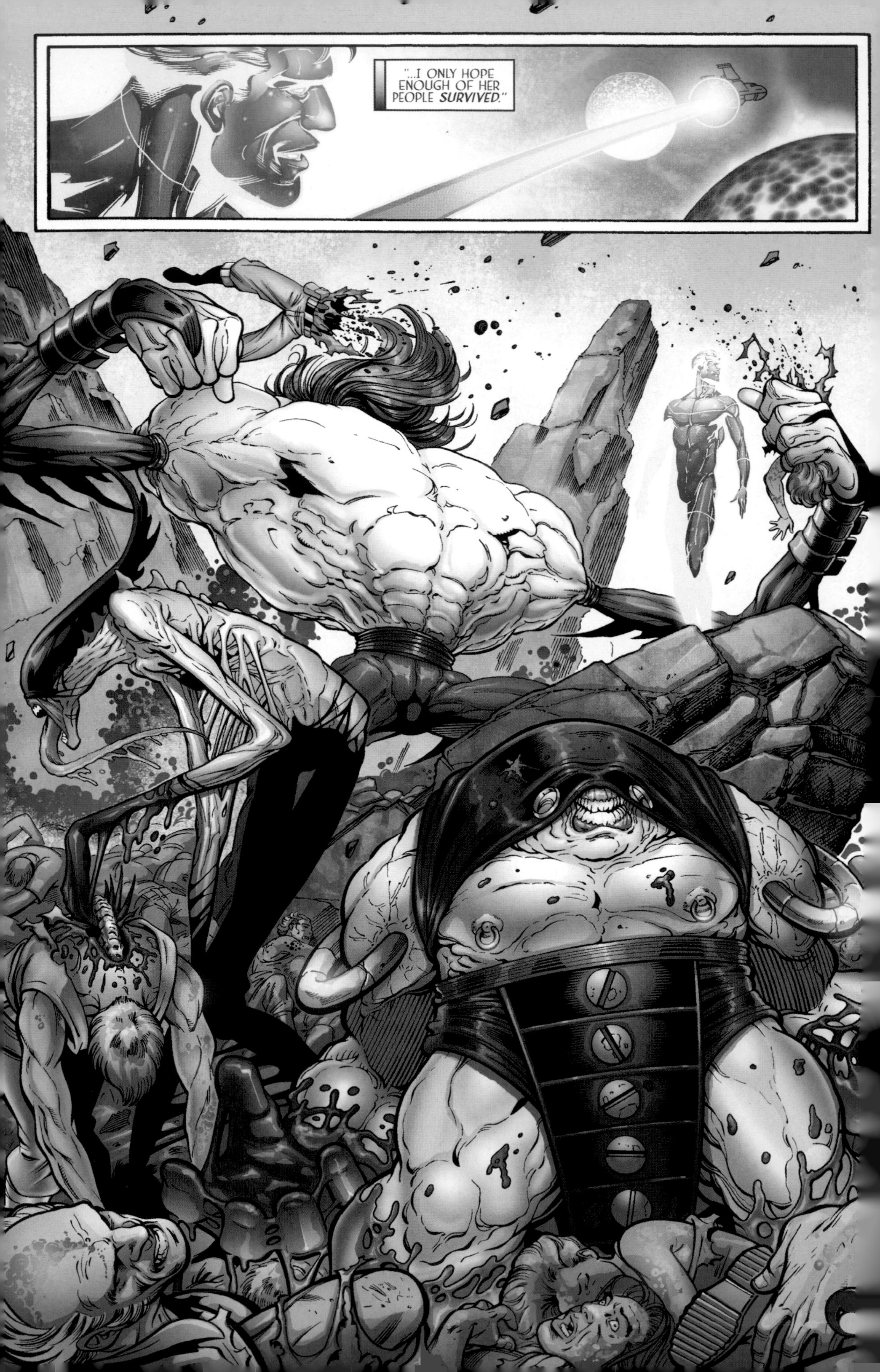
"...I ONLY HOPE ENOUGH OF HER PEOPLE SURVIVED."

STORYTELLERS

TONY BEDARD
WRITER

PAUL PELLETIER
PENCILER

DAVE MEIKIS
INKER

JAMES ROCHELLE
COLORIST

TROY PETERI
LETTERER

The
CrossGen
Universe
created by
Mark Alessi &
Gina M. Villa

MARK ALESSI Publisher & Chief Executive Officer * GINA M. VILLA Chief Operating Officer
MICHAEL A. BEATTIE Chief Financial Officer * JENNIFER HERNANDEZ General Counsel
TONY PANACCIO Vice President Product Development * CHRIS OARR Vice President Sales & Marketing
JAMES BREITBEIL Director Marketing & Distribution * IAN M. FELLER Director Corporate Communications
COURTLAND WHITED MIS Director * GABO MENDOZA Internet Services Director
CHARLES DECKER Director Production Control * BRIAN M. SOLTIS Controller
BRANDON PETERSON Vice President Special Projects * BARBARA KESEL Head Writer
BART SEARS Art Director * PAM DAVIES Vice President Production
SYLVIA BRETZ Production Supervisor Advertising/Web * ERIN FLANAGAN Web Designer
JANET BECHTLE Production Supervisor Books * RANDY MARTIN Production Designer
MICHELLE PUGLIESE Freelance Coordinator

Chapter 3

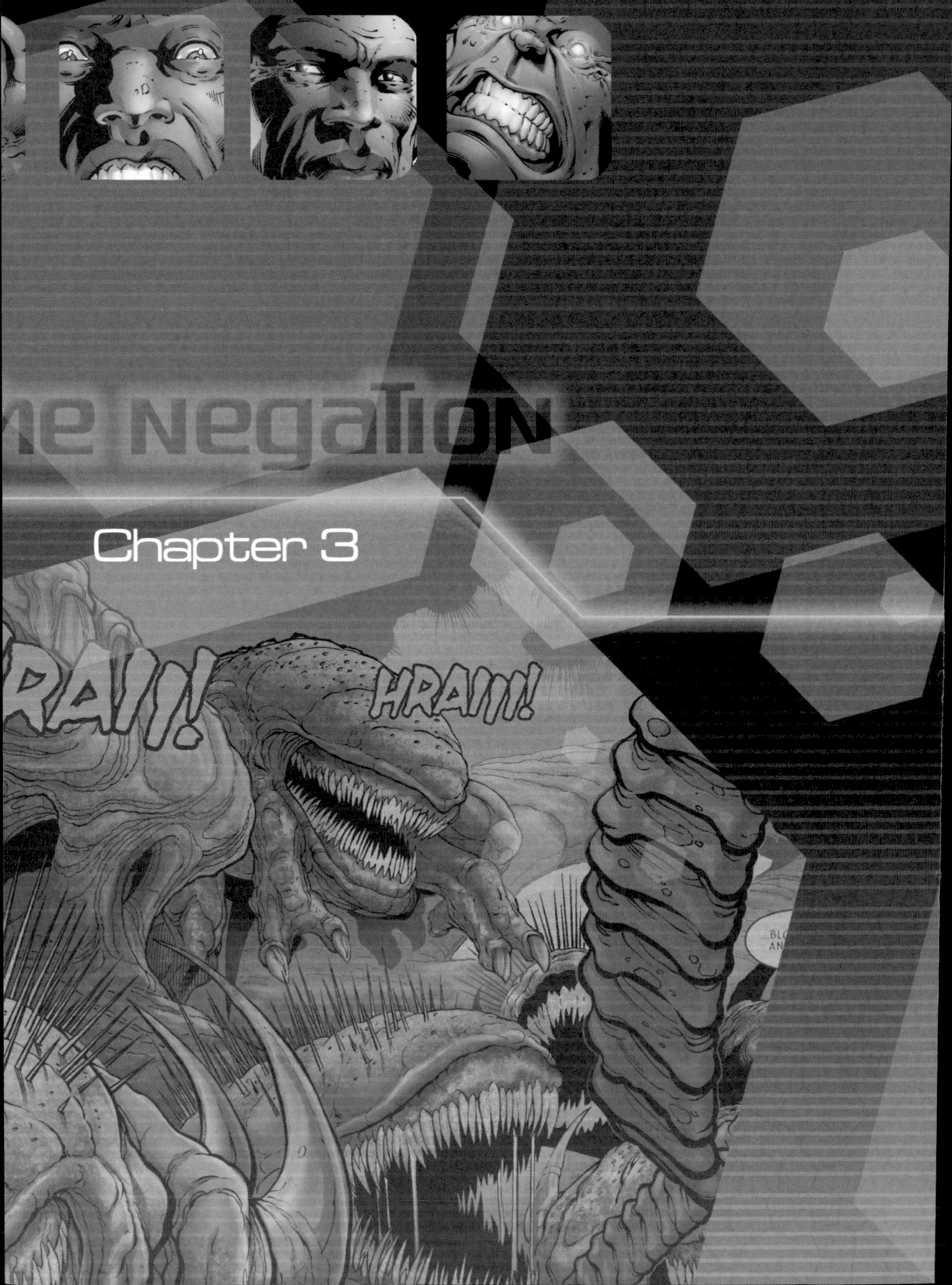
NEGATION
RAII!
HRAIII!

KEY ISSUE

NEGATION®

15
MARCH
$2.95
$4.75 CAN

Tony Bedard

Paul Pelletier

Dave Meikis

James Rochelle

Issue 15
March 2003

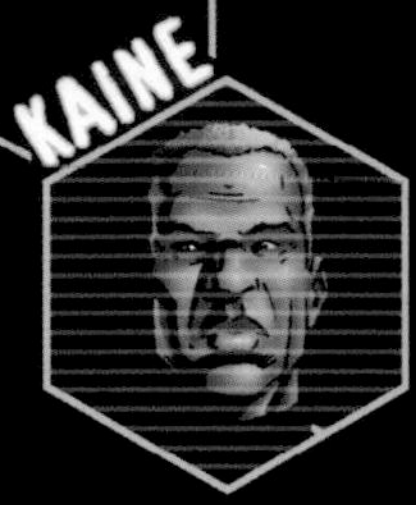
KAINE

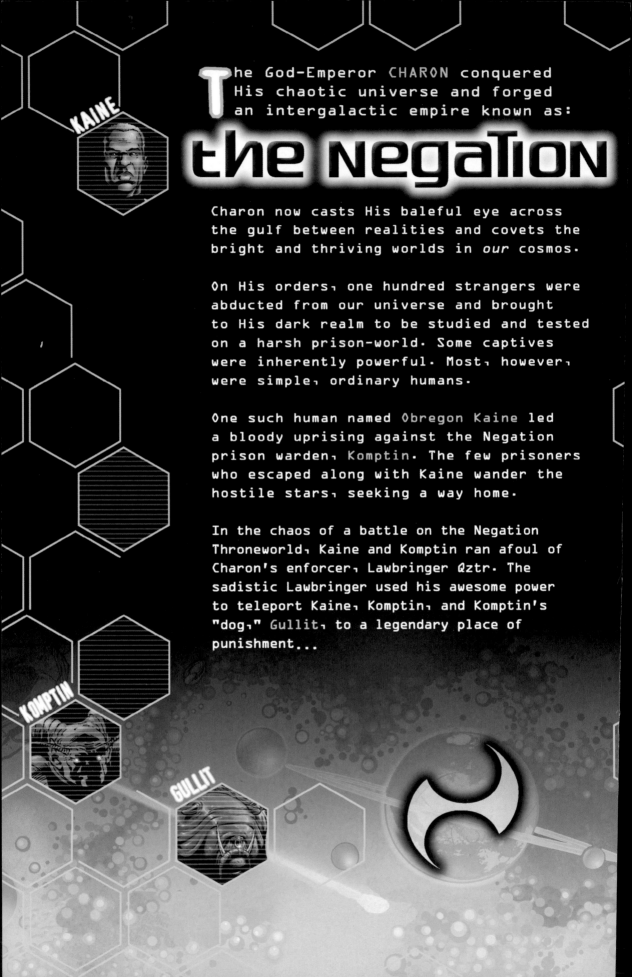

The God-Emperor CHARON conquered His chaotic universe and forged an intergalactic empire known as:

the Negation

Charon now casts His baleful eye across the gulf between realities and covets the bright and thriving worlds in *our* cosmos.

On His orders, one hundred strangers were abducted from our universe and brought to His dark realm to be studied and tested on a harsh prison-world. Some captives were inherently powerful. Most, however, were simple, ordinary humans.

One such human named Obregon Kaine led a bloody uprising against the Negation prison warden, Komptin. The few prisoners who escaped along with Kaine wander the hostile stars, seeking a way home.

In the chaos of a battle on the Negation Throneworld, Kaine and Komptin ran afoul of Charon's enforcer, Lawbringer Qztr. The sadistic Lawbringer used his awesome power to teleport Kaine, Komptin, and Komptin's "dog," Gullit, to a legendary place of punishment...

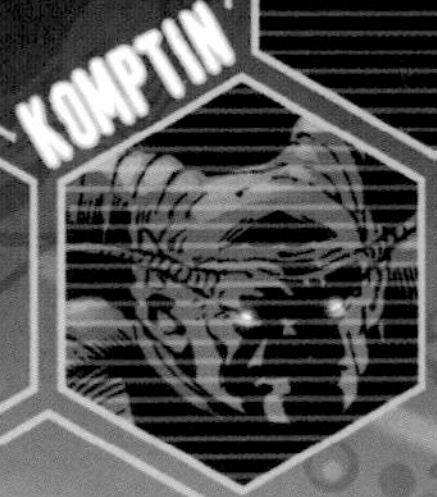
KOMPTIN

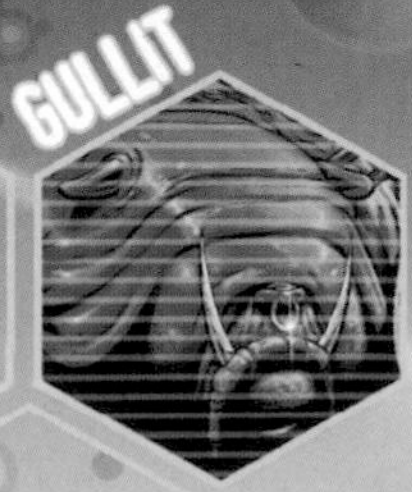
GULLIT

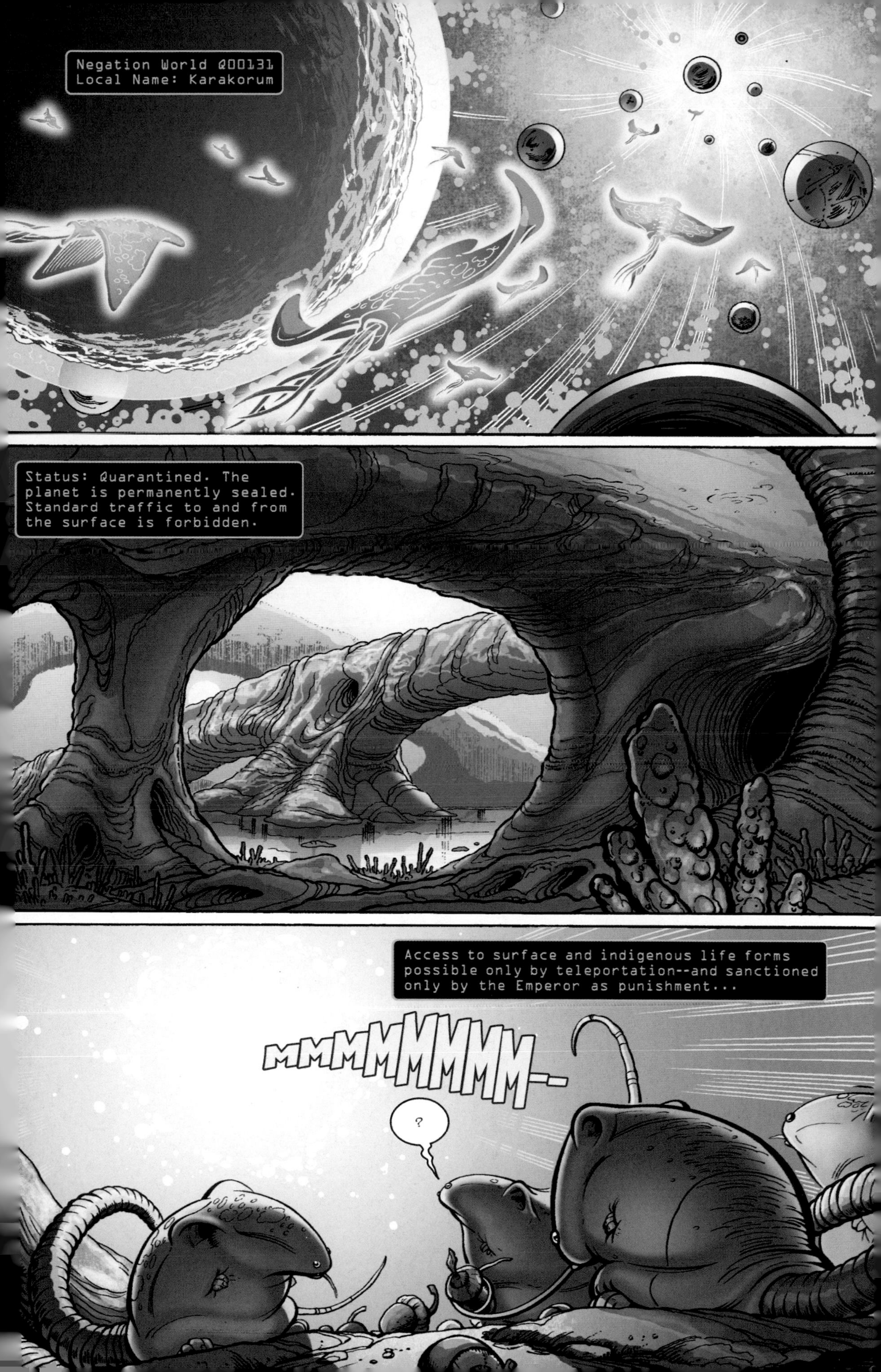
Negation World Q00131
Local Name: Karakorum
Status: Quarantined. The planet is permanently sealed. Standard traffic to and from the surface is forbidden.
Access to surface and indigenous life forms possible only by teleportation--and sanctioned only by the Emperor as punishment...
MMMMMMMMMM--
?

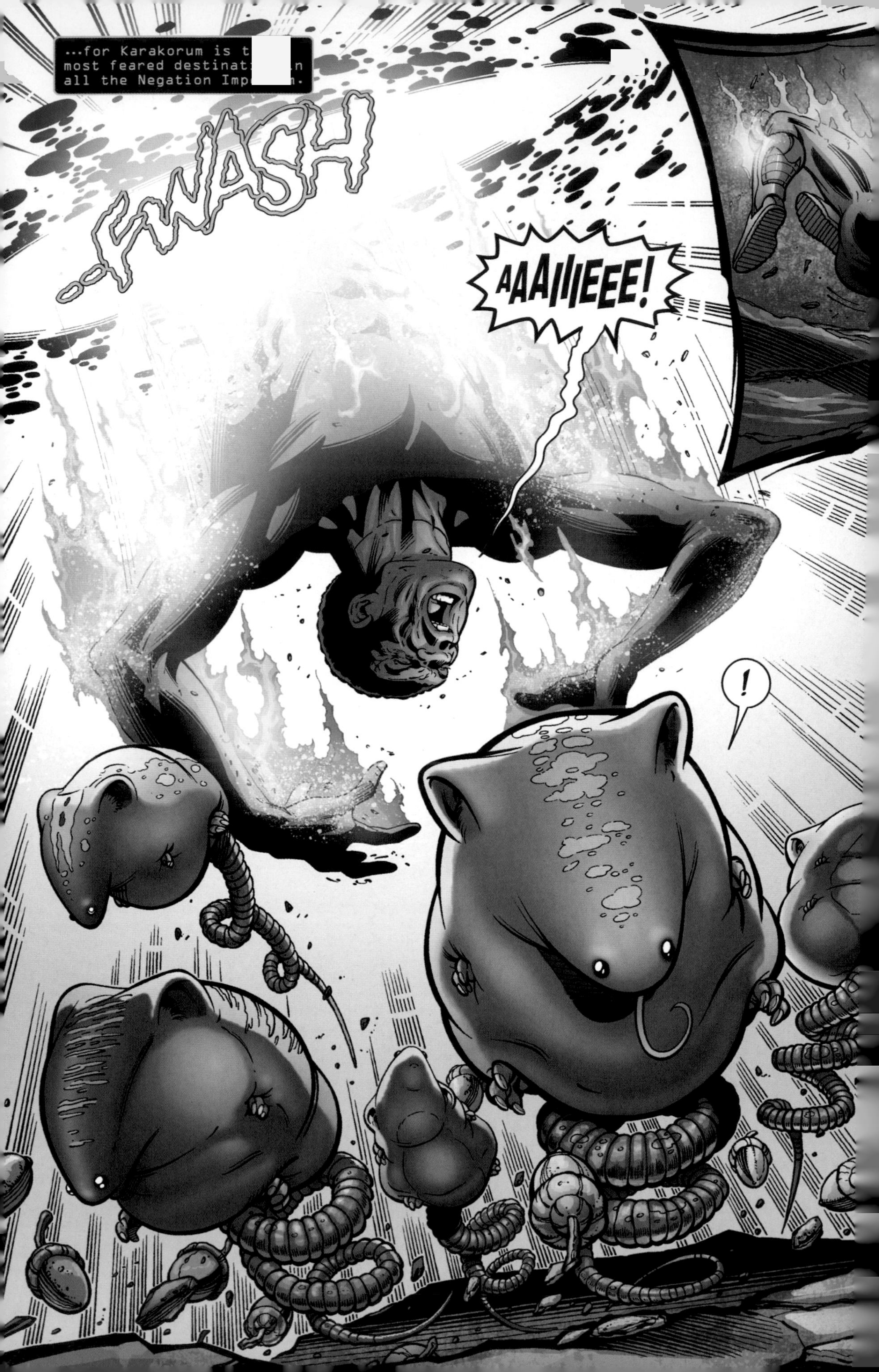
...for Karakorum is t most feared destinat n all the Negation Imp n.
FWASH
AAAIIIIEEE!
!

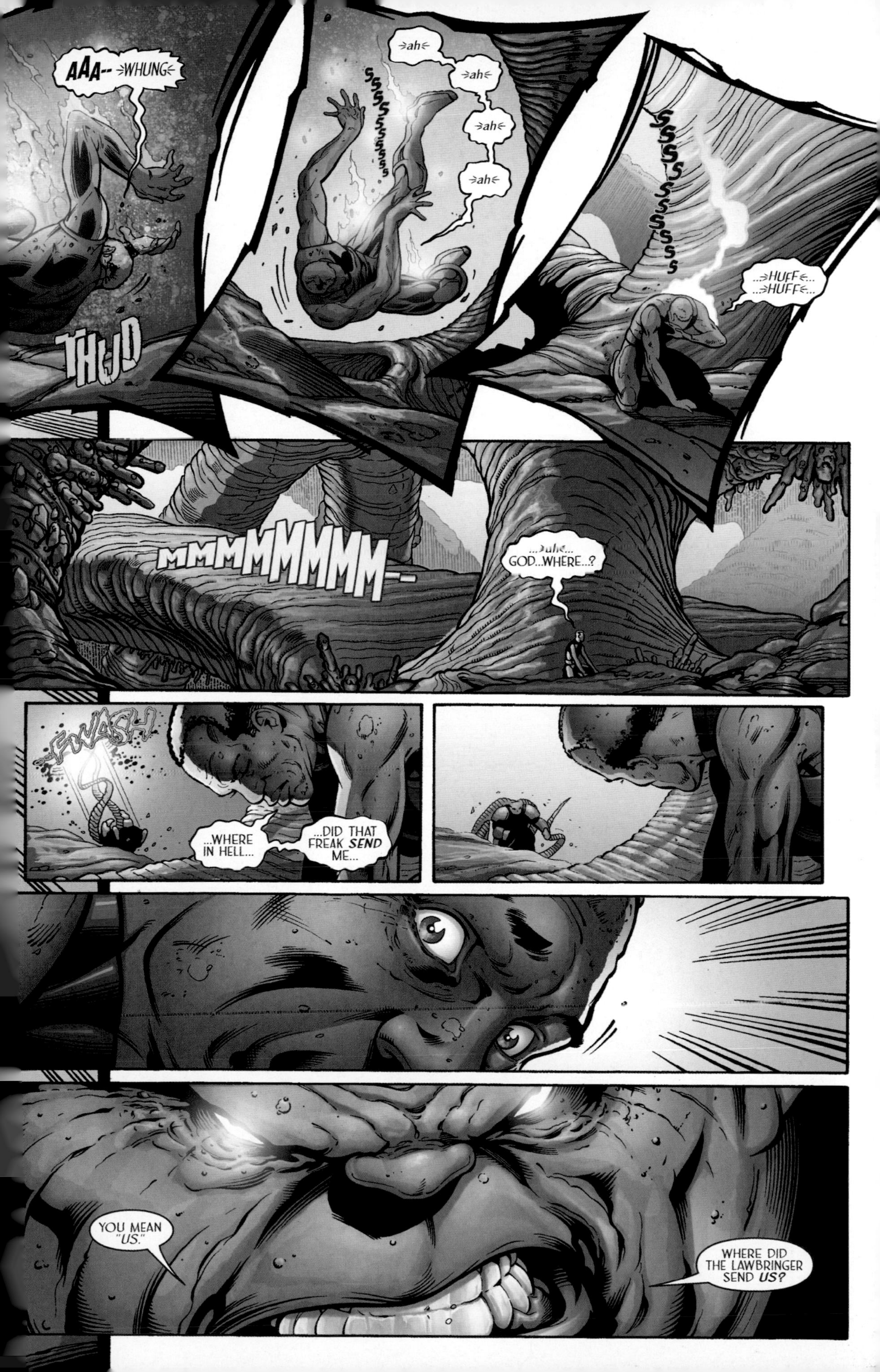
AAA-- WHUNG
THUD
ah
ah
ah
ah
SSSSSSSSSS
SSSSSSSSSSS
...HUFF...
...HUFF...
MMMMMMMMMM--
GOD...WHERE...?
FWASH
...WHERE IN HELL...
...DID THAT FREAK SEND ME...
YOU MEAN "US."
WHERE DID THE LAWBRINGER SEND US?

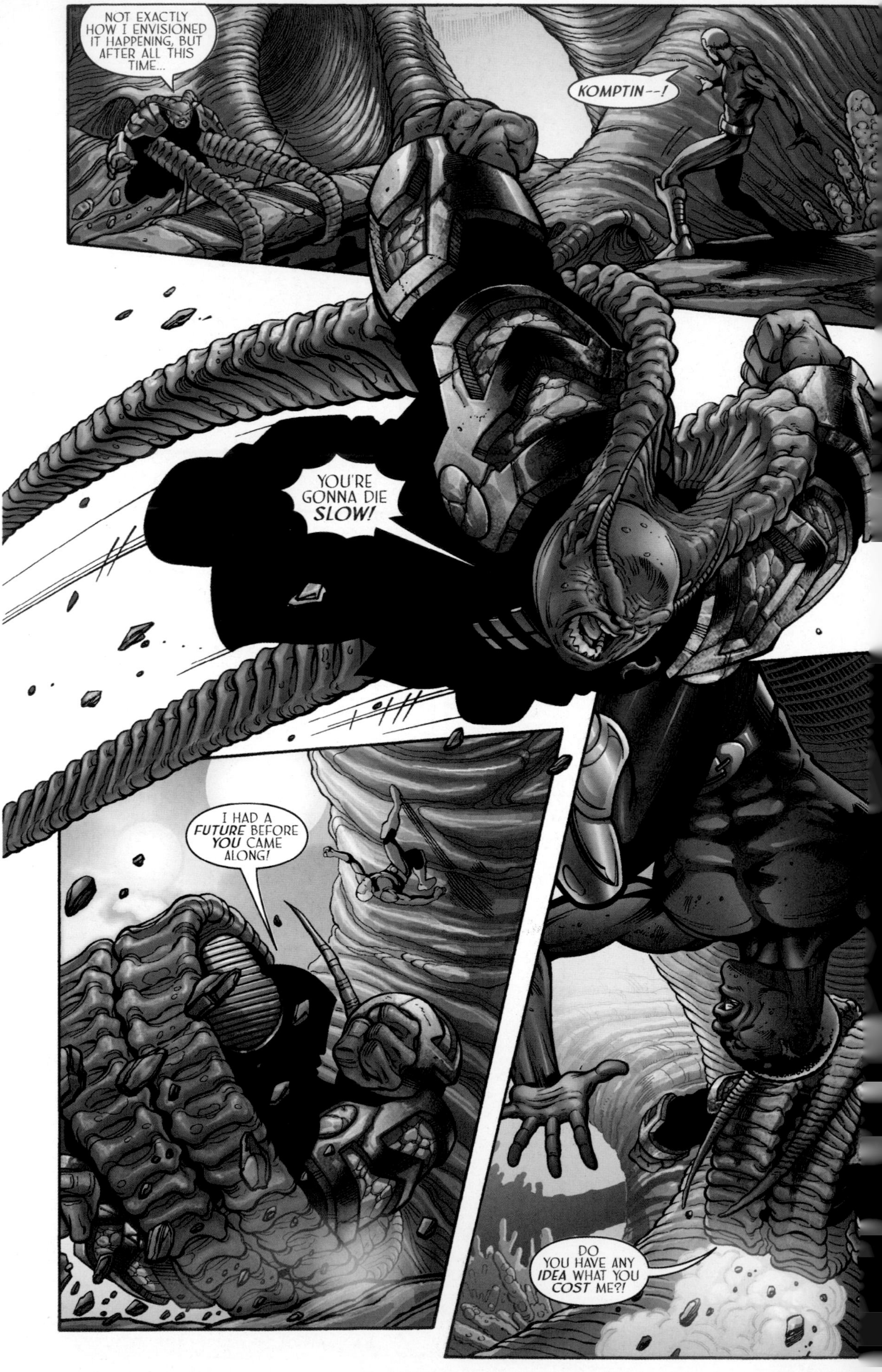
NOT EXACTLY HOW I ENVISIONED IT HAPPENING, BUT AFTER ALL THIS TIME...
KOMPTIN--!
YOU'RE GONNA DIE SLOW!
I HAD A FUTURE BEFORE YOU CAME ALONG!
DO YOU HAVE ANY IDEA WHAT YOU COST ME?!

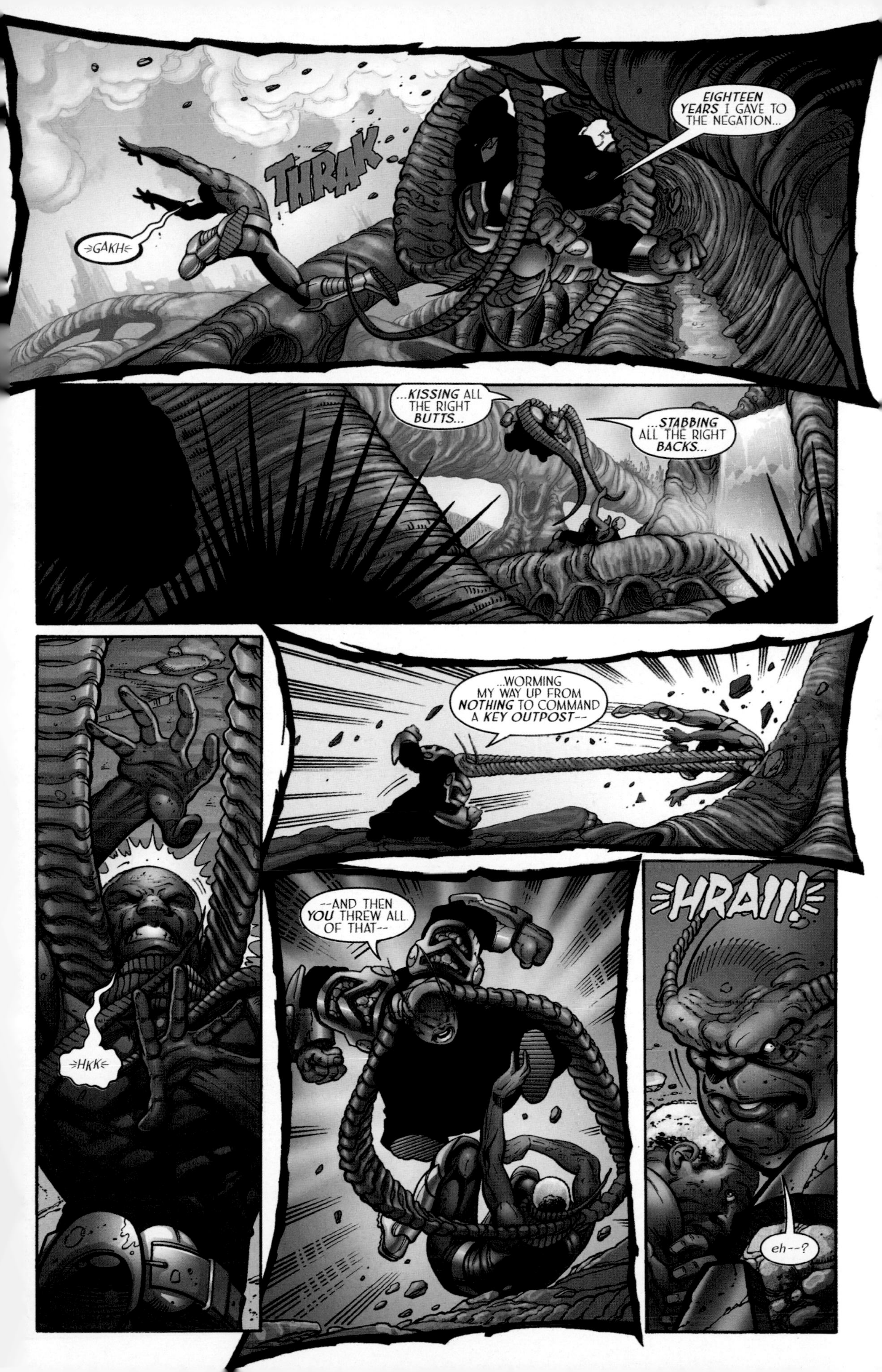
THRAK
EIGHTEEN YEARS I GAVE TO THE NEGATION...
GAKH
...KISSING ALL THE RIGHT BUTTS...
...STABBING ALL THE RIGHT BACKS...
...WORMING MY WAY UP FROM NOTHING TO COMMAND A KEY OUTPOST--
HKK
--AND THEN YOU THREW ALL OF THAT--
HRAII!
eh--?

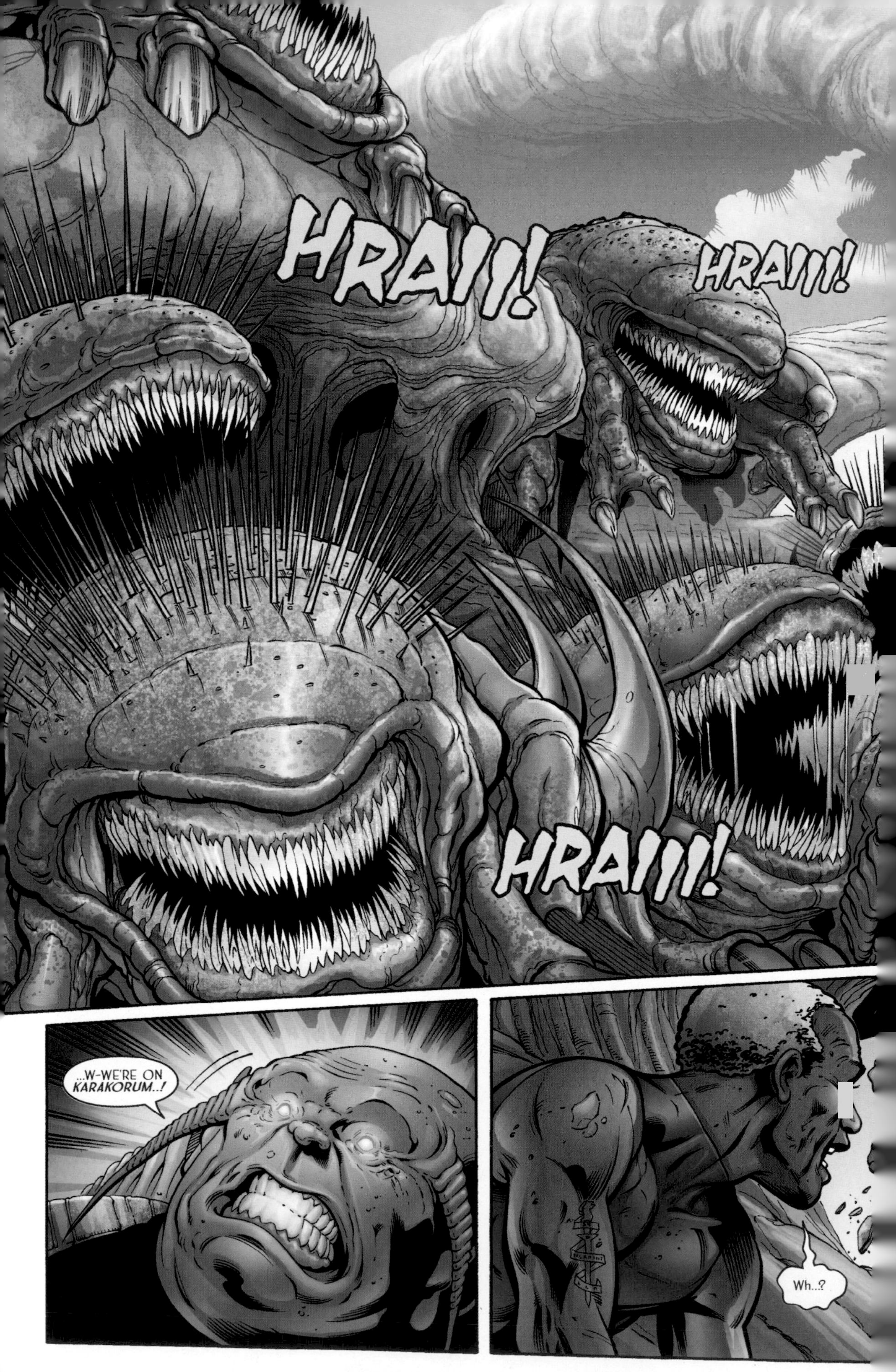
HRAIII!
HRAIII!
HRAIII!
...W-WE'RE ON KARAKORUM..!
Wh..?

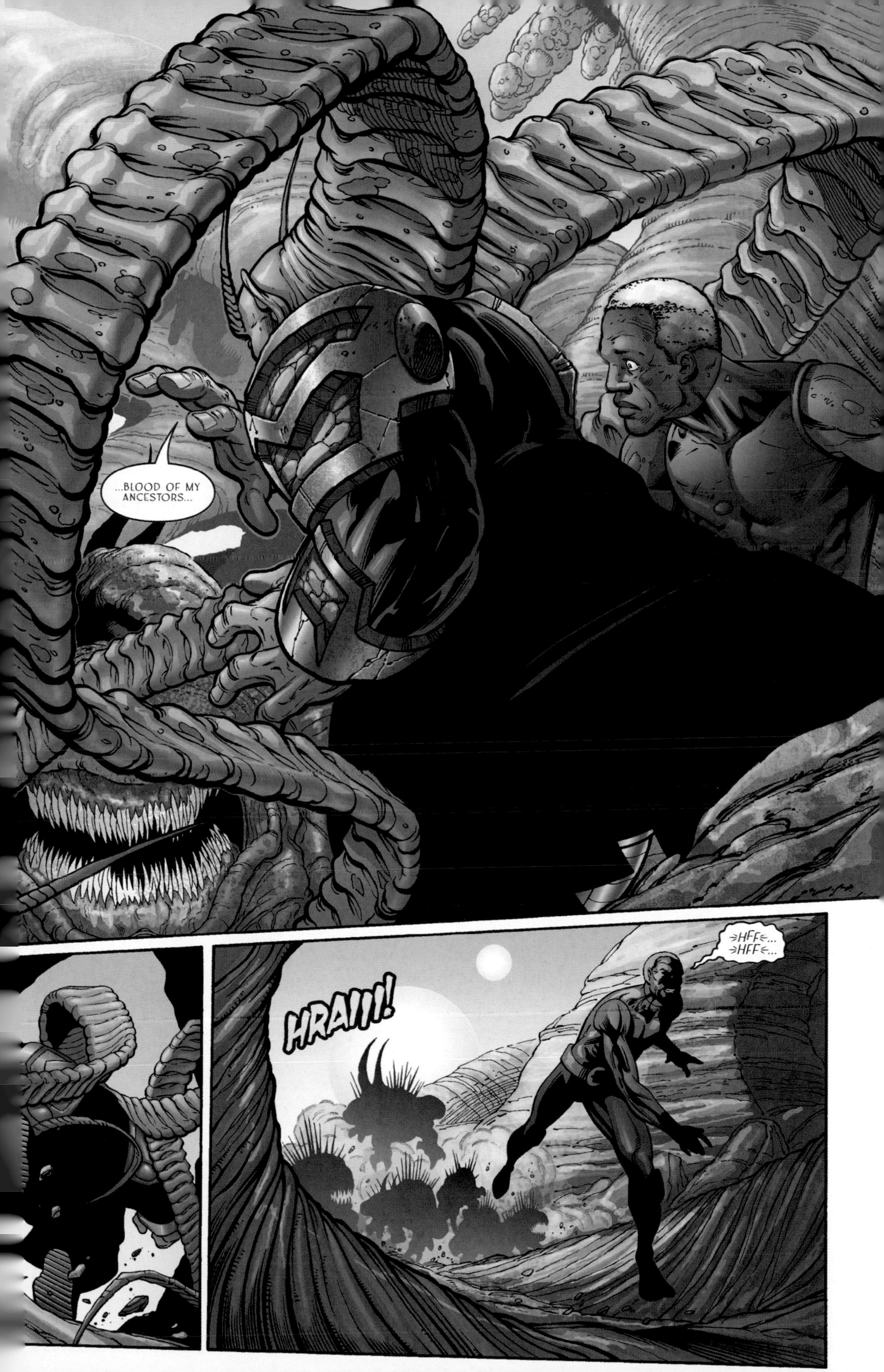
...BLOOD OF MY ANCESTORS...
HRAIII!
HFF... HFF...

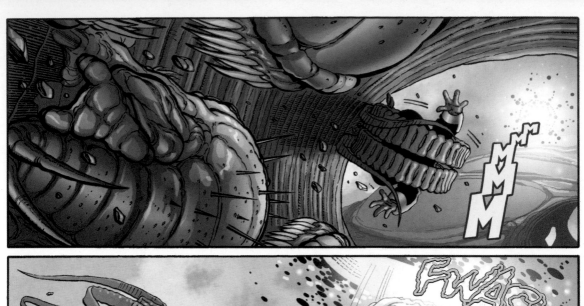

GULLIT! THANK THE STARS—HE PUNISHED YOU, TOO!

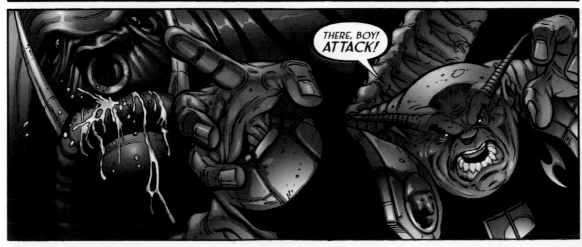

THERE, BOY! ATTACK!

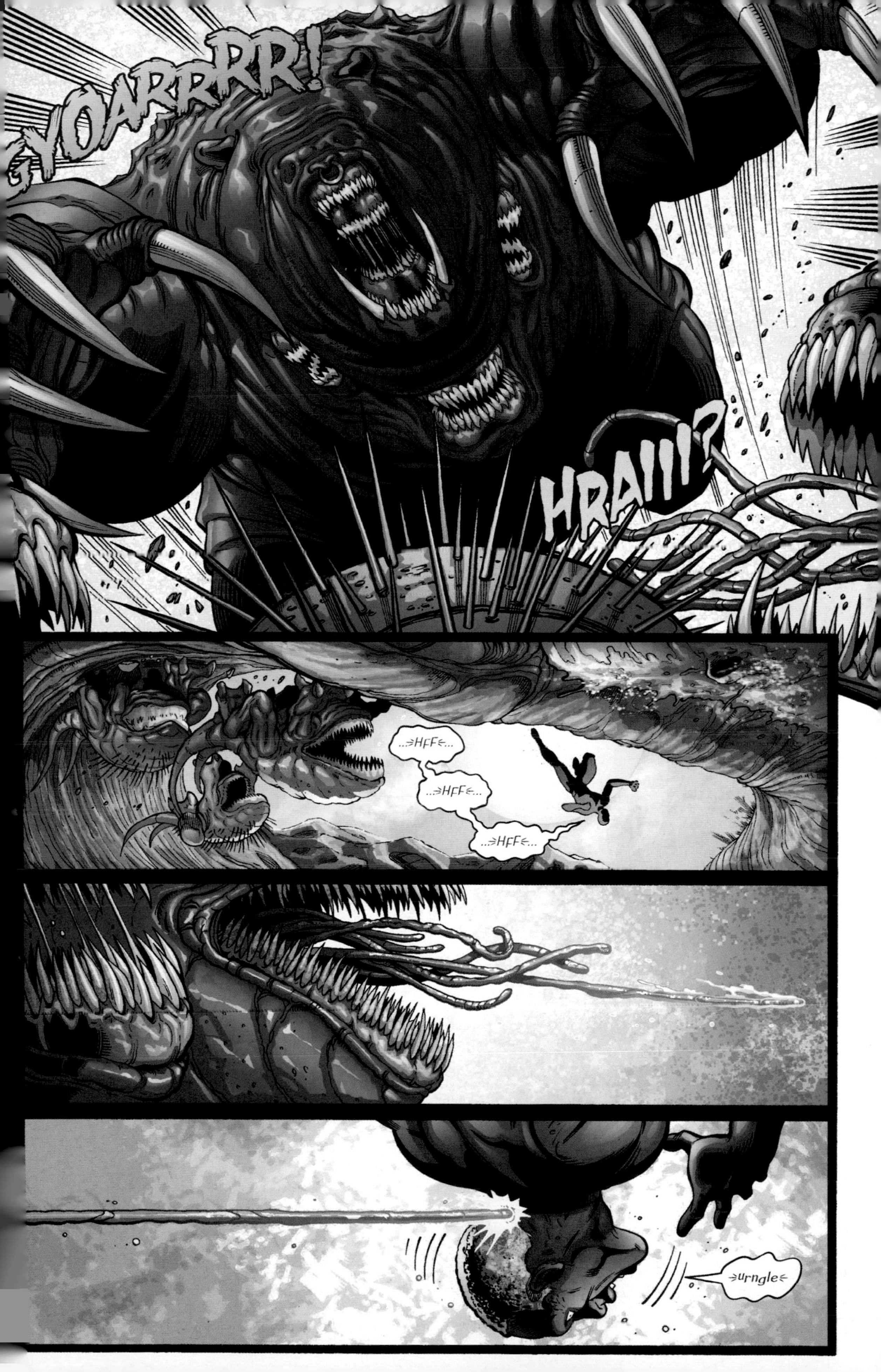

YOARRRR!
HRAIII?
...HFF...
...HFF...
...HFF...
urngle

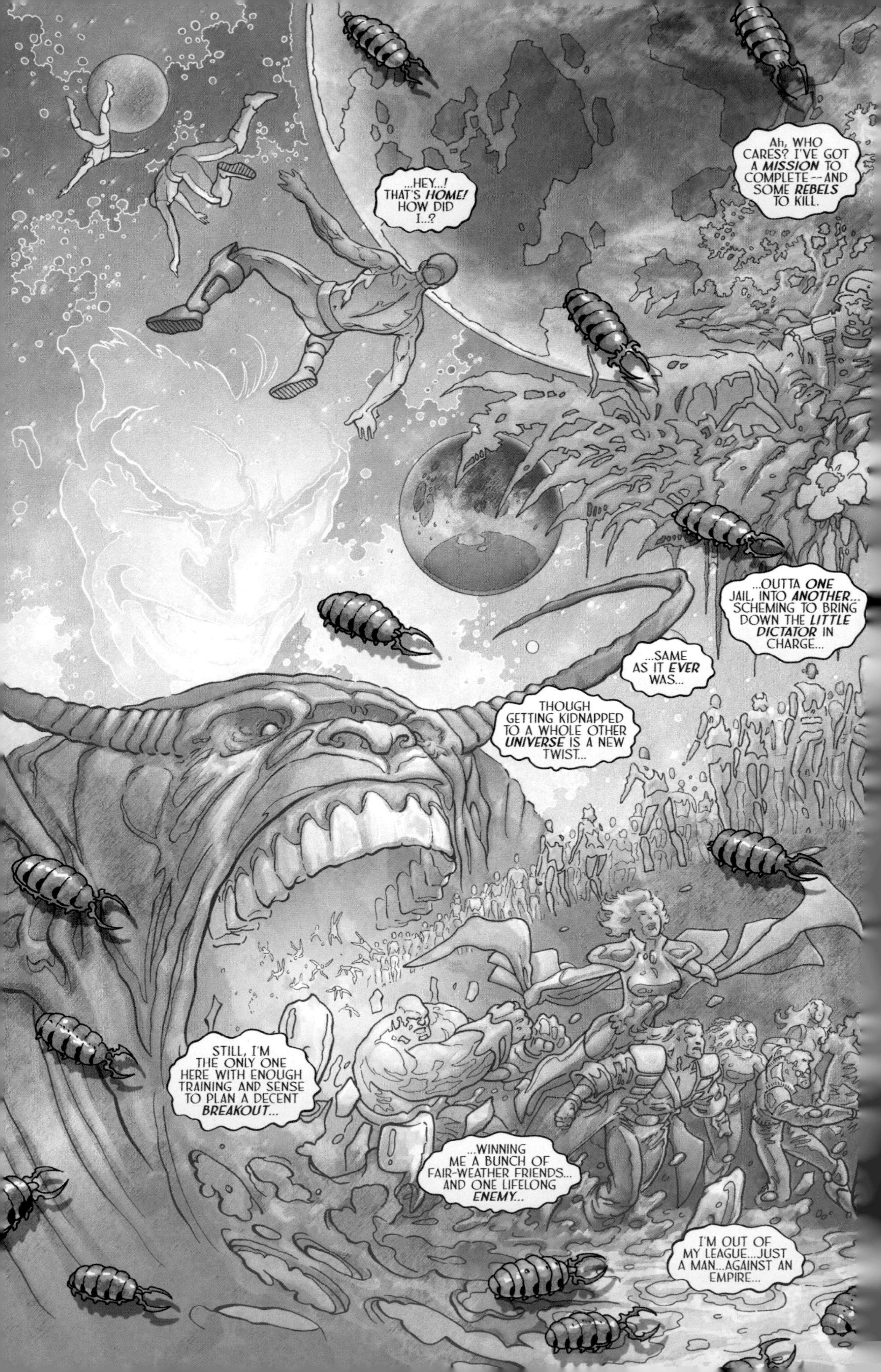
...HEY...! THAT'S HOME! HOW DID I...?
Ah, WHO CARES? I'VE GOT A MISSION TO COMPLETE--AND SOME REBELS TO KILL.
...OUTTA ONE JAIL, INTO ANOTHER... SCHEMING TO BRING DOWN THE LITTLE DICTATOR IN CHARGE...
...SAME AS IT EVER WAS...
THOUGH GETTING KIDNAPPED TO A WHOLE OTHER UNIVERSE IS A NEW TWIST...
STILL, I'M THE ONLY ONE HERE WITH ENOUGH TRAINING AND SENSE TO PLAN A DECENT BREAKOUT...
...WINNING ME A BUNCH OF FAIR-WEATHER FRIENDS... AND ONE LIFELONG ENEMY...
I'M OUT OF MY LEAGUE...JUST A MAN...AGAINST AN EMPIRE...

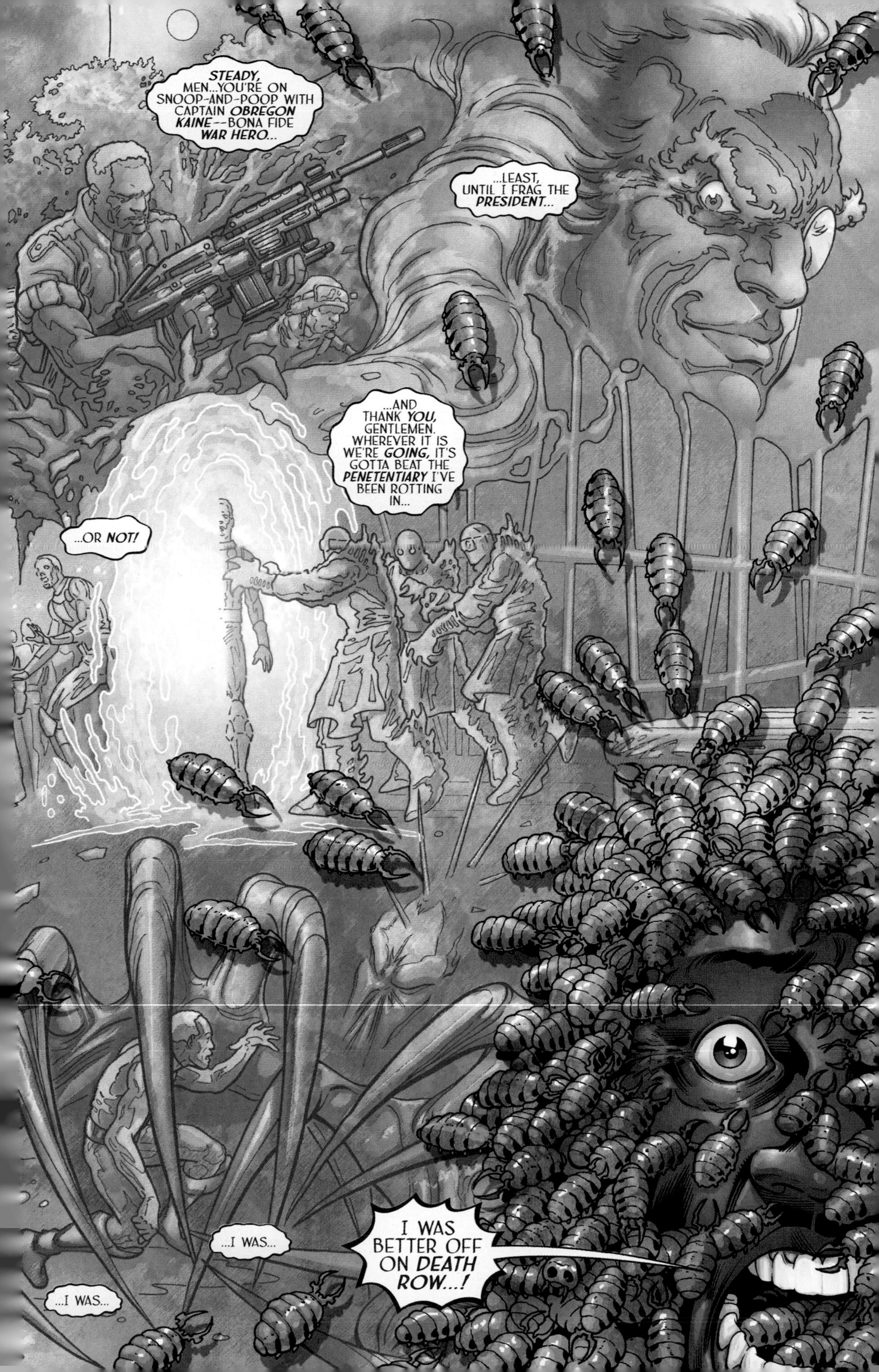
STEADY, MEN...YOU'RE ON SNOOP-AND-POOP WITH CAPTAIN OBREGON KAINE--BONA FIDE WAR HERO...
...LEAST, UNTIL I FRAG THE PRESIDENT...
...AND THANK YOU, GENTLEMEN. WHEREVER IT IS WE'RE GOING, IT'S GOTTA BEAT THE PENETENTIARY I'VE BEEN ROTTING IN...
...OR NOT!
...I WAS...
...I WAS...
I WAS BETTER OFF ON DEATH ROW...!

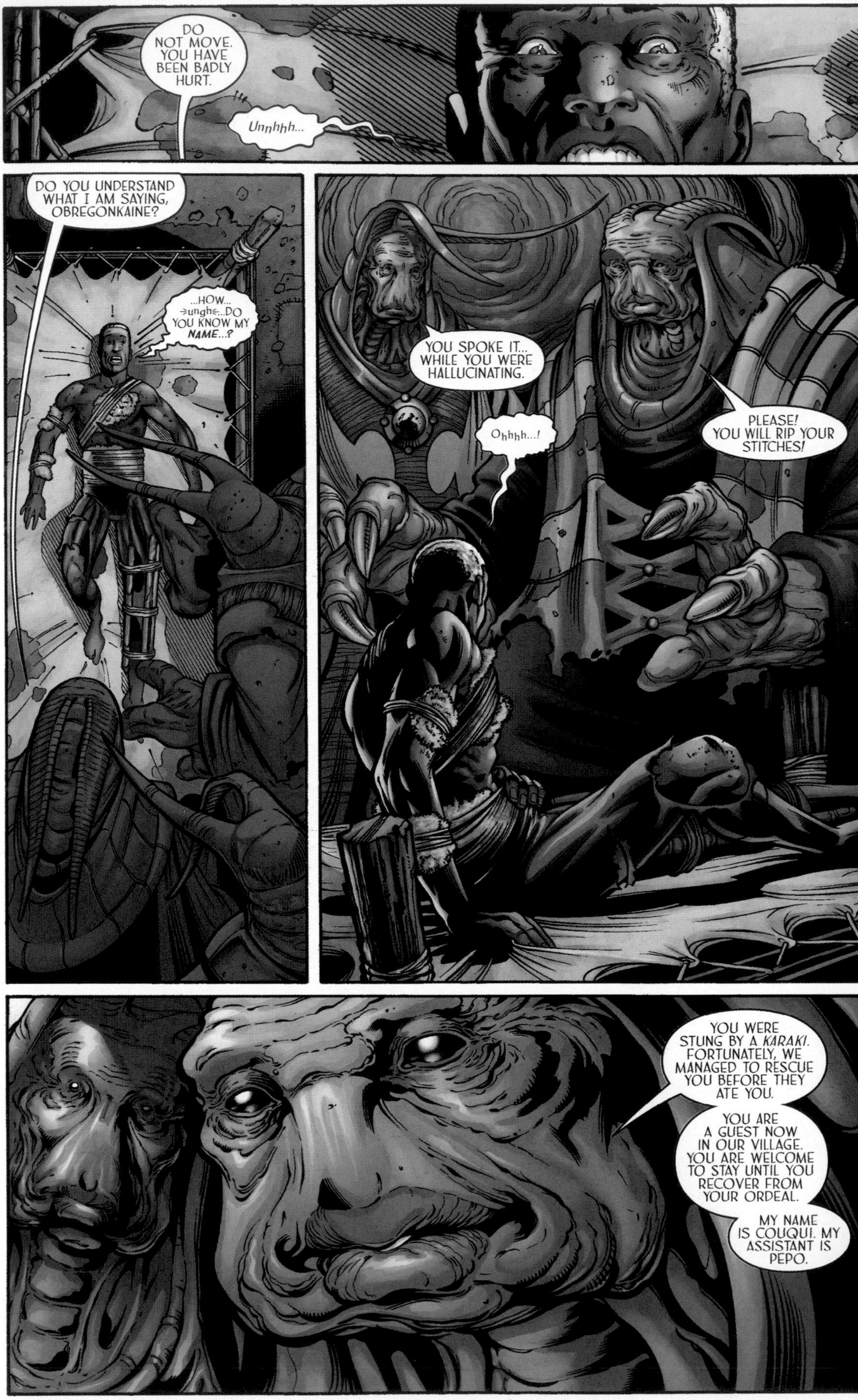
DO NOT MOVE. YOU HAVE BEEN BADLY HURT.
Unnhhh...
DO YOU UNDERSTAND WHAT I AM SAYING, OBREGONKAINE?
...HOW... ≥ungh≤...DO YOU KNOW MY NAME...?
YOU SPOKE IT... WHILE YOU WERE HALLUCINATING.
Ohhhh...!
PLEASE! YOU WILL RIP YOUR STITCHES!
YOU WERE STUNG BY A KARAKI. FORTUNATELY, WE MANAGED TO RESCUE YOU BEFORE THEY ATE YOU.
YOU ARE A GUEST NOW IN OUR VILLAGE. YOU ARE WELCOME TO STAY UNTIL YOU RECOVER FROM YOUR ORDEAL.
MY NAME IS COUQUI. MY ASSISTANT IS PEPO.

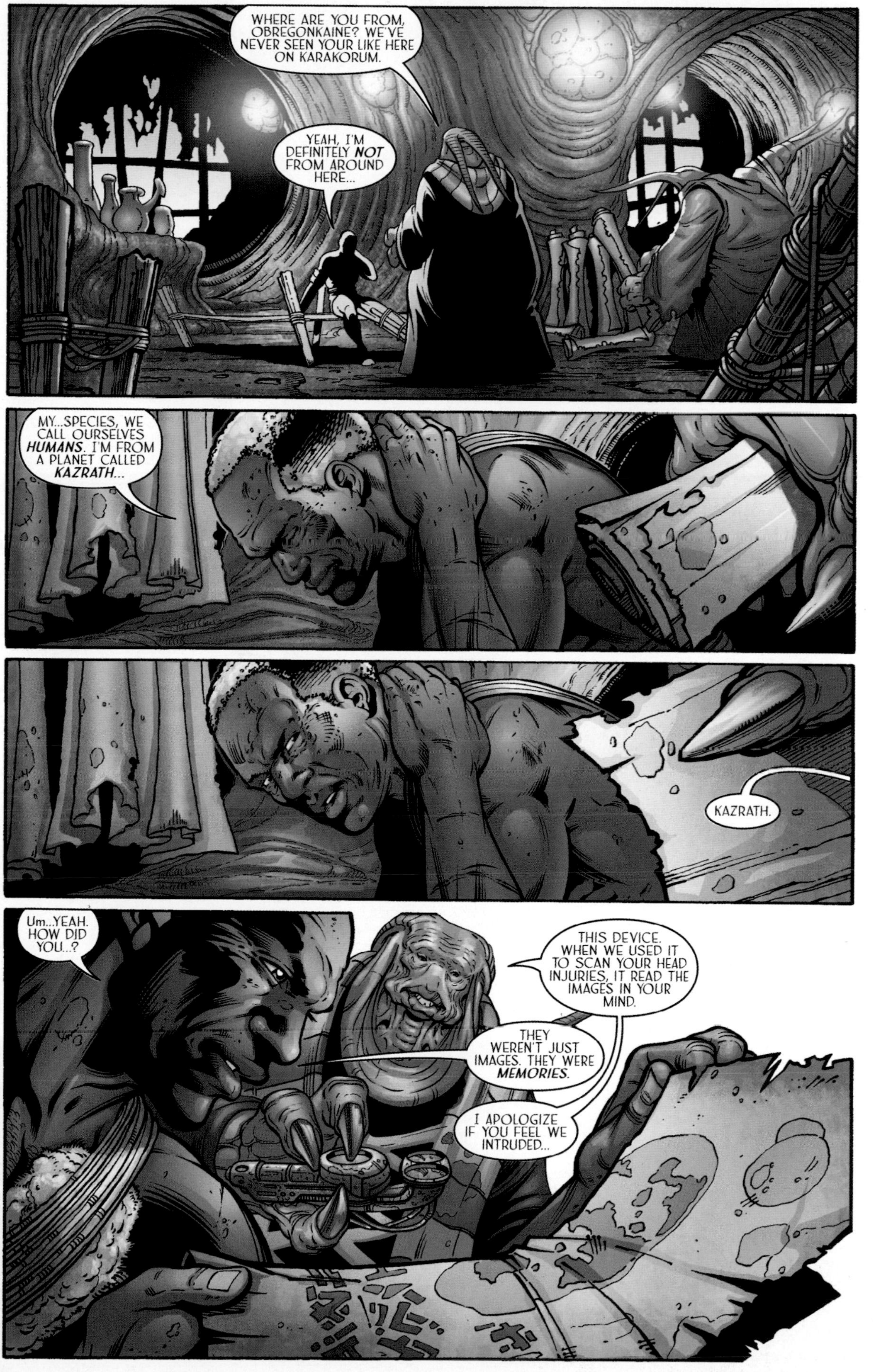
WHERE ARE YOU FROM, OBREGONKAINE? WE'VE NEVER SEEN YOUR LIKE HERE ON KARAKORUM.
YEAH, I'M DEFINITELY *NOT* FROM AROUND HERE...
MY...SPECIES, WE CALL OURSELVES *HUMANS*. I'M FROM A PLANET CALLED *KAZRATH*...
KAZRATH.
Um...YEAH. HOW DID YOU...?
THIS DEVICE. WHEN WE USED IT TO SCAN YOUR HEAD INJURIES, IT READ THE IMAGES IN YOUR MIND.
THEY WEREN'T JUST IMAGES. THEY WERE *MEMORIES*.
I APOLOGIZE IF YOU FEEL WE INTRUDED...

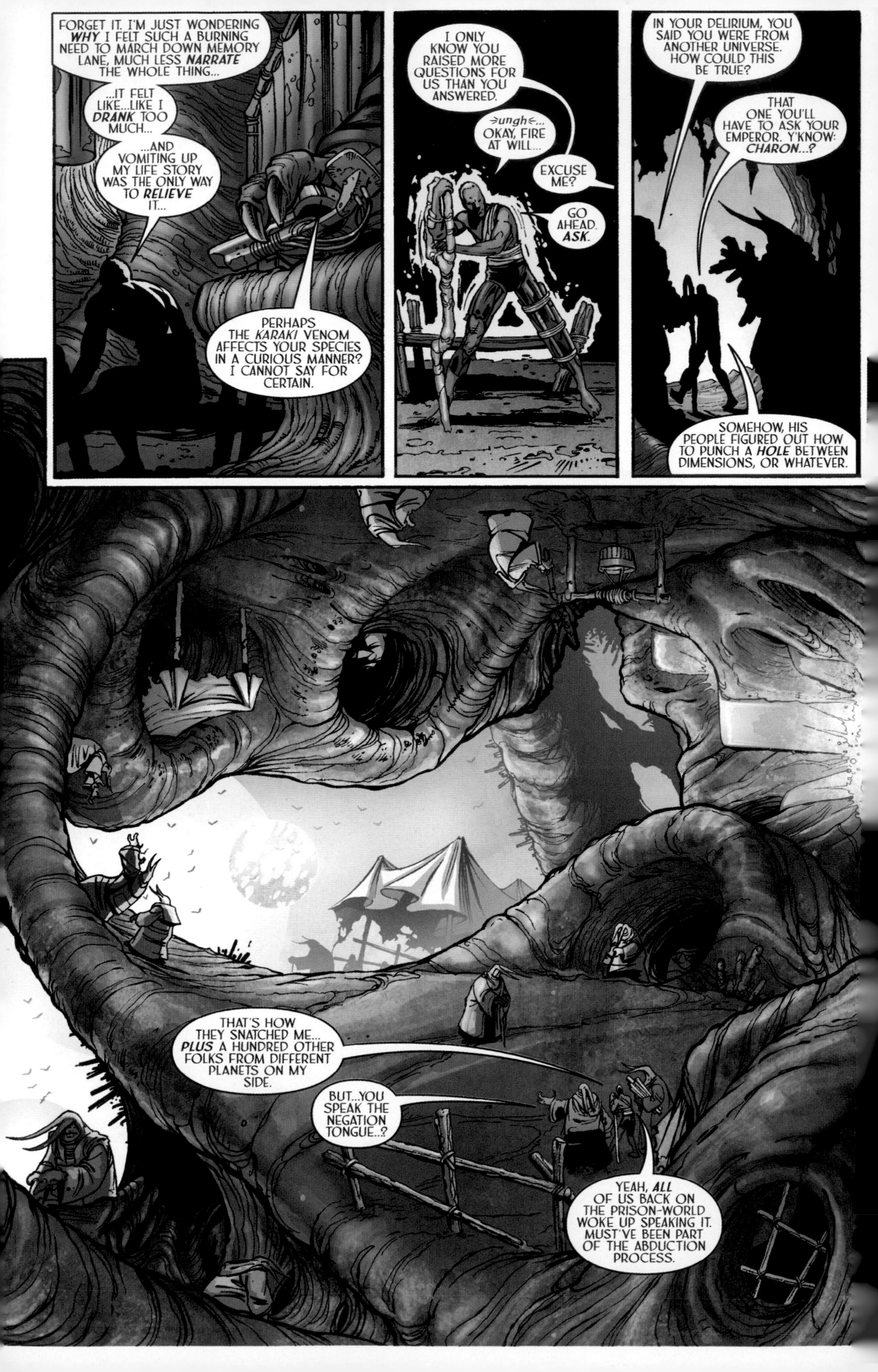

FORGET IT. I'M JUST WONDERING WHY I FELT SUCH A BURNING NEED TO MARCH DOWN MEMORY LANE, MUCH LESS NARRATE THE WHOLE THING...
...IT FELT LIKE...LIKE I DRANK TOO MUCH...
...AND VOMITING UP MY LIFE STORY WAS THE ONLY WAY TO RELIEVE IT...
PERHAPS THE KARAKI VENOM AFFECTS YOUR SPECIES IN A CURIOUS MANNER? I CANNOT SAY FOR CERTAIN.
I ONLY KNOW YOU RAISED MORE QUESTIONS FOR US THAN YOU ANSWERED.
ungh... OKAY, FIRE AT WILL...
EXCUSE ME?
GO AHEAD. ASK.
IN YOUR DELIRIUM, YOU SAID YOU WERE FROM ANOTHER UNIVERSE. HOW COULD THIS BE TRUE?
THAT ONE YOU'LL HAVE TO ASK YOUR EMPEROR. Y'KNOW: CHARON...?
SOMEHOW, HIS PEOPLE FIGURED OUT HOW TO PUNCH A HOLE BETWEEN DIMENSIONS, OR WHATEVER.
THAT'S HOW THEY SNATCHED ME... PLUS A HUNDRED OTHER FOLKS FROM DIFFERENT PLANETS ON MY SIDE.
BUT...YOU SPEAK THE NEGATION TONGUE...?
YEAH, ALL OF US BACK ON THE PRISON-WORLD WOKE UP SPEAKING IT. MUST'VE BEEN PART OF THE ABDUCTION PROCESS.

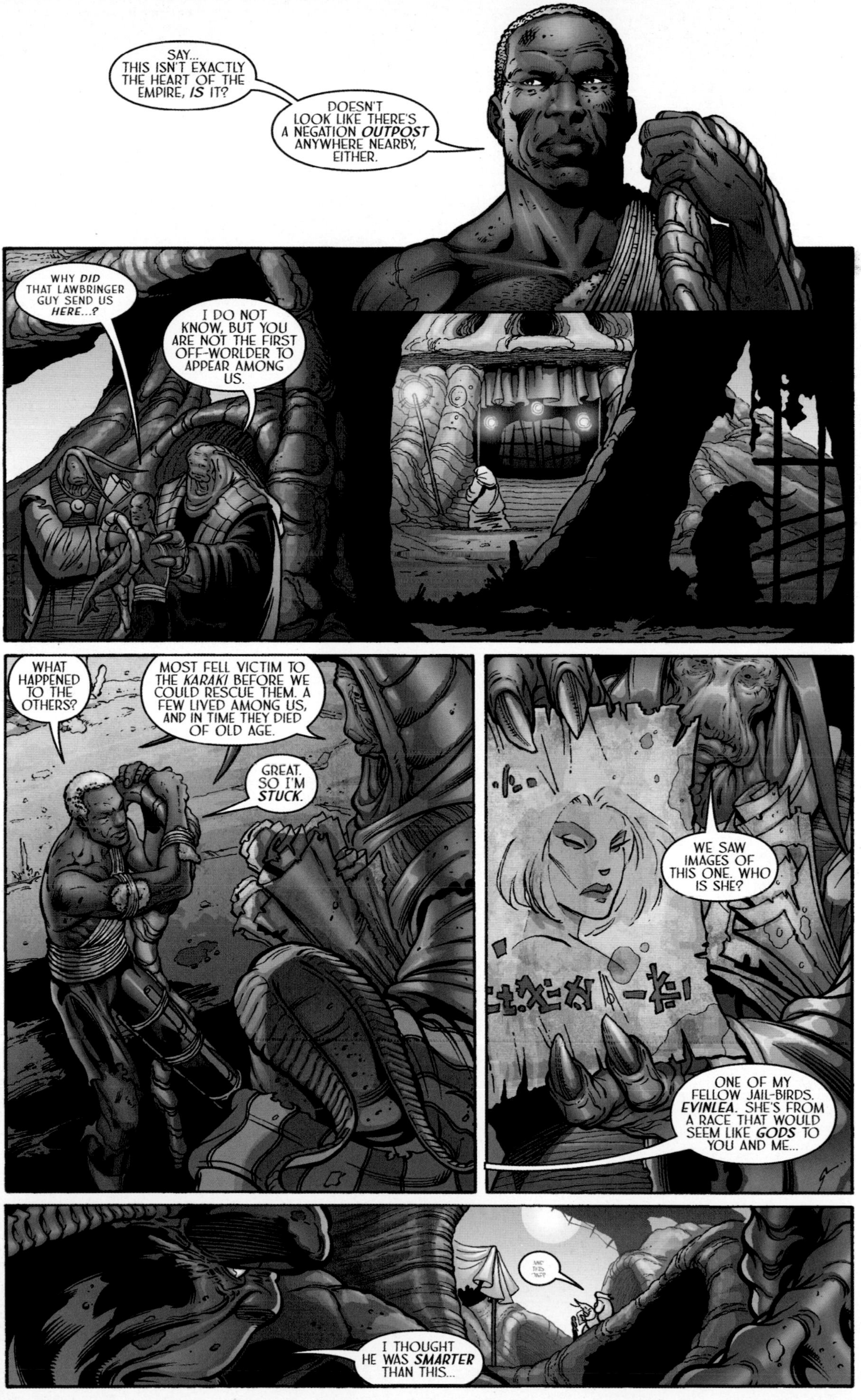

SAY... THIS ISN'T EXACTLY THE HEART OF THE EMPIRE, *IS* IT?
DOESN'T LOOK LIKE THERE'S A NEGATION *OUTPOST* ANYWHERE NEARBY, EITHER.
WHY *DID* THAT LAWBRINGER GUY SEND US *HERE...?*
I DO NOT KNOW, BUT YOU ARE NOT THE FIRST OFF-WORLDER TO APPEAR AMONG US.
WHAT HAPPENED TO THE OTHERS?
MOST FELL VICTIM TO THE *KARAKI* BEFORE WE COULD RESCUE THEM. A FEW LIVED AMONG US, AND IN TIME THEY DIED OF OLD AGE.
GREAT. SO I'M *STUCK.*
WE SAW IMAGES OF THIS ONE. WHO IS SHE?
ONE OF MY FELLOW JAIL-BIRDS. *EVINLEA.* SHE'S FROM A RACE THAT WOULD SEEM LIKE *GODS* TO YOU AND ME...
I THOUGHT HE WAS *SMARTER* THAN THIS...

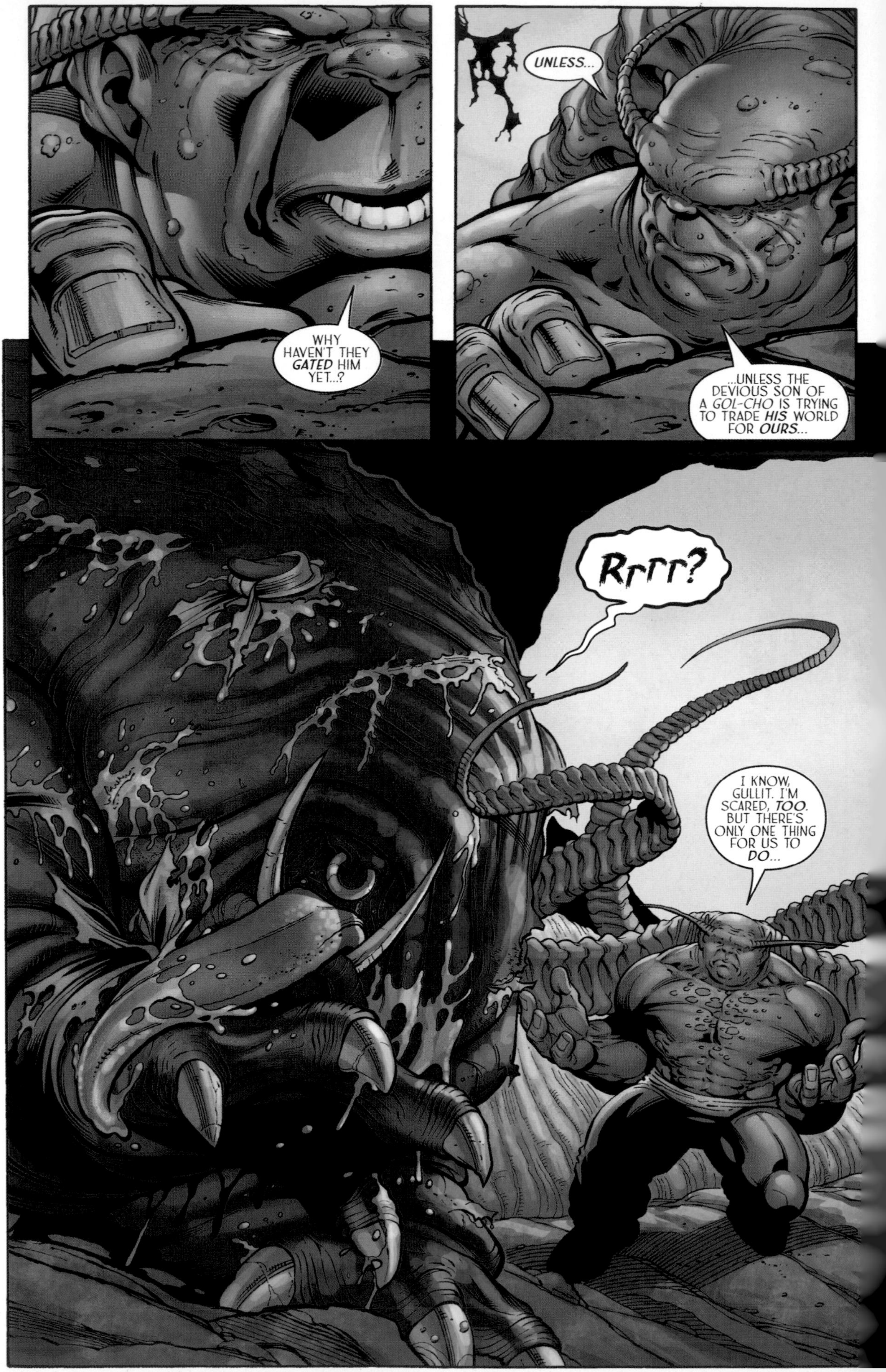
WHY HAVEN'T THEY GATED HIM YET...?
UNLESS...
...UNLESS THE DEVIOUS SON OF A GOL-CHO IS TRYING TO TRADE HIS WORLD FOR OURS...
Rrrr?
I KNOW, GULLIT. I'M SCARED, TOO. BUT THERE'S ONLY ONE THING FOR US TO DO...

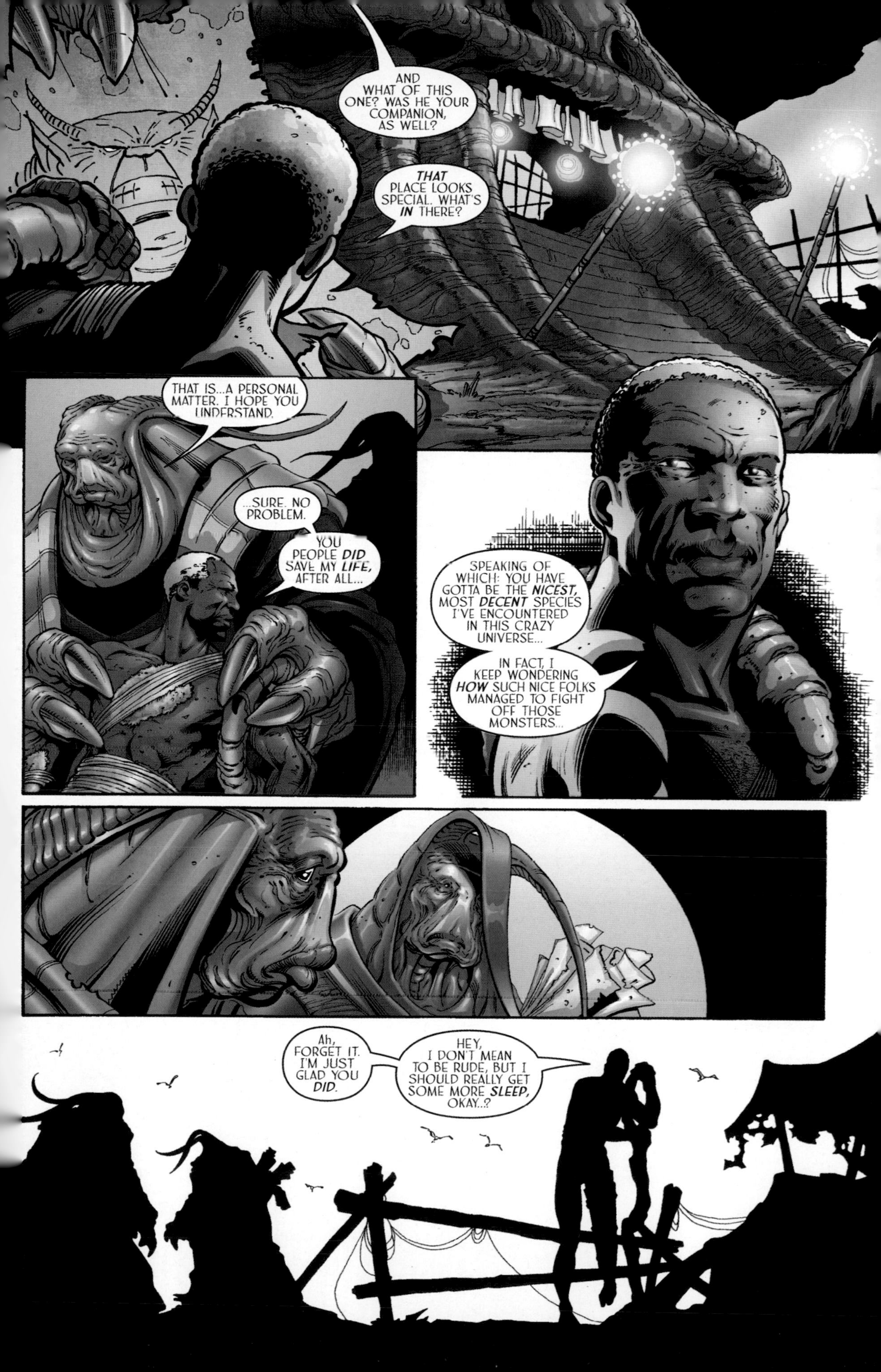
AND WHAT OF THIS ONE? WAS HE YOUR COMPANION, AS WELL?
THAT PLACE LOOKS SPECIAL. WHAT'S IN THERE?
THAT IS...A PERSONAL MATTER. I HOPE YOU UNDERSTAND.
...SURE. NO PROBLEM.
YOU PEOPLE DID SAVE MY LIFE, AFTER ALL...
SPEAKING OF WHICH: YOU HAVE GOTTA BE THE NICEST, MOST DECENT SPECIES I'VE ENCOUNTERED IN THIS CRAZY UNIVERSE...
IN FACT, I KEEP WONDERING HOW SUCH NICE FOLKS MANAGED TO FIGHT OFF THOSE MONSTERS...
Ah, FORGET IT. I'M JUST GLAD YOU DID.
HEY, I DON'T MEAN TO BE RUDE, BUT I SHOULD REALLY GET SOME MORE SLEEP, OKAY...?

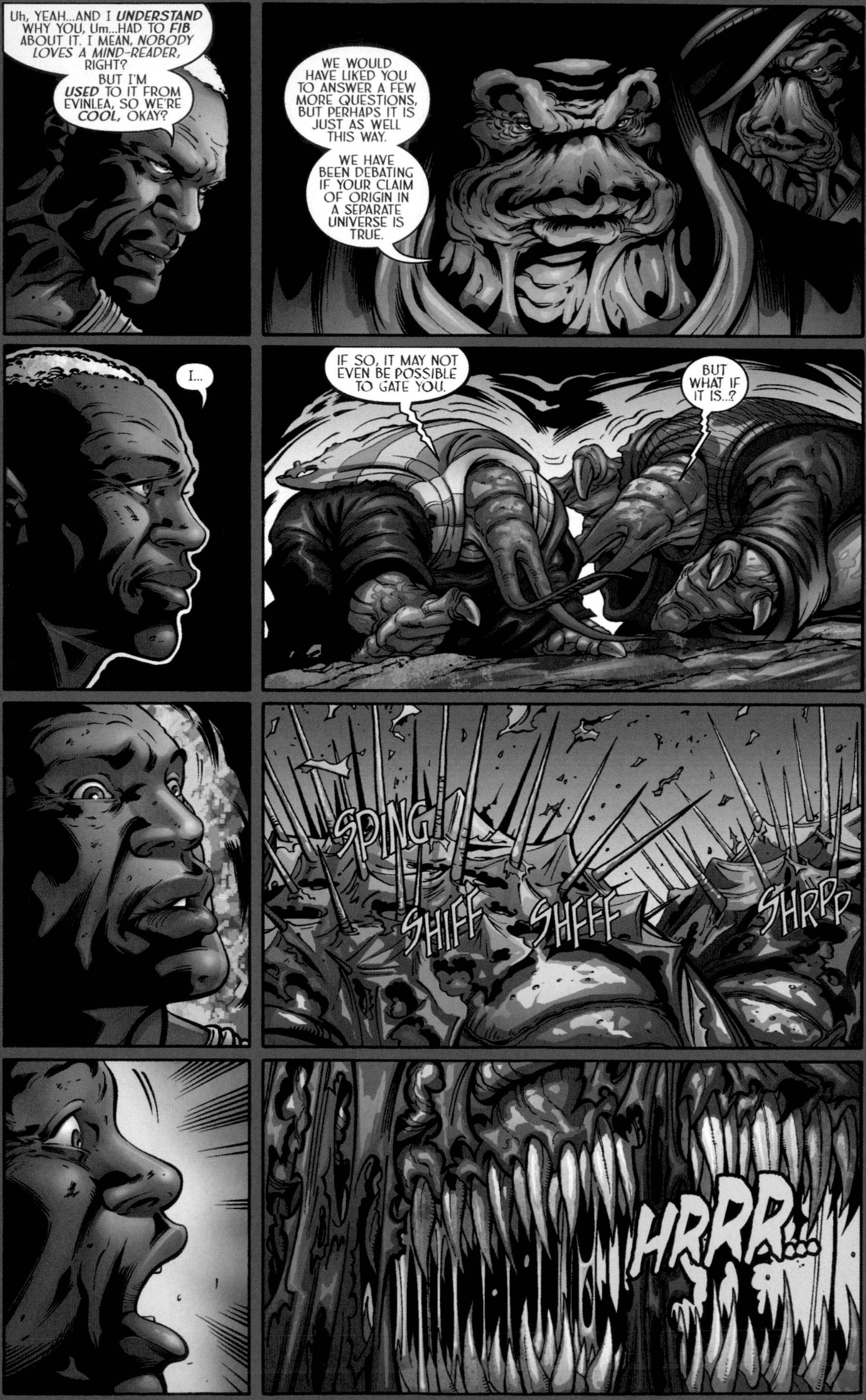
Uh, YEAH...AND I UNDERSTAND WHY YOU, Um...HAD TO FIB ABOUT IT. I MEAN, NOBODY LOVES A MIND-READER, RIGHT?
BUT I'M USED TO IT FROM EVINLEA, SO WE'RE COOL, OKAY?
WE WOULD HAVE LIKED YOU TO ANSWER A FEW MORE QUESTIONS, BUT PERHAPS IT IS JUST AS WELL THIS WAY.
WE HAVE BEEN DEBATING IF YOUR CLAIM OF ORIGIN IN A SEPARATE UNIVERSE IS TRUE.
I...
IF SO, IT MAY NOT EVEN BE POSSIBLE TO GATE YOU.
BUT WHAT IF IT IS..?
SPING
SHIFF
SHFFF
SHRPP
HRRR...

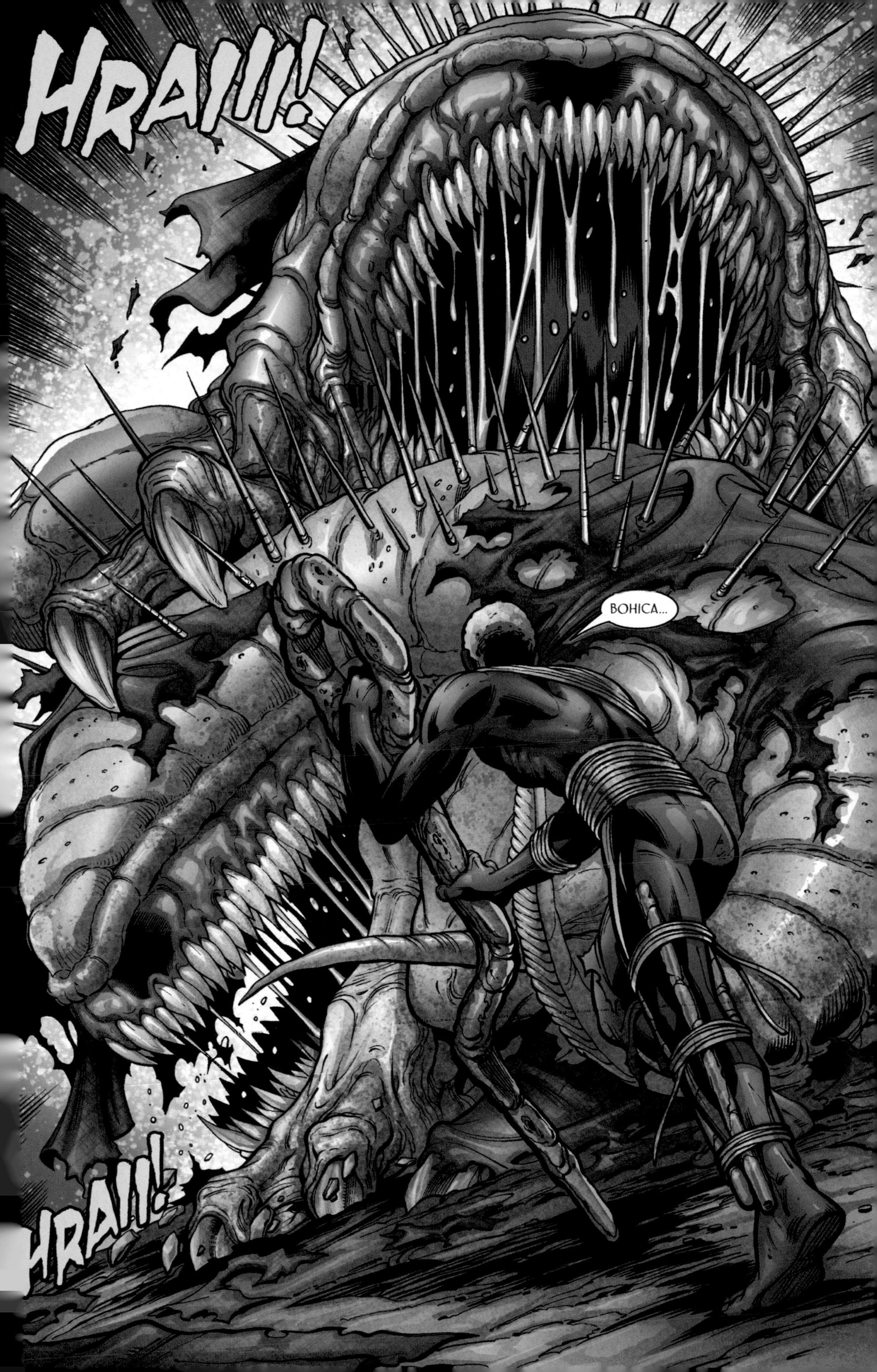
HRAIII!
BOHICA...
HRAII!

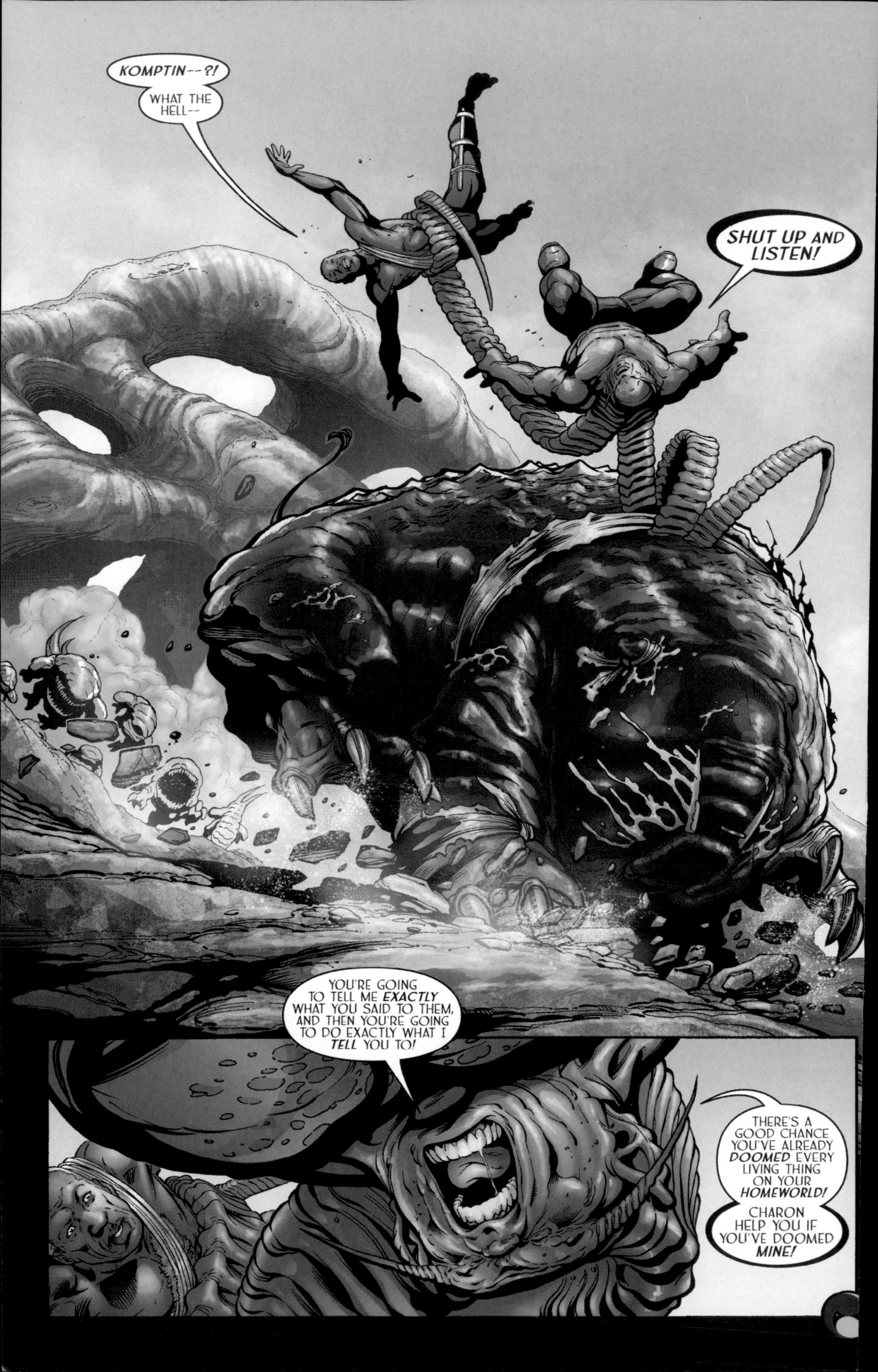
KOMPTIN--?!
WHAT THE HELL--
SHUT UP AND LISTEN!
YOU'RE GOING TO TELL ME EXACTLY WHAT YOU SAID TO THEM, AND THEN YOU'RE GOING TO DO EXACTLY WHAT I TELL YOU TO!
THERE'S A GOOD CHANCE YOU'VE ALREADY DOOMED EVERY LIVING THING ON YOUR HOMEWORLD!
CHARON HELP YOU IF YOU'VE DOOMED MINE!

STORYTELLERS

TONY BEDARD
WRITER

PAUL PELLETIER
PENCILER

DAVE MEIKIS
INKER

JAMES ROCHELLE
COLORIST

TROY PETERI
LETTERER

The
CrossGen
Universe
created by
Mark Alessi &
Gina M. Villa

MARK ALESSI Publisher & Chief Executive Officer * GINA M. VILLA Chief Operating Officer
MICHAEL A. BEATTIE Chief Financial Officer * JENNIFER HERNANDEZ General Counsel * TONY PANACCIO Vice President Product Development
CHRIS OARR Vice President Sales & Marketing * ROBERT BOYD Director Marketing * JAMES BREITBEIL Director Marketing & Distribution
IAN M. FELLER Director Corporate Communications * COURTLAND WHITED MIS Director * GABO MENDOZA Internet Services Director
CHARLES DECKER Director Production Control * BRIAN M. SOLTIS Controller * BRANDON PETERSON Vice President Special Projects
BARBARA KESEL Head Writer * BART SEARS Art Director * MICHELLE PUGLIESE Freelance Coordinator
MICHAEL ATIYEH, BUTCH GUICE, DAVE LANPHEAR, RICK MAGYAR, LAURA MARTIN, MARK PENNINGTON, ANDY SMITH Assistant Art Directors
PAM DAVIES Vice President Production * SYLVIA BRETZ Production Supervisor Advertising/Web * ERIN FLANAGAN Web Designer
JANET BECHTLE Production Supervisor Books * RANDY MARTIN Production Designer

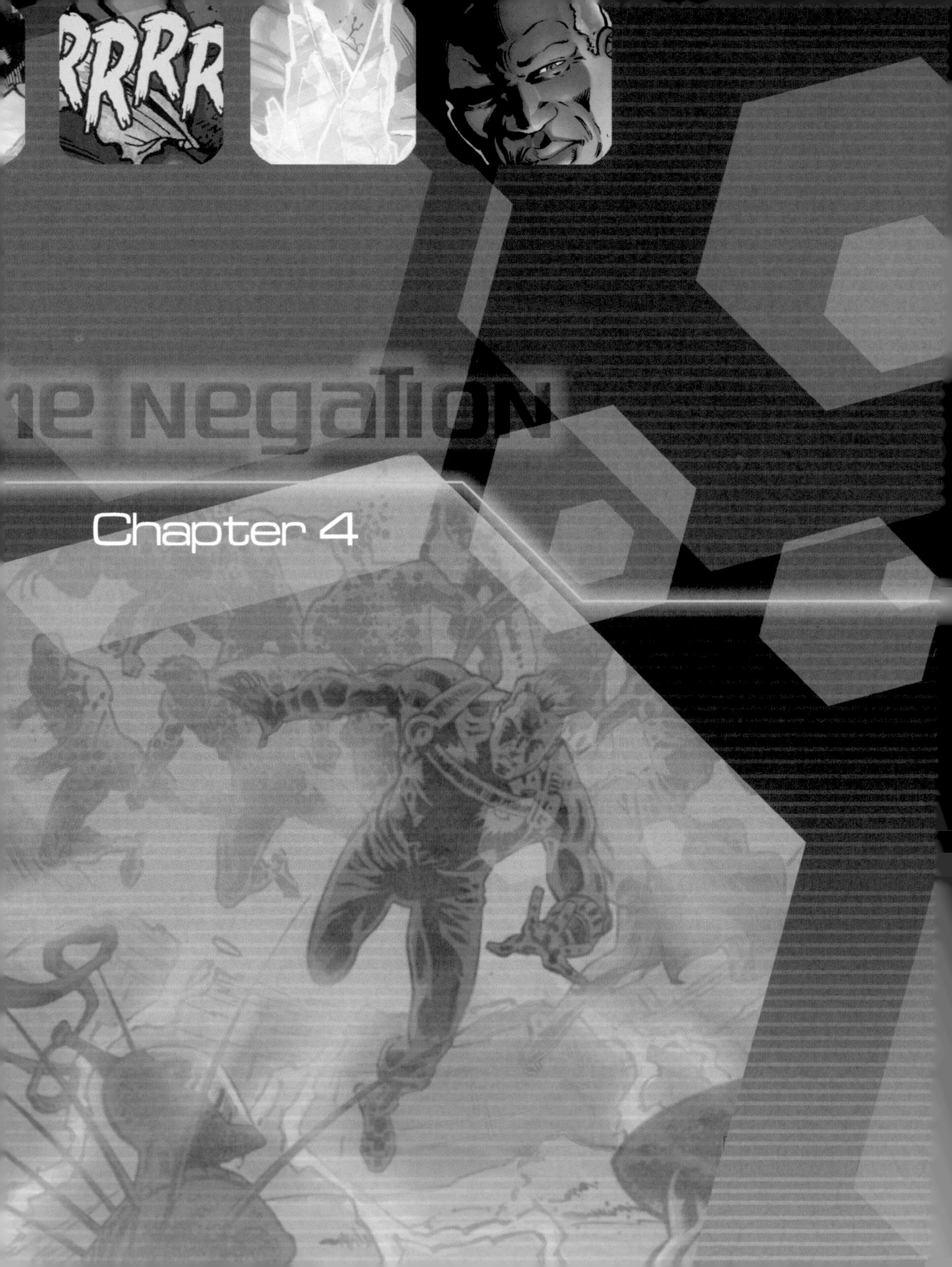
RRRR
ne Negation

Chapter 4

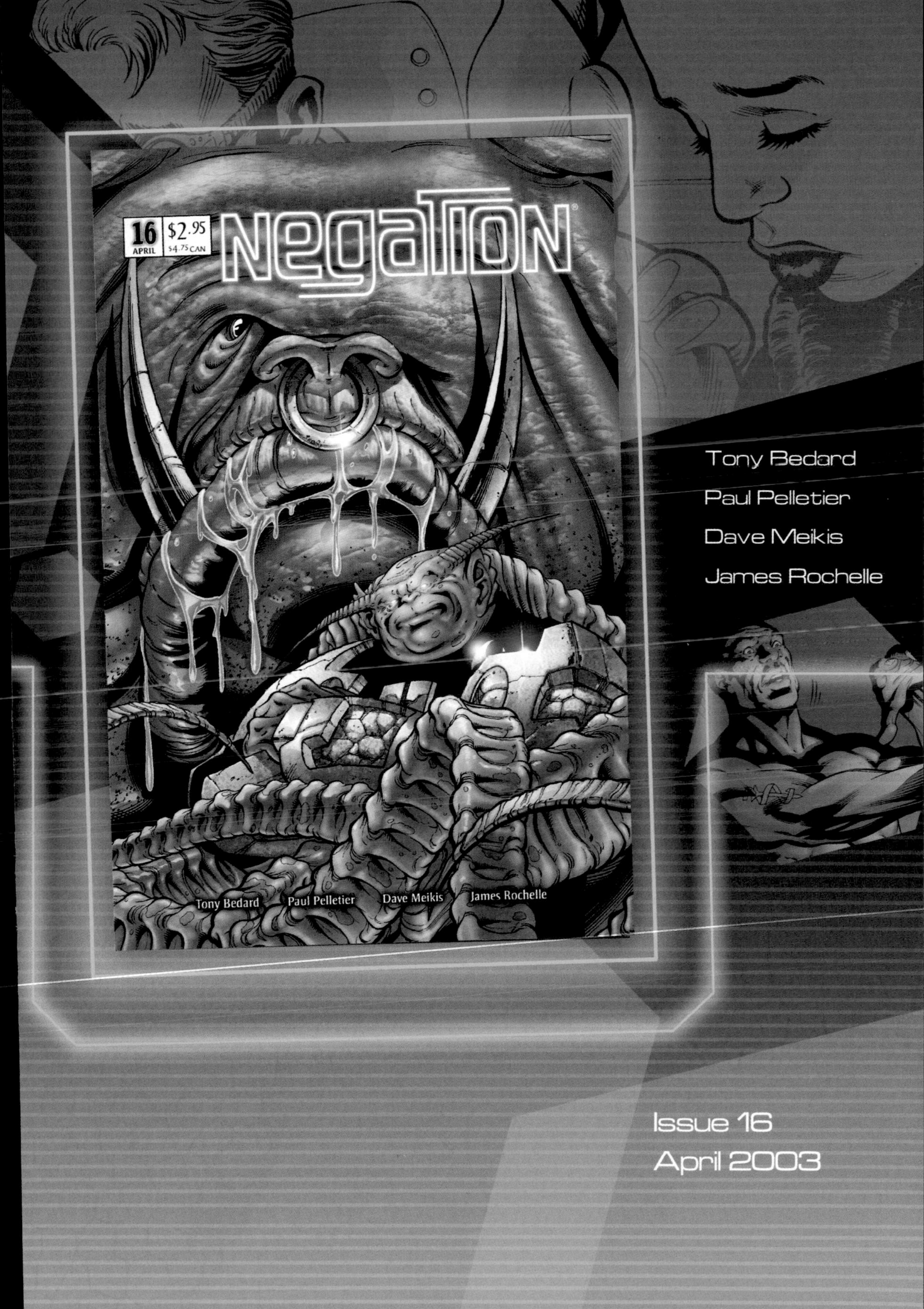
16
APRIL
$2.95
$4.75 CAN
Negation
Tony Bedard
Paul Pelletier
Dave Meikis
James Rochelle
Tony Bedard
Paul Pelletier
Dave Meikis
James Rochelle
Issue 16
April 2003

KAINE

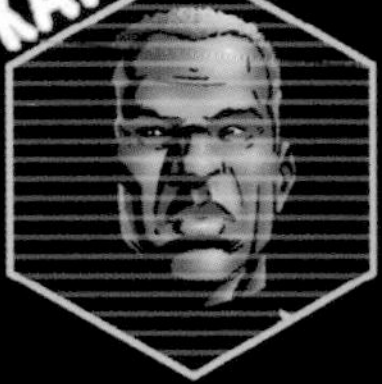

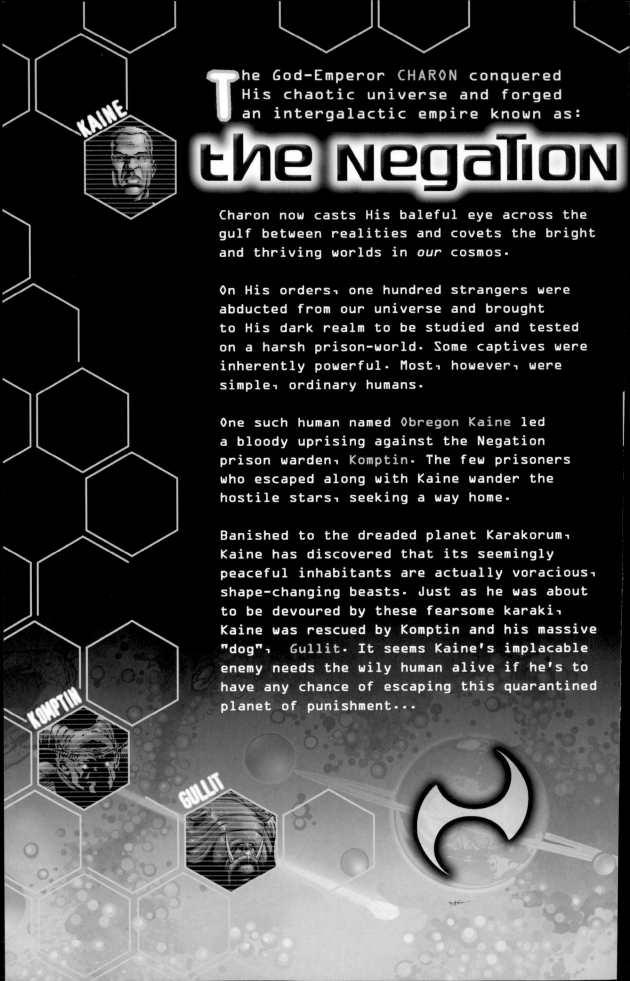

The God-Emperor CHARON conquered His chaotic universe and forged an intergalactic empire known as:

the NegaTION

Charon now casts His baleful eye across the gulf between realities and covets the bright and thriving worlds in *our* cosmos.

On His orders, one hundred strangers were abducted from our universe and brought to His dark realm to be studied and tested on a harsh prison-world. Some captives were inherently powerful. Most, however, were simple, ordinary humans.

One such human named Obregon Kaine led a bloody uprising against the Negation prison warden, Komptin. The few prisoners who escaped along with Kaine wander the hostile stars, seeking a way home.

Banished to the dreaded planet Karakorum, Kaine has discovered that its seemingly peaceful inhabitants are actually voracious, shape-changing beasts. Just as he was about to be devoured by these fearsome karaki, Kaine was rescued by Komptin and his massive "dog", Gullit. It seems Kaine's implacable enemy needs the wily human alive if he's to have any chance of escaping this quarantined planet of punishment...

KOMPTIN

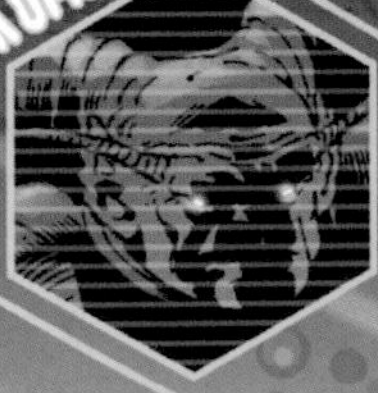

GULLIT

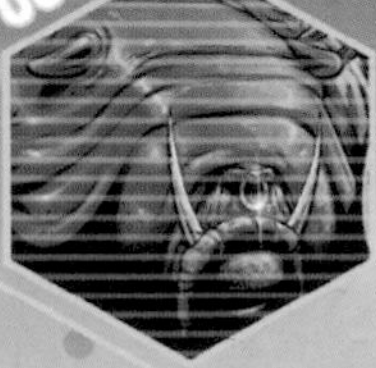

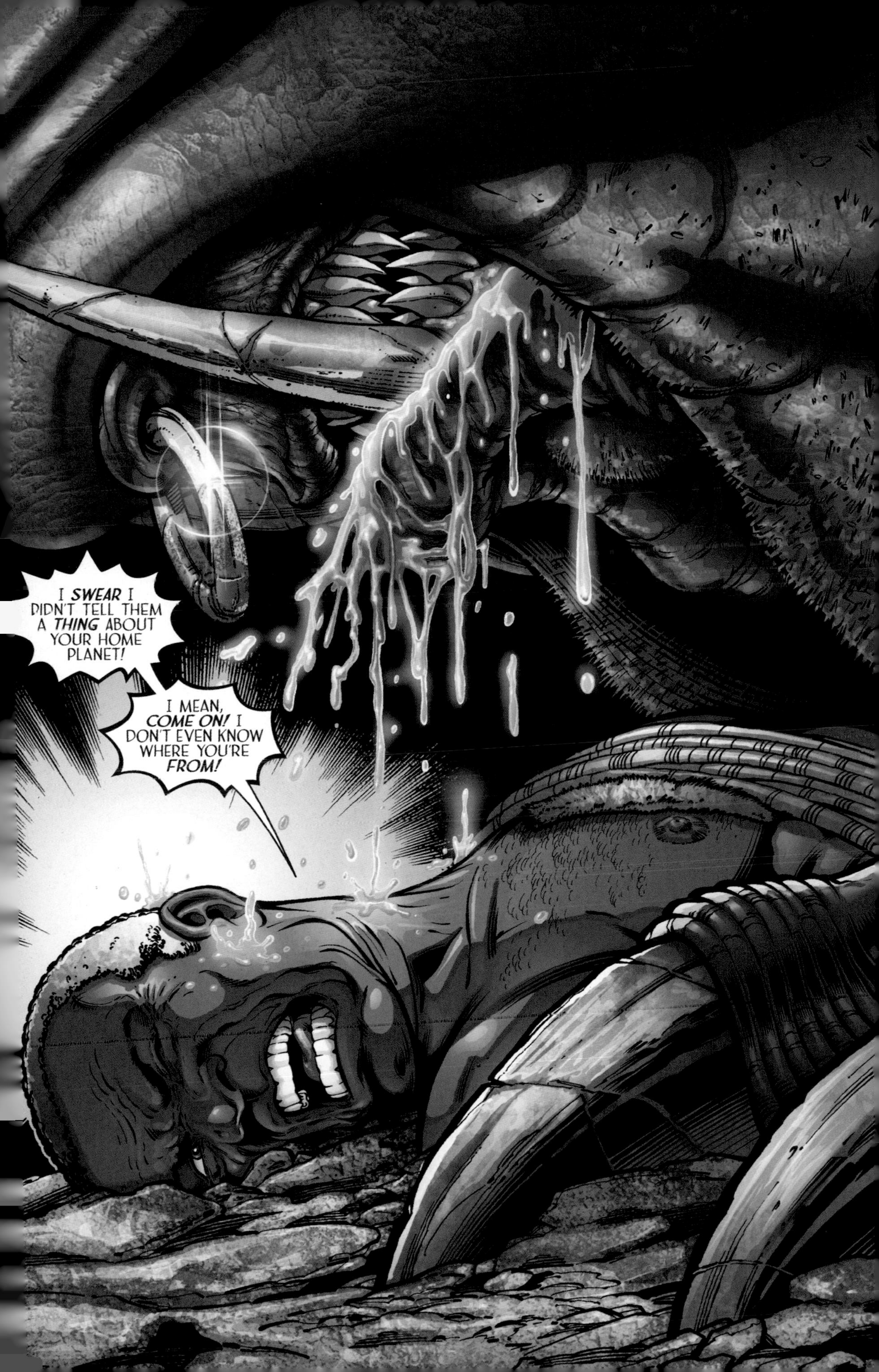
I SWEAR I DIDN'T TELL THEM A THING ABOUT YOUR HOME PLANET!
I MEAN, COME ON! I DON'T EVEN KNOW WHERE YOU'RE FROM!

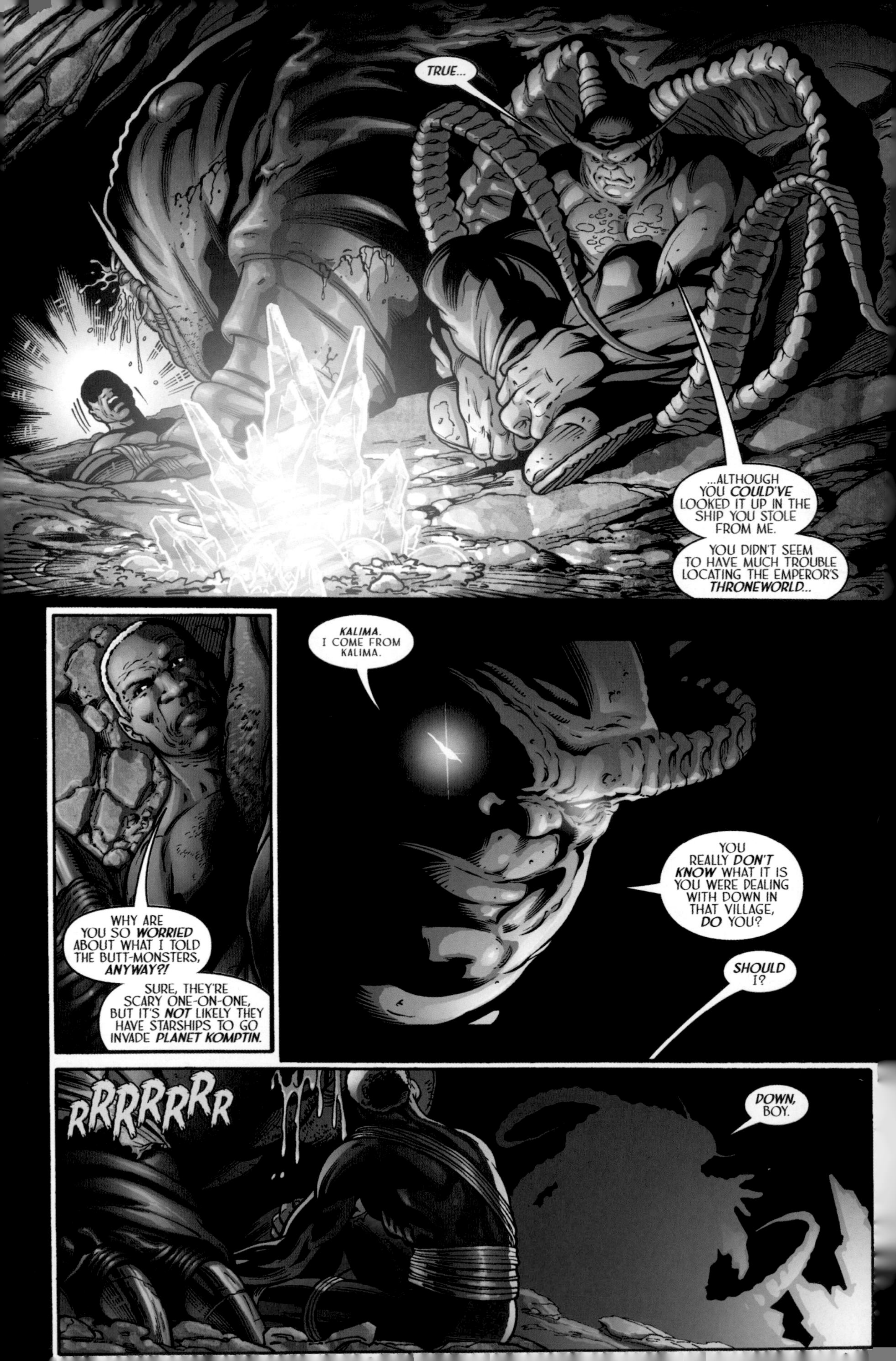
TRUE...
...ALTHOUGH YOU COULD'VE LOOKED IT UP IN THE SHIP YOU STOLE FROM ME.
YOU DIDN'T SEEM TO HAVE MUCH TROUBLE LOCATING THE EMPEROR'S THRONEWORLD...
WHY ARE YOU SO WORRIED ABOUT WHAT I TOLD THE BUTT-MONSTERS, ANYWAY?!
SURE, THEY'RE SCARY ONE-ON-ONE, BUT IT'S NOT LIKELY THEY HAVE STARSHIPS TO GO INVADE PLANET KOMPTIN.
KALIMA. I COME FROM KALIMA.
YOU REALLY DON'T KNOW WHAT IT IS YOU WERE DEALING WITH DOWN IN THAT VILLAGE, DO YOU?
SHOULD I?
RRRRRRR
DOWN, BOY.

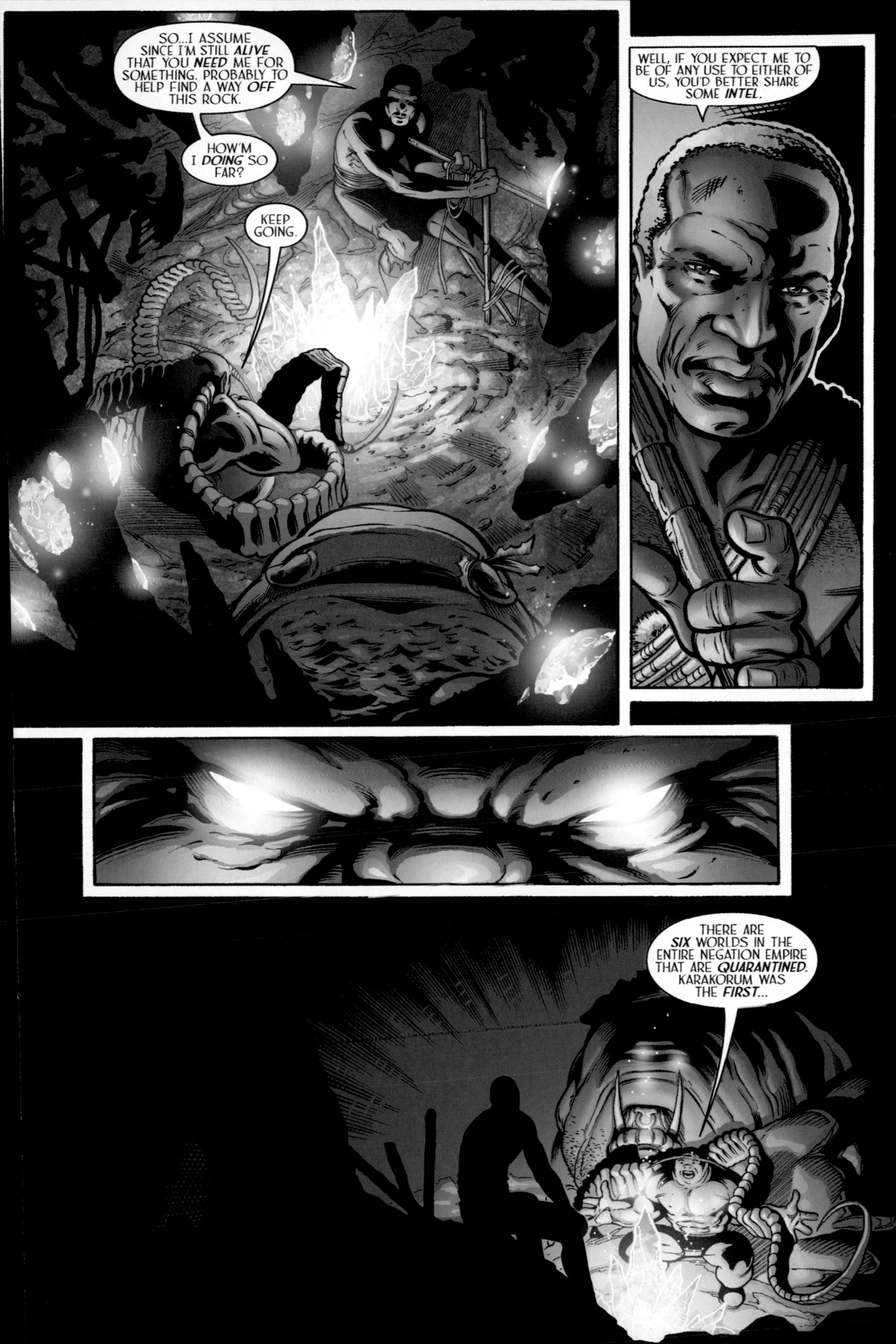
SO...I ASSUME SINCE I'M STILL ALIVE THAT YOU NEED ME FOR SOMETHING. PROBABLY TO HELP FIND A WAY OFF THIS ROCK.
HOW'M I DOING SO FAR?
KEEP GOING.
WELL, IF YOU EXPECT ME TO BE OF ANY USE TO EITHER OF US, YOU'D BETTER SHARE SOME INTEL.
THERE ARE SIX WORLDS IN THE ENTIRE NEGATION EMPIRE THAT ARE QUARANTINED. KARAKORUM WAS THE FIRST...

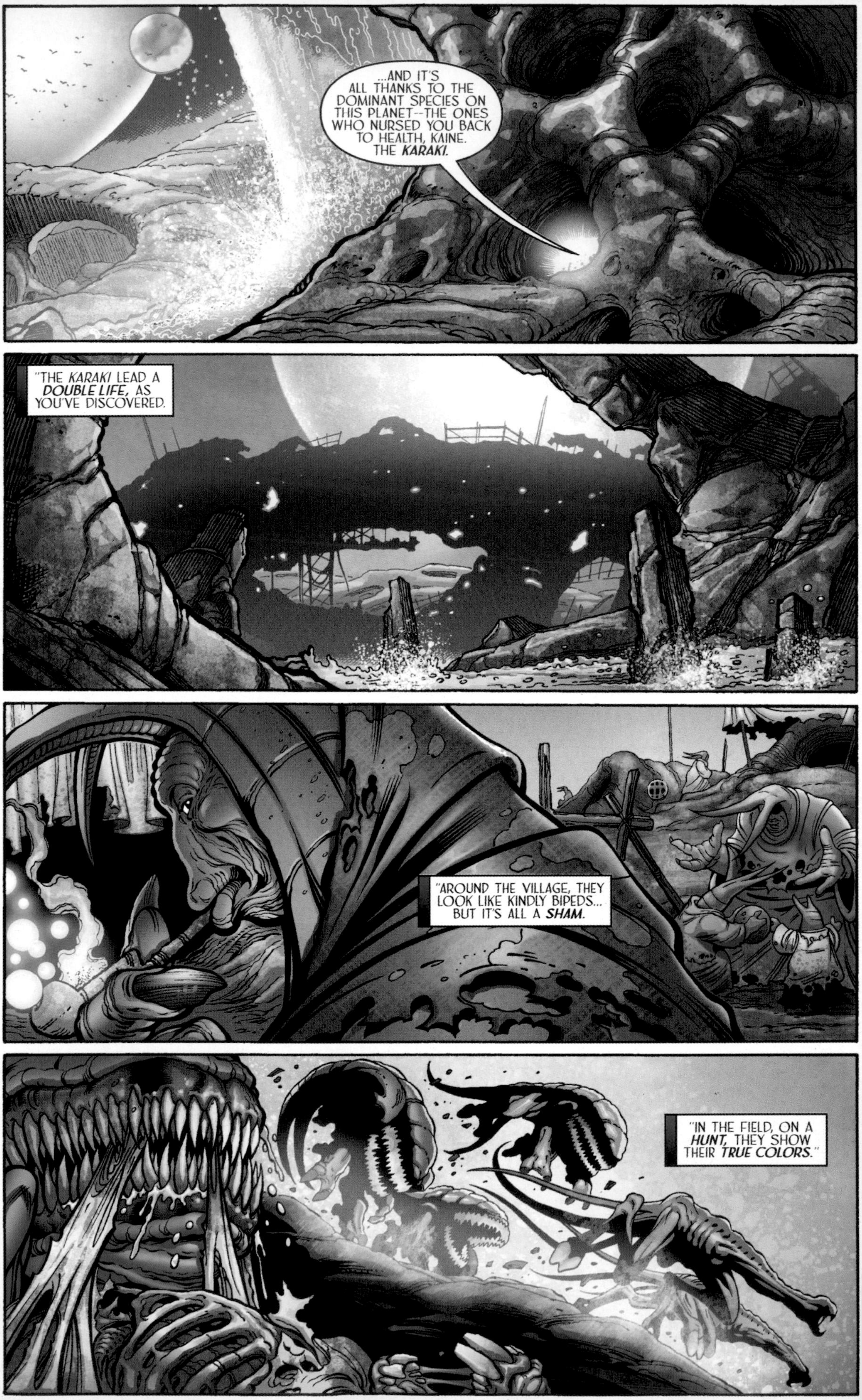

...AND IT'S ALL THANKS TO THE DOMINANT SPECIES ON THIS PLANET--THE ONES WHO NURSED YOU BACK TO HEALTH, KAINE. THE *KARAKI.*
"THE *KARAKI* LEAD A *DOUBLE LIFE,* AS YOU'VE DISCOVERED.
"AROUND THE VILLAGE, THEY LOOK LIKE KINDLY BIPEDS... BUT IT'S ALL A *SHAM.*
"IN THE FIELD, ON A *HUNT,* THEY SHOW THEIR *TRUE COLORS.*"

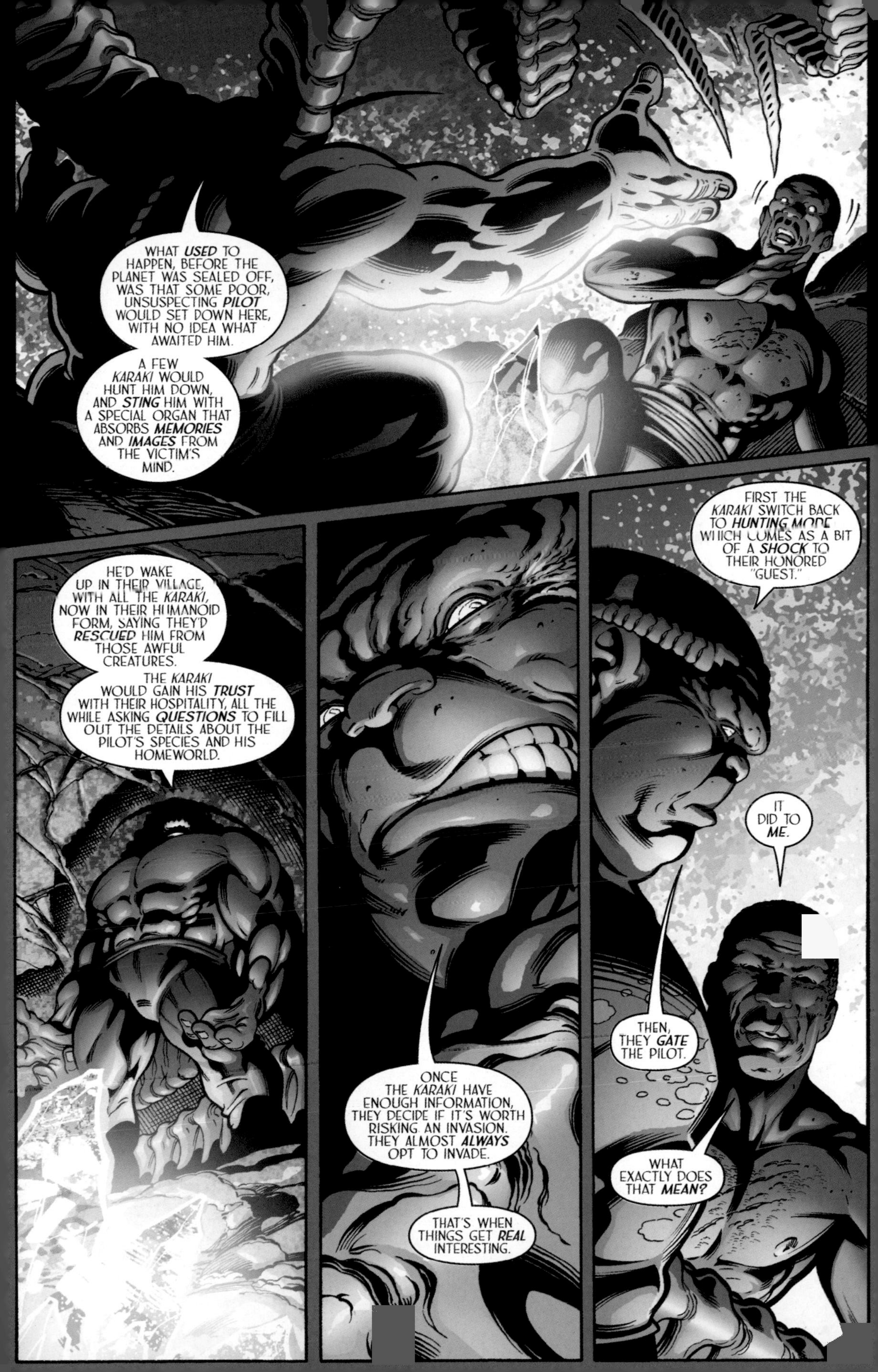
WHAT *USED* TO HAPPEN, BEFORE THE PLANET WAS SEALED OFF, WAS THAT SOME POOR, UNSUSPECTING *PILOT* WOULD SET DOWN HERE, WITH NO IDEA WHAT AWAITED HIM.
A FEW *KARAKI* WOULD HUNT HIM DOWN, AND *STING* HIM WITH A SPECIAL ORGAN THAT ABSORBS *MEMORIES* AND *IMAGES* FROM THE VICTIM'S MIND.
HE'D WAKE UP IN THEIR VILLAGE, WITH ALL THE *KARAKI*, NOW IN THEIR HUMANOID FORM, SAYING THEY'D *RESCUED* HIM FROM THOSE AWFUL CREATURES.
THE *KARAKI* WOULD GAIN HIS *TRUST* WITH THEIR HOSPITALITY, ALL THE WHILE ASKING *QUESTIONS* TO FILL OUT THE DETAILS ABOUT THE PILOT'S SPECIES AND HIS HOMEWORLD.
ONCE THE *KARAKI* HAVE ENOUGH INFORMATION, THEY DECIDE IF IT'S WORTH RISKING AN INVASION. THEY ALMOST *ALWAYS* OPT TO INVADE.
THAT'S WHEN THINGS GET *REAL* INTERESTING.
FIRST THE *KARAKI* SWITCH BACK TO *HUNTING MODE* WHICH COMES AS A BIT OF A *SHOCK* TO THEIR HONORED "GUEST."
IT DID TO *ME*.
THEN, THEY *GATE* THE PILOT.
WHAT EXACTLY DOES THAT *MEAN?*

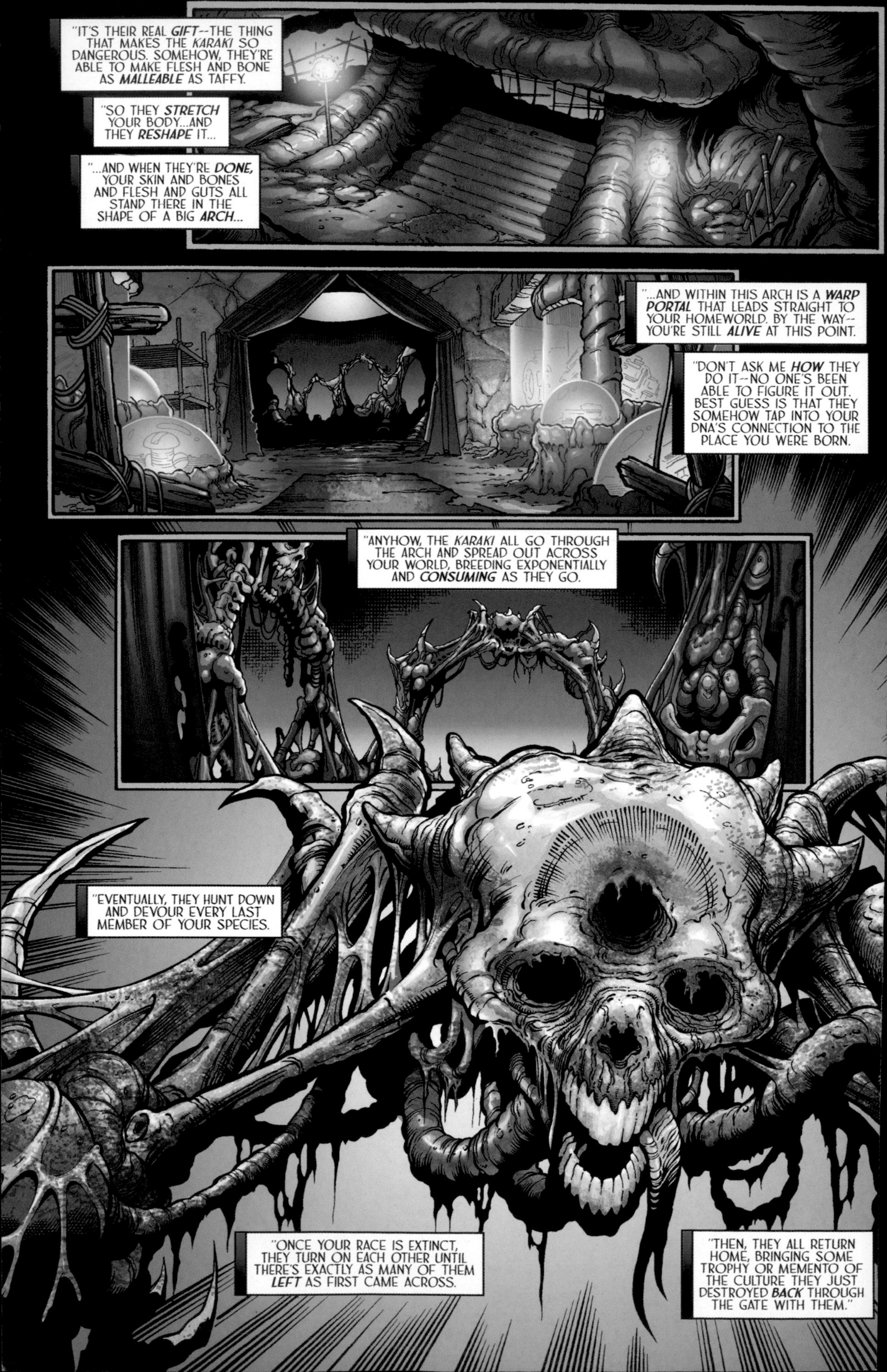
"IT'S THEIR REAL GIFT--THE THING THAT MAKES THE KARAKI SO DANGEROUS. SOMEHOW, THEY'RE ABLE TO MAKE FLESH AND BONE AS MALLEABLE AS TAFFY.
"SO THEY STRETCH YOUR BODY...AND THEY RESHAPE IT...
"...AND WHEN THEY'RE DONE, YOUR SKIN AND BONES AND FLESH AND GUTS ALL STAND THERE IN THE SHAPE OF A BIG ARCH...
"...AND WITHIN THIS ARCH IS A WARP PORTAL THAT LEADS STRAIGHT TO YOUR HOMEWORLD. BY THE WAY--YOU'RE STILL ALIVE AT THIS POINT.
"DON'T ASK ME HOW THEY DO IT--NO ONE'S BEEN ABLE TO FIGURE IT OUT. BEST GUESS IS THAT THEY SOMEHOW TAP INTO YOUR DNA'S CONNECTION TO THE PLACE YOU WERE BORN.
"ANYHOW, THE KARAKI ALL GO THROUGH THE ARCH AND SPREAD OUT ACROSS YOUR WORLD, BREEDING EXPONENTIALLY AND CONSUMING AS THEY GO.
"EVENTUALLY, THEY HUNT DOWN AND DEVOUR EVERY LAST MEMBER OF YOUR SPECIES.
"ONCE YOUR RACE IS EXTINCT, THEY TURN ON EACH OTHER UNTIL THERE'S EXACTLY AS MANY OF THEM LEFT AS FIRST CAME ACROSS.
"THEN, THEY ALL RETURN HOME, BRINGING SOME TROPHY OR MEMENTO OF THE CULTURE THEY JUST DESTROYED BACK THROUGH THE GATE WITH THEM."

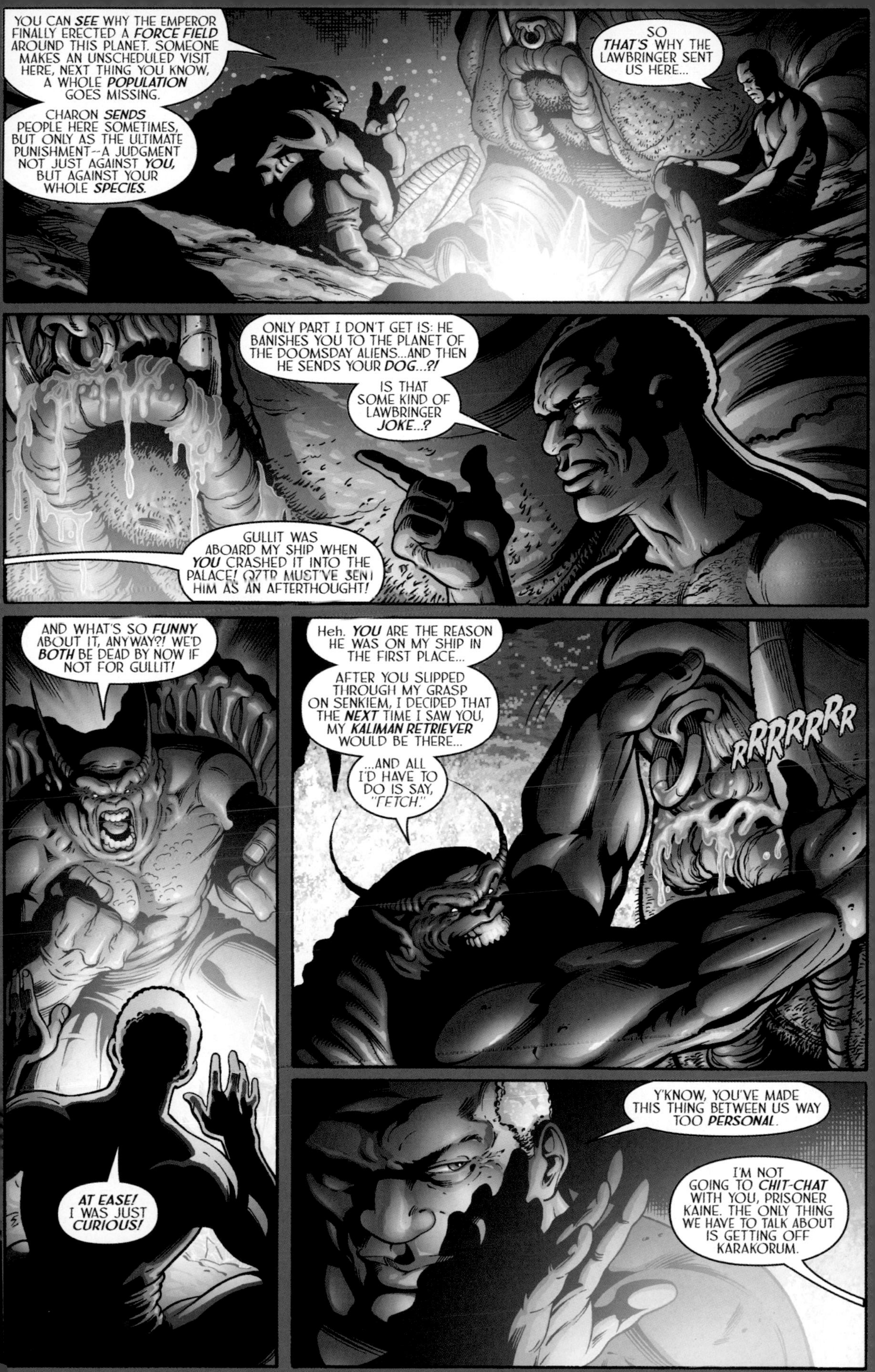
YOU CAN SEE WHY THE EMPEROR FINALLY ERECTED A FORCE FIELD AROUND THIS PLANET. SOMEONE MAKES AN UNSCHEDULED VISIT HERE, NEXT THING YOU KNOW, A WHOLE POPULATION GOES MISSING.
CHARON SENDS PEOPLE HERE SOMETIMES, BUT ONLY AS THE ULTIMATE PUNISHMENT--A JUDGMENT NOT JUST AGAINST YOU, BUT AGAINST YOUR WHOLE SPECIES.
SO THAT'S WHY THE LAWBRINGER SENT US HERE...
ONLY PART I DON'T GET IS: HE BANISHES YOU TO THE PLANET OF THE DOOMSDAY ALIENS...AND THEN HE SENDS YOUR DOG...?!
IS THAT SOME KIND OF LAWBRINGER JOKE...?
GULLIT WAS ABOARD MY SHIP WHEN YOU CRASHED IT INTO THE PALACE! OZTR MUST'VE SENT HIM AS AN AFTERTHOUGHT!
AND WHAT'S SO FUNNY ABOUT IT, ANYWAY?! WE'D BOTH BE DEAD BY NOW IF NOT FOR GULLIT!
AT EASE! I WAS JUST CURIOUS!
Heh. YOU ARE THE REASON HE WAS ON MY SHIP IN THE FIRST PLACE...
AFTER YOU SLIPPED THROUGH MY GRASP ON SENKIEM, I DECIDED THAT THE NEXT TIME I SAW YOU, MY KALIMAN RETRIEVER WOULD BE THERE...
...AND ALL I'D HAVE TO DO IS SAY, "FETCH."
RRRRRRR
Y'KNOW, YOU'VE MADE THIS THING BETWEEN US WAY TOO PERSONAL.
I'M NOT GOING TO CHIT-CHAT WITH YOU, PRISONER KAINE. THE ONLY THING WE HAVE TO TALK ABOUT IS GETTING OFF KARAKORUM.

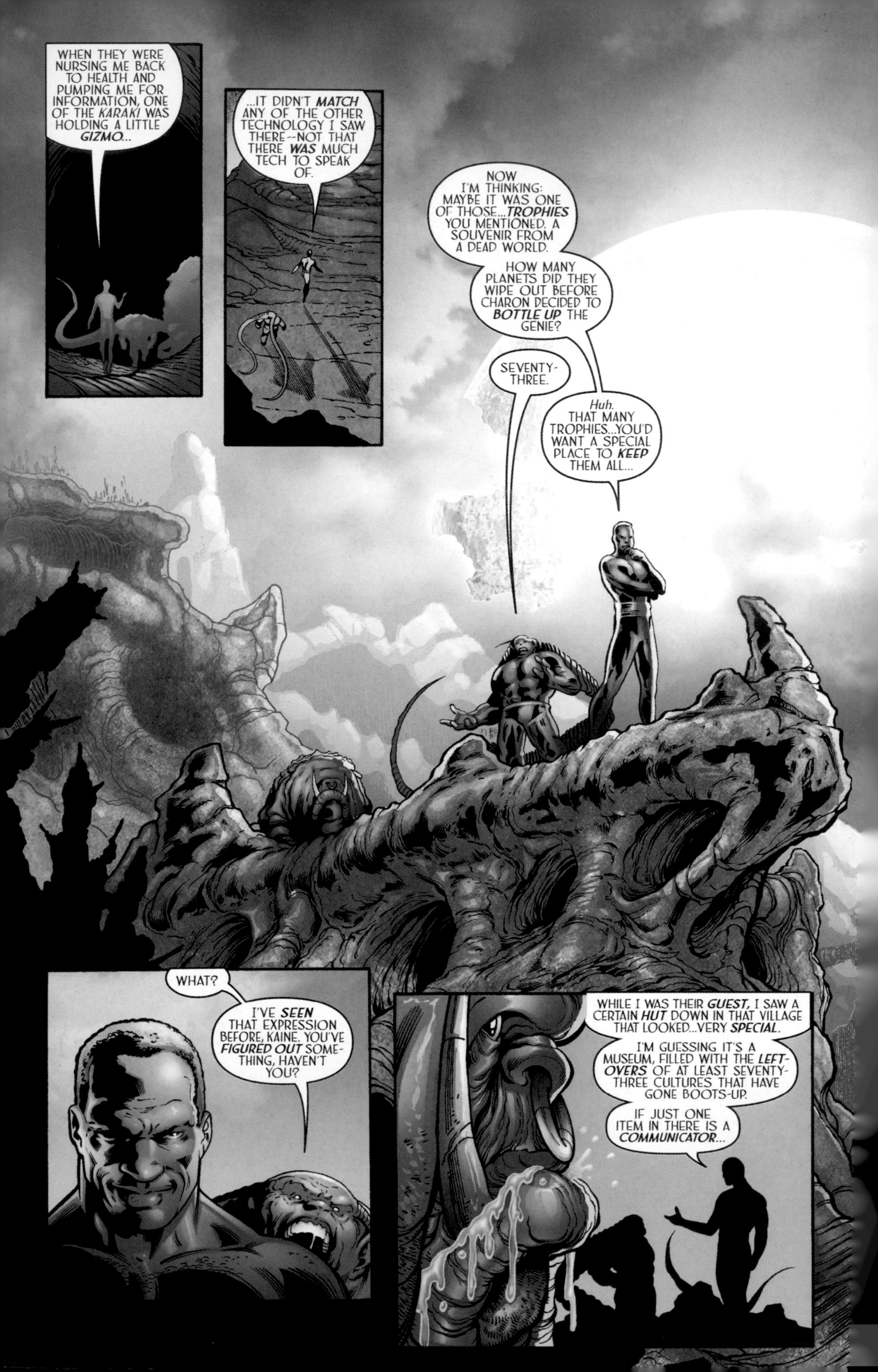

WHEN THEY WERE NURSING ME BACK TO HEALTH AND PUMPING ME FOR INFORMATION, ONE OF THE *KARAKI* WAS HOLDING A LITTLE ***GIZMO***...
...IT DIDN'T ***MATCH*** ANY OF THE OTHER TECHNOLOGY I SAW THERE--NOT THAT THERE ***WAS*** MUCH TECH TO SPEAK OF.
NOW I'M THINKING: MAYBE IT WAS ONE OF THOSE...***TROPHIES*** YOU MENTIONED. A SOUVENIR FROM A DEAD WORLD.
HOW MANY PLANETS DID THEY WIPE OUT BEFORE CHARON DECIDED TO ***BOTTLE UP*** THE GENIE?
SEVENTY-THREE.
Huh. THAT MANY TROPHIES...YOU'D WANT A SPECIAL PLACE TO ***KEEP*** THEM ALL...
WHAT?
I'VE ***SEEN*** THAT EXPRESSION BEFORE, KAINE. YOU'VE ***FIGURED OUT*** SOME-THING, HAVEN'T YOU?
WHILE I WAS THEIR ***GUEST,*** I SAW A CERTAIN ***HUT*** DOWN IN THAT VILLAGE THAT LOOKED...VERY ***SPECIAL***.
I'M GUESSING IT'S A MUSEUM, FILLED WITH THE ***LEFT-OVERS*** OF AT LEAST SEVENTY-THREE CULTURES THAT HAVE GONE BOOTS-UP.
IF JUST ONE ITEM IN THERE IS A ***COMMUNICATOR***...

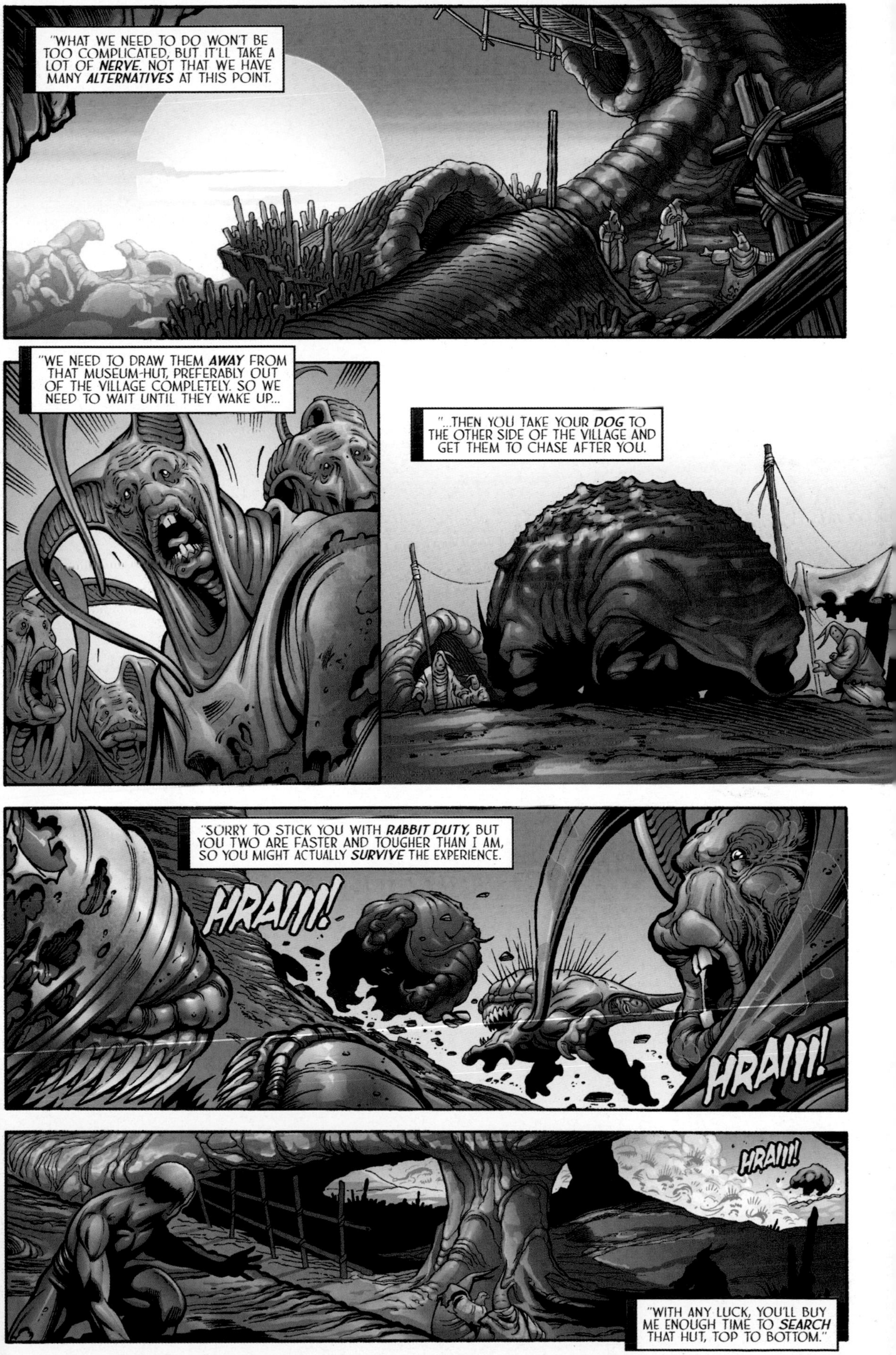
"WHAT WE NEED TO DO WON'T BE TOO COMPLICATED, BUT IT'LL TAKE A LOT OF NERVE. NOT THAT WE HAVE MANY ALTERNATIVES AT THIS POINT.
"WE NEED TO DRAW THEM AWAY FROM THAT MUSEUM-HUT, PREFERABLY OUT OF THE VILLAGE COMPLETELY. SO WE NEED TO WAIT UNTIL THEY WAKE UP...
"...THEN YOU TAKE YOUR DOG TO THE OTHER SIDE OF THE VILLAGE AND GET THEM TO CHASE AFTER YOU.
"SORRY TO STICK YOU WITH RABBIT DUTY, BUT YOU TWO ARE FASTER AND TOUGHER THAN I AM, SO YOU MIGHT ACTUALLY SURVIVE THE EXPERIENCE.
HRAIII!
HRAIII!
HRAIII!
"WITH ANY LUCK, YOU'LL BUY ME ENOUGH TIME TO SEARCH THAT HUT, TOP TO BOTTOM."

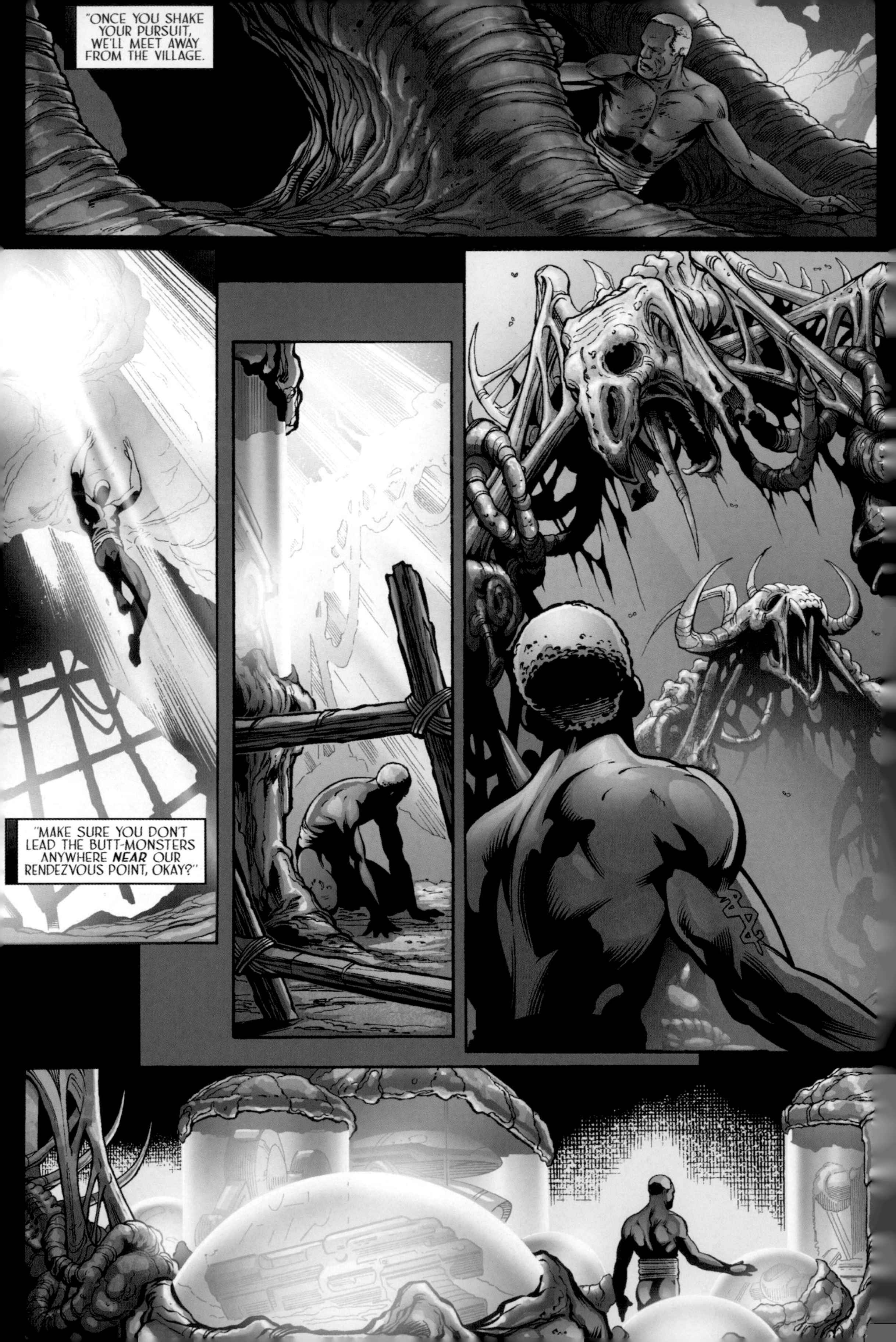
"ONCE YOU SHAKE YOUR PURSUIT, WE'LL MEET AWAY FROM THE VILLAGE.
"MAKE SURE YOU DON'T LEAD THE BUTT-MONSTERS ANYWHERE NEAR OUR RENDEZVOUS POINT, OKAY?"

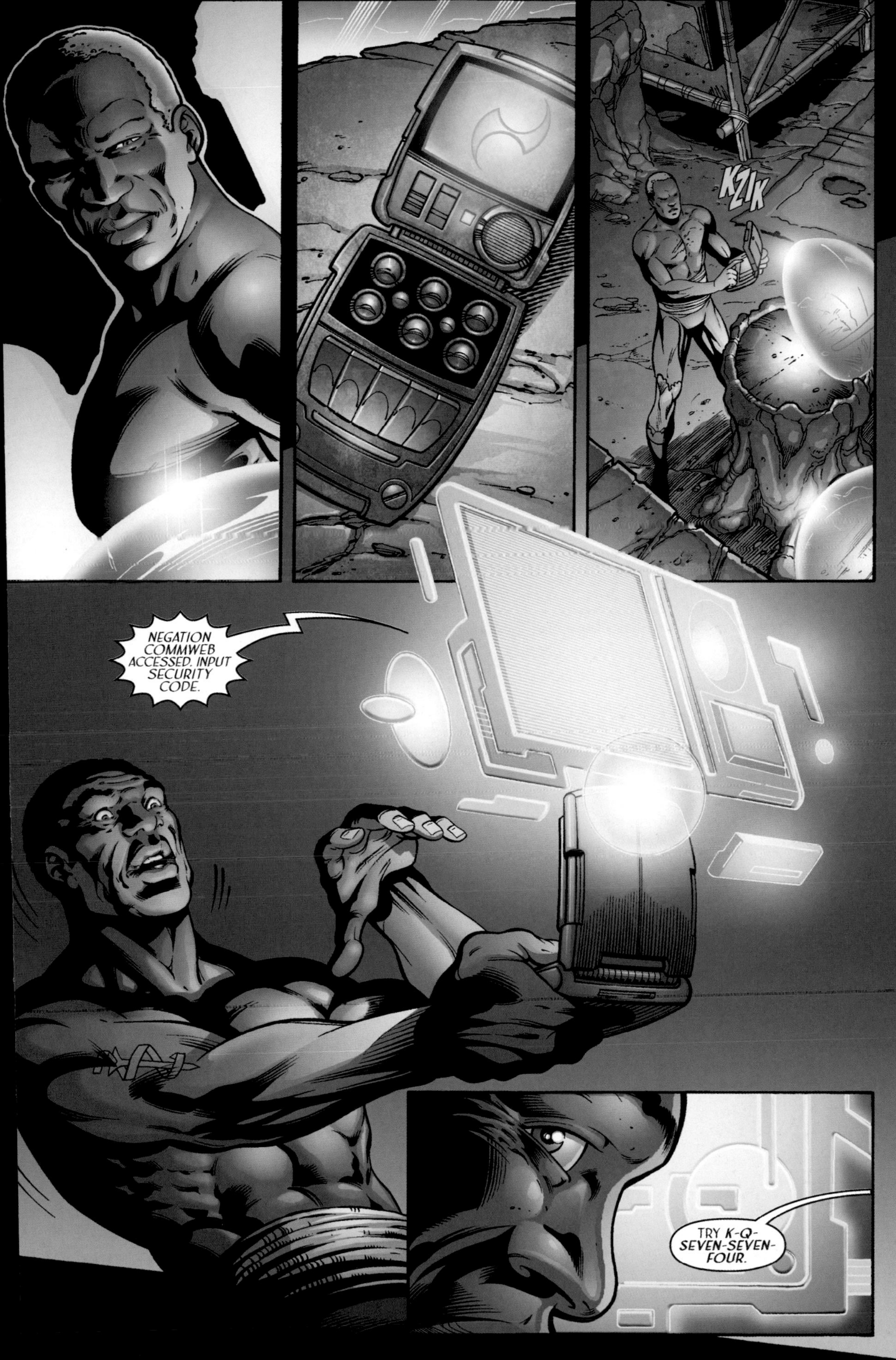
KZIK
NEGATION COMMWEB ACCESSED. INPUT SECURITY CODE.
TRY K-Q-SEVEN-SEVEN-FOUR.

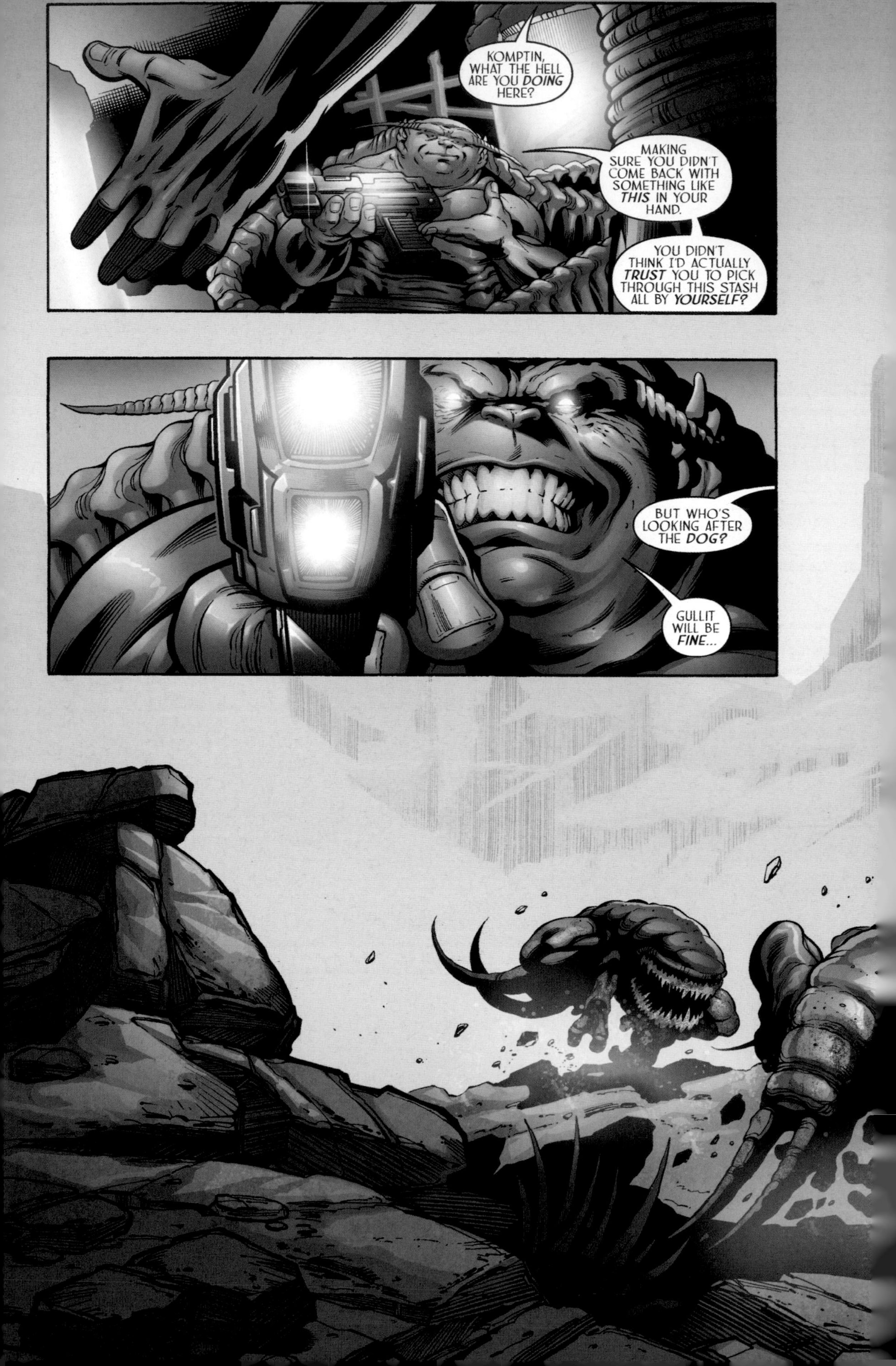
KOMPTIN, WHAT THE HELL ARE YOU DOING HERE?
MAKING SURE YOU DIDN'T COME BACK WITH SOMETHING LIKE THIS IN YOUR HAND.
YOU DIDN'T THINK I'D ACTUALLY TRUST YOU TO PICK THROUGH THIS STASH ALL BY YOURSELF?
BUT WHO'S LOOKING AFTER THE DOG?
GULLIT WILL BE FINE...

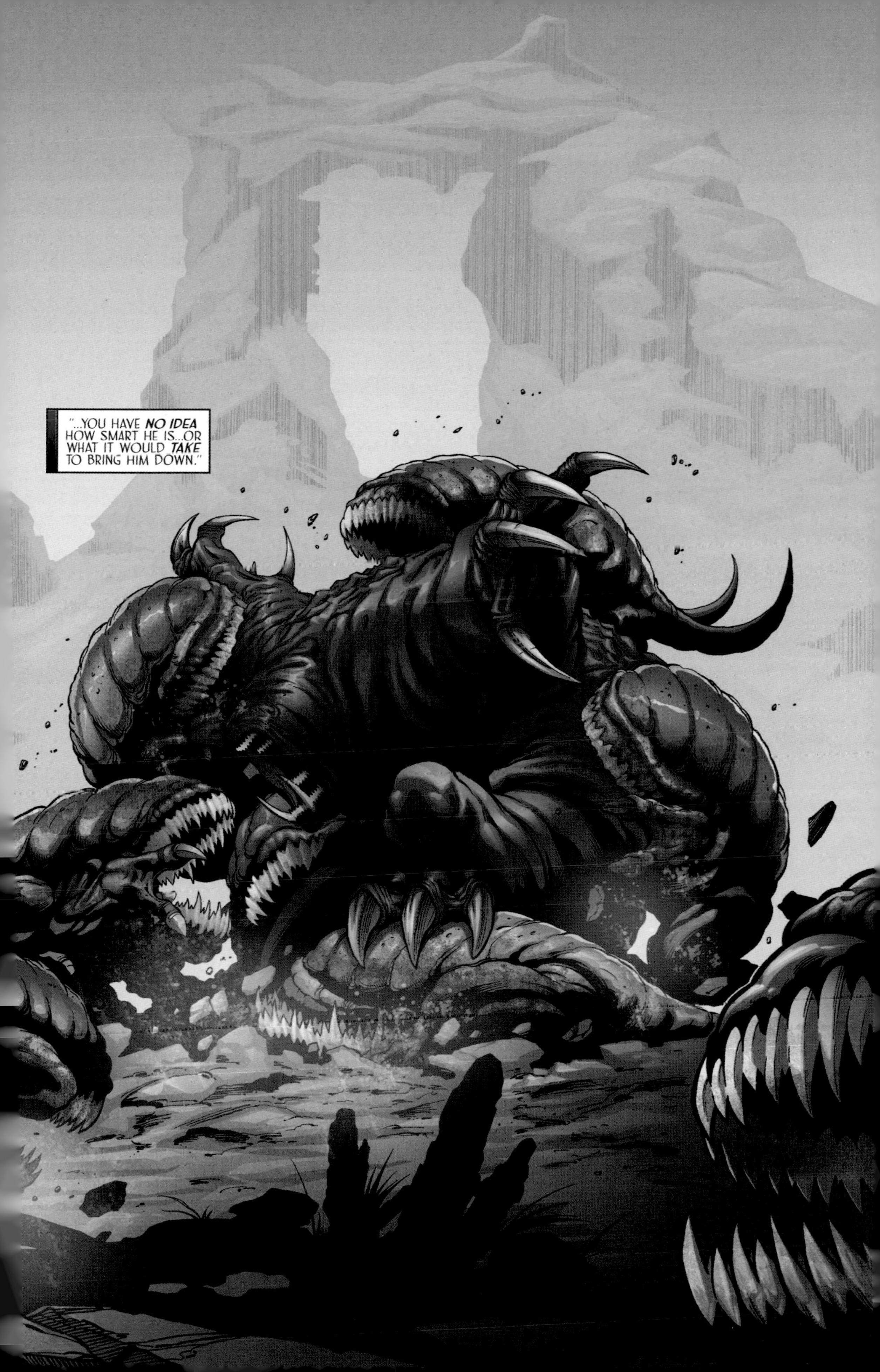
"...YOU HAVE NO IDEA HOW SMART HE IS...OR WHAT IT WOULD TAKE TO BRING HIM DOWN."

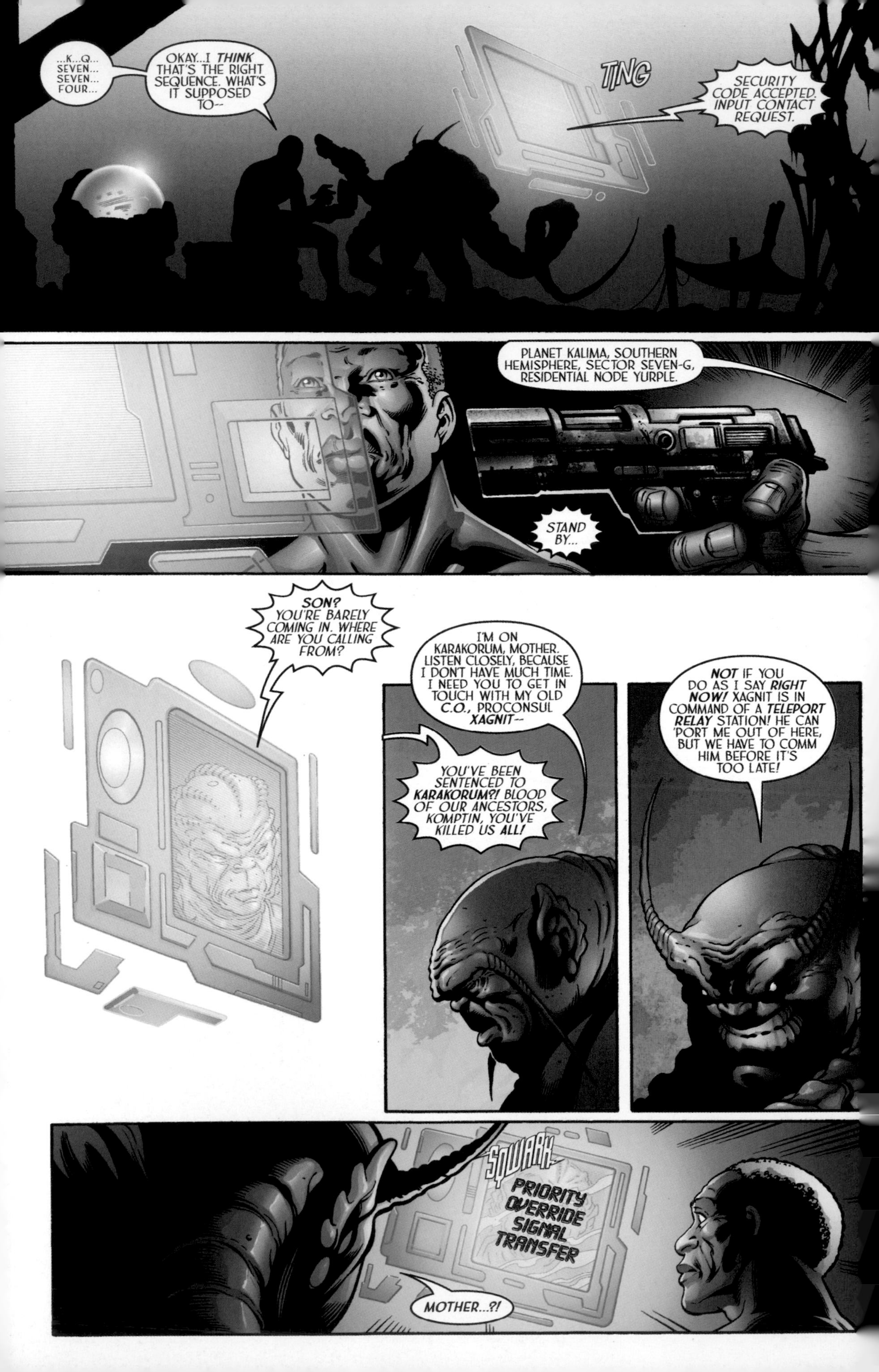
...K...Q... SEVEN... SEVEN... FOUR...
OKAY...I THINK THAT'S THE RIGHT SEQUENCE. WHAT'S IT SUPPOSED TO--
TING
SECURITY CODE ACCEPTED. INPUT CONTACT REQUEST.
PLANET KALIMA, SOUTHERN HEMISPHERE, SECTOR SEVEN-G, RESIDENTIAL NODE YURPLE.
STAND BY...
SON? YOU'RE BARELY COMING IN. WHERE ARE YOU CALLING FROM?
I'M ON KARAKORUM, MOTHER. LISTEN CLOSELY, BECAUSE I DON'T HAVE MUCH TIME. I NEED YOU TO GET IN TOUCH WITH MY OLD C.O., PROCONSUL XAGNIT--
YOU'VE BEEN SENTENCED TO KARAKORUM?! BLOOD OF OUR ANCESTORS, KOMPTIN, YOU'VE KILLED US ALL!
NOT IF YOU DO AS I SAY RIGHT NOW! XAGNIT IS IN COMMAND OF A TELEPORT RELAY STATION! HE CAN 'PORT ME OUT OF HERE, BUT WE HAVE TO COMM HIM BEFORE IT'S TOO LATE!
SQWARK
PRIORITY OVERRIDE SIGNAL TRANSFER
MOTHER...?!

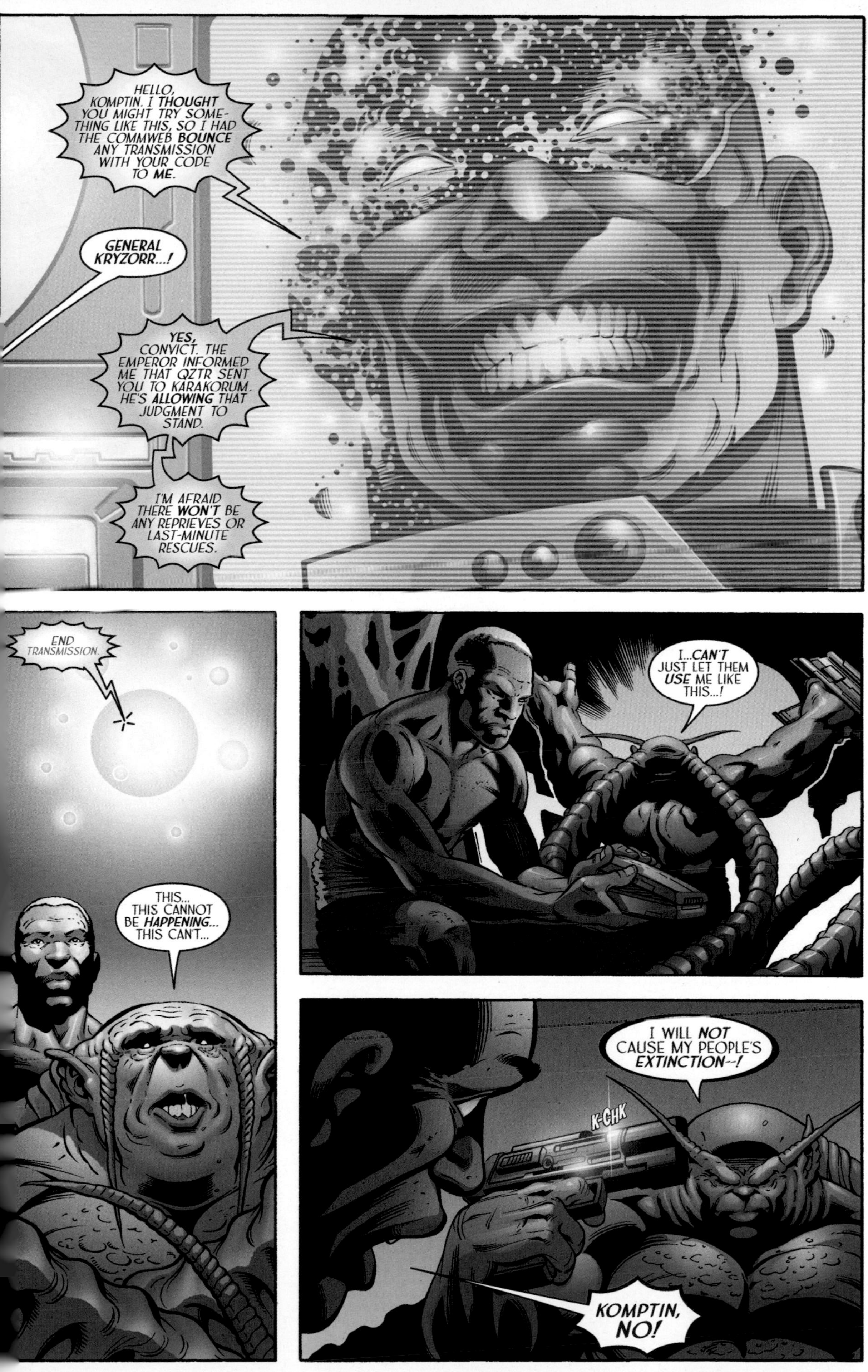
HELLO, KOMPTIN. I THOUGHT YOU MIGHT TRY SOMETHING LIKE THIS, SO I HAD THE COMMWEB BOUNCE ANY TRANSMISSION WITH YOUR CODE TO ME.
GENERAL KRYZORR...!
YES, CONVICT. THE EMPEROR INFORMED ME THAT QZTR SENT YOU TO KARAKORUM. HE'S ALLOWING THAT JUDGMENT TO STAND.
I'M AFRAID THERE WON'T BE ANY REPRIEVES OR LAST-MINUTE RESCUES.
END TRANSMISSION.
THIS... THIS CANNOT BE HAPPENING... THIS CAN'T...
I...CAN'T JUST LET THEM USE ME LIKE THIS...!
I WILL NOT CAUSE MY PEOPLE'S EXTINCTION--!
K-CHK
KOMPTIN, NO!

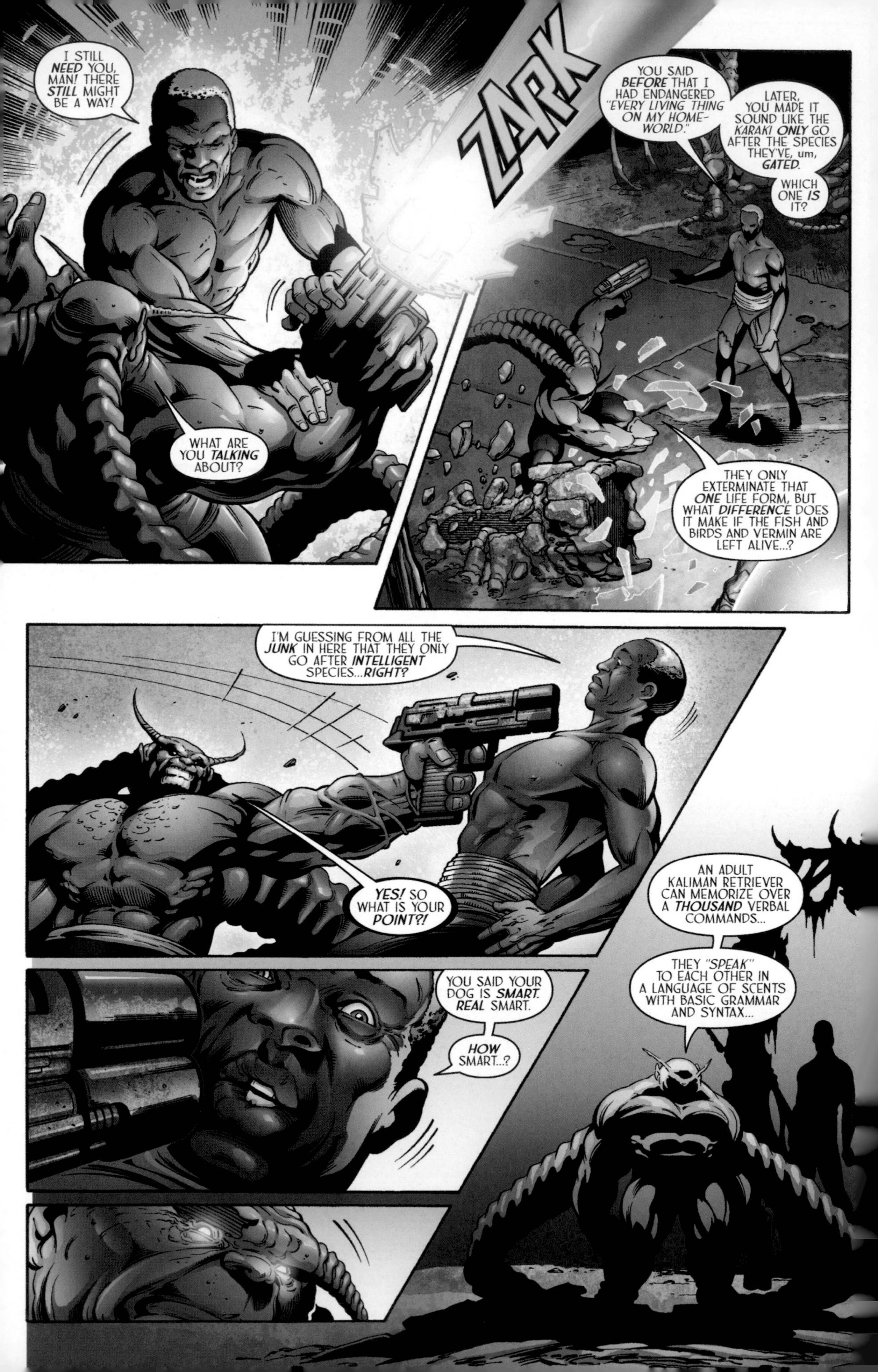
I STILL NEED YOU, MAN! THERE STILL MIGHT BE A WAY!
WHAT ARE YOU TALKING ABOUT?
ZARK
YOU SAID BEFORE THAT I HAD ENDANGERED "EVERY LIVING THING ON MY HOME-WORLD."
LATER, YOU MADE IT SOUND LIKE THE KARAKI ONLY GO AFTER THE SPECIES THEY'VE, um, GATED.
WHICH ONE IS IT?
THEY ONLY EXTERMINATE THAT ONE LIFE FORM, BUT WHAT DIFFERENCE DOES IT MAKE IF THE FISH AND BIRDS AND VERMIN ARE LEFT ALIVE...?
I'M GUESSING FROM ALL THE JUNK IN HERE THAT THEY ONLY GO AFTER INTELLIGENT SPECIES...RIGHT?
YES! SO WHAT IS YOUR POINT?!
YOU SAID YOUR DOG IS SMART. REAL SMART.
HOW SMART...?
AN ADULT KALIMAN RETRIEVER CAN MEMORIZE OVER A THOUSAND VERBAL COMMANDS...
THEY "SPEAK" TO EACH OTHER IN A LANGUAGE OF SCENTS WITH BASIC GRAMMAR AND SYNTAX...

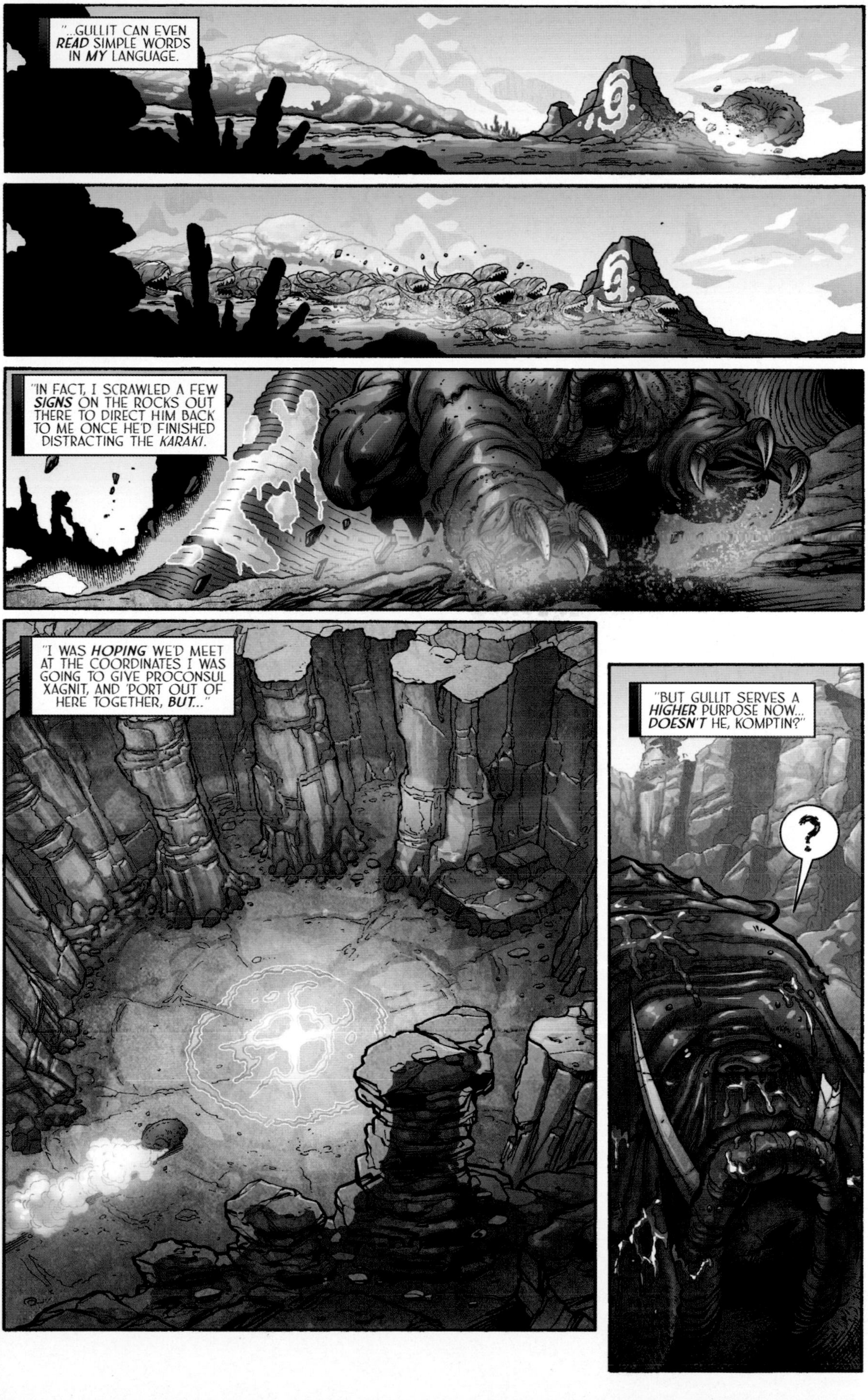
"...GULLIT CAN EVEN READ SIMPLE WORDS IN MY LANGUAGE.
"IN FACT, I SCRAWLED A FEW SIGNS ON THE ROCKS OUT THERE TO DIRECT HIM BACK TO ME ONCE HE'D FINISHED DISTRACTING THE KARAKI.
"I WAS HOPING WE'D MEET AT THE COORDINATES I WAS GOING TO GIVE PROCONSUL XAGNIT, AND 'PORT OUT OF HERE TOGETHER, BUT..."
"BUT GULLIT SERVES A HIGHER PURPOSE NOW... DOESN'T HE, KOMPTIN?"
?

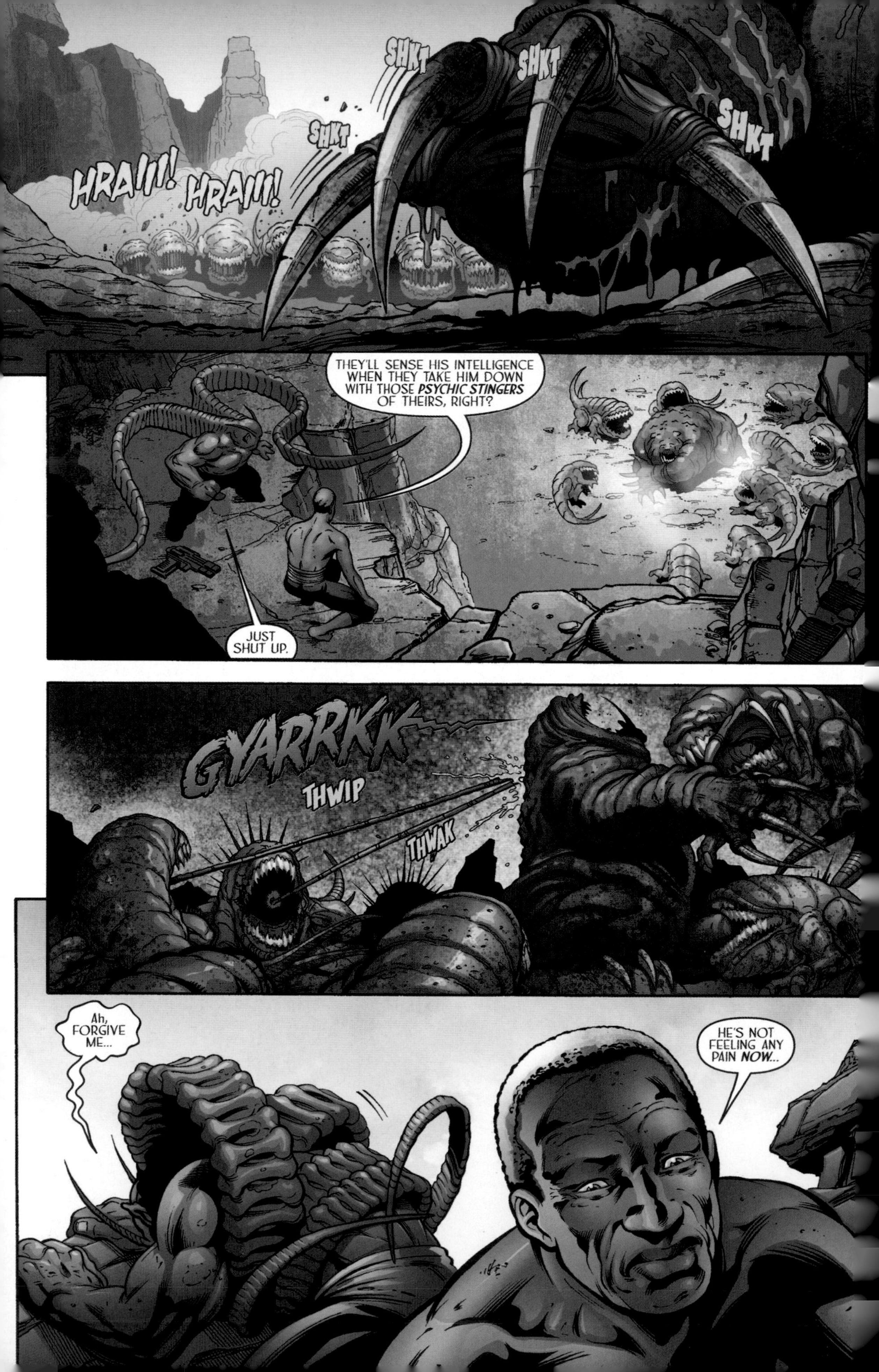
SHKT
SHKT
SHKT
SHKT
HRA!!!! HRA!!!!
THEY'LL SENSE HIS INTELLIGENCE WHEN THEY TAKE HIM DOWN WITH THOSE PSYCHIC STINGERS OF THEIRS, RIGHT?
JUST SHUT UP.
GYARRKK
THWIP
THWAK
Ah, FORGIVE ME...
HE'S NOT FEELING ANY PAIN NOW...

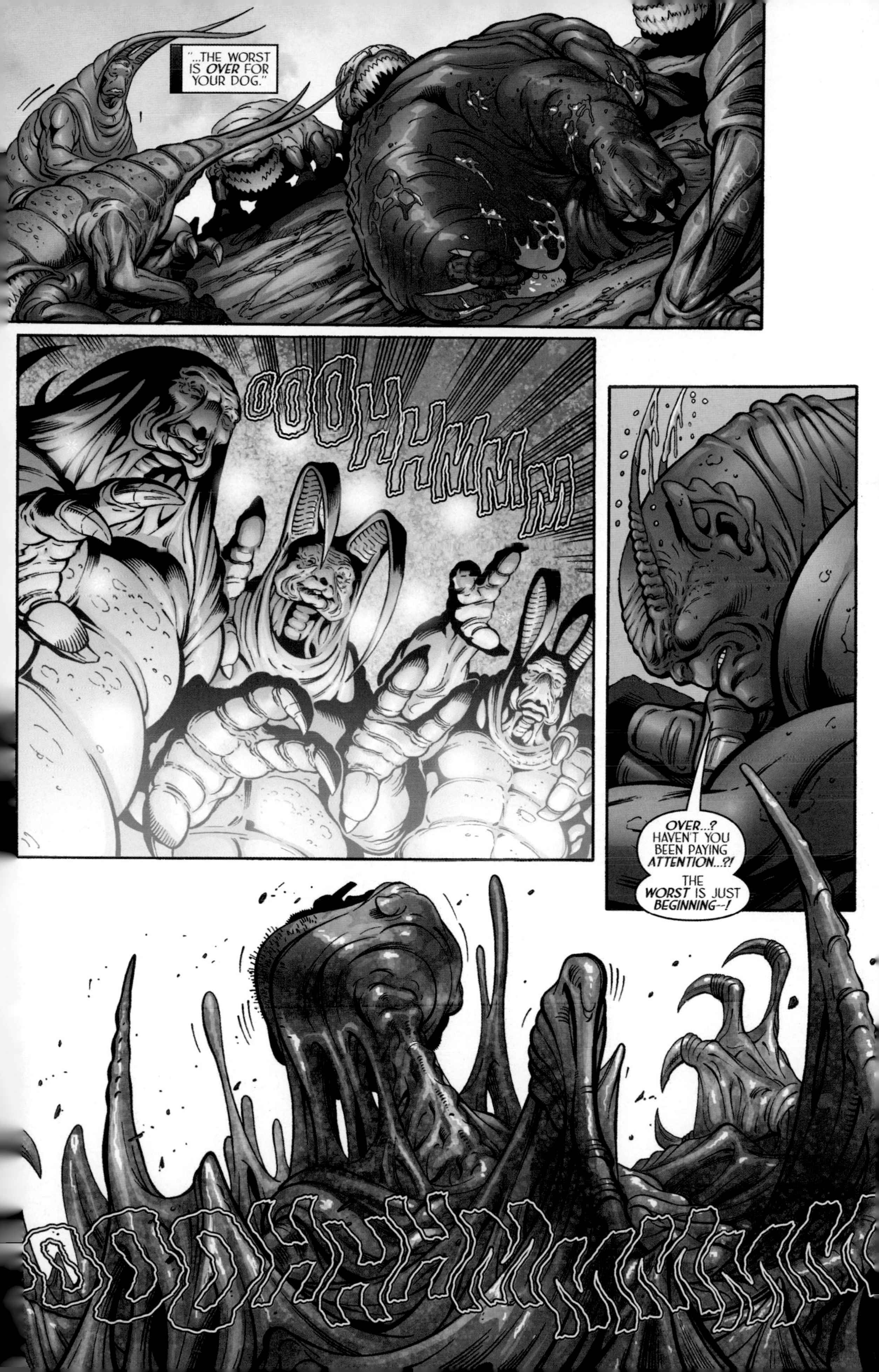
"...THE WORST IS OVER FOR YOUR DOG."
OOOHHMMMM
OVER...? HAVEN'T YOU BEEN PAYING ATTENTION...?!
THE WORST IS JUST BEGINNING--!
OOOHHMMMMMMMM

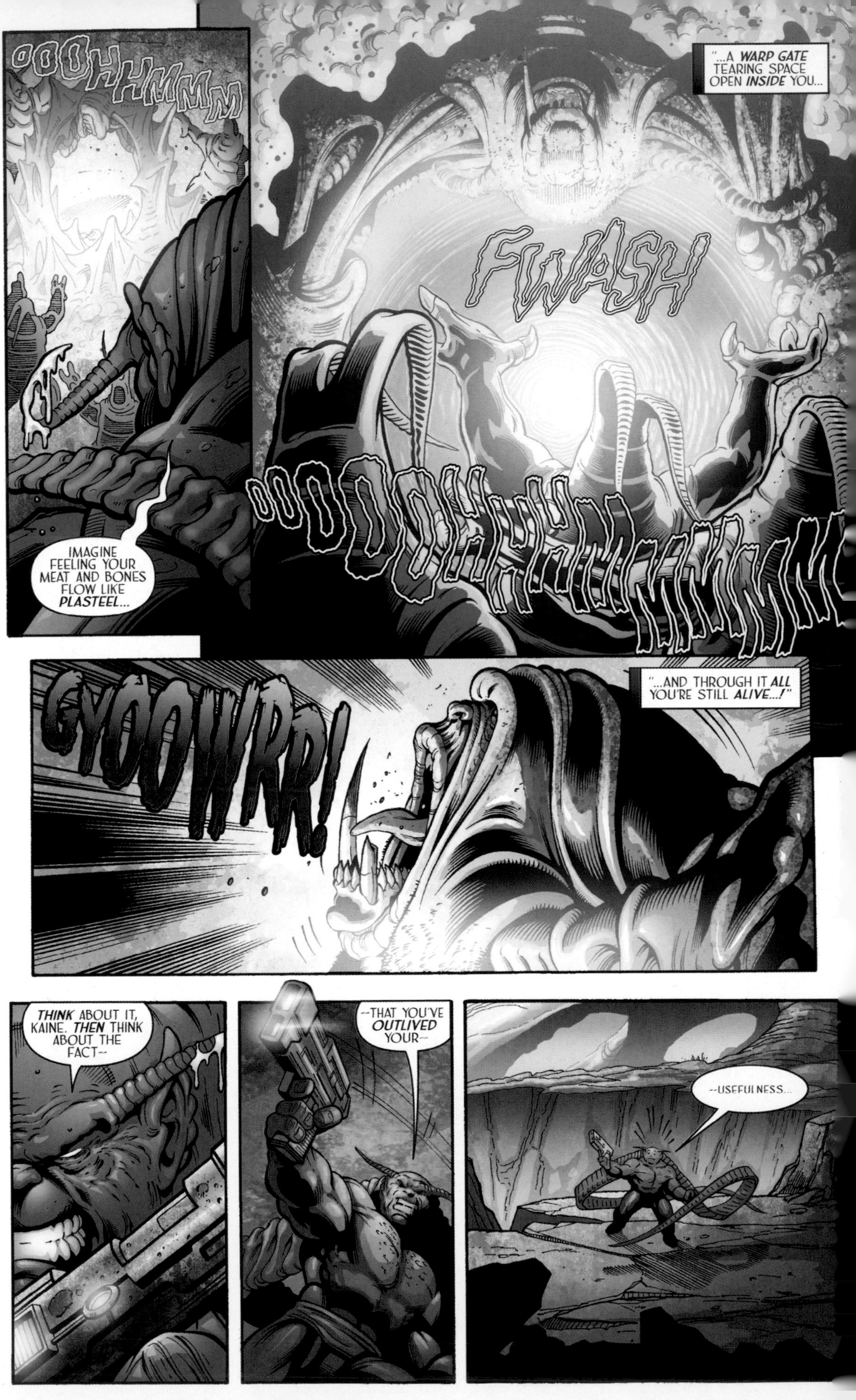
OOOHHMMM
"...A WARP GATE TEARING SPACE OPEN INSIDE YOU...
FWASH
IMAGINE FEELING YOUR MEAT AND BONES FLOW LIKE PLASTEEL...
OOOOOOHHHMMMMMMM
"...AND THROUGH IT ALL YOU'RE STILL ALIVE...!"
GYOOWRR!
THINK ABOUT IT, KAINE. THEN THINK ABOUT THE FACT--
--THAT YOU'VE OUTLIVED YOUR--
--USEFULNESS...

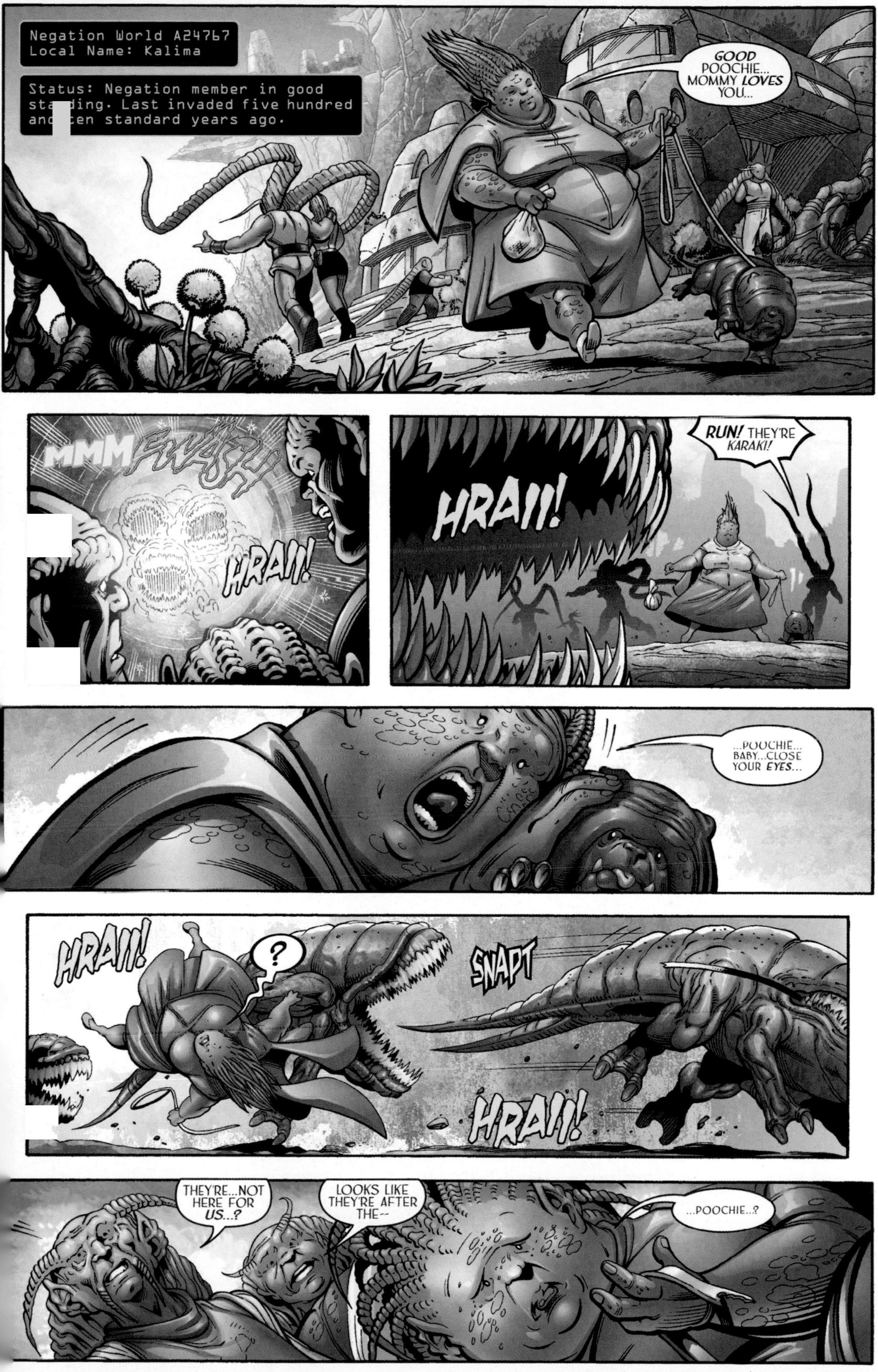
Negation World A24767
Local Name: Kalima
Status: Negation member in good standing. Last invaded five hundred and ten standard years ago.
GOOD POOCHIE... MOMMY LOVES YOU...
MMMFWASH
HRAII!
HRAII!
RUN! THEY'RE KARAKI!
...POOCHIE... BABY...CLOSE YOUR EYES...
HRAII!
?
SNAPT
HRAII!
THEY'RE...NOT HERE FOR US...?
LOOKS LIKE THEY'RE AFTER THE--
...POOCHIE..?

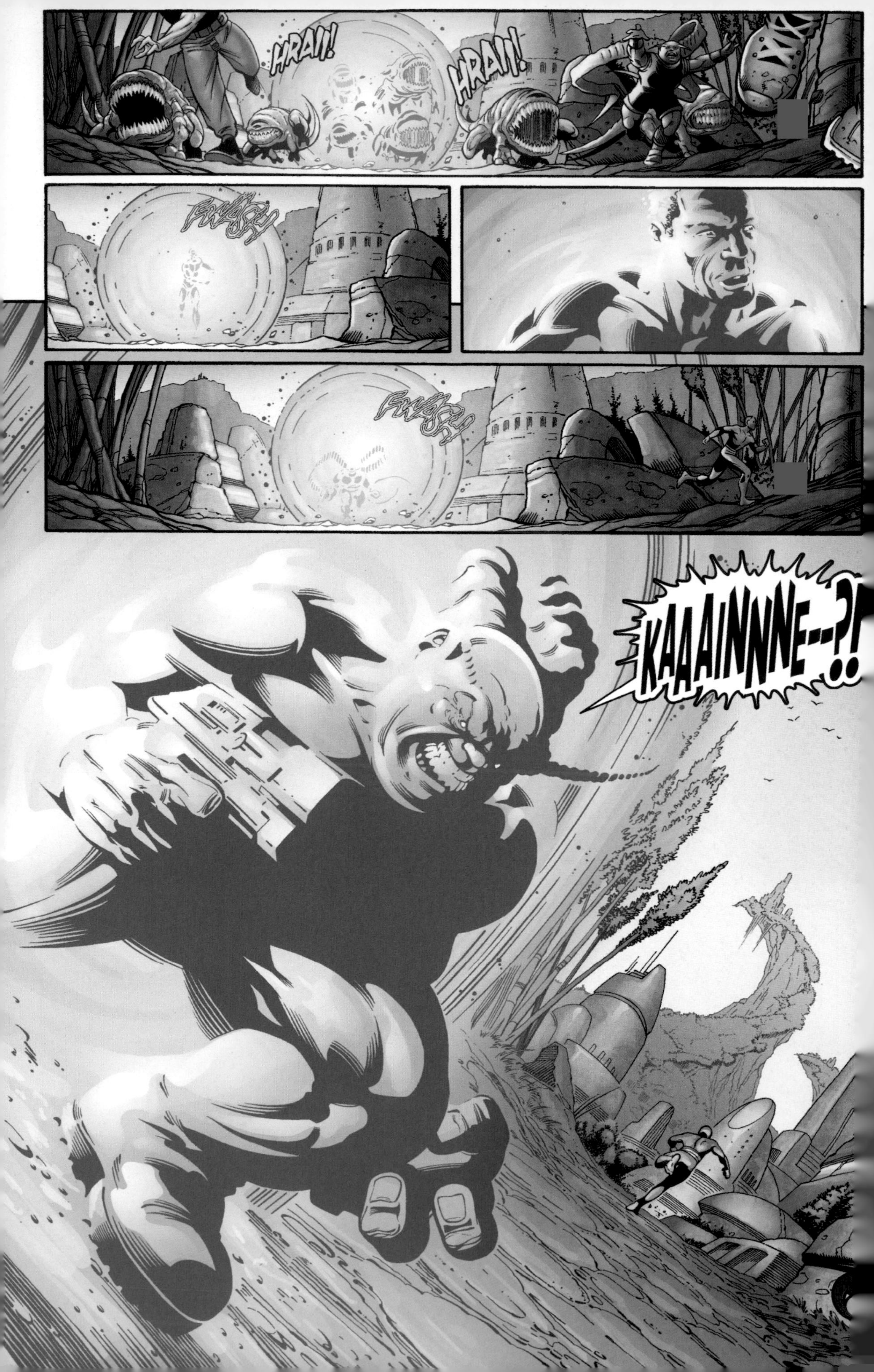
HRAII!
HRAII!
FWASH
FWASH
KAAAINNNE--?!

STORYTELLERS

TONY BEDARD
WRITER

PAUL PELLETIER
PENCILER

DAVE MEIKIS
INKER

JAMES ROCHELLE
COLORIST

TROY PETERI
LETTERER

The CrossGen Universe created by Mark Alessi & Gina M. Villa

MARK ALESSI Publisher & Chief Executive Officer * GINA M. VILLA Chief Operating Officer * MICHAEL A. BEATTIE Chief Financial Officer
JENNIFER HERNANDEZ General Counsel * JIM STIKELEATHER Chief Technical Officer * TONY PANACCIO Vice President Product Development
CHRIS OARR Vice President Sales & Marketing * ROBERT BOYD Director Marketing * JAMES BREITBEIL Director Marketing & Distribution
IAN M. FELLER Director Corporate Communications * COURTLAND WHITED MIS Director * GABO MENDOZA Internet Services Director
CHARLES DECKER Director Production Control * BRIAN M. SOLTIS Controller * BRANDON PETERSON Vice President Special Projects
BARBARA KESEL Head Writer * BART SEARS Art Director * MICHELLE PUGLIESE Freelance Coordinator
MICHAEL ATIYEH, BUTCH GUICE, DAVE LANPHEAR, RICK MAGYAR, LAURA MARTIN, MARK PENNINGTON, ANDY SMITH Assistant Art Directors
M DAVIES Vice President Production * SYLVIA BRETZ Production Supervisor Advertising/Web * JANET BECHTLE Production Supervisor Books
RANDY MARTIN & ERIN FLANAGAN Production Designers * MARISOL QUINTANA Production Assistant

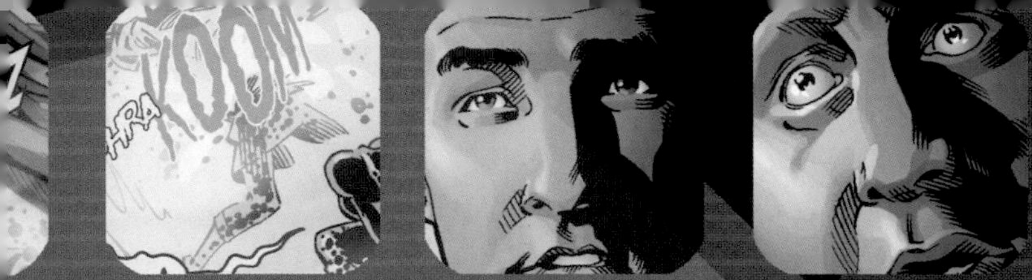
HRA KOOM

he Negation

Chapter 5

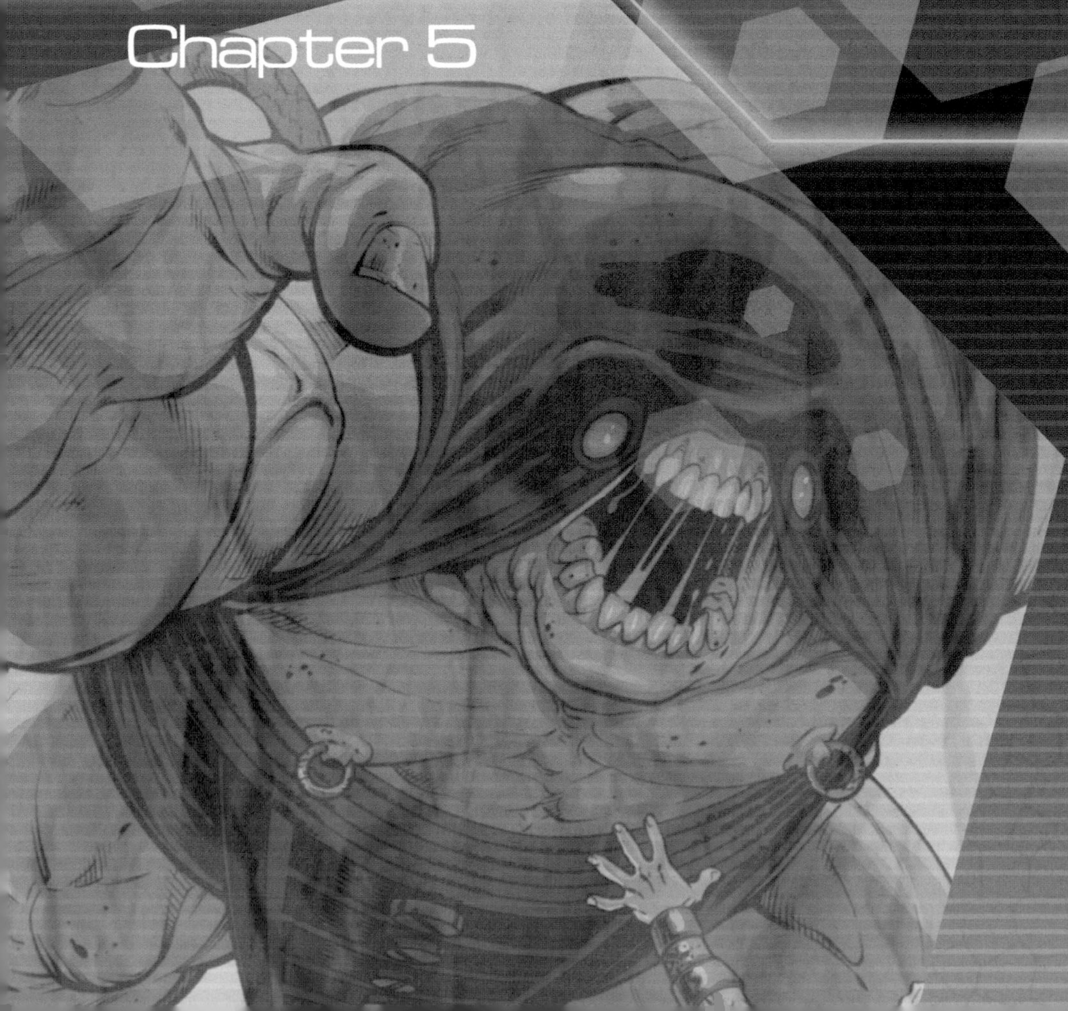

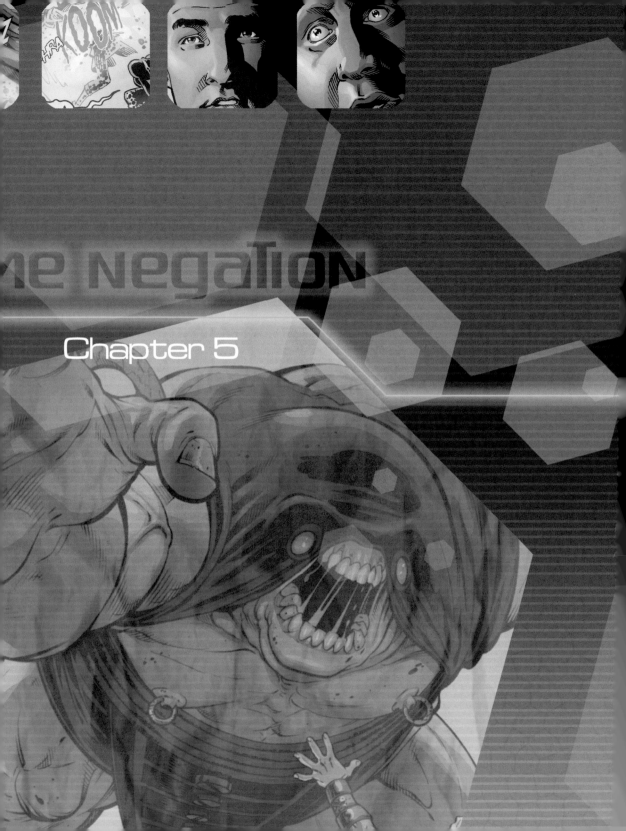

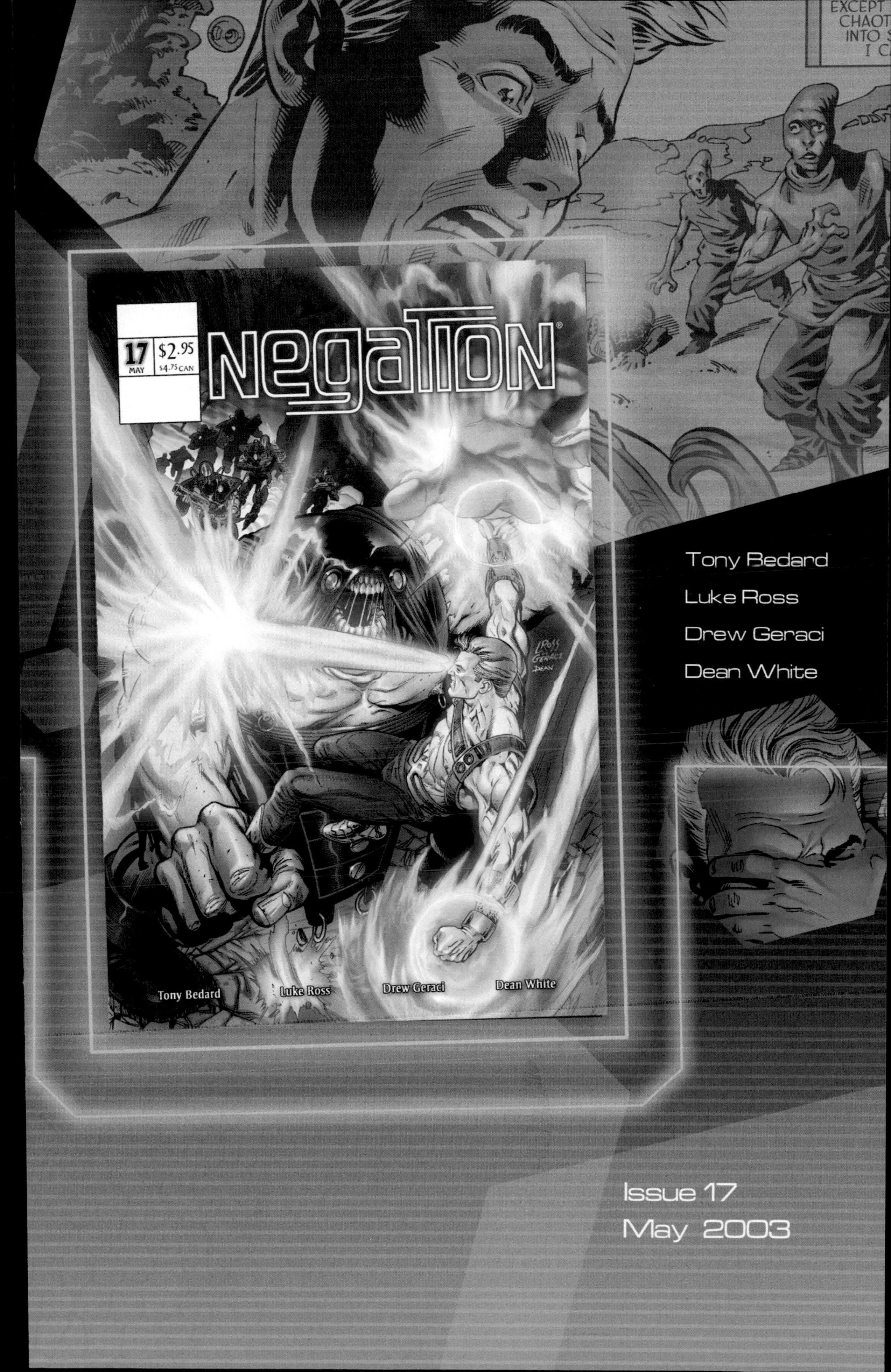

17 MAY
$2.95
$4.75 CAN
Negation
Tony Bedard
Luke Ross
Drew Geraci
Dean White
L Ross
Geraci
Dean
Tony Bedard
Luke Ross
Drew Geraci
Dean White
Issue 17
May 2003

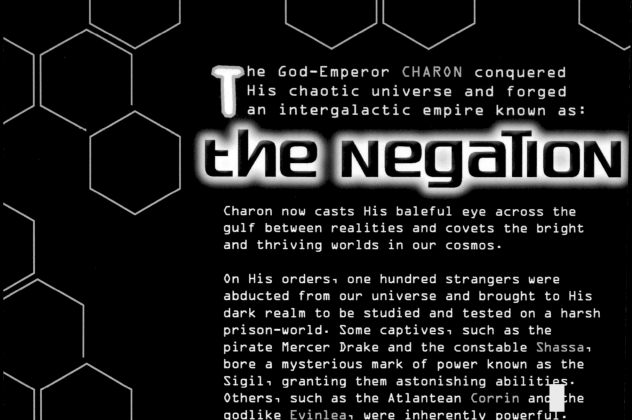

The God-Emperor CHARON conquered His chaotic universe and forged an intergalactic empire known as:

the negation

Charon now casts His baleful eye across the gulf between realities and covets the bright and thriving worlds in our cosmos.

On His orders, one hundred strangers were abducted from our universe and brought to His dark realm to be studied and tested on a harsh prison-world. Some captives, such as the pirate Mercer Drake and the constable Shassa, bore a mysterious mark of power known as the Sigil, granting them astonishing abilities. Others, such as the Atlantean Corrin and the godlike Evinlea, were inherently powerful. Most, however, were simple, ordinary humans.

One such human named Obregon Kaine led a bloody uprising against the Negation prison warden, Komptin. The few prisoners who escaped with their lives now wander the hostile stars, seeking a way home.

Forced to withdraw from the Negation Throneworld without Kaine, the escapees rush to a rendezvous point, hoping to meet up with other survivors from their daring raid against Charon Himself. Their loss of Kaine is tempered by the knowledge that they rescued baby Memi from the clutches of the Negation, along with a mysterious newcomer, Gammid of Atlantis, whose power and history will have a profound impact upon their lives...

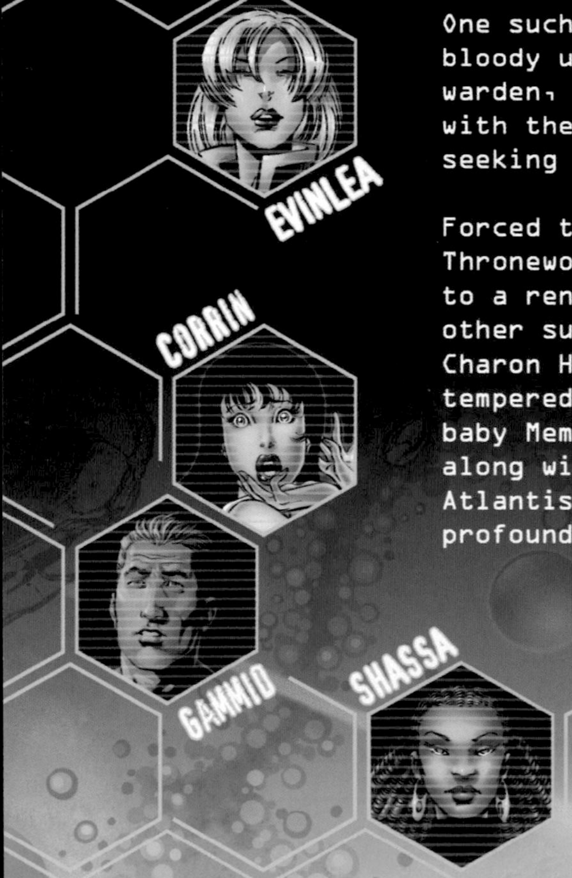

EVINLEA

CORRIN

GAMMID SHASSA

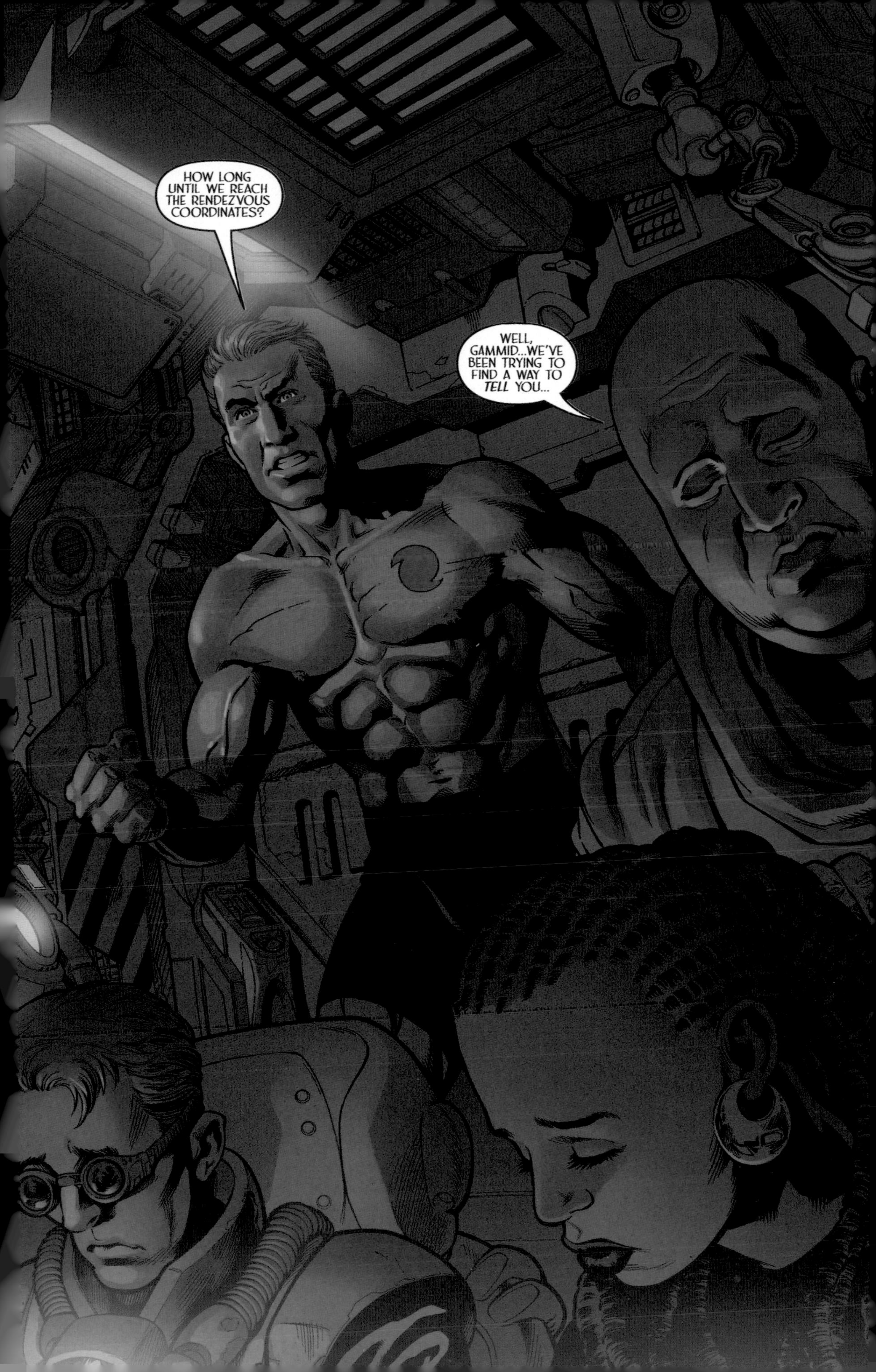
HOW LONG UNTIL WE REACH THE RENDEZVOUS COORDINATES?
WELL, GAMMID...WE'VE BEEN TRYING TO FIND A WAY TO *TELL* YOU...

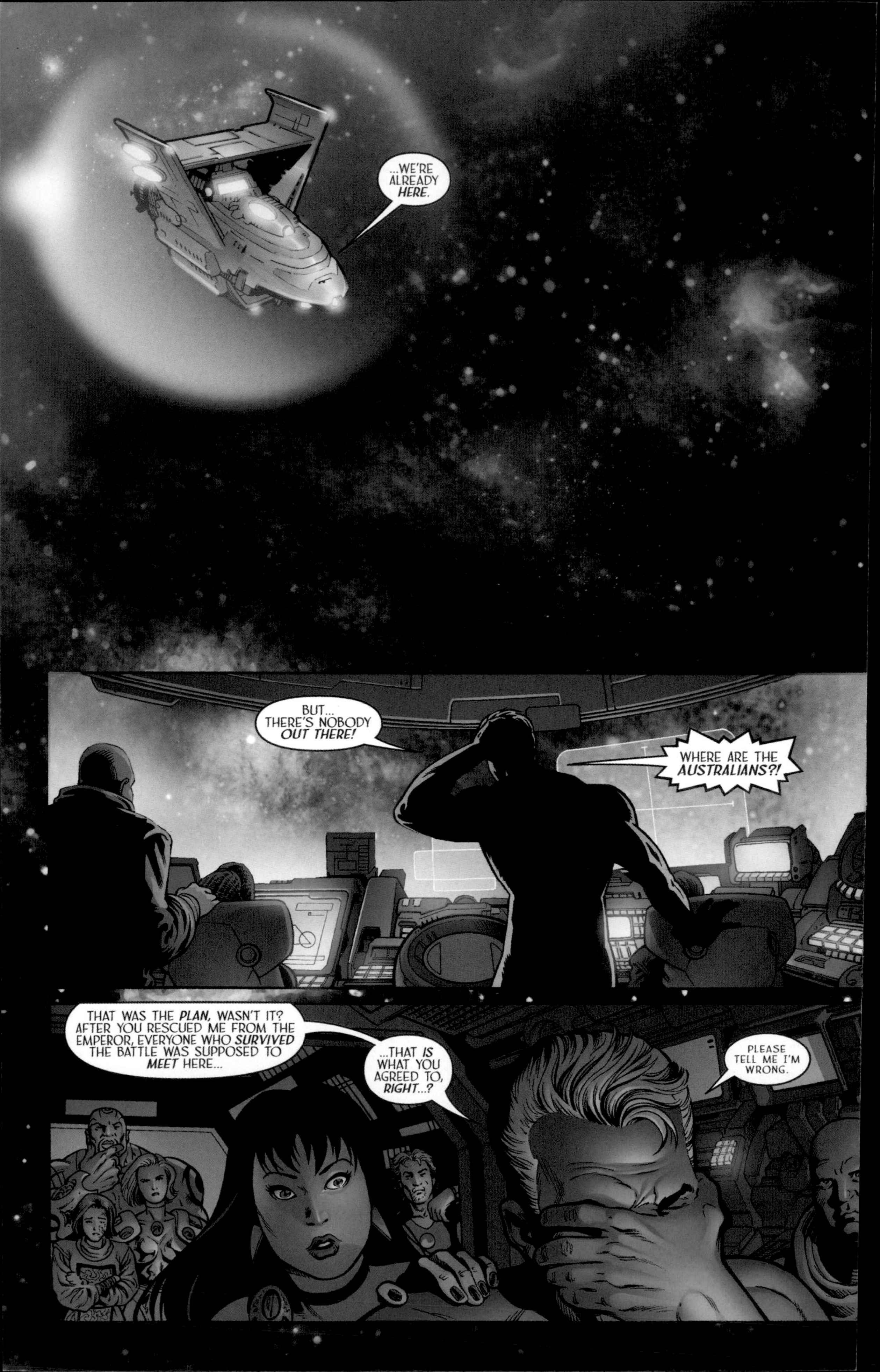
...WE'RE ALREADY HERE.
BUT... THERE'S NOBODY OUT THERE!
WHERE ARE THE AUSTRALIANS?!
THAT WAS THE PLAN, WASN'T IT? AFTER YOU RESCUED ME FROM THE EMPEROR, EVERYONE WHO SURVIVED THE BATTLE WAS SUPPOSED TO MEET HERE...
...THAT IS WHAT YOU AGREED TO, RIGHT...?
PLEASE TELL ME I'M WRONG.

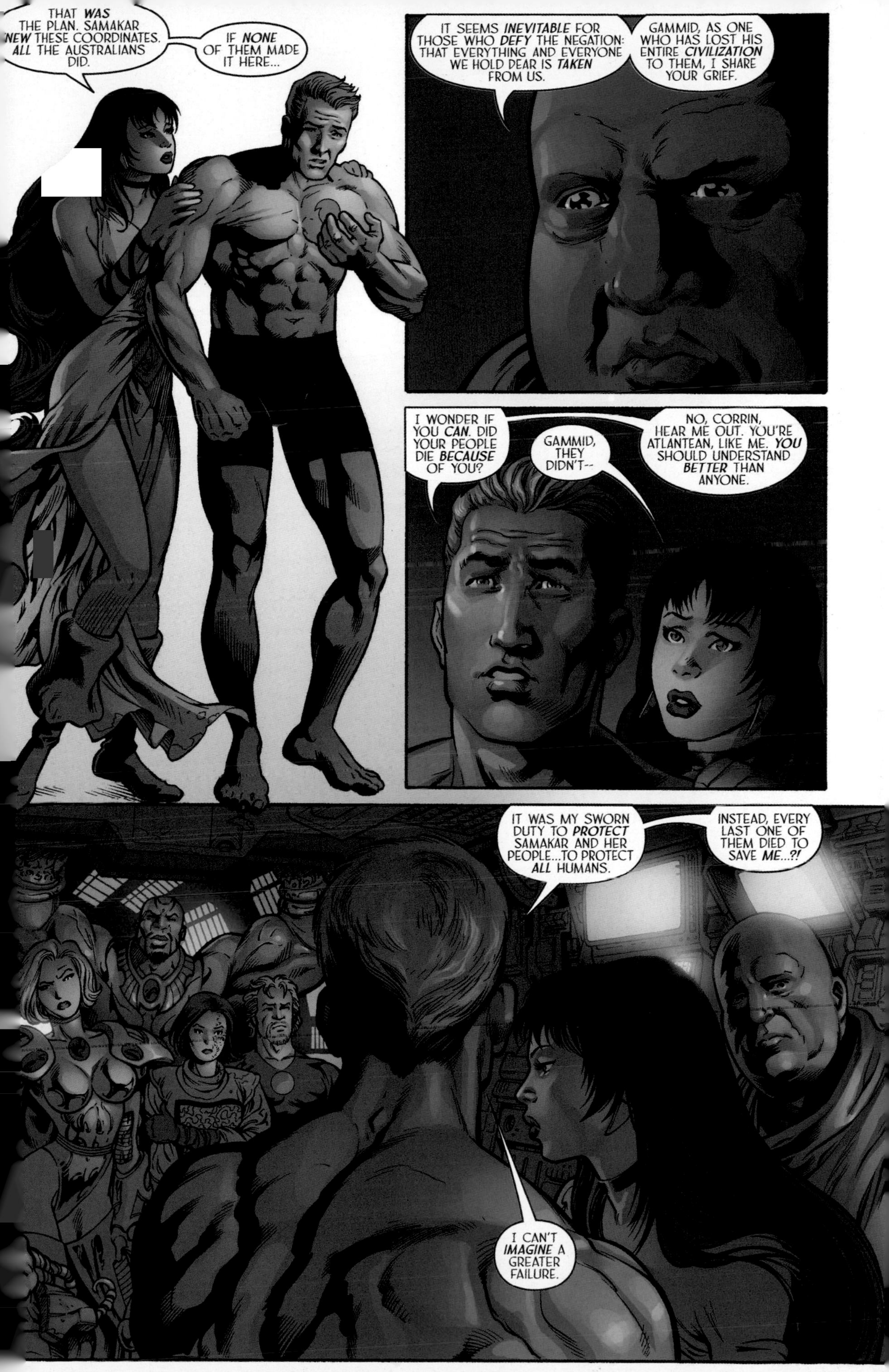

THAT WAS THE PLAN. SAMAKAR NEW THESE COORDINATES. ALL THE AUSTRALIANS DID.
IF NONE OF THEM MADE IT HERE...
IT SEEMS INEVITABLE FOR THOSE WHO DEFY THE NEGATION: THAT EVERYTHING AND EVERYONE WE HOLD DEAR IS TAKEN FROM US.
GAMMID, AS ONE WHO HAS LOST HIS ENTIRE CIVILIZATION TO THEM, I SHARE YOUR GRIEF.
I WONDER IF YOU CAN. DID YOUR PEOPLE DIE BECAUSE OF YOU?
GAMMID, THEY DIDN'T--
NO, CORRIN, HEAR ME OUT. YOU'RE ATLANTEAN, LIKE ME. YOU SHOULD UNDERSTAND BETTER THAN ANYONE.
IT WAS MY SWORN DUTY TO PROTECT SAMAKAR AND HER PEOPLE...TO PROTECT ALL HUMANS.
INSTEAD, EVERY LAST ONE OF THEM DIED TO SAVE ME...?!
I CAN'T IMAGINE A GREATER FAILURE.

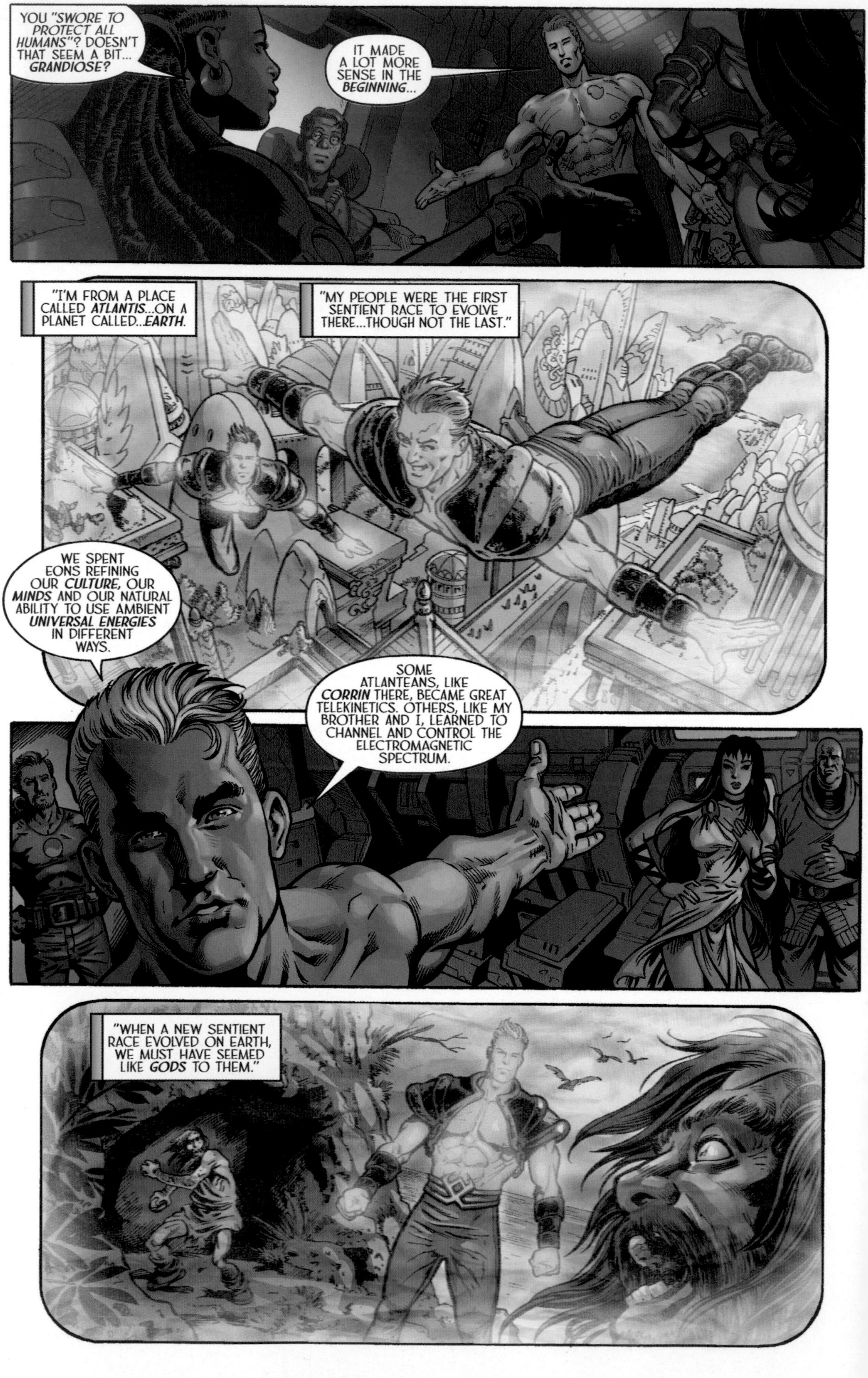
YOU "SWORE TO PROTECT ALL HUMANS"? DOESN'T THAT SEEM A BIT... GRANDIOSE?
IT MADE A LOT MORE SENSE IN THE BEGINNING...
"I'M FROM A PLACE CALLED ATLANTIS...ON A PLANET CALLED...EARTH.
"MY PEOPLE WERE THE FIRST SENTIENT RACE TO EVOLVE THERE...THOUGH NOT THE LAST."
WE SPENT EONS REFINING OUR CULTURE, OUR MINDS AND OUR NATURAL ABILITY TO USE AMBIENT UNIVERSAL ENERGIES IN DIFFERENT WAYS.
SOME ATLANTEANS, LIKE CORRIN THERE, BECAME GREAT TELEKINETICS. OTHERS, LIKE MY BROTHER AND I, LEARNED TO CHANNEL AND CONTROL THE ELECTROMAGNETIC SPECTRUM.
"WHEN A NEW SENTIENT RACE EVOLVED ON EARTH, WE MUST HAVE SEEMED LIKE GODS TO THEM."

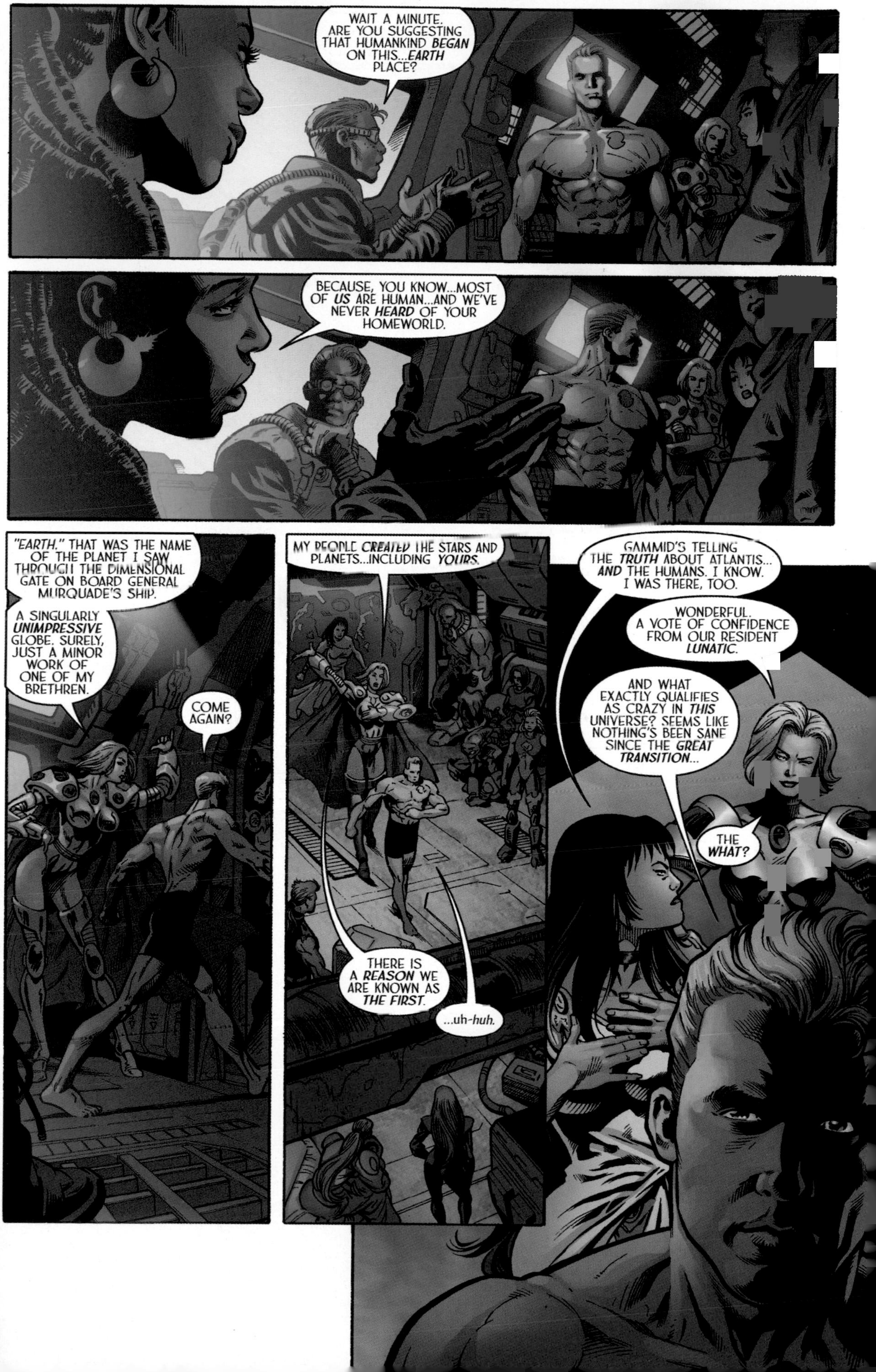

WAIT A MINUTE. ARE YOU SUGGESTING THAT HUMANKIND *BEGAN* ON THIS...*EARTH* PLACE?
BECAUSE, YOU KNOW...MOST OF *US* ARE HUMAN...AND WE'VE NEVER *HEARD* OF YOUR HOMEWORLD.
"EARTH." THAT WAS THE NAME OF THE PLANET I SAW THROUGH THE DIMENSIONAL GATE ON BOARD GENERAL MURQUADE'S SHIP.
A SINGULARLY *UNIMPRESSIVE* GLOBE. SURELY, JUST A MINOR WORK OF ONE OF MY BRETHREN.
COME AGAIN?
MY PEOPLE *CREATED* THE STARS AND PLANETS...INCLUDING *YOURS*.
THERE IS A *REASON* WE ARE KNOWN AS *THE FIRST*.
...uh-*huh*.
GAMMID'S TELLING THE *TRUTH* ABOUT ATLANTIS... *AND* THE HUMANS. I KNOW. I WAS THERE, TOO.
WONDERFUL. A VOTE OF CONFIDENCE FROM OUR RESIDENT *LUNATIC*.
AND WHAT EXACTLY QUALIFIES AS CRAZY IN *THIS* UNIVERSE? SEEMS LIKE NOTHING'S BEEN SANE SINCE THE *GREAT TRANSITION*...
THE *WHAT?*

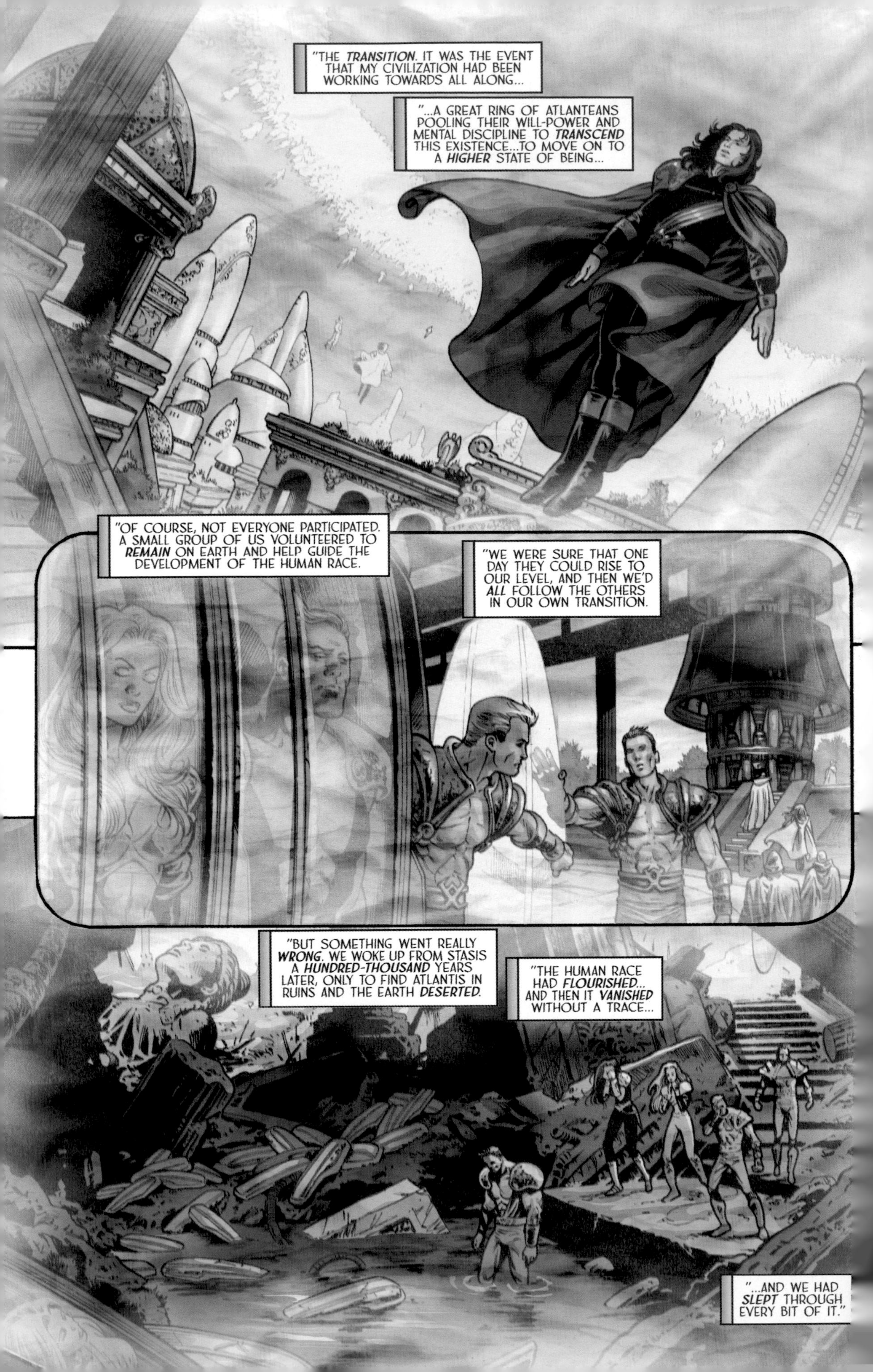
"THE TRANSITION. IT WAS THE EVENT THAT MY CIVILIZATION HAD BEEN WORKING TOWARDS ALL ALONG...
"...A GREAT RING OF ATLANTEANS POOLING THEIR WILL-POWER AND MENTAL DISCIPLINE TO TRANSCEND THIS EXISTENCE...TO MOVE ON TO A HIGHER STATE OF BEING...
"OF COURSE, NOT EVERYONE PARTICIPATED. A SMALL GROUP OF US VOLUNTEERED TO REMAIN ON EARTH AND HELP GUIDE THE DEVELOPMENT OF THE HUMAN RACE.
"WE WERE SURE THAT ONE DAY THEY COULD RISE TO OUR LEVEL, AND THEN WE'D ALL FOLLOW THE OTHERS IN OUR OWN TRANSITION.
"BUT SOMETHING WENT REALLY WRONG. WE WOKE UP FROM STASIS A HUNDRED-THOUSAND YEARS LATER, ONLY TO FIND ATLANTIS IN RUINS AND THE EARTH DESERTED.
"THE HUMAN RACE HAD FLOURISHED... AND THEN IT VANISHED WITHOUT A TRACE...
"...AND WE HAD SLEPT THROUGH EVERY BIT OF IT."

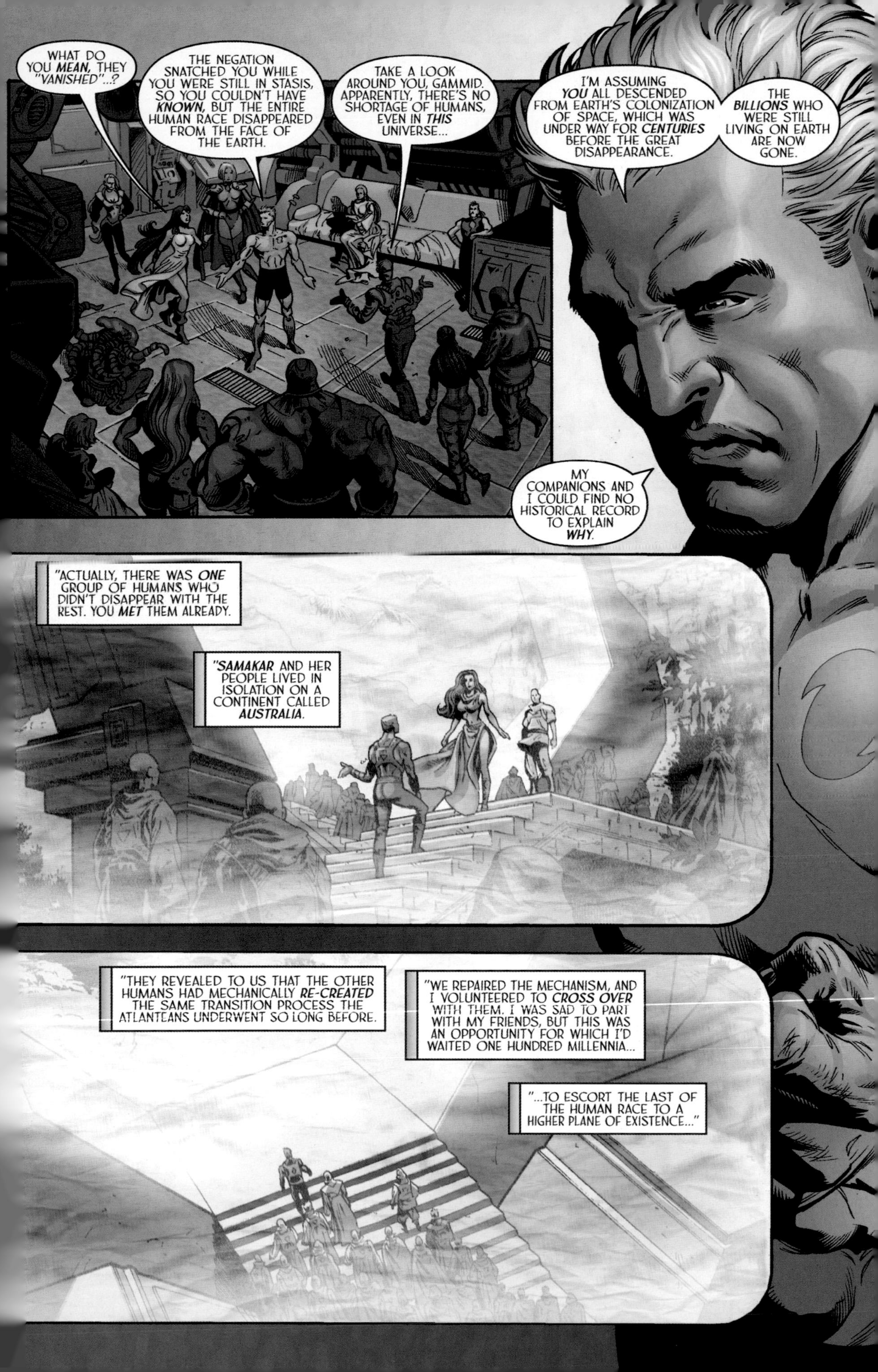
WHAT DO YOU MEAN, THEY "VANISHED"...?
THE NEGATION SNATCHED YOU WHILE YOU WERE STILL IN STASIS, SO YOU COULDN'T HAVE KNOWN, BUT THE ENTIRE HUMAN RACE DISAPPEARED FROM THE FACE OF THE EARTH.
TAKE A LOOK AROUND YOU, GAMMID. APPARENTLY, THERE'S NO SHORTAGE OF HUMANS, EVEN IN THIS UNIVERSE...
I'M ASSUMING YOU ALL DESCENDED FROM EARTH'S COLONIZATION OF SPACE, WHICH WAS UNDER WAY FOR CENTURIES BEFORE THE GREAT DISAPPEARANCE.
THE BILLIONS WHO WERE STILL LIVING ON EARTH ARE NOW GONE.
MY COMPANIONS AND I COULD FIND NO HISTORICAL RECORD TO EXPLAIN WHY.
"ACTUALLY, THERE WAS ONE GROUP OF HUMANS WHO DIDN'T DISAPPEAR WITH THE REST. YOU MET THEM ALREADY.
"SAMAKAR AND HER PEOPLE LIVED IN ISOLATION ON A CONTINENT CALLED AUSTRALIA.
"THEY REVEALED TO US THAT THE OTHER HUMANS HAD MECHANICALLY RE-CREATED THE SAME TRANSITION PROCESS THE ATLANTEANS UNDERWENT SO LONG BEFORE.
"WE REPAIRED THE MECHANISM, AND I VOLUNTEERED TO CROSS OVER WITH THEM. I WAS SAD TO PART WITH MY FRIENDS, BUT THIS WAS AN OPPORTUNITY FOR WHICH I'D WAITED ONE HUNDRED MILLENNIA...
"...TO ESCORT THE LAST OF THE HUMAN RACE TO A HIGHER PLANE OF EXISTENCE..."

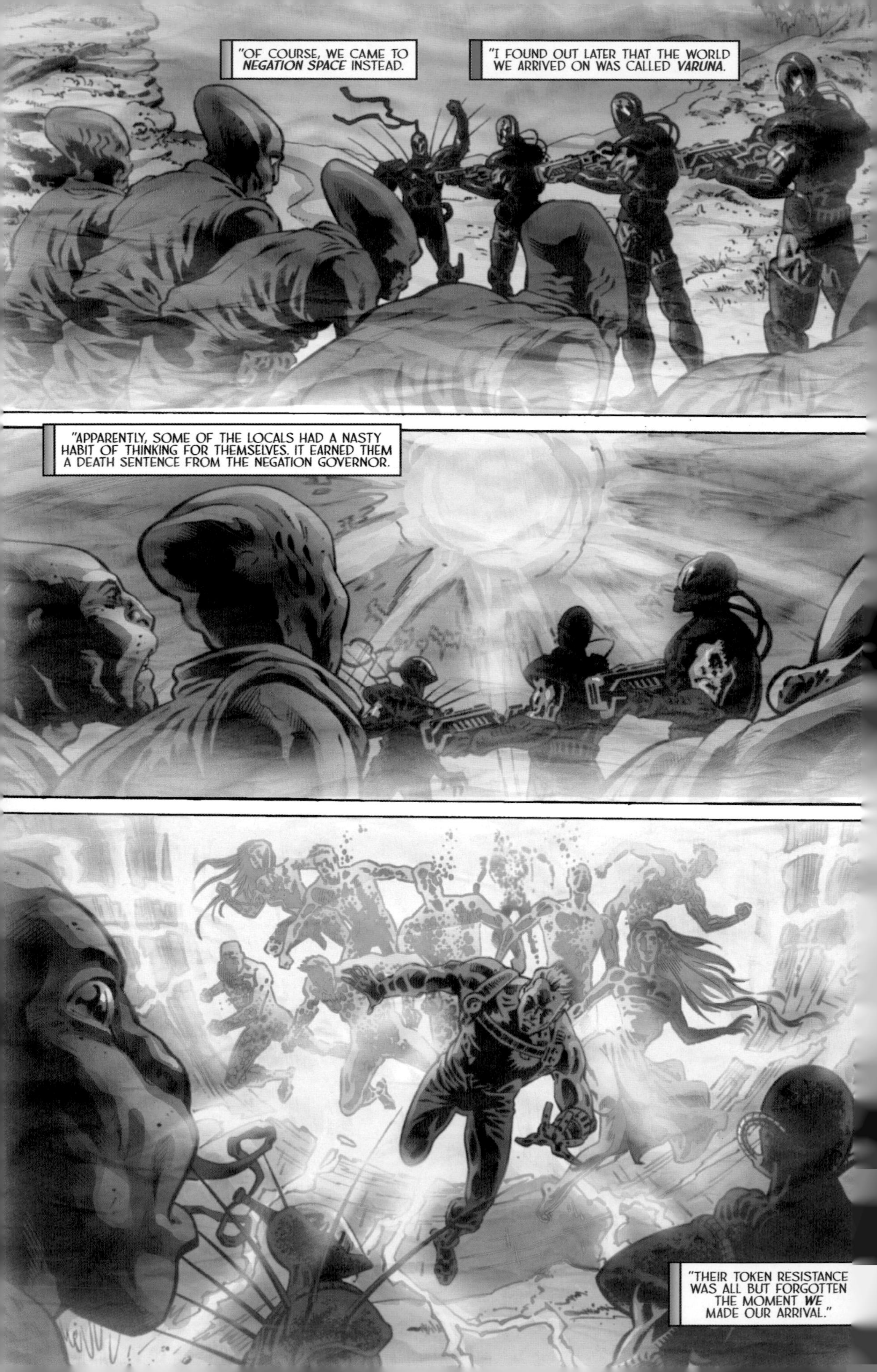
"OF COURSE, WE CAME TO NEGATION SPACE INSTEAD.
"I FOUND OUT LATER THAT THE WORLD WE ARRIVED ON WAS CALLED VARUNA.
"APPARENTLY, SOME OF THE LOCALS HAD A NASTY HABIT OF THINKING FOR THEMSELVES. IT EARNED THEM A DEATH SENTENCE FROM THE NEGATION GOVERNOR.
"THEIR TOKEN RESISTANCE WAS ALL BUT FORGOTTEN THE MOMENT WE MADE OUR ARRIVAL."

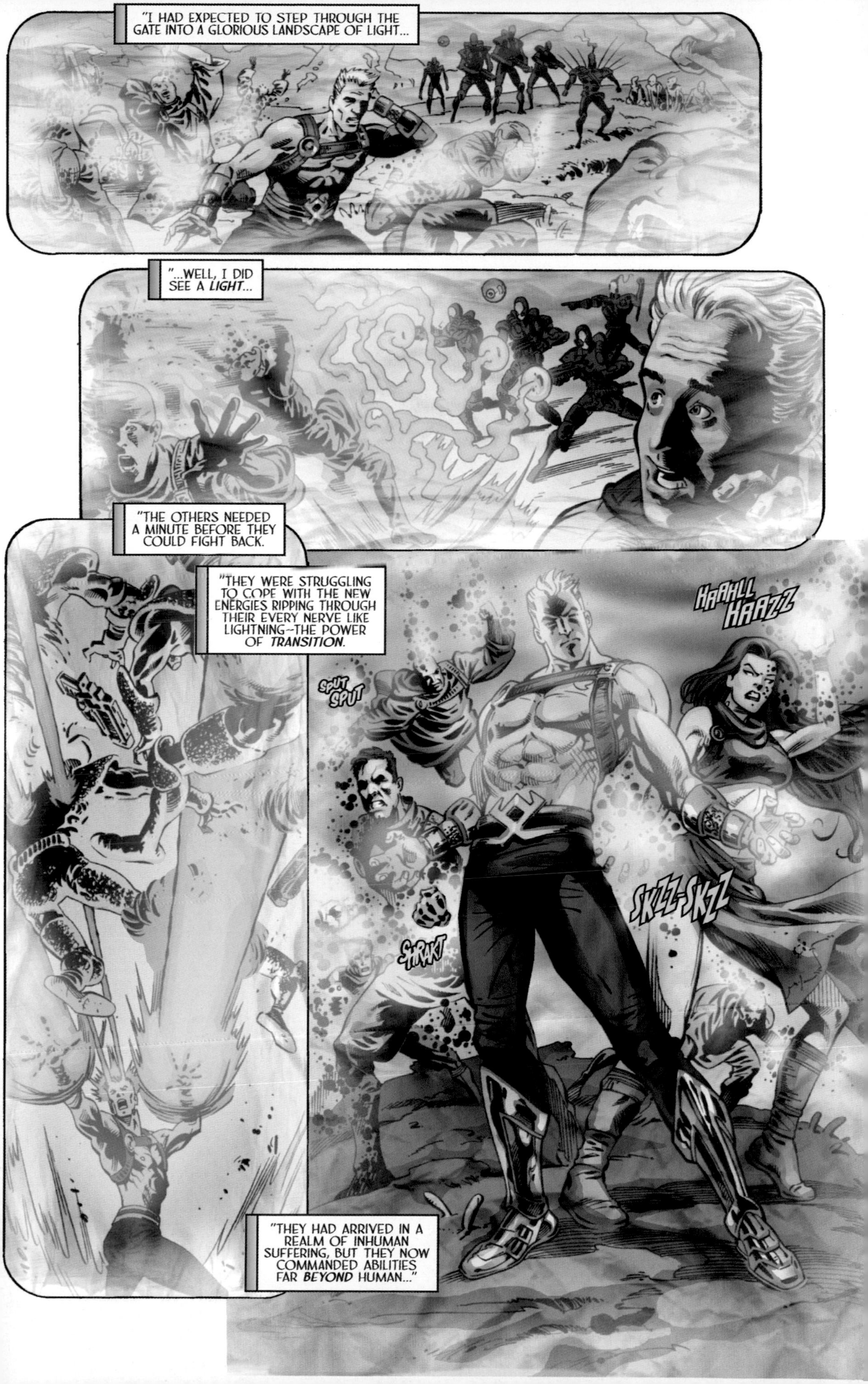
"I HAD EXPECTED TO STEP THROUGH THE GATE INTO A GLORIOUS LANDSCAPE OF LIGHT...
"...WELL, I DID SEE A *LIGHT*...
"THE OTHERS NEEDED A MINUTE BEFORE THEY COULD FIGHT BACK.
"THEY WERE STRUGGLING TO COPE WITH THE NEW ENERGIES RIPPING THROUGH THEIR EVERY NERVE LIKE LIGHTNING--THE POWER OF *TRANSITION*.
HAAHLL HAAZZ
SPUT SPUT
SKZZ-SKZZ
SHRAKT
"THEY HAD ARRIVED IN A REALM OF INHUMAN SUFFERING, BUT THEY NOW COMMANDED ABILITIES FAR *BEYOND* HUMAN..."

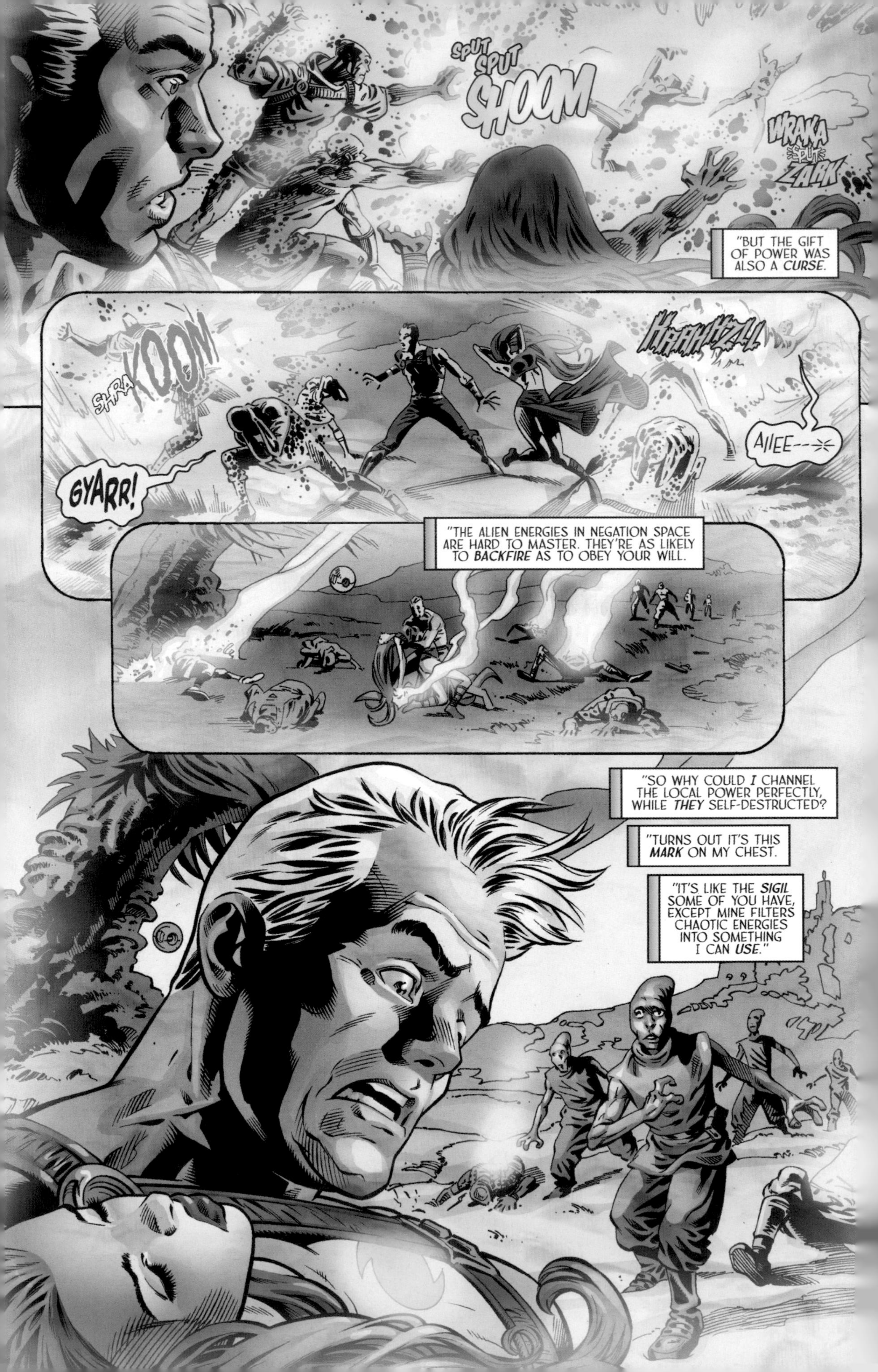
SPUT SPUT SHOOM
WRAKA SPUT ZARK
"BUT THE GIFT OF POWER WAS ALSO A CURSE.
SHRAKOOM
HRAHHZZZL
AIIEE--
GYARR!
"THE ALIEN ENERGIES IN NEGATION SPACE ARE HARD TO MASTER. THEY'RE AS LIKELY TO BACKFIRE AS TO OBEY YOUR WILL.
"SO WHY COULD I CHANNEL THE LOCAL POWER PERFECTLY, WHILE THEY SELF-DESTRUCTED?
"TURNS OUT IT'S THIS MARK ON MY CHEST.
"IT'S LIKE THE SIGIL SOME OF YOU HAVE, EXCEPT MINE FILTERS CHAOTIC ENERGIES INTO SOMETHING I CAN USE."

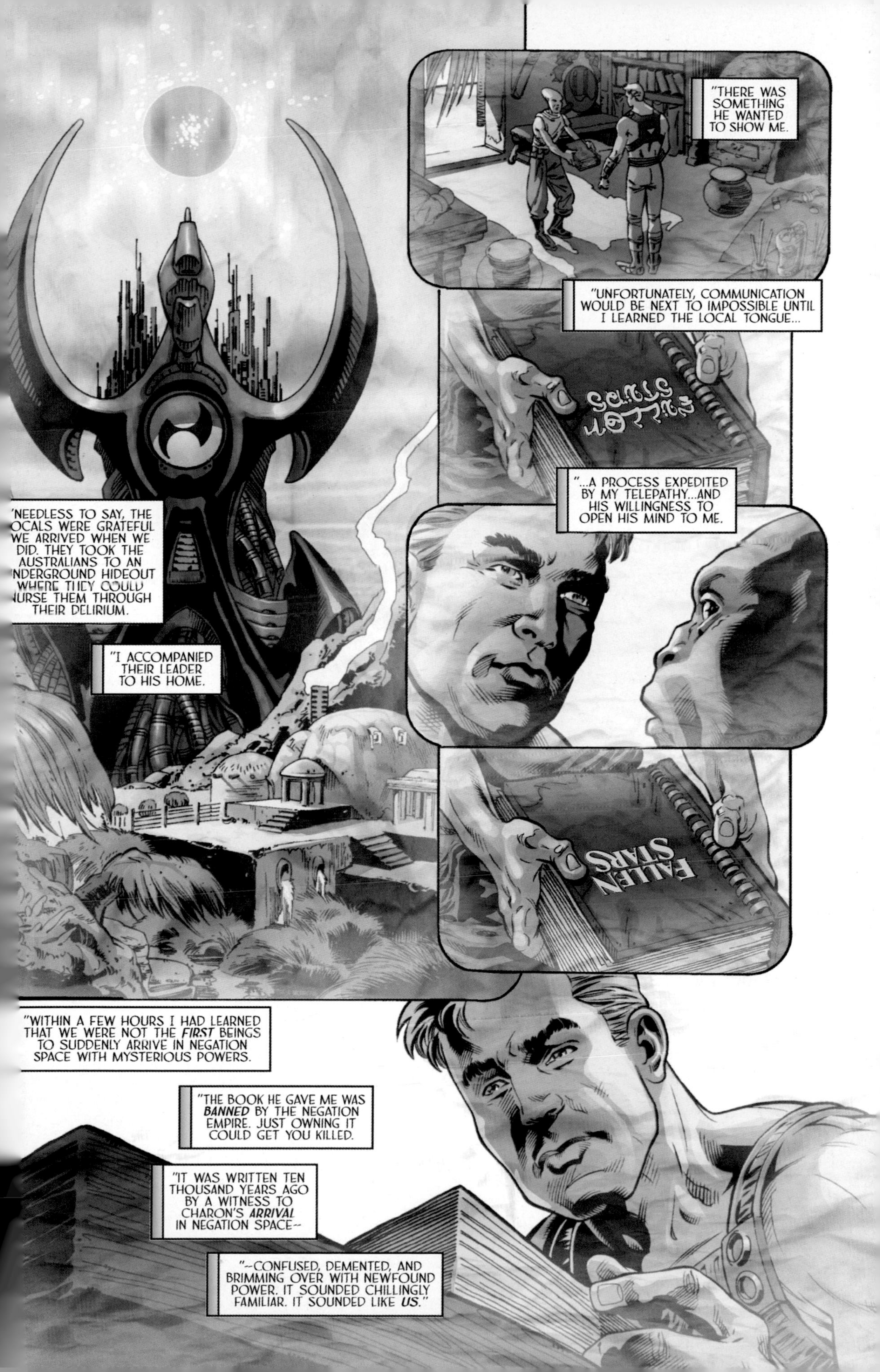

"THERE WAS SOMETHING HE WANTED TO SHOW ME.
"UNFORTUNATELY, COMMUNICATION WOULD BE NEXT TO IMPOSSIBLE UNTIL I LEARNED THE LOCAL TONGUE...
"...A PROCESS EXPEDITED BY MY TELEPATHY...AND HIS WILLINGNESS TO OPEN HIS MIND TO ME.
FALLEN STARS
'NEEDLESS TO SAY, THE OCALS WERE GRATEFUL WE ARRIVED WHEN WE DID. THEY TOOK THE AUSTRALIANS TO AN NDERGROUND HIDEOUT WHERE THEY COULD URSE THEM THROUGH THEIR DELIRIUM.
"I ACCOMPANIED THEIR LEADER TO HIS HOME.
"WITHIN A FEW HOURS I HAD LEARNED THAT WE WERE NOT THE FIRST BEINGS TO SUDDENLY ARRIVE IN NEGATION SPACE WITH MYSTERIOUS POWERS.
"THE BOOK HE GAVE ME WAS BANNED BY THE NEGATION EMPIRE. JUST OWNING IT COULD GET YOU KILLED.
"IT WAS WRITTEN TEN THOUSAND YEARS AGO BY A WITNESS TO CHARON'S ARRIVAL IN NEGATION SPACE--
"--CONFUSED, DEMENTED, AND BRIMMING OVER WITH NEWFOUND POWER. IT SOUNDED CHILLINGLY FAMILIAR. IT SOUNDED LIKE US."

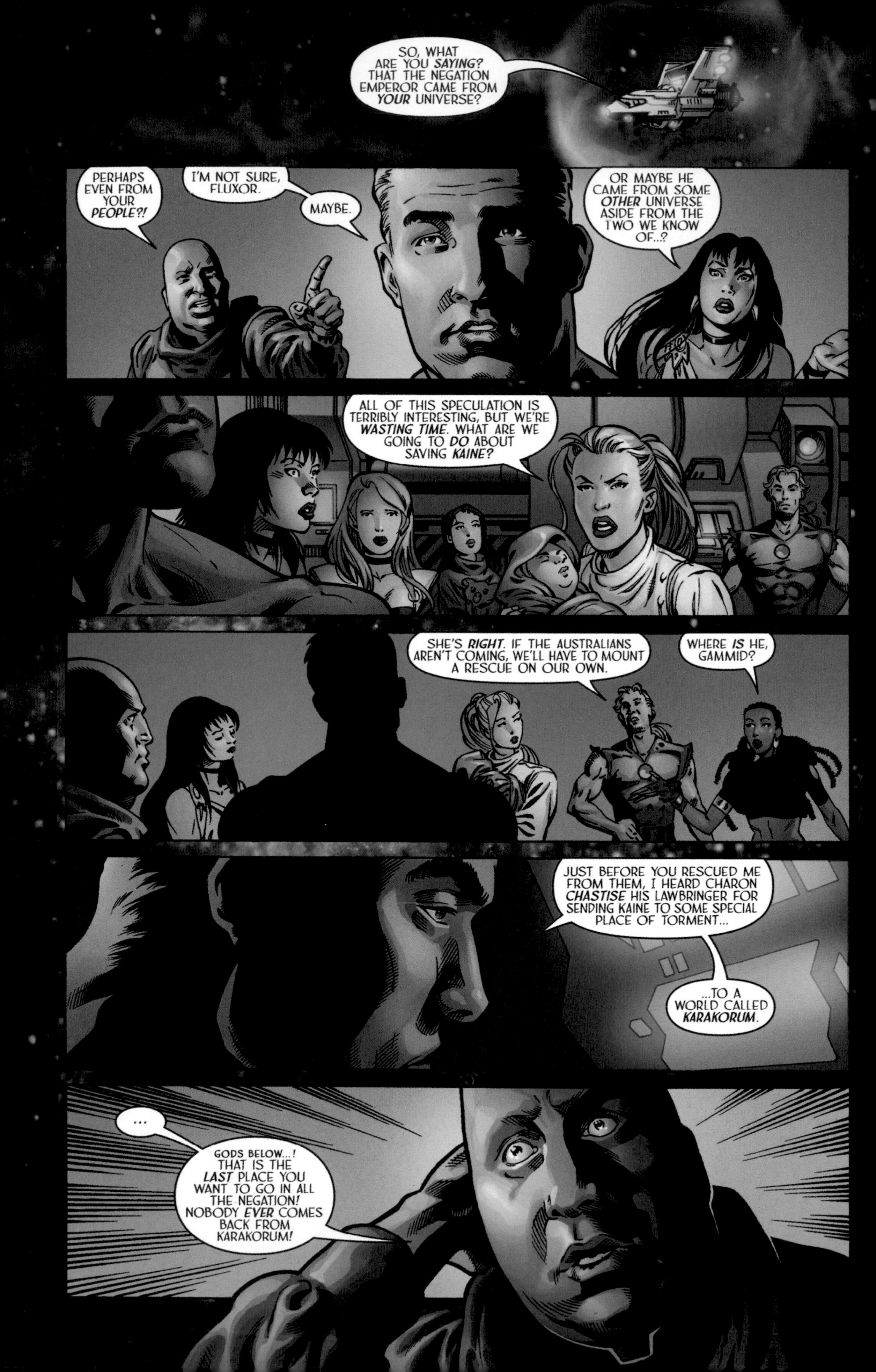
SO, WHAT ARE YOU *SAYING?* THAT THE NEGATION EMPEROR CAME FROM *YOUR* UNIVERSE?
I'M NOT SURE, FLUXOR.
PERHAPS EVEN FROM YOUR *PEOPLE?!*
MAYBE.
OR MAYBE HE CAME FROM SOME *OTHER* UNIVERSE ASIDE FROM THE TWO WE KNOW OF...?
ALL OF THIS SPECULATION IS TERRIBLY INTERESTING, BUT WE'RE *WASTING TIME*. WHAT ARE WE GOING TO *DO* ABOUT SAVING *KAINE?*
SHE'S *RIGHT*. IF THE AUSTRALIANS AREN'T COMING, WE'LL HAVE TO MOUNT A RESCUE ON OUR OWN.
WHERE *IS* HE, GAMMID?
JUST BEFORE YOU RESCUED ME FROM THEM, I HEARD CHARON *CHASTISE* HIS LAWBRINGER FOR SENDING KAINE TO SOME SPECIAL PLACE OF TORMENT...
...TO A WORLD CALLED *KARAKORUM*.
...
GODS BELOW...! THAT IS THE *LAST* PLACE YOU WANT TO GO IN ALL THE NEGATION! NOBODY *EVER* COMES BACK FROM KARAKORUM!

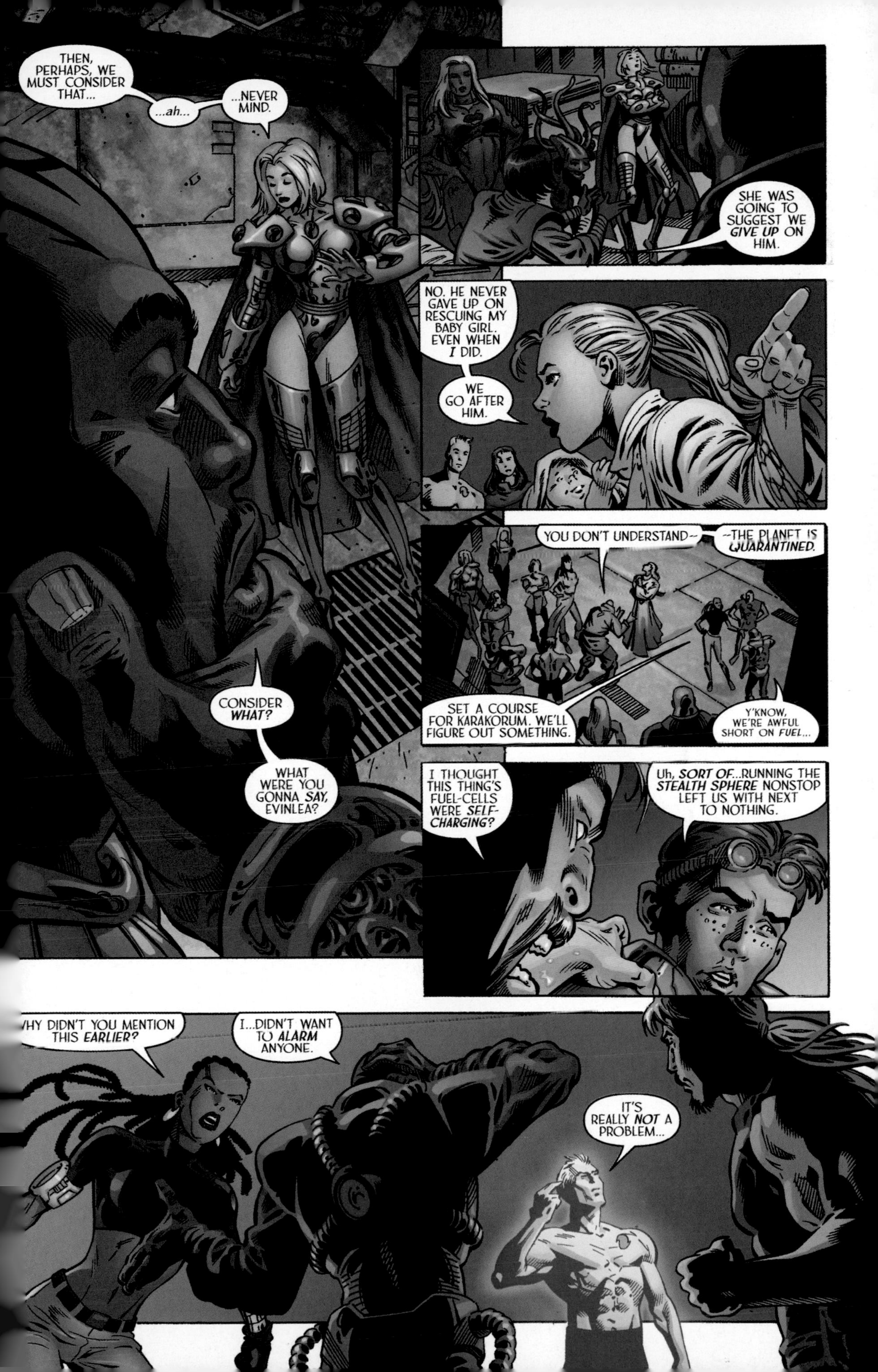
THEN, PERHAPS, WE MUST CONSIDER THAT...
...ah...
...NEVER MIND.
SHE WAS GOING TO SUGGEST WE GIVE UP ON HIM.
CONSIDER WHAT?
WHAT WERE YOU GONNA SAY, EVINLEA?
NO. HE NEVER GAVE UP ON RESCUING MY BABY GIRL. EVEN WHEN I DID.
WE GO AFTER HIM.
YOU DON'T UNDERSTAND--
--THE PLANET IS QUARANTINED.
SET A COURSE FOR KARAKORUM. WE'LL FIGURE OUT SOMETHING.
Y'KNOW, WE'RE AWFUL SHORT ON FUEL...
I THOUGHT THIS THING'S FUEL-CELLS WERE SELF-CHARGING?
Uh, SORT OF...RUNNING THE STEALTH SPHERE NONSTOP LEFT US WITH NEXT TO NOTHING.
WHY DIDN'T YOU MENTION THIS EARLIER?
I...DIDN'T WANT TO ALARM ANYONE.
IT'S REALLY NOT A PROBLEM...

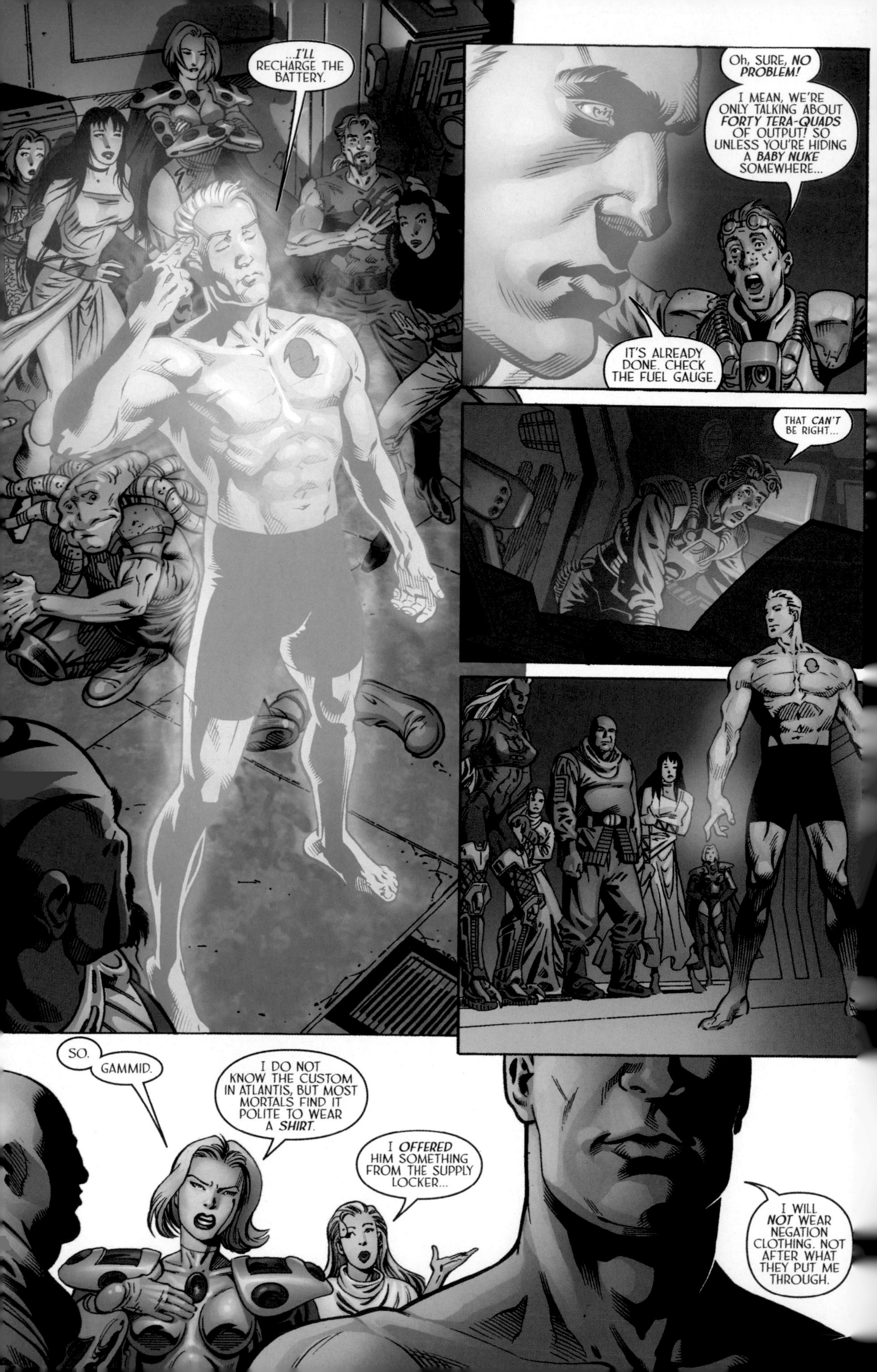
...I'LL RECHARGE THE BATTERY.
Oh, SURE, NO PROBLEM!
I MEAN, WE'RE ONLY TALKING ABOUT FORTY TERA-QUADS OF OUTPUT! SO UNLESS YOU'RE HIDING A BABY NUKE SOMEWHERE...
IT'S ALREADY DONE. CHECK THE FUEL GAUGE.
THAT CAN'T BE RIGHT...
SO.
GAMMID.
I DO NOT KNOW THE CUSTOM IN ATLANTIS, BUT MOST MORTALS FIND IT POLITE TO WEAR A SHIRT.
I OFFERED HIM SOMETHING FROM THE SUPPLY LOCKER...
I WILL NOT WEAR NEGATION CLOTHING. NOT AFTER WHAT THEY PUT ME THROUGH.

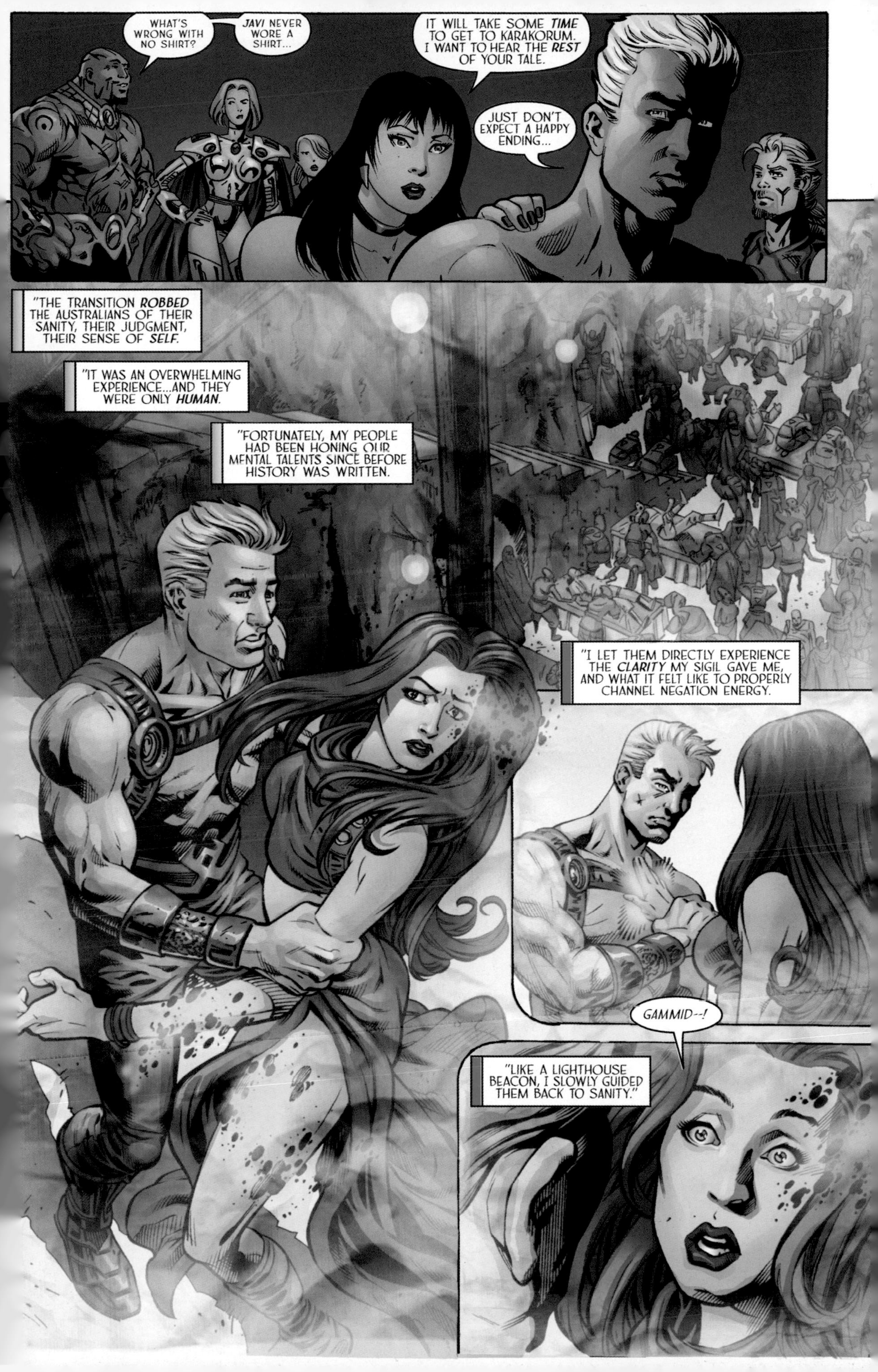
WHAT'S WRONG WITH NO SHIRT?
JAVI NEVER WORE A SHIRT...
IT WILL TAKE SOME TIME TO GET TO KARAKORUM. I WANT TO HEAR THE REST OF YOUR TALE.
JUST DON'T EXPECT A HAPPY ENDING...
"THE TRANSITION ROBBED THE AUSTRALIANS OF THEIR SANITY, THEIR JUDGMENT, THEIR SENSE OF SELF.
"IT WAS AN OVERWHELMING EXPERIENCE...AND THEY WERE ONLY HUMAN.
"FORTUNATELY, MY PEOPLE HAD BEEN HONING OUR MENTAL TALENTS SINCE BEFORE HISTORY WAS WRITTEN.
"I LET THEM DIRECTLY EXPERIENCE THE CLARITY MY SIGIL GAVE ME, AND WHAT IT FELT LIKE TO PROPERLY CHANNEL NEGATION ENERGY.
GAMMID--!
"LIKE A LIGHTHOUSE BEACON, I SLOWLY GUIDED THEM BACK TO SANITY."

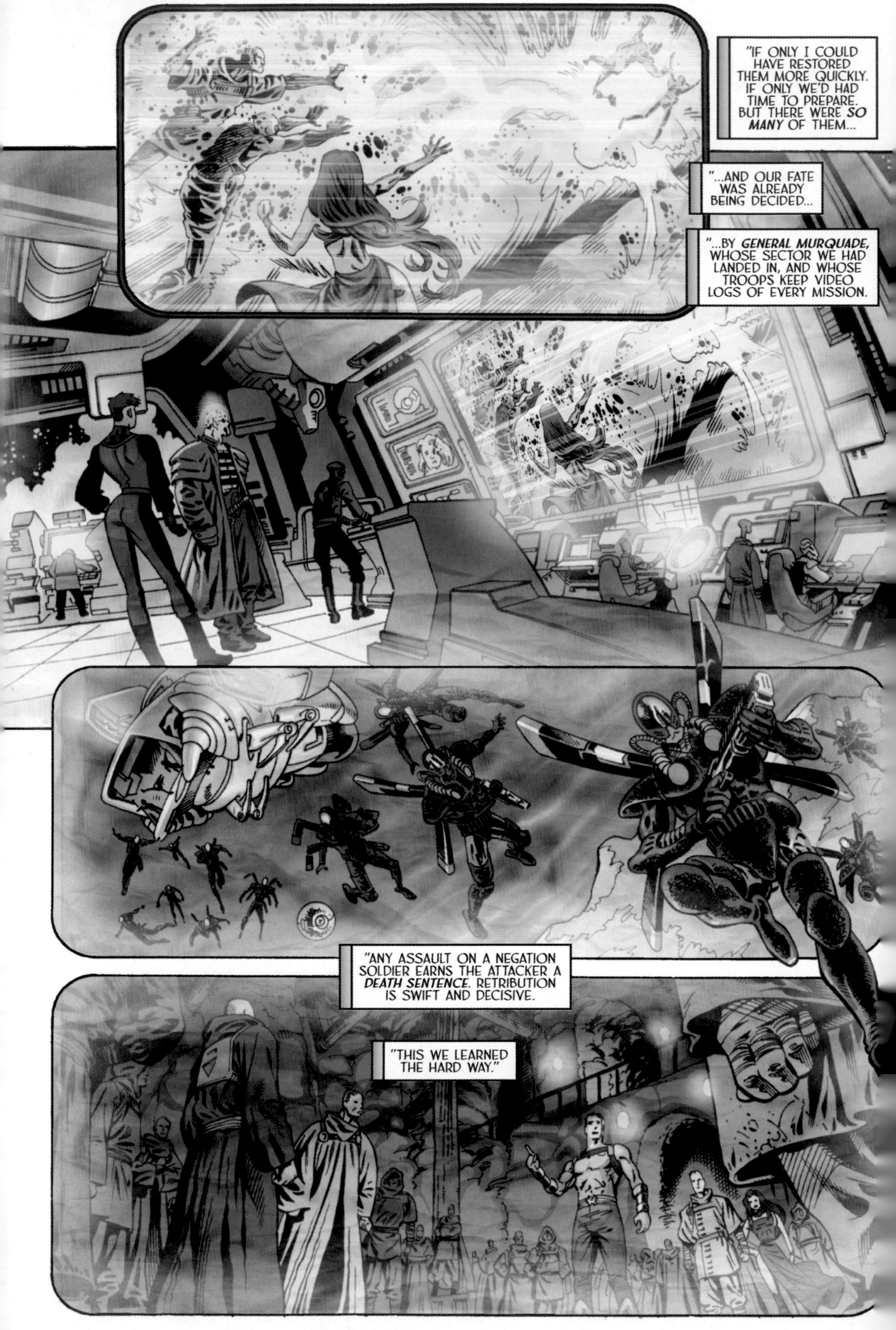
"IF ONLY I COULD HAVE RESTORED THEM MORE QUICKLY. IF ONLY WE'D HAD TIME TO PREPARE. BUT THERE WERE *SO MANY* OF THEM...
"...AND OUR FATE WAS ALREADY BEING DECIDED...
"...BY *GENERAL MURQUADE,* WHOSE SECTOR WE HAD LANDED IN, AND WHOSE TROOPS KEEP VIDEO LOGS OF EVERY MISSION.
"ANY ASSAULT ON A NEGATION SOLDIER EARNS THE ATTACKER A *DEATH SENTENCE*. RETRIBUTION IS SWIFT AND DECISIVE.
"THIS WE LEARNED THE HARD WAY."

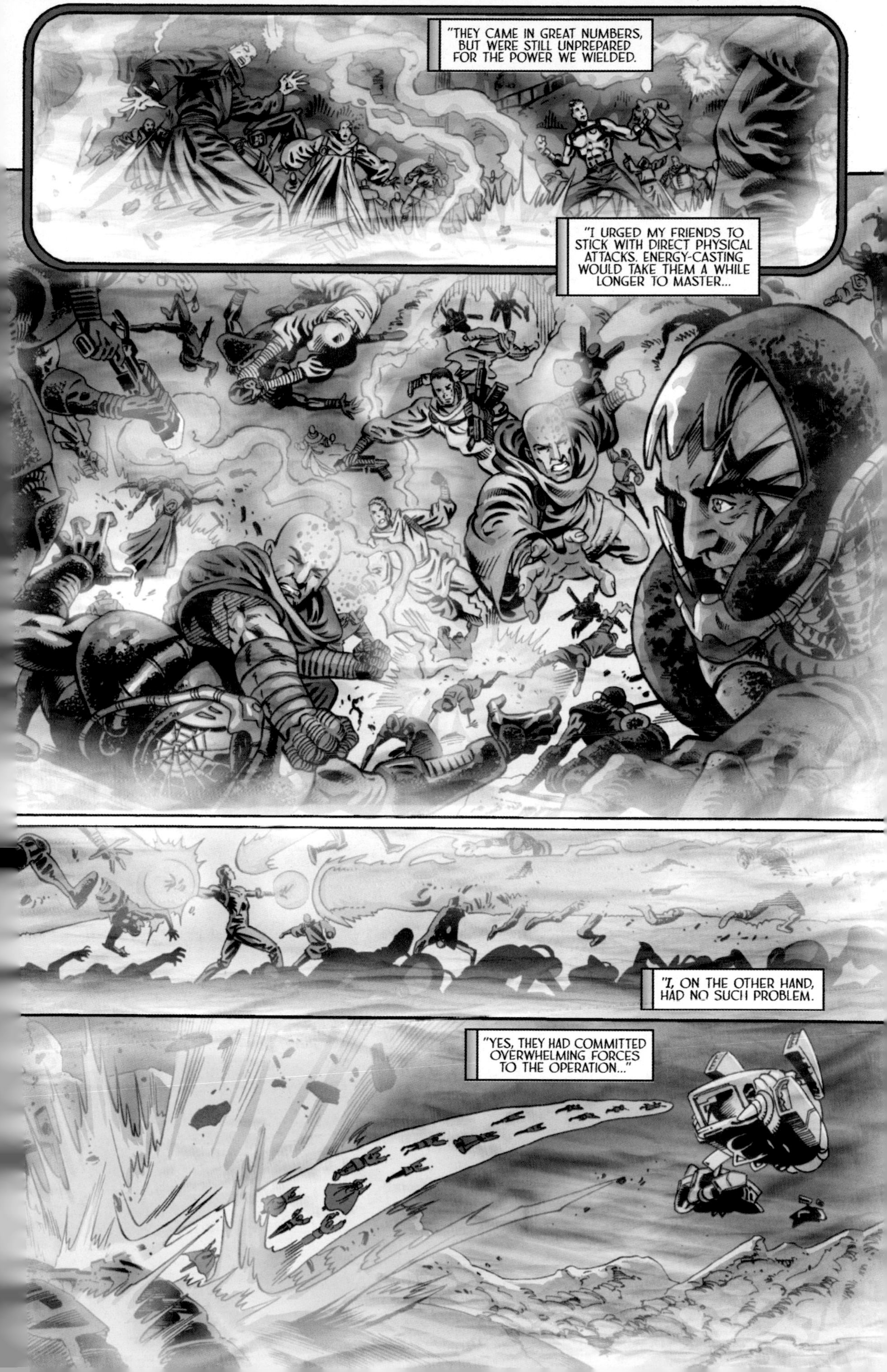
"THEY CAME IN GREAT NUMBERS, BUT WERE STILL UNPREPARED FOR THE POWER WE WIELDED.
"I URGED MY FRIENDS TO STICK WITH DIRECT PHYSICAL ATTACKS. ENERGY-CASTING WOULD TAKE THEM A WHILE LONGER TO MASTER...
"I, ON THE OTHER HAND, HAD NO SUCH PROBLEM.
"YES, THEY HAD COMMITTED OVERWHELMING FORCES TO THE OPERATION..."

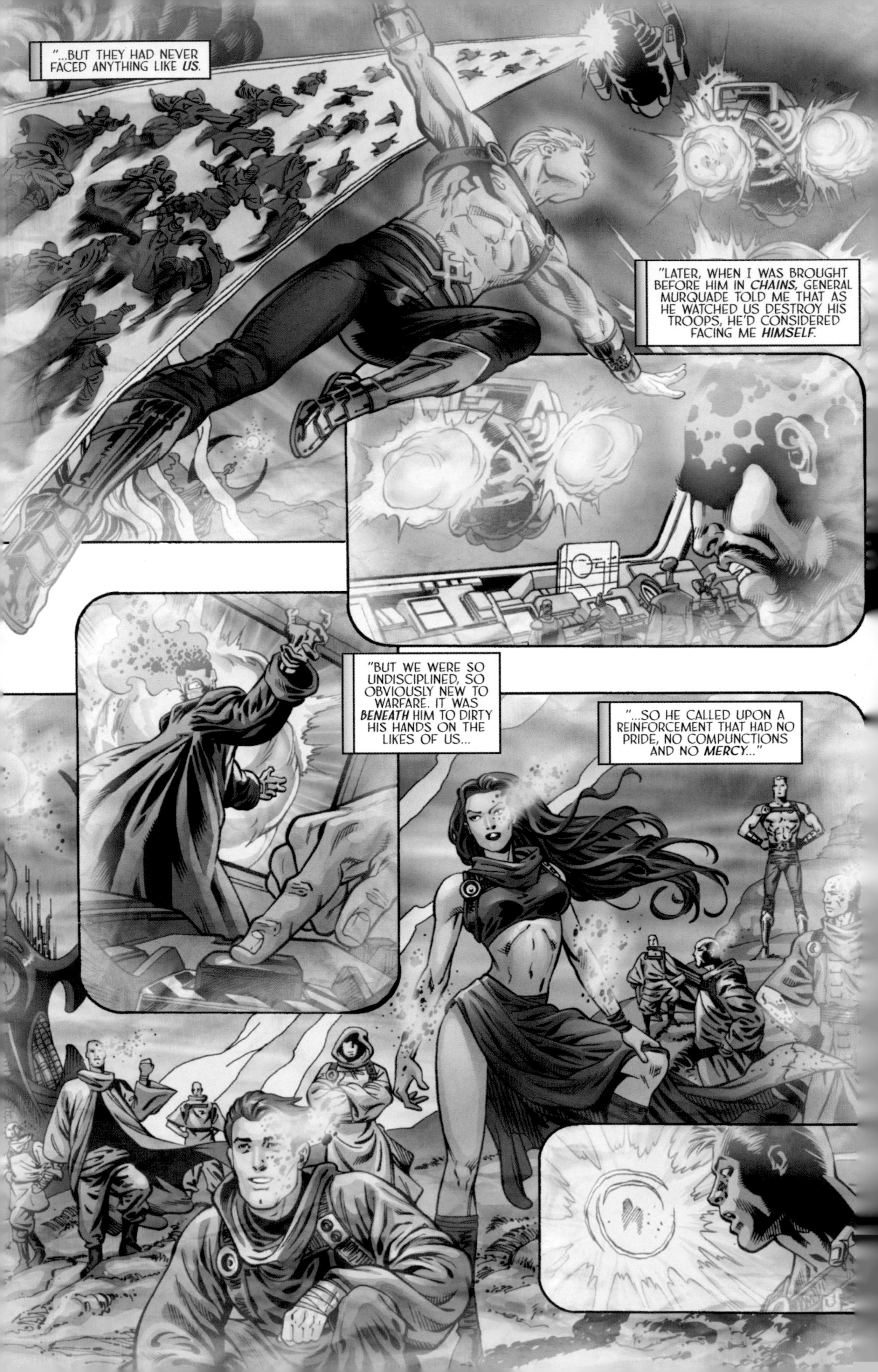
"...BUT THEY HAD NEVER FACED ANYTHING LIKE US.
"LATER, WHEN I WAS BROUGHT BEFORE HIM IN CHAINS, GENERAL MURQUADE TOLD ME THAT AS HE WATCHED US DESTROY HIS TROOPS, HE'D CONSIDERED FACING ME HIMSELF.
"BUT WE WERE SO UNDISCIPLINED, SO OBVIOUSLY NEW TO WARFARE. IT WAS BENEATH HIM TO DIRTY HIS HANDS ON THE LIKES OF US...
"...SO HE CALLED UPON A REINFORCEMENT THAT HAD NO PRIDE, NO COMPUNCTIONS AND NO MERCY..."

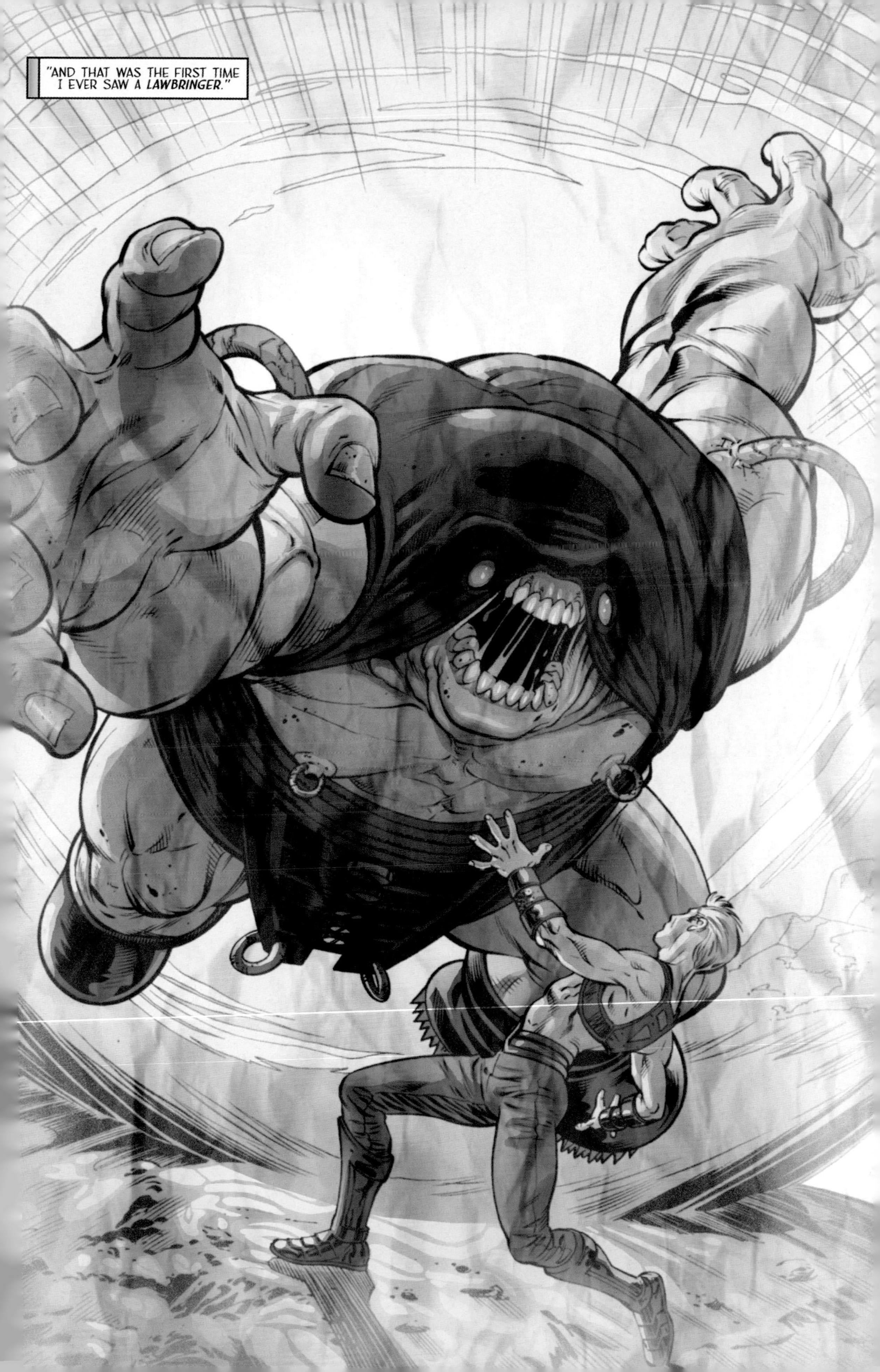
"AND THAT WAS THE FIRST TIME I EVER SAW A LAWBRINGER."

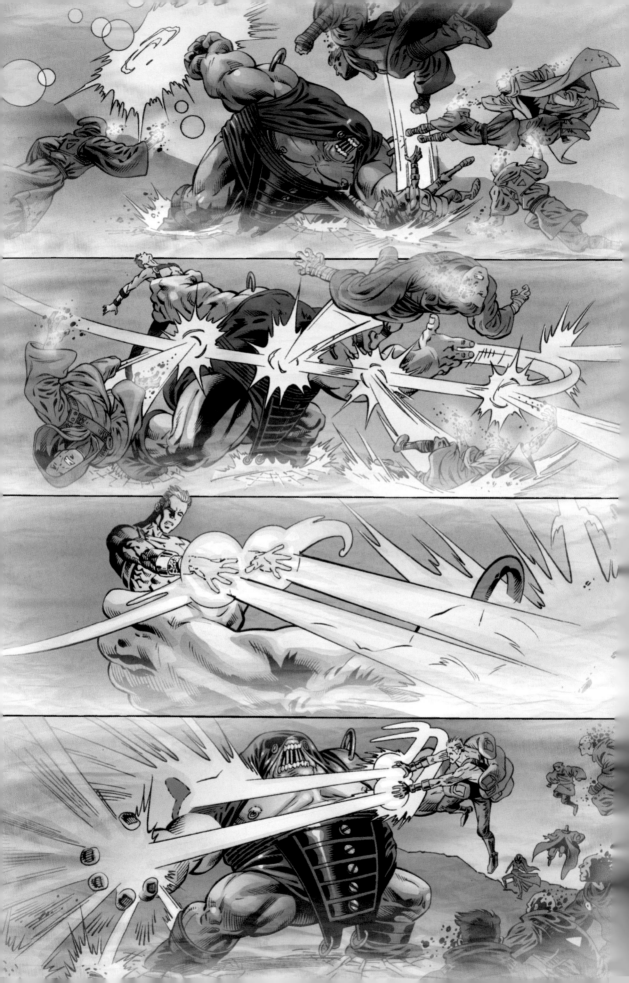

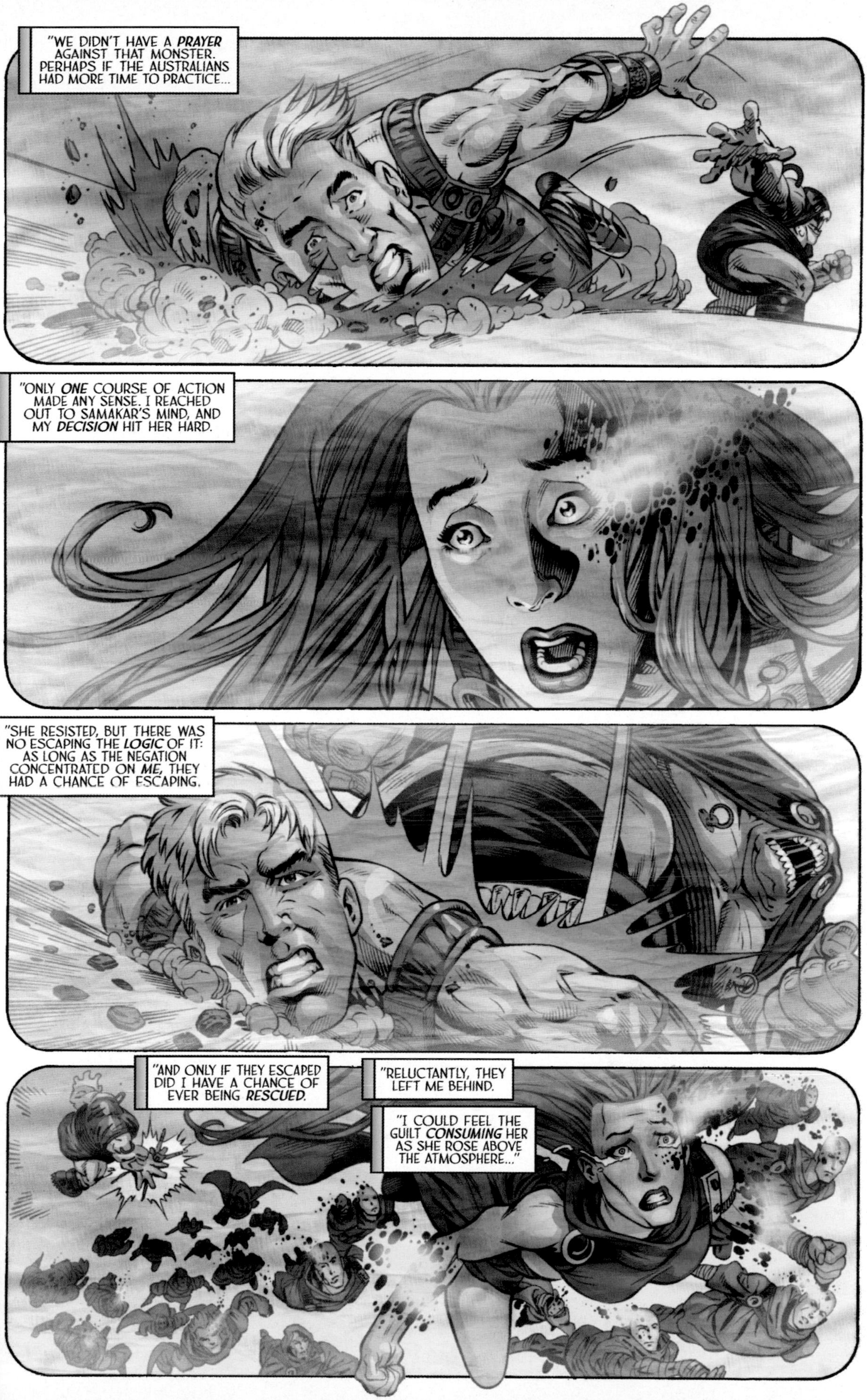
"WE DIDN'T HAVE A PRAYER AGAINST THAT MONSTER. PERHAPS IF THE AUSTRALIANS HAD MORE TIME TO PRACTICE...
"ONLY ONE COURSE OF ACTION MADE ANY SENSE. I REACHED OUT TO SAMAKAR'S MIND, AND MY DECISION HIT HER HARD.
"SHE RESISTED, BUT THERE WAS NO ESCAPING THE LOGIC OF IT: AS LONG AS THE NEGATION CONCENTRATED ON ME, THEY HAD A CHANCE OF ESCAPING.
"AND ONLY IF THEY ESCAPED DID I HAVE A CHANCE OF EVER BEING RESCUED.
"RELUCTANTLY, THEY LEFT ME BEHIND.
"I COULD FEEL THE GUILT CONSUMING HER AS SHE ROSE ABOVE THE ATMOSPHERE..."

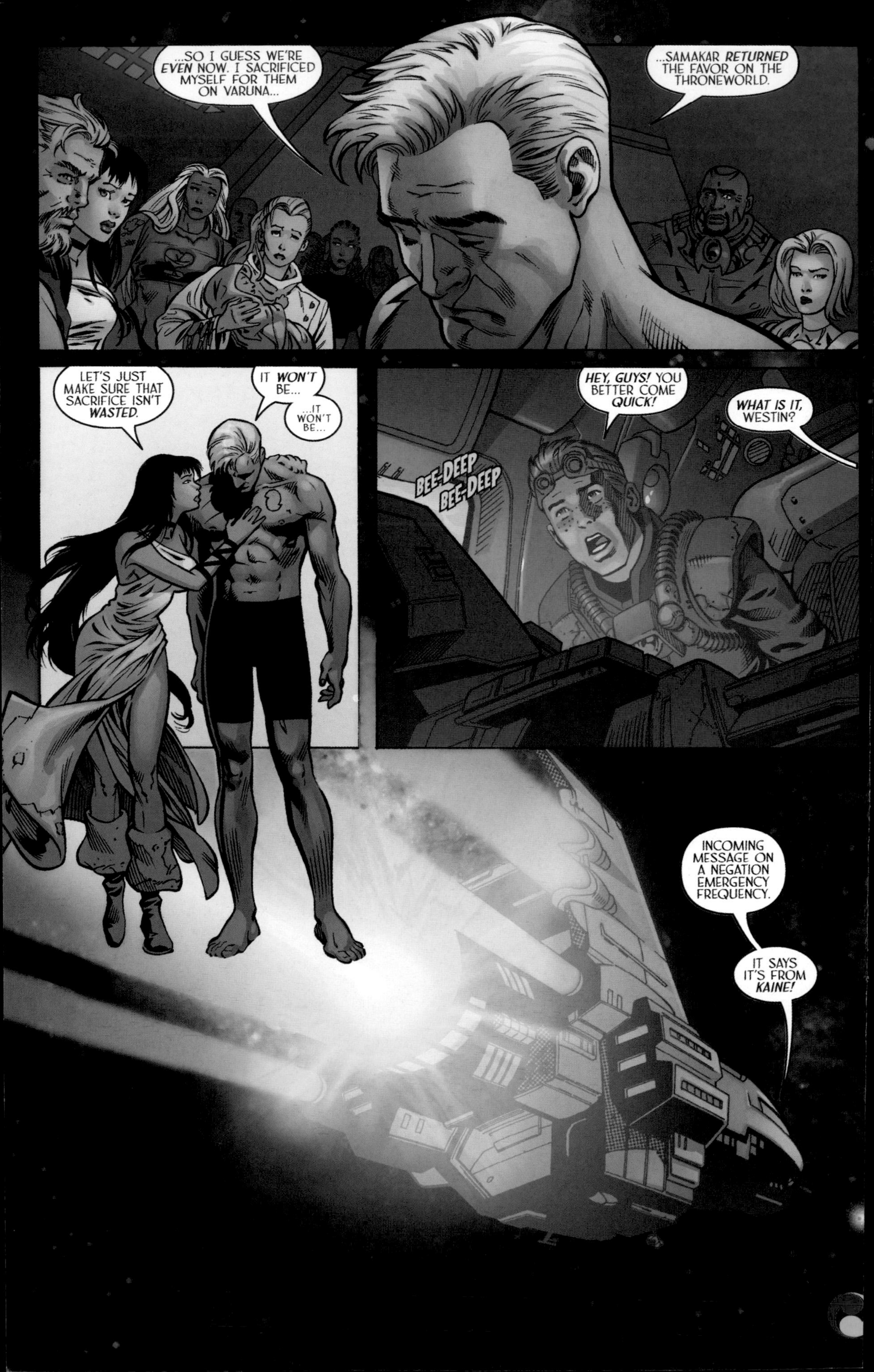
...SO I GUESS WE'RE EVEN NOW. I SACRIFICED MYSELF FOR THEM ON VARUNA...
...SAMAKAR RETURNED THE FAVOR ON THE THRONEWORLD.
LET'S JUST MAKE SURE THAT SACRIFICE ISN'T WASTED.
IT WON'T BE...
...IT WON'T BE...
HEY, GUYS! YOU BETTER COME QUICK!
BEE-DEEP BEE-DEEP
WHAT IS IT, WESTIN?
INCOMING MESSAGE ON A NEGATION EMERGENCY FREQUENCY.
IT SAYS IT'S FROM KAINE!

STORYTELLERS

TONY BEDARD
WRITER

LUKE ROSS
GUEST PENCILER

DREW GERACI
WITH JOHN HOLDREDGE
GUEST INKERS

DEAN WHITE
GUEST COLORIST

TROY PETERI
LETTERER

The CrossGen Universe created by Mark Alessi & Gina M. Villa

Publisher & CEO • **Mark Alessi**
   Director of Conventions & Facilities • **John Smith**
Senior Vice President Chief Creative Officer • **Gina M. Villa**
   Vice President Writing Development • **Barbara Kesel**
   Director Ancillary Publishing • **Ian M. Feller**
   Director of Production Control • **Charles Decker**
Senior Vice President Chief Financial Officer • **Michael A. Beattie**
   Controller • **Brian Soltis**
   Director of Human Resources • **Karla Barnett**
   Office Manager • **Shirley Burdett**
Senior Vice President General Counsel • **Jennifer Hernandez**
Senior Vice President Chief Technology Officer • **Jim Stikeleather**
   Director of Information Technology • **Courtland Whited**
   Internet Services Director • **Gabo Mendoza**
Senior Vice President Product Development • **Tony Panaccio**
   Director of Marketing & Communications • **Bill Rosemann**

Vice President Sales • **Chris Oarr**
   Director of Sales Book Trade • **Robert Boyd**
   Director of Sales Direct & Foreign Markets • **James Breitbeil**
Vice President Special Projects • **Brandon Peterson**
Vice President Art Director • **Bart Sears**
   Assistant Art Directors • **Michael Atiyeh, Butch Guice,**
   Dave Lanphear, Rick Magyar, Laura Martin,
   Mark Pennington, Andy Smith
   Freelance Coordinator • **Michelle Pugliese**
Vice President Production • **Pam Davies**
   Production Supervisor Advertising/Web • **Sylvia Bretz**
   Production Supervisor Books • **Janet Bechtle**
   Production Designers • **Erin Flanagan** & **Randy Martin**
   Production Assistant • **Marisol Quintana**

ME NEGATION

Chapter 5

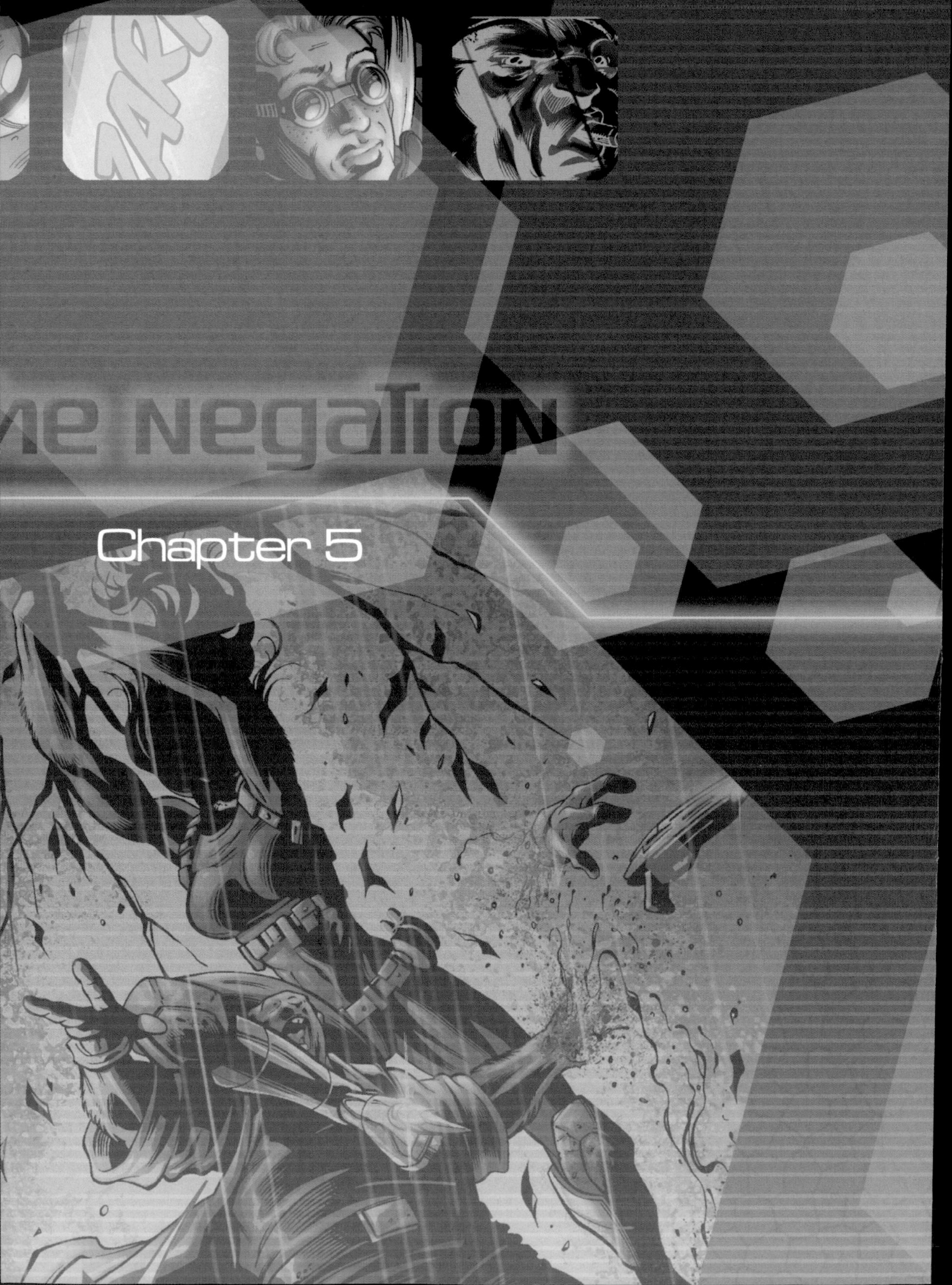

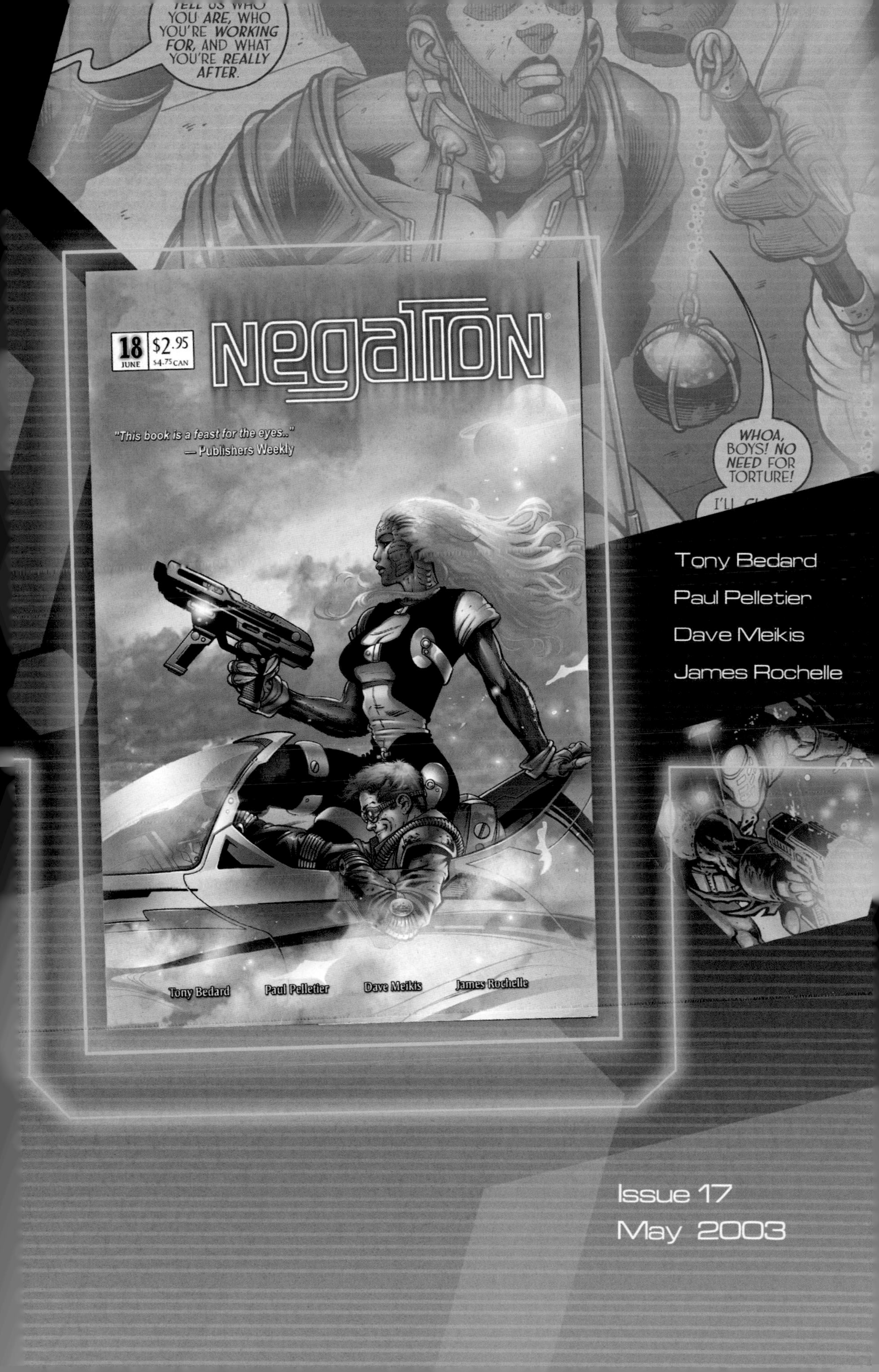
TELL US WHO YOU ARE, WHO YOU'RE WORKING FOR, AND WHAT YOU'RE REALLY AFTER.
WHOA, BOYS! NO NEED FOR TORTURE!
18 JUNE
$2.95 $4.75 CAN
NEGATION
"This book is a feast for the eyes.." — Publishers Weekly
Tony Bedard Paul Pelletier Dave Meikis James Rochelle
Tony Bedard
Paul Pelletier
Dave Meikis
James Rochelle
Issue 17
May 2003

The God-Emperor CHARON conquered His chaotic universe and forged an intergalactic empire known as:

the NegaTION

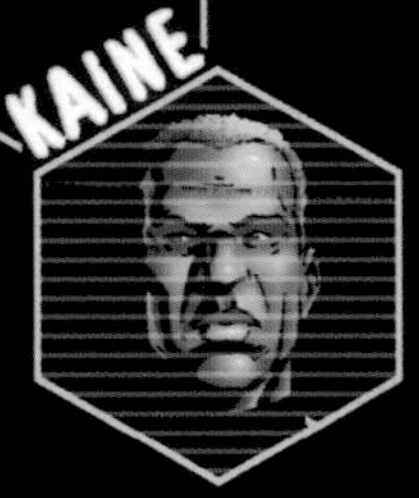
KAINE

Charon now casts His baleful eye across the gulf between realities and covets the bright and thriving worlds in our cosmos.

On His orders, one hundred strangers were abducted from our universe and brought to His dark realm to be studied and tested on a harsh prison-world. Some captives, such as the scam artist Westin, bore a mysterious mark of power known as the Sigil, granting them astonishing abilities. Others, such as the Saurian Lizard Lady, came from inherently powerful races. Most, however, were simple, ordinary humans.

One such human named Obregon Kaine led a bloody uprising against their Negation captors. The few prisoners who escaped with their lives now wander the hostile stars, seeking a way home.

Joined by a powerful newcomer, Gammid of Atlantis, the fugitives receive a distress call from Kaine, whom they feared irretrievably lost. But before they can mount a rescue, they must first acquire some crucial supplies and equipment...

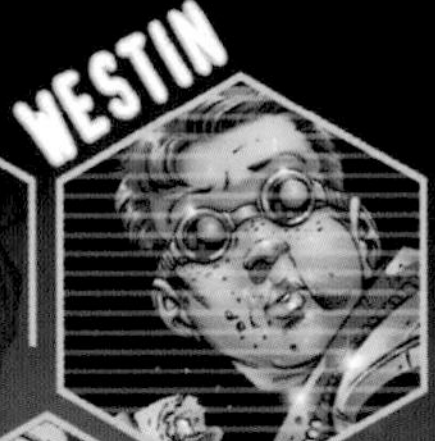
WESTIN

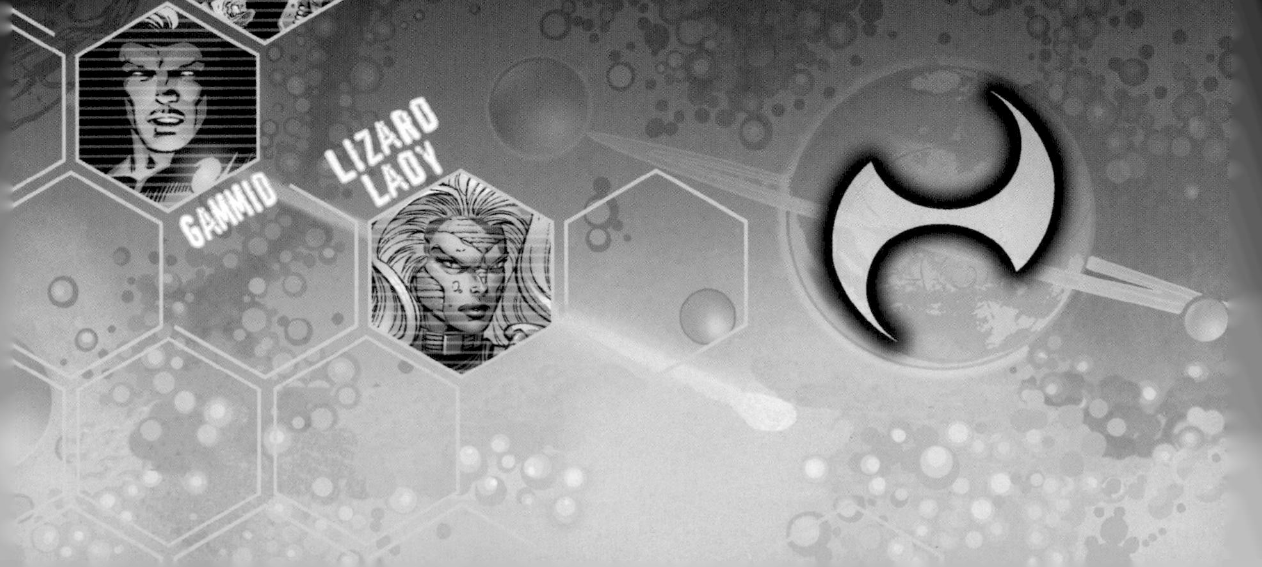
GAMMID
LIZARD LADY

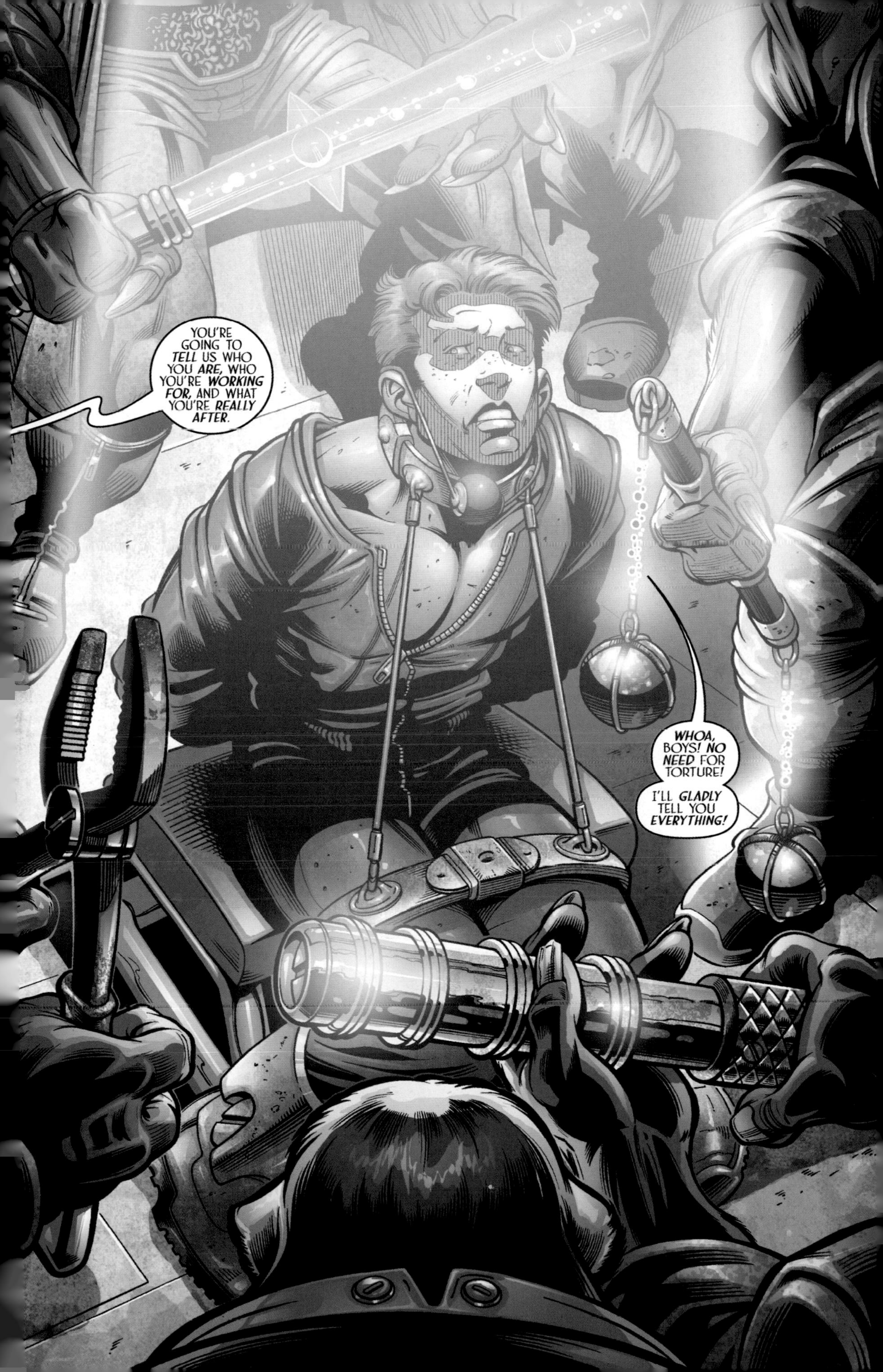
YOU'RE GOING TO TELL US WHO YOU ARE, WHO YOU'RE WORKING FOR, AND WHAT YOU'RE REALLY AFTER.
WHOA, BOYS! NO NEED FOR TORTURE!
I'LL GLADLY TELL YOU EVERYTHING!

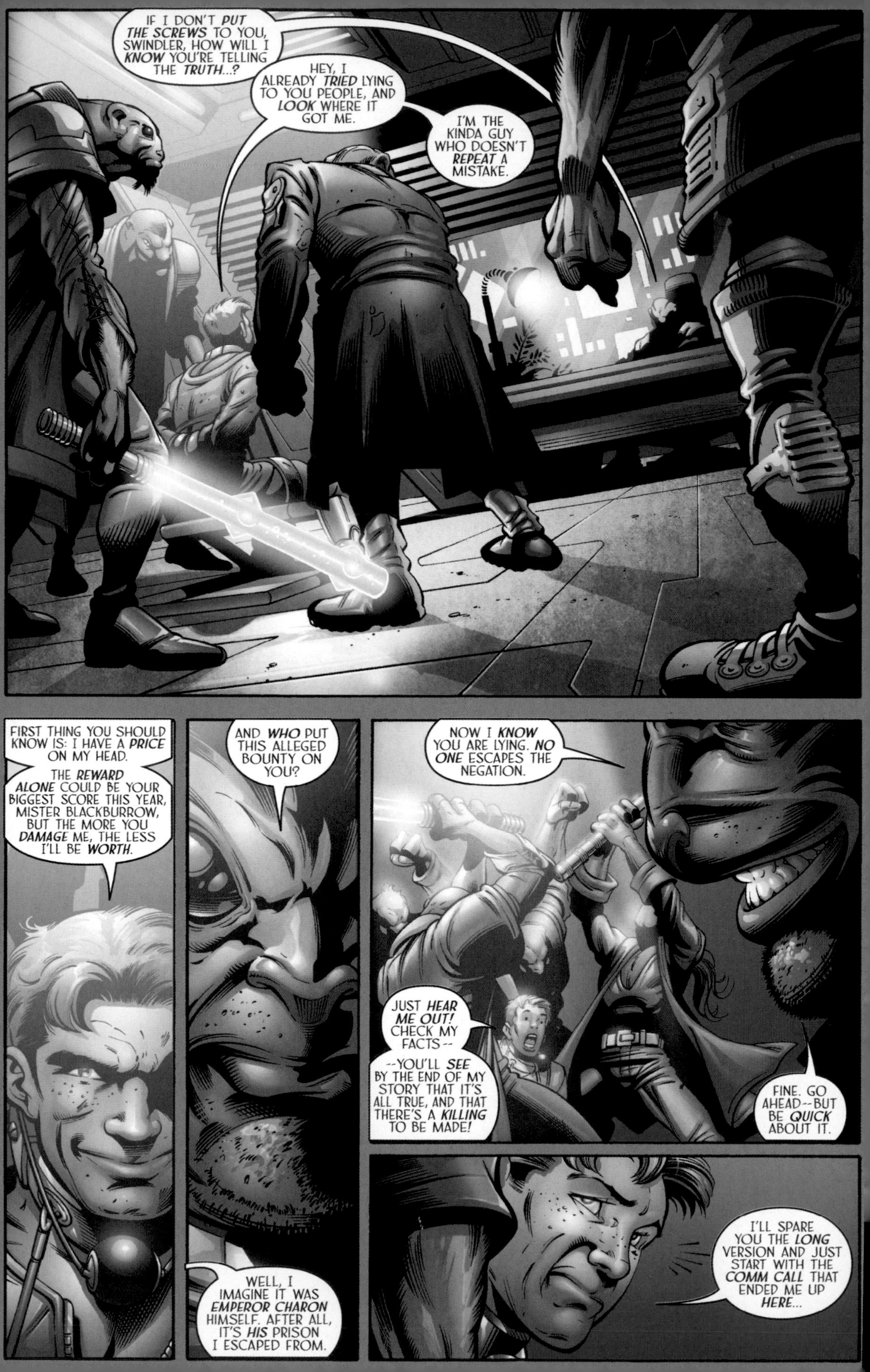
IF I DON'T PUT THE SCREWS TO YOU, SWINDLER, HOW WILL I KNOW YOU'RE TELLING THE TRUTH...?
HEY, I ALREADY TRIED LYING TO YOU PEOPLE, AND LOOK WHERE IT GOT ME.
I'M THE KINDA GUY WHO DOESN'T REPEAT A MISTAKE.
FIRST THING YOU SHOULD KNOW IS: I HAVE A PRICE ON MY HEAD.
THE REWARD ALONE COULD BE YOUR BIGGEST SCORE THIS YEAR, MISTER BLACKBURROW, BUT THE MORE YOU DAMAGE ME, THE LESS I'LL BE WORTH.
AND WHO PUT THIS ALLEGED BOUNTY ON YOU?
WELL, I IMAGINE IT WAS EMPEROR CHARON HIMSELF. AFTER ALL, IT'S HIS PRISON I ESCAPED FROM.
NOW I KNOW YOU ARE LYING. NO ONE ESCAPES THE NEGATION.
JUST HEAR ME OUT! CHECK MY FACTS--
--YOU'LL SEE BY THE END OF MY STORY THAT IT'S ALL TRUE, AND THAT THERE'S A KILLING TO BE MADE!
FINE. GO AHEAD--BUT BE QUICK ABOUT IT.
I'LL SPARE YOU THE LONG VERSION AND JUST START WITH THE COMM CALL THAT ENDED ME UP HERE...

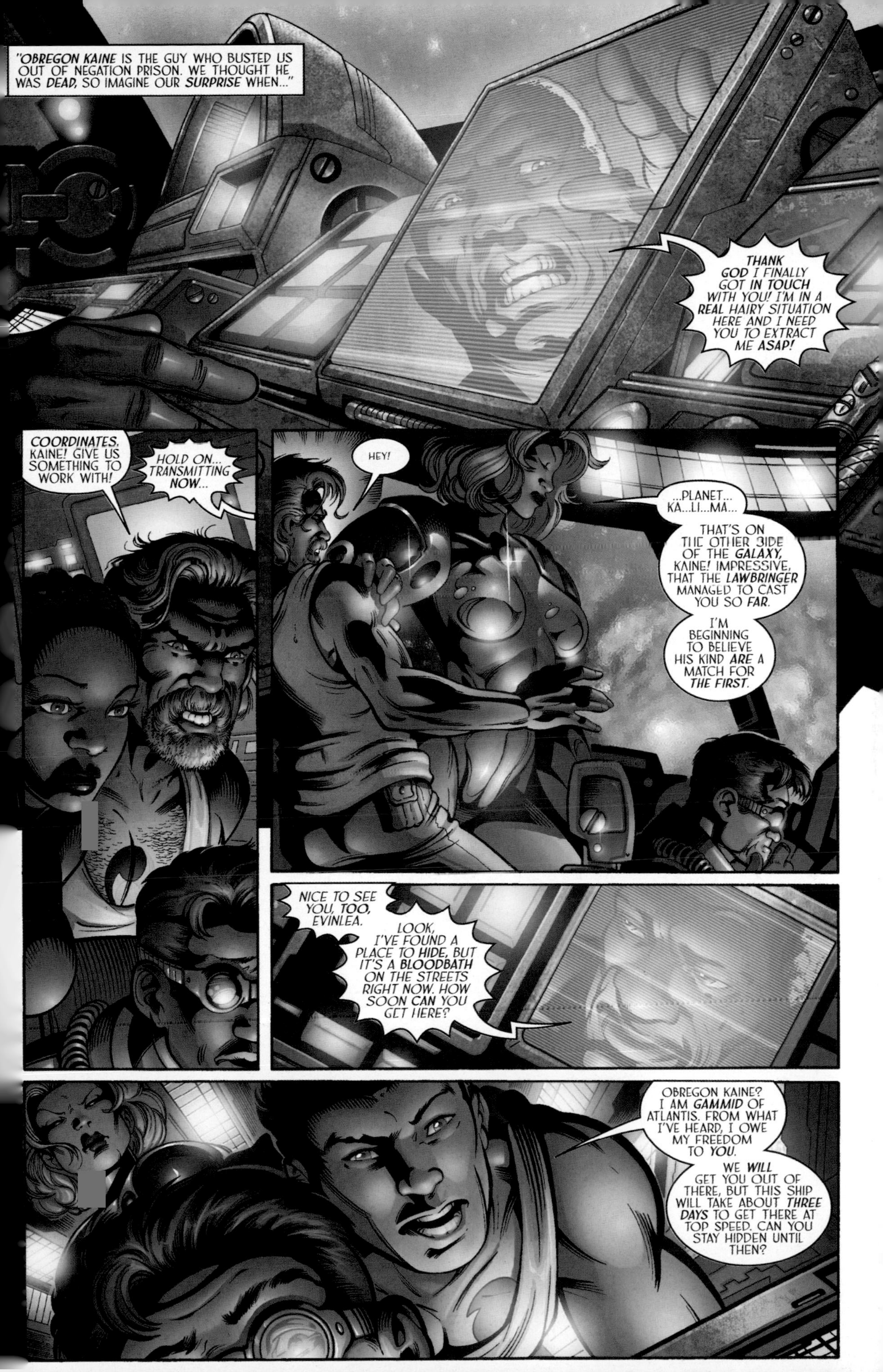
"OBREGON KAINE IS THE GUY WHO BUSTED US OUT OF NEGATION PRISON. WE THOUGHT HE WAS DEAD, SO IMAGINE OUR SURPRISE WHEN..."
THANK GOD I FINALLY GOT IN TOUCH WITH YOU! I'M IN A REAL HAIRY SITUATION HERE AND I NEED YOU TO EXTRACT ME ASAP!
COORDINATES, KAINE! GIVE US SOMETHING TO WORK WITH!
HOLD ON... TRANSMITTING NOW...
HEY!
...PLANET... KA...LI...MA...
THAT'S ON THE OTHER SIDE OF THE GALAXY, KAINE! IMPRESSIVE, THAT THE LAWBRINGER MANAGED TO CAST YOU SO FAR.
I'M BEGINNING TO BELIEVE HIS KIND ARE A MATCH FOR THE FIRST.
NICE TO SEE YOU, TOO, EVINLEA.
LOOK, I'VE FOUND A PLACE TO HIDE, BUT IT'S A BLOODBATH ON THE STREETS RIGHT NOW. HOW SOON CAN YOU GET HERE?
OBREGON KAINE? I AM GAMMID OF ATLANTIS. FROM WHAT I'VE HEARD, I OWE MY FREEDOM TO YOU.
WE WILL GET YOU OUT OF THERE, BUT THIS SHIP WILL TAKE ABOUT THREE DAYS TO GET THERE AT TOP SPEED. CAN YOU STAY HIDDEN UNTIL THEN?

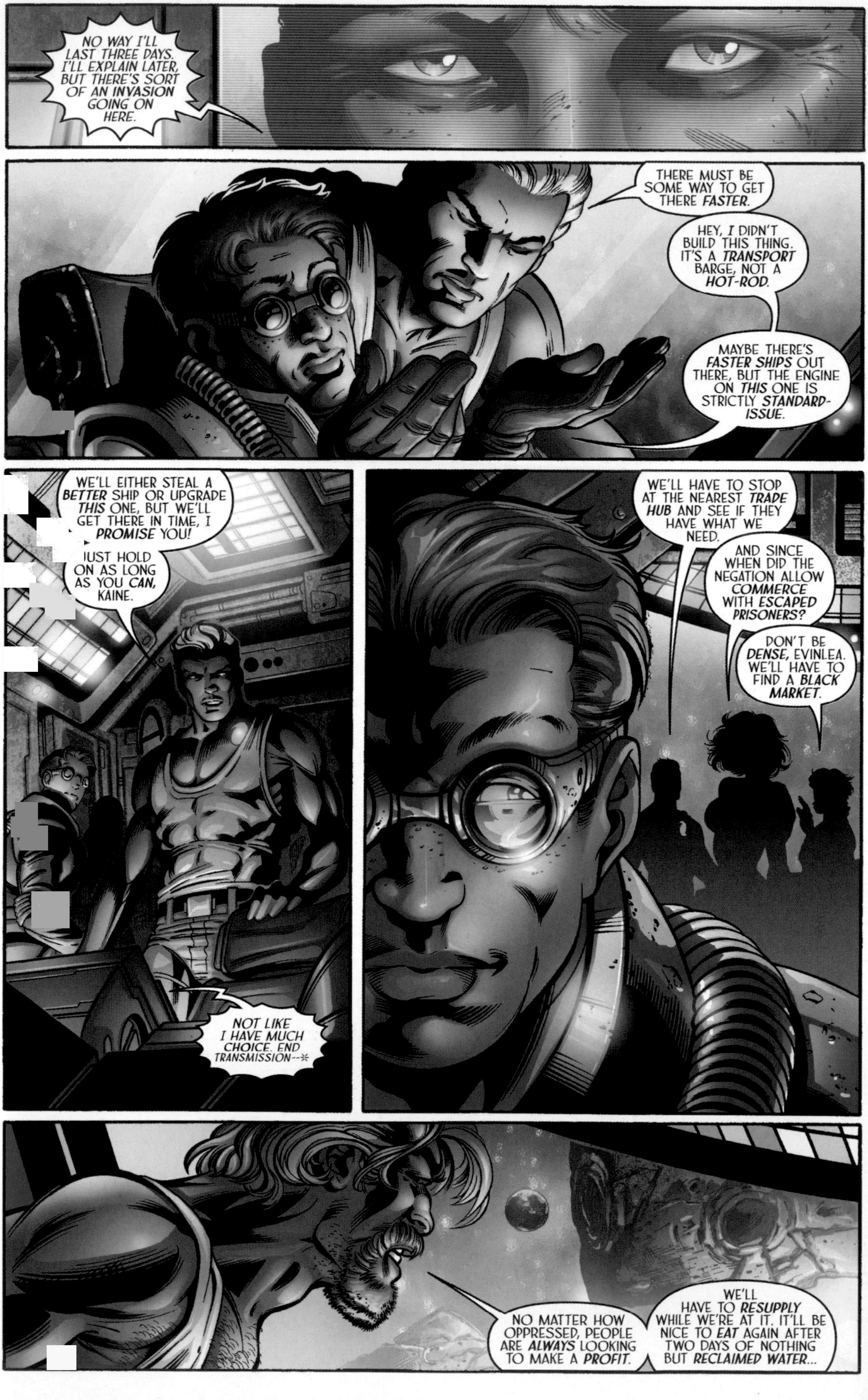
NO WAY I'LL LAST THREE DAYS. I'LL EXPLAIN LATER, BUT THERE'S SORT OF AN INVASION GOING ON HERE.
THERE MUST BE SOME WAY TO GET THERE FASTER.
HEY, I DIDN'T BUILD THIS THING. IT'S A TRANSPORT BARGE, NOT A HOT-ROD.
MAYBE THERE'S FASTER SHIPS OUT THERE, BUT THE ENGINE ON THIS ONE IS STRICTLY STANDARD-ISSUE.
WE'LL EITHER STEAL A BETTER SHIP OR UPGRADE THIS ONE, BUT WE'LL GET THERE IN TIME, I PROMISE YOU!
JUST HOLD ON AS LONG AS YOU CAN, KAINE.
NOT LIKE I HAVE MUCH CHOICE. END TRANSMISSION--*
WE'LL HAVE TO STOP AT THE NEAREST TRADE HUB AND SEE IF THEY HAVE WHAT WE NEED.
AND SINCE WHEN DID THE NEGATION ALLOW COMMERCE WITH ESCAPED PRISONERS?
DON'T BE DENSE, EVINLEA. WE'LL HAVE TO FIND A BLACK MARKET.
NO MATTER HOW OPPRESSED, PEOPLE ARE ALWAYS LOOKING TO MAKE A PROFIT.
WE'LL HAVE TO RESUPPLY WHILE WE'RE AT IT. IT'LL BE NICE TO EAT AGAIN AFTER TWO DAYS OF NOTHING BUT RECLAIMED WATER...

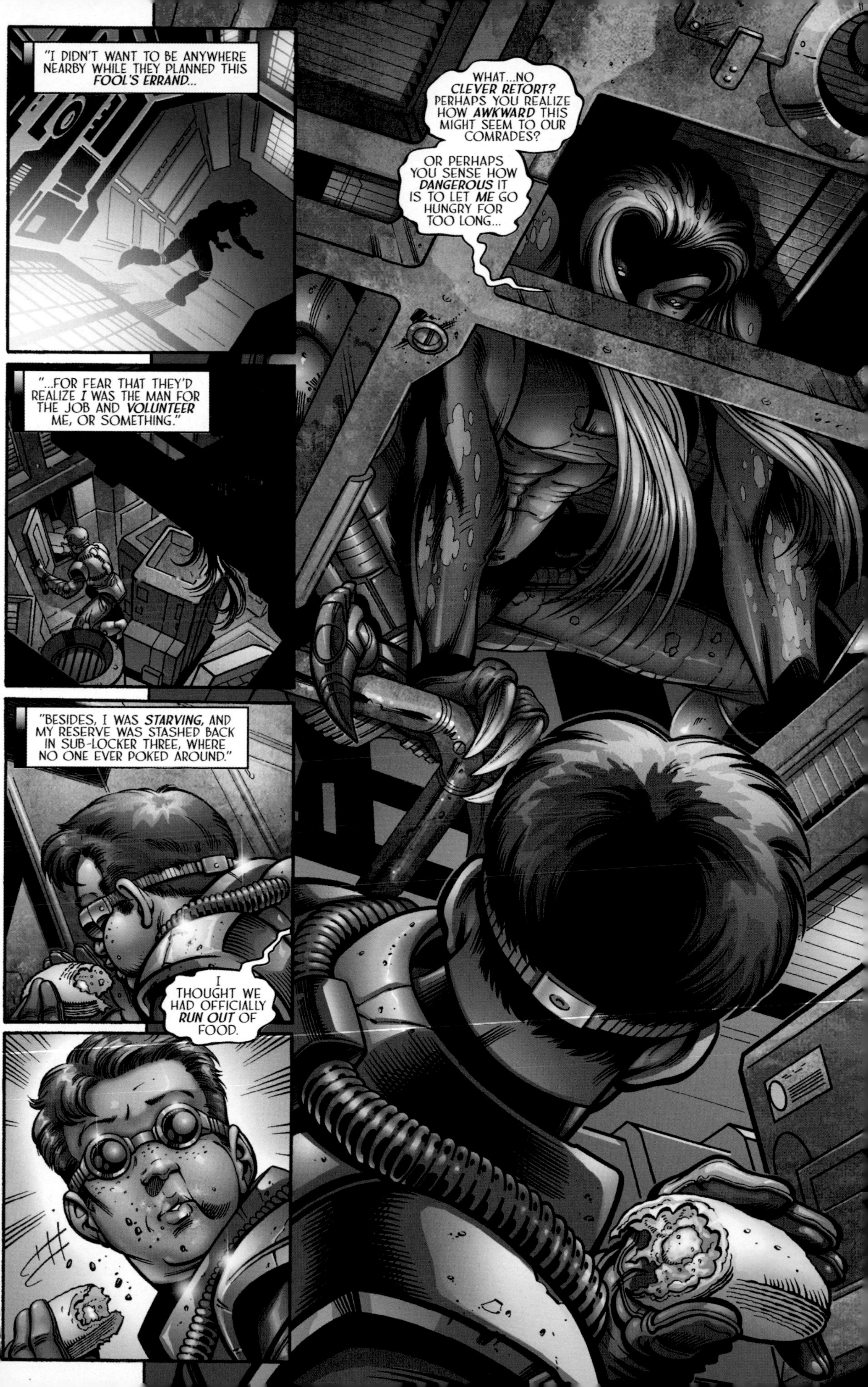
"I DIDN'T WANT TO BE ANYWHERE NEARBY WHILE THEY PLANNED THIS *FOOL'S ERRAND*...
"...FOR FEAR THAT THEY'D REALIZE *I* WAS THE MAN FOR THE JOB AND *VOLUNTEER* ME, OR SOMETHING."
"BESIDES, I WAS *STARVING*, AND MY RESERVE WAS STASHED BACK IN SUB-LOCKER THREE, WHERE NO ONE EVER POKED AROUND."
I THOUGHT WE HAD OFFICIALLY *RUN OUT* OF FOOD.
WHAT...NO *CLEVER RETORT?* PERHAPS YOU REALIZE HOW *AWKWARD* THIS MIGHT SEEM TO OUR COMRADES?
OR PERHAPS YOU SENSE HOW *DANGEROUS* IT IS TO LET *ME* GO HUNGRY FOR TOO LONG...

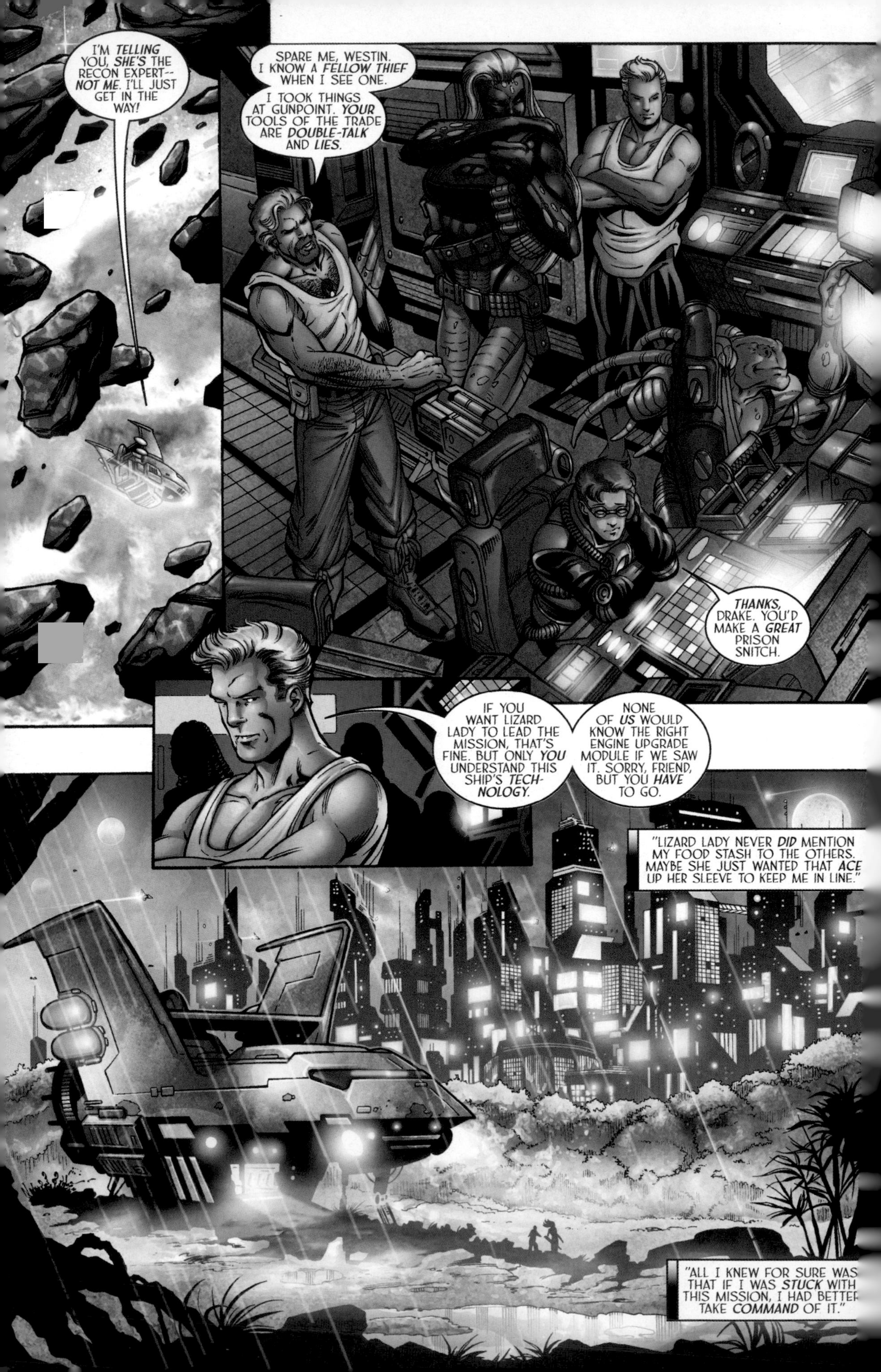
I'M TELLING YOU, SHE'S THE RECON EXPERT-- NOT ME. I'LL JUST GET IN THE WAY!
SPARE ME, WESTIN. I KNOW A FELLOW THIEF WHEN I SEE ONE.
I TOOK THINGS AT GUNPOINT. YOUR TOOLS OF THE TRADE ARE DOUBLE-TALK AND LIES.
THANKS, DRAKE. YOU'D MAKE A GREAT PRISON SNITCH.
IF YOU WANT LIZARD LADY TO LEAD THE MISSION, THAT'S FINE. BUT ONLY YOU UNDERSTAND THIS SHIP'S TECH-NOLOGY.
NONE OF US WOULD KNOW THE RIGHT ENGINE UPGRADE MODULE IF WE SAW IT. SORRY, FRIEND, BUT YOU HAVE TO GO.
"LIZARD LADY NEVER DID MENTION MY FOOD STASH TO THE OTHERS. MAYBE SHE JUST WANTED THAT ACE UP HER SLEEVE TO KEEP ME IN LINE."
"ALL I KNEW FOR SURE WAS THAT IF I WAS STUCK WITH THIS MISSION, I HAD BETTER TAKE COMMAND OF IT."

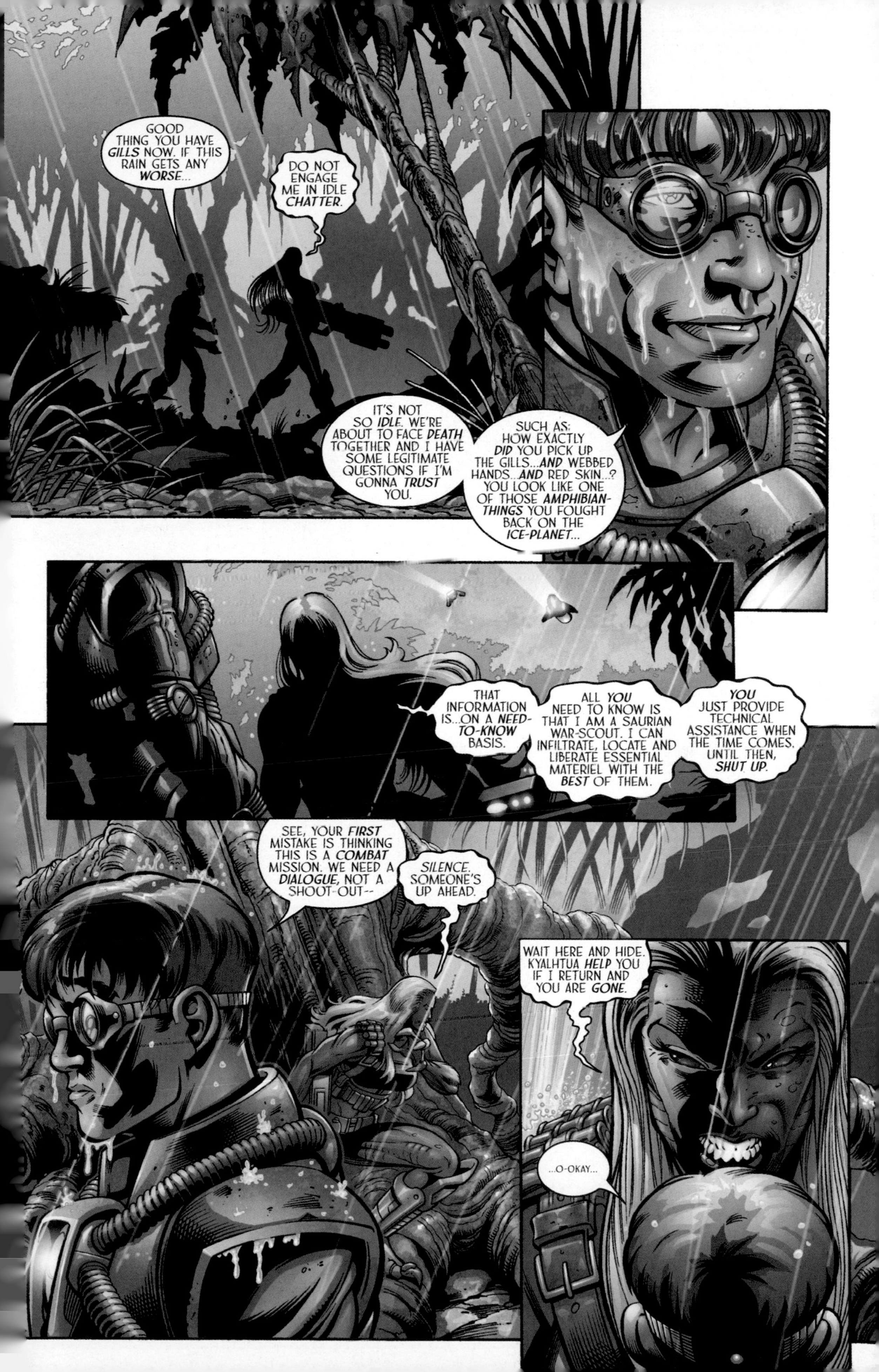
GOOD THING YOU HAVE GILLS NOW. IF THIS RAIN GETS ANY WORSE...
DO NOT ENGAGE ME IN IDLE CHATTER.
IT'S NOT SO IDLE. WE'RE ABOUT TO FACE DEATH TOGETHER AND I HAVE SOME LEGITIMATE QUESTIONS IF I'M GONNA TRUST YOU.
SUCH AS: HOW EXACTLY DID YOU PICK UP THE GILLS...AND WEBBED HANDS...AND RED SKIN...? YOU LOOK LIKE ONE OF THOSE AMPHIBIAN-THINGS YOU FOUGHT BACK ON THE ICE-PLANET...
THAT INFORMATION IS...ON A NEED-TO-KNOW BASIS.
ALL YOU NEED TO KNOW IS THAT I AM A SAURIAN WAR-SCOUT. I CAN INFILTRATE, LOCATE AND LIBERATE ESSENTIAL MATERIEL WITH THE BEST OF THEM.
YOU JUST PROVIDE TECHNICAL ASSISTANCE WHEN THE TIME COMES. UNTIL THEN, SHUT UP.
SEE, YOUR FIRST MISTAKE IS THINKING THIS IS A COMBAT MISSION. WE NEED A DIALOGUE, NOT A SHOOT-OUT--
SILENCE. SOMEONE'S UP AHEAD.
WAIT HERE AND HIDE. KYALHTUA HELP YOU IF I RETURN AND YOU ARE GONE.
...O-OKAY...

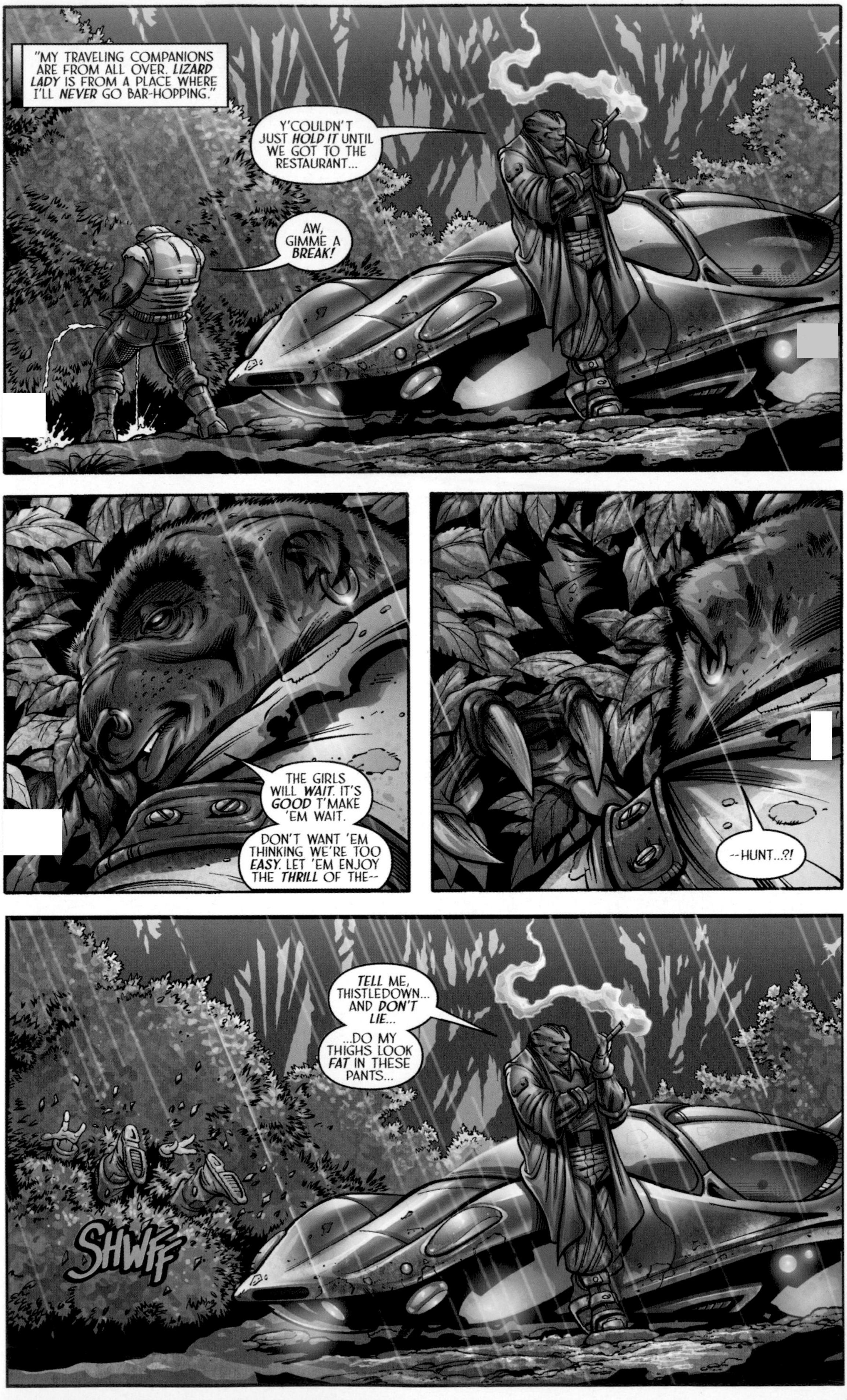
"MY TRAVELING COMPANIONS ARE FROM ALL OVER. LIZARD LADY IS FROM A PLACE WHERE I'LL NEVER GO BAR-HOPPING."
Y'COULDN'T JUST HOLD IT UNTIL WE GOT TO THE RESTAURANT...
AW, GIMME A BREAK!
THE GIRLS WILL WAIT. IT'S GOOD T'MAKE 'EM WAIT.
DON'T WANT 'EM THINKING WE'RE TOO EASY. LET 'EM ENJOY THE THRILL OF THE--
--HUNT...?!
TELL ME, THISTLEDOWN... AND DON'T LIE...
...DO MY THIGHS LOOK FAT IN THESE PANTS...
SHWFF

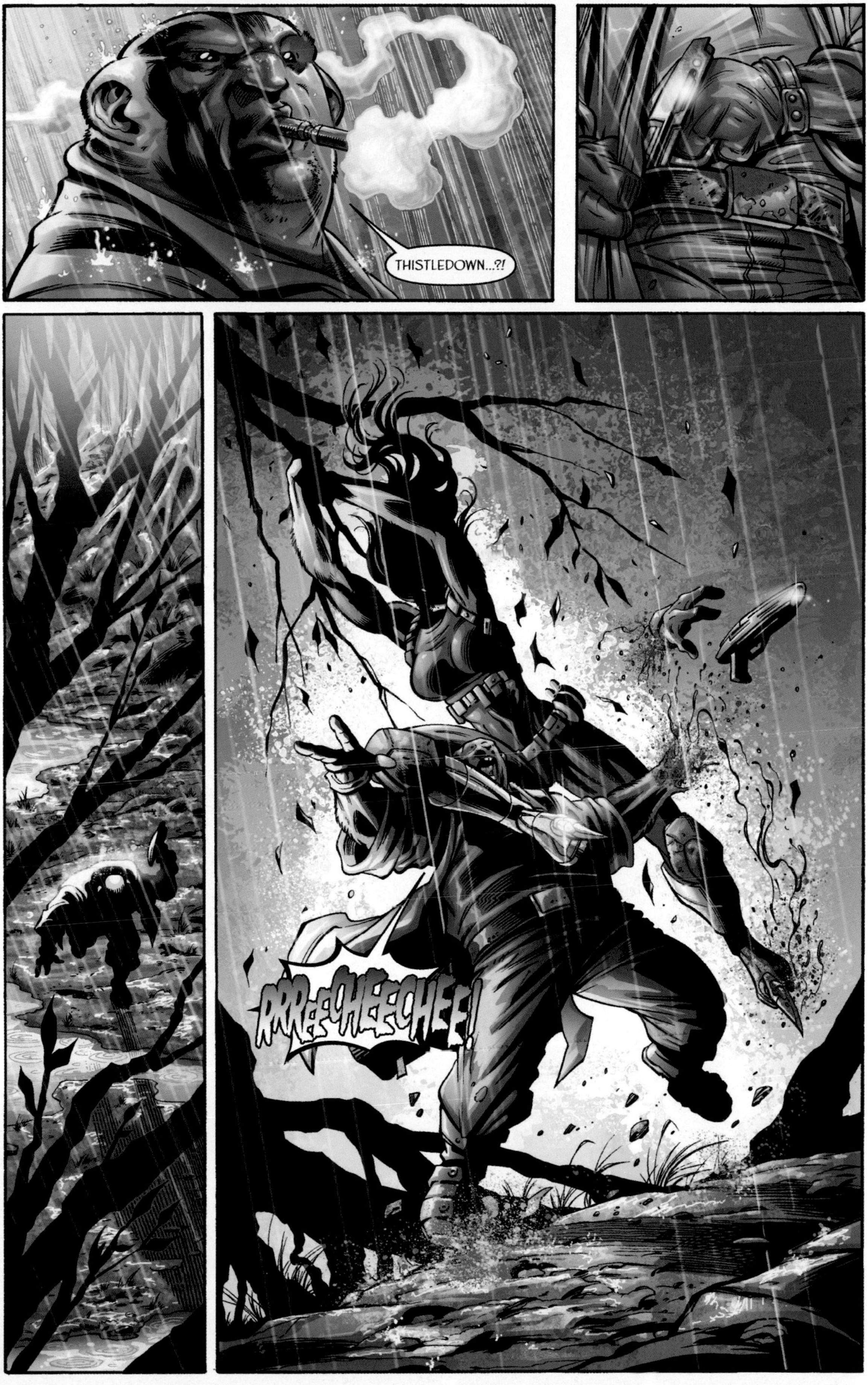
THISTLEDOWN...?!
RRR-EE-CHEE-CHEE!

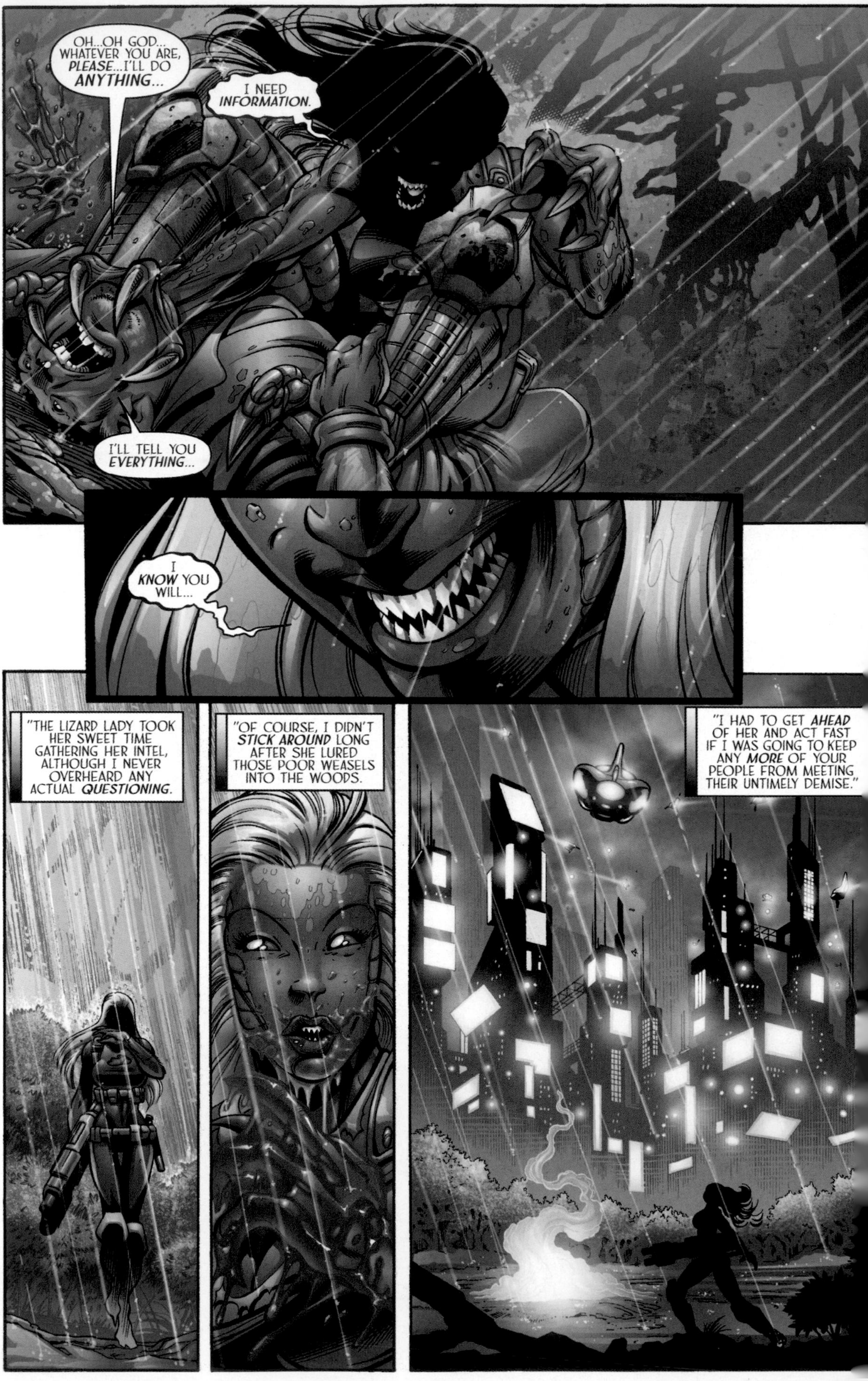

OH...OH GOD... WHATEVER YOU ARE, PLEASE...I'LL DO ANYTHING...
I NEED INFORMATION.
I'LL TELL YOU EVERYTHING...
I KNOW YOU WILL...
"THE LIZARD LADY TOOK HER SWEET TIME GATHERING HER INTEL, ALTHOUGH I NEVER OVERHEARD ANY ACTUAL QUESTIONING.
"OF COURSE, I DIDN'T STICK AROUND LONG AFTER SHE LURED THOSE POOR WEASELS INTO THE WOODS.
"I HAD TO GET AHEAD OF HER AND ACT FAST IF I WAS GOING TO KEEP ANY MORE OF YOUR PEOPLE FROM MEETING THEIR UNTIMELY DEMISE."

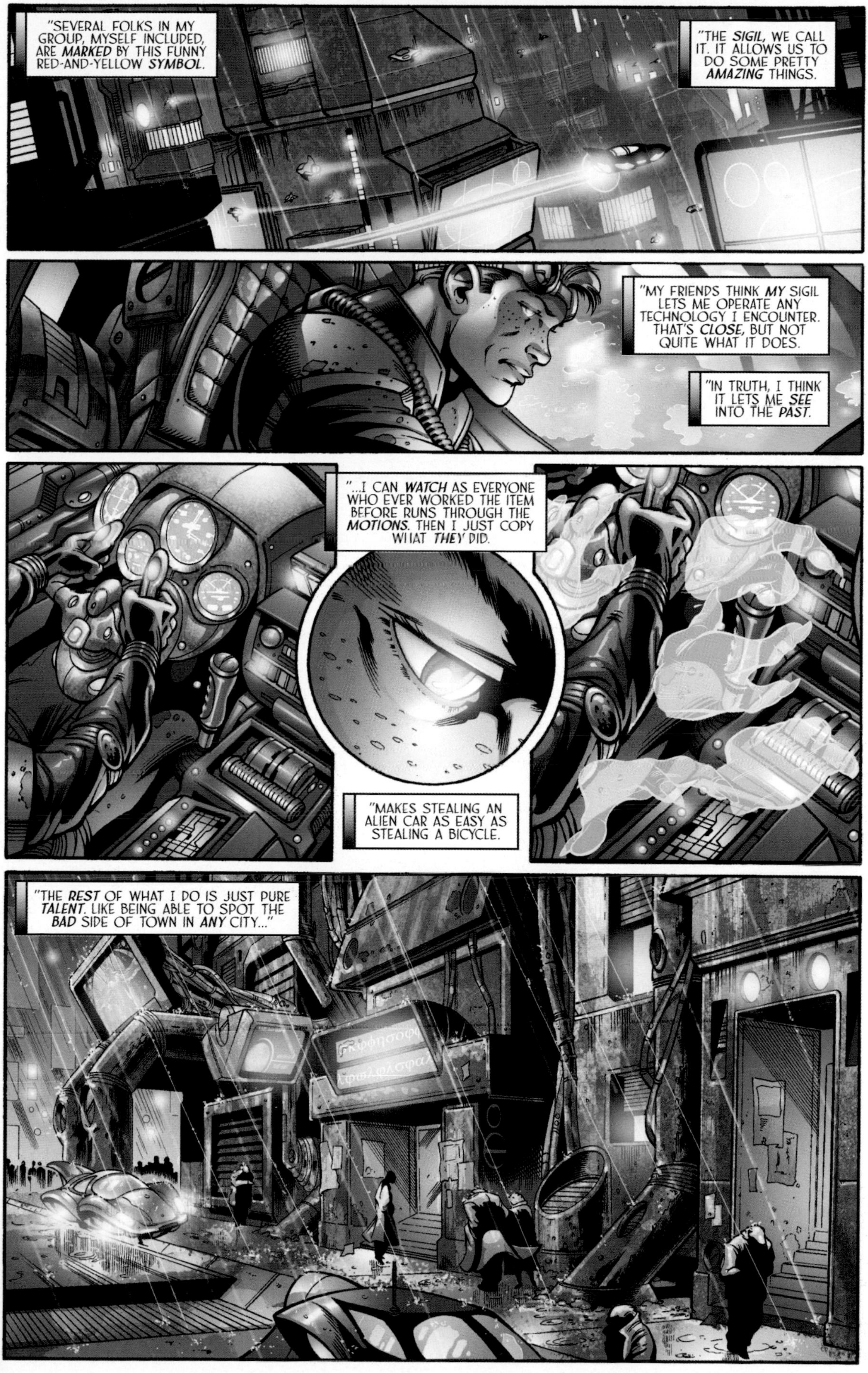
"SEVERAL FOLKS IN MY GROUP, MYSELF INCLUDED, ARE MARKED BY THIS FUNNY RED-AND-YELLOW SYMBOL.
"THE SIGIL, WE CALL IT. IT ALLOWS US TO DO SOME PRETTY AMAZING THINGS.
"MY FRIENDS THINK MY SIGIL LETS ME OPERATE ANY TECHNOLOGY I ENCOUNTER. THAT'S CLOSE, BUT NOT QUITE WHAT IT DOES.
"IN TRUTH, I THINK IT LETS ME SEE INTO THE PAST.
"...I CAN WATCH AS EVERYONE WHO EVER WORKED THE ITEM BEFORE RUNS THROUGH THE MOTIONS. THEN I JUST COPY WHAT THEY DID.
"MAKES STEALING AN ALIEN CAR AS EASY AS STEALING A BICYCLE.
"THE REST OF WHAT I DO IS JUST PURE TALENT. LIKE BEING ABLE TO SPOT THE BAD SIDE OF TOWN IN ANY CITY..."

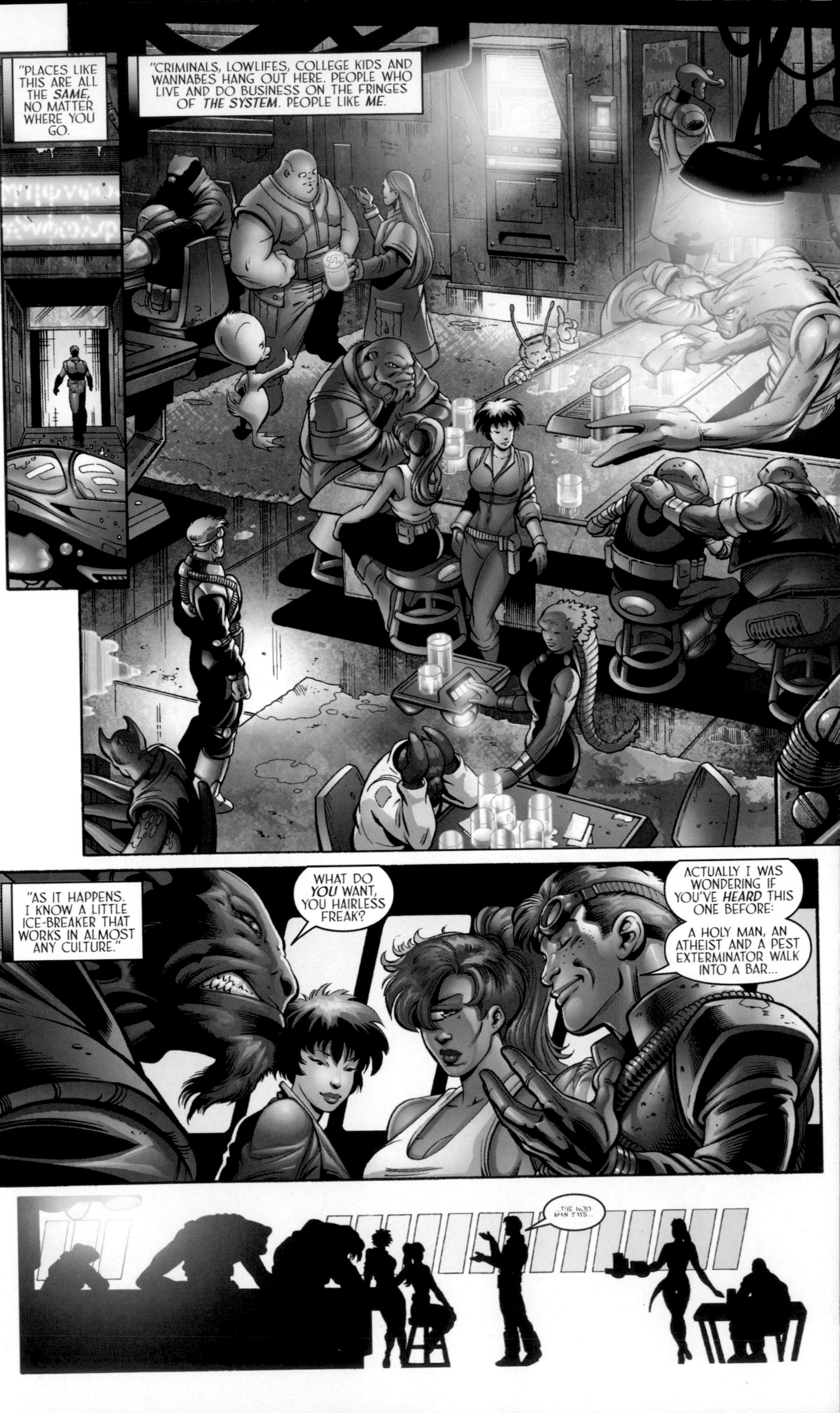
"PLACES LIKE THIS ARE ALL THE *SAME*, NO MATTER WHERE YOU GO.
"CRIMINALS, LOWLIFES, COLLEGE KIDS AND WANNABES HANG OUT HERE. PEOPLE WHO LIVE AND DO BUSINESS ON THE FRINGES OF *THE SYSTEM*. PEOPLE LIKE *ME*.
"AS IT HAPPENS. I KNOW A LITTLE ICE-BREAKER THAT WORKS IN ALMOST ANY CULTURE."
WHAT DO *YOU* WANT, YOU HAIRLESS FREAK?
ACTUALLY I WAS WONDERING IF YOU'VE *HEARD* THIS ONE BEFORE:
A HOLY MAN, AN ATHEIST AND A PEST EXTERMINATOR WALK INTO A BAR...
...THE HOLY MAN SAYS...

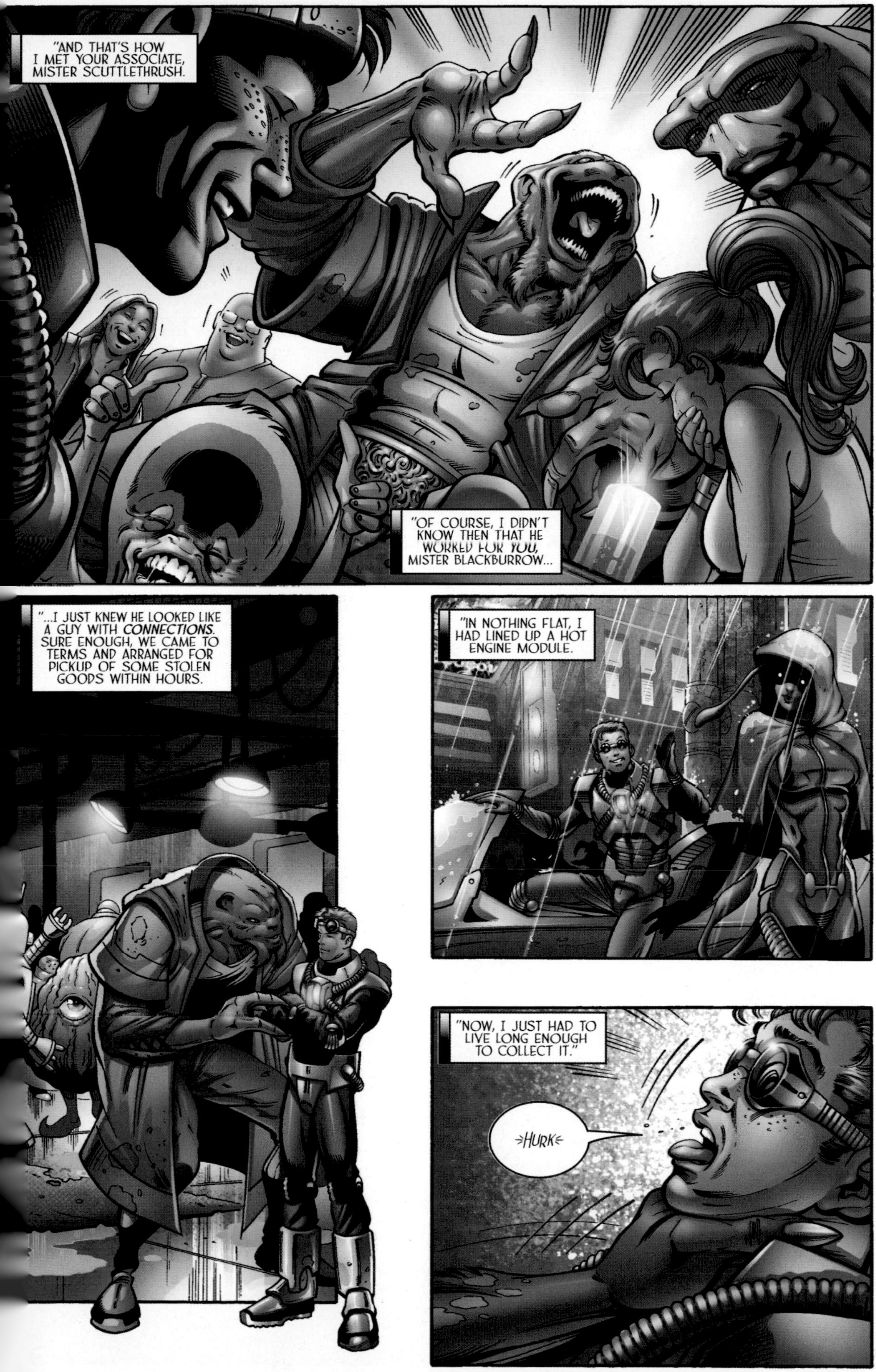
"AND THAT'S HOW I MET YOUR ASSOCIATE, MISTER SCUTTLETHRUSH.
"OF COURSE, I DIDN'T KNOW THEN THAT HE WORKED FOR YOU, MISTER BLACKBURROW...
"...I JUST KNEW HE LOOKED LIKE A GUY WITH CONNECTIONS. SURE ENOUGH, WE CAME TO TERMS AND ARRANGED FOR PICKUP OF SOME STOLEN GOODS WITHIN HOURS.
"IN NOTHING FLAT, I HAD LINED UP A HOT ENGINE MODULE.
"NOW, I JUST HAD TO LIVE LONG ENOUGH TO COLLECT IT."
HURK

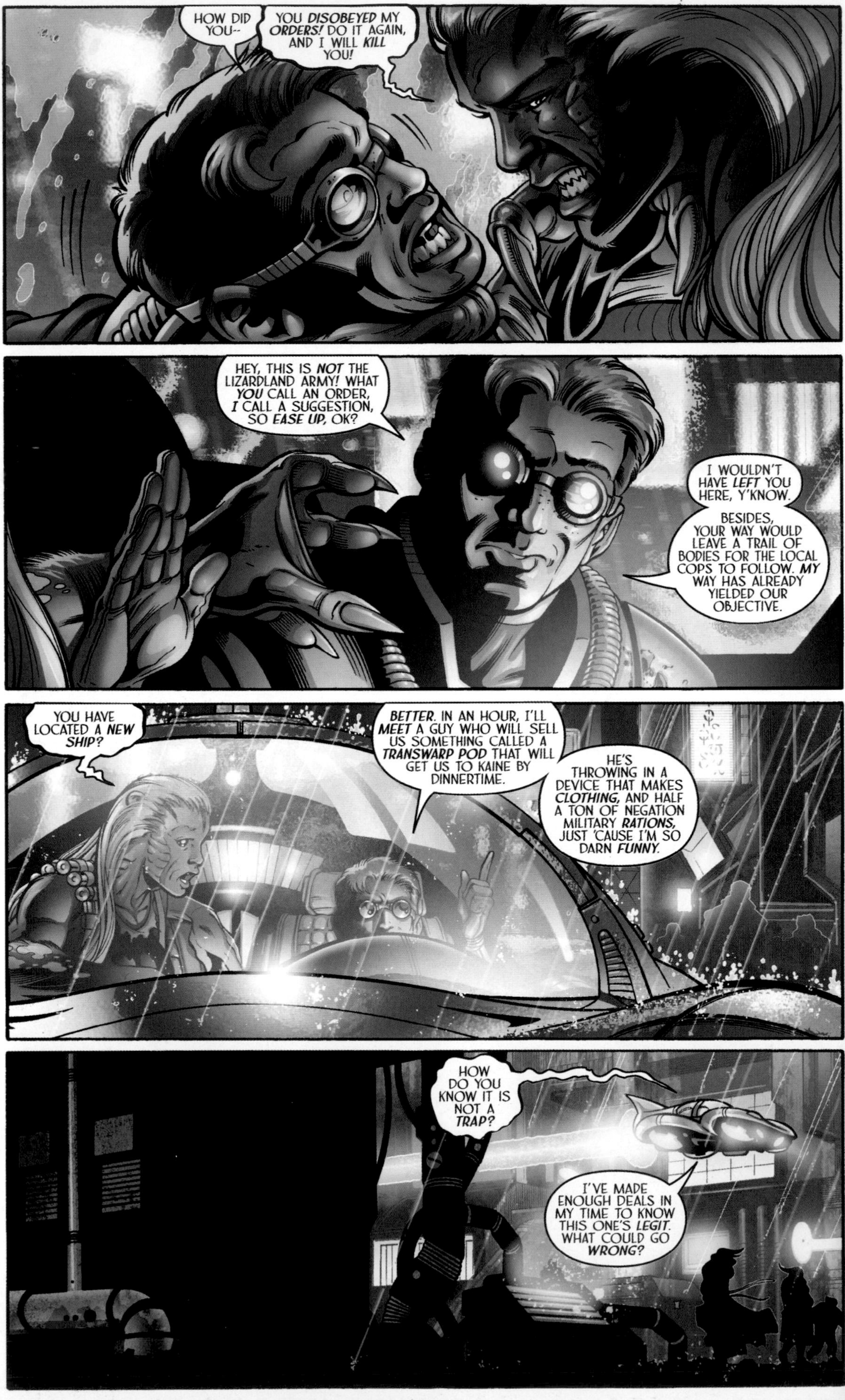
HOW DID YOU--
YOU *DISOBEYED* MY *ORDERS!* DO IT AGAIN, AND I WILL *KILL* YOU!
HEY, THIS IS *NOT* THE LIZARDLAND ARMY! WHAT *YOU* CALL AN ORDER, *I* CALL A SUGGESTION, SO *EASE UP*, OK?
I WOULDN'T HAVE *LEFT* YOU HERE, Y'KNOW.
BESIDES, YOUR WAY WOULD LEAVE A TRAIL OF BODIES FOR THE LOCAL COPS TO FOLLOW. *MY* WAY HAS ALREADY YIELDED OUR OBJECTIVE.
YOU HAVE LOCATED A *NEW SHIP?*
BETTER. IN AN HOUR, I'LL *MEET* A GUY WHO WILL SELL US SOMETHING CALLED A *TRANSWARP POD* THAT WILL GET US TO KAINE BY DINNERTIME.
HE'S THROWING IN A DEVICE THAT MAKES *CLOTHING,* AND HALF A TON OF NEGATION MILITARY *RATIONS,* JUST 'CAUSE I'M SO DARN *FUNNY*.
HOW DO YOU KNOW IT IS NOT A *TRAP?*
I'VE MADE ENOUGH DEALS IN MY TIME TO KNOW THIS ONE'S *LEGIT*. WHAT COULD GO *WRONG?*

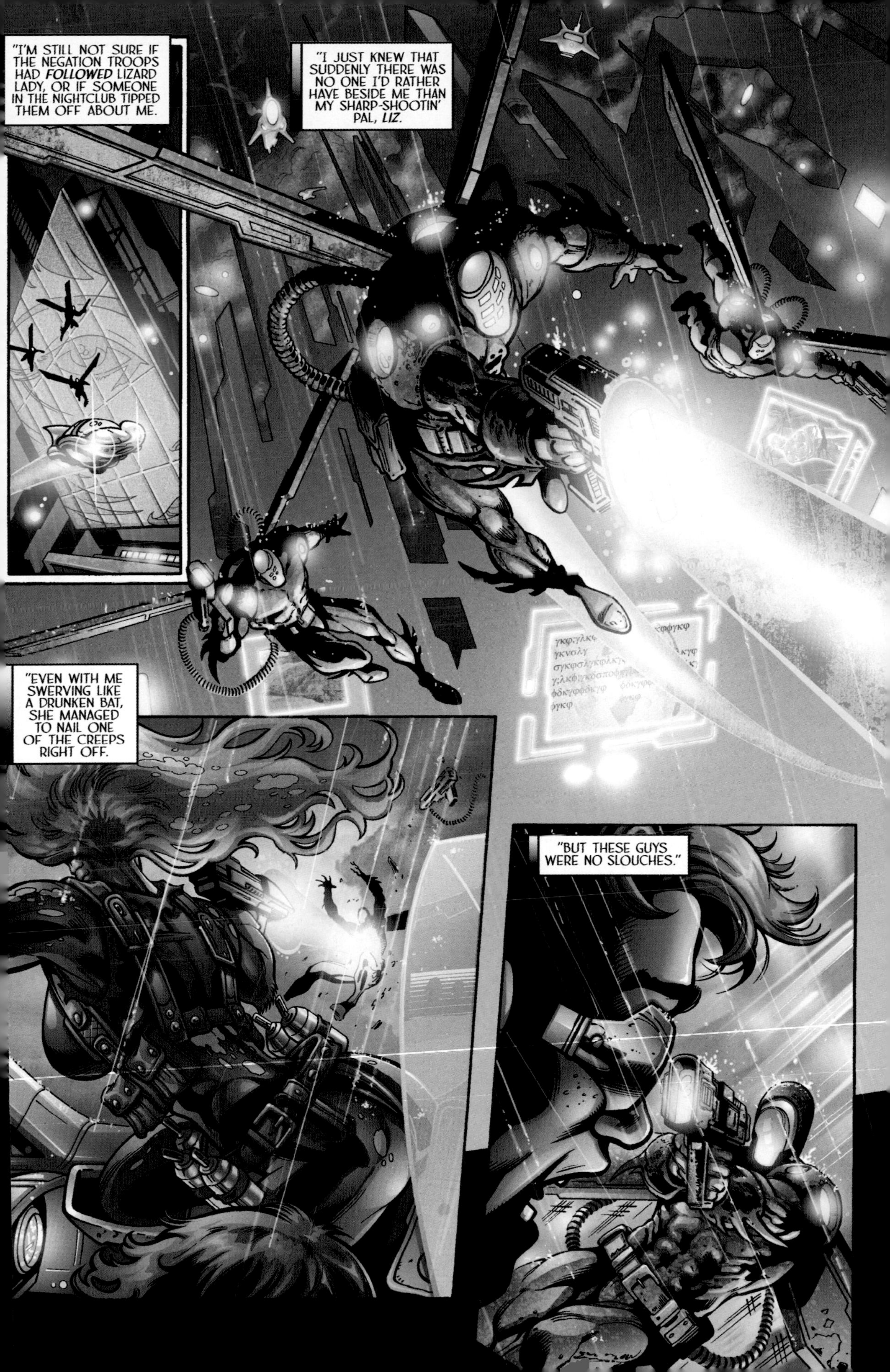
"I'M STILL NOT SURE IF THE NEGATION TROOPS HAD FOLLOWED LIZARD LADY, OR IF SOMEONE IN THE NIGHTCLUB TIPPED THEM OFF ABOUT ME.
"I JUST KNEW THAT SUDDENLY THERE WAS NO ONE I'D RATHER HAVE BESIDE ME THAN MY SHARP-SHOOTIN' PAL, LIZ.
"EVEN WITH ME SWERVING LIKE A DRUNKEN BAT, SHE MANAGED TO NAIL ONE OF THE CREEPS RIGHT OFF.
"BUT THESE GUYS WERE NO SLOUCHES."

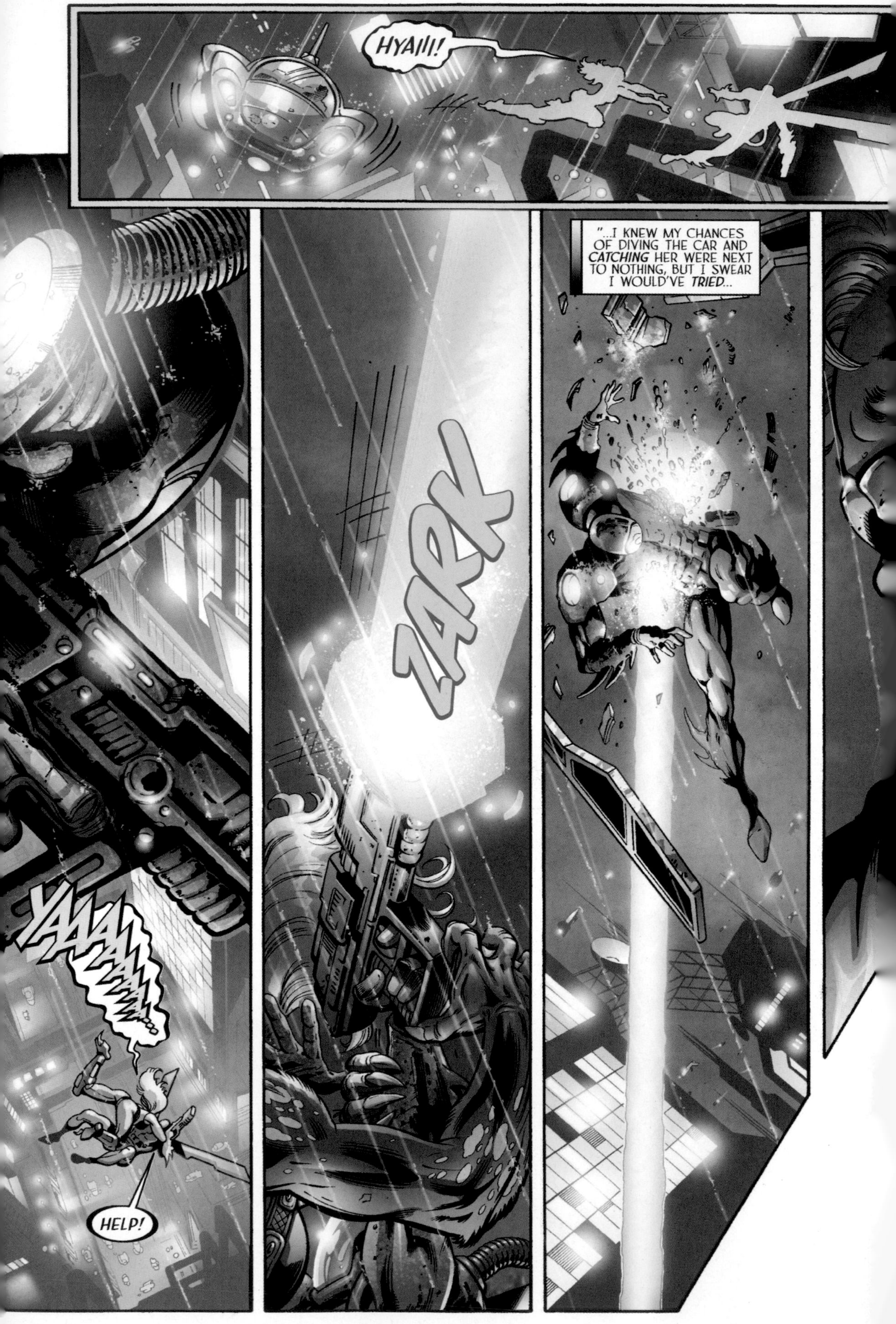
HYA!!!!
YAAAAAAAAAA...
HELP!
ZARK
"...I KNEW MY CHANCES OF DIVING THE CAR AND CATCHING HER WERE NEXT TO NOTHING, BUT I SWEAR I WOULD'VE TRIED...

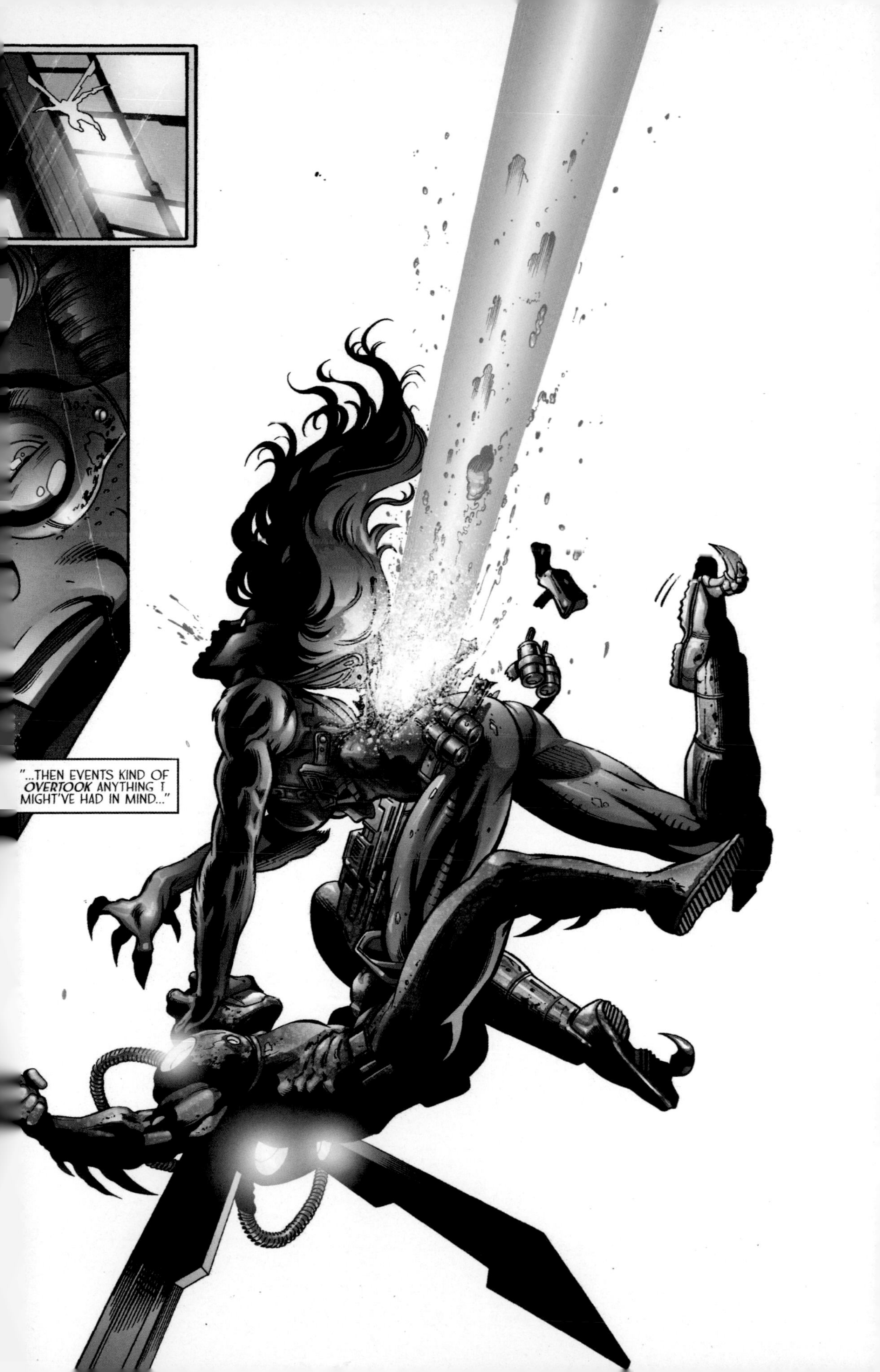
"...THEN EVENTS KIND OF
OVERTOOK ANYTHING I
MIGHT'VE HAD IN MIND..."

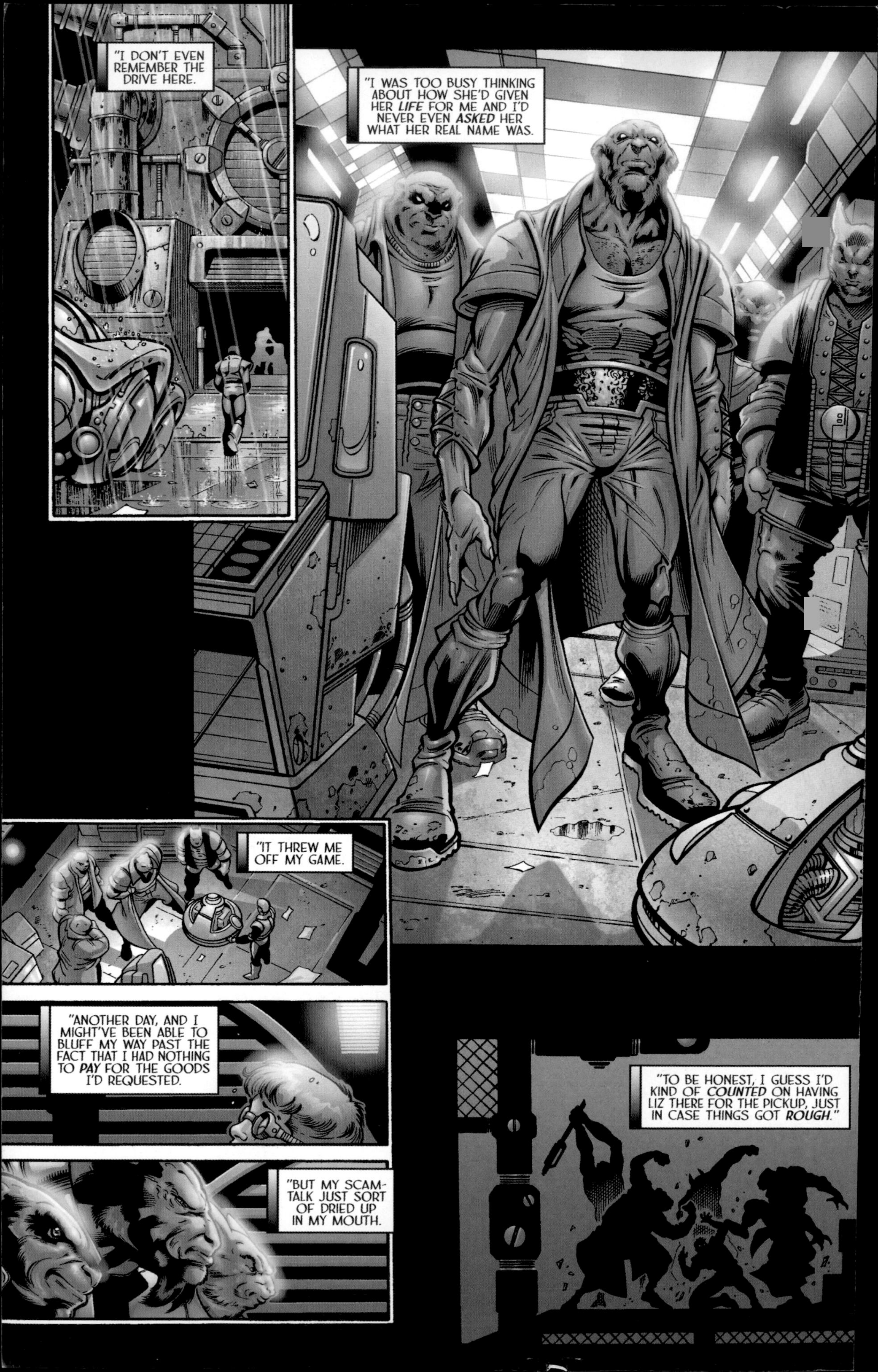
"I DON'T EVEN REMEMBER THE DRIVE HERE.
"I WAS TOO BUSY THINKING ABOUT HOW SHE'D GIVEN HER *LIFE* FOR ME AND I'D NEVER EVEN *ASKED* HER WHAT HER REAL NAME WAS.
"IT THREW ME OFF MY GAME.
"ANOTHER DAY, AND I MIGHT'VE BEEN ABLE TO BLUFF MY WAY PAST THE FACT THAT I HAD NOTHING TO *PAY* FOR THE GOODS I'D REQUESTED.
"BUT MY SCAM-TALK JUST SORT OF DRIED UP IN MY MOUTH.
"TO BE HONEST, I GUESS I'D KIND OF *COUNTED* ON HAVING LIZ THERE FOR THE PICKUP, JUST IN CASE THINGS GOT *ROUGH*."

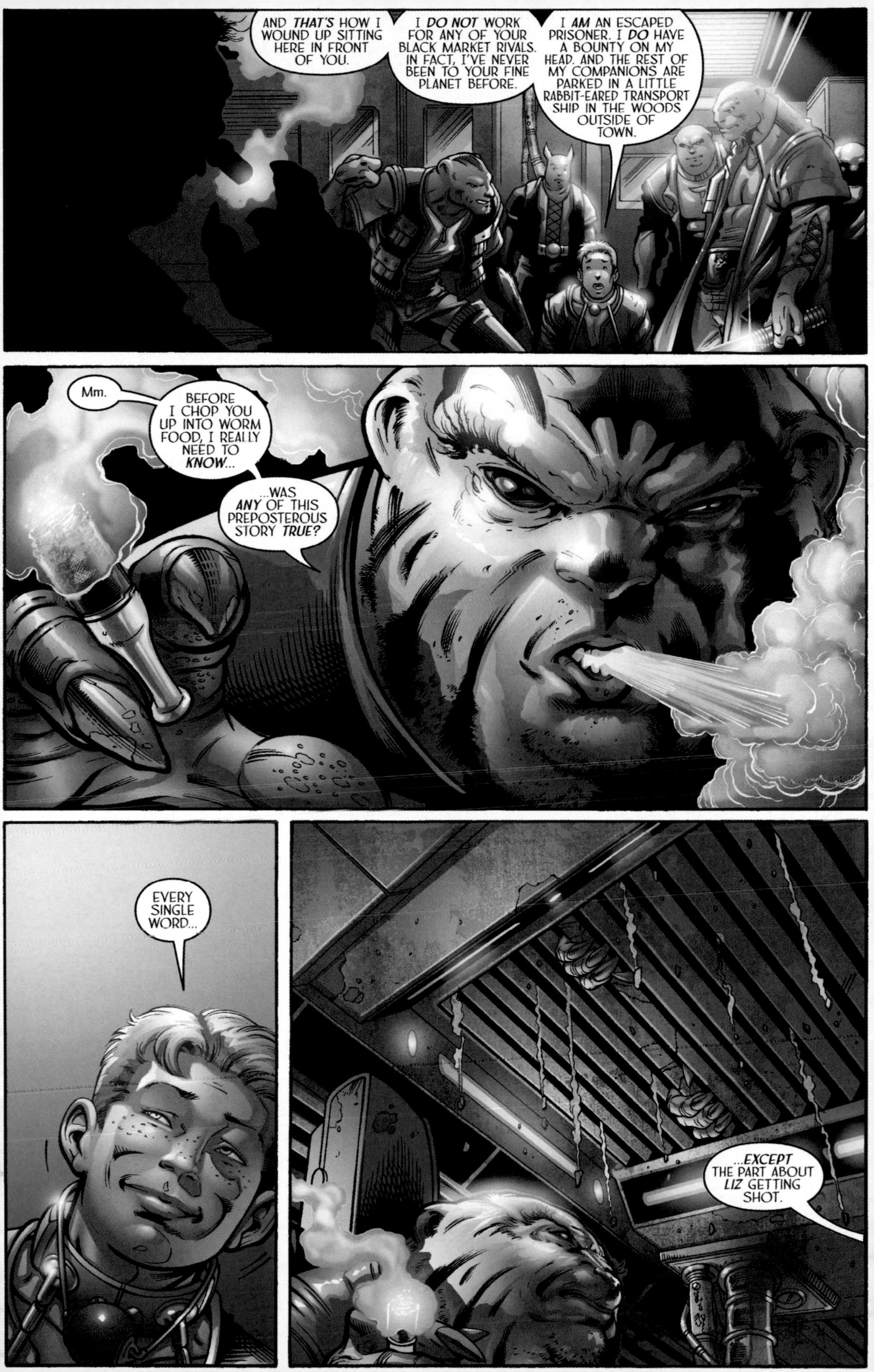
AND *THAT'S* HOW I WOUND UP SITTING HERE IN FRONT OF YOU.
I *DO NOT* WORK FOR ANY OF YOUR BLACK MARKET RIVALS. IN FACT, I'VE NEVER BEEN TO YOUR FINE PLANET BEFORE.
I *AM* AN ESCAPED PRISONER. I *DO* HAVE A BOUNTY ON MY HEAD. AND THE REST OF MY COMPANIONS ARE PARKED IN A LITTLE RABBIT-EARED TRANSPORT SHIP IN THE WOODS OUTSIDE OF TOWN.
Mm.
BEFORE I CHOP YOU UP INTO WORM FOOD, I REALLY NEED TO *KNOW*...
...WAS *ANY* OF THIS PREPOSTEROUS STORY *TRUE?*
EVERY SINGLE WORD...
...*EXCEPT* THE PART ABOUT *LIZ* GETTING SHOT.

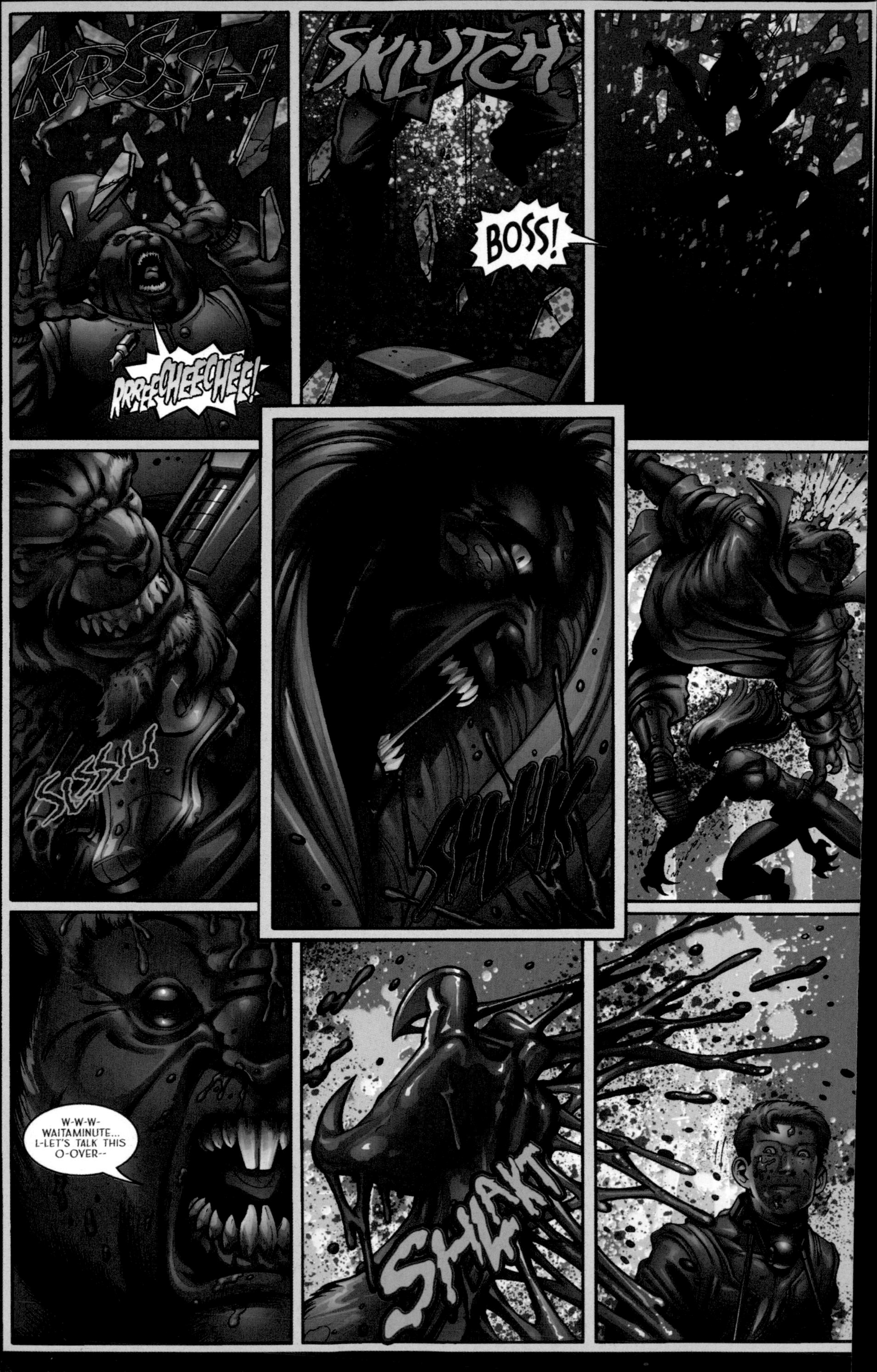
KRSSSH
RRREECHEECHEE!
SKLUTCH
BOSS!
SSSSH
SHLUK
W-W-W-
WAITAMINUTE...
L-LET'S TALK THIS
O-OVER--
SHCKT

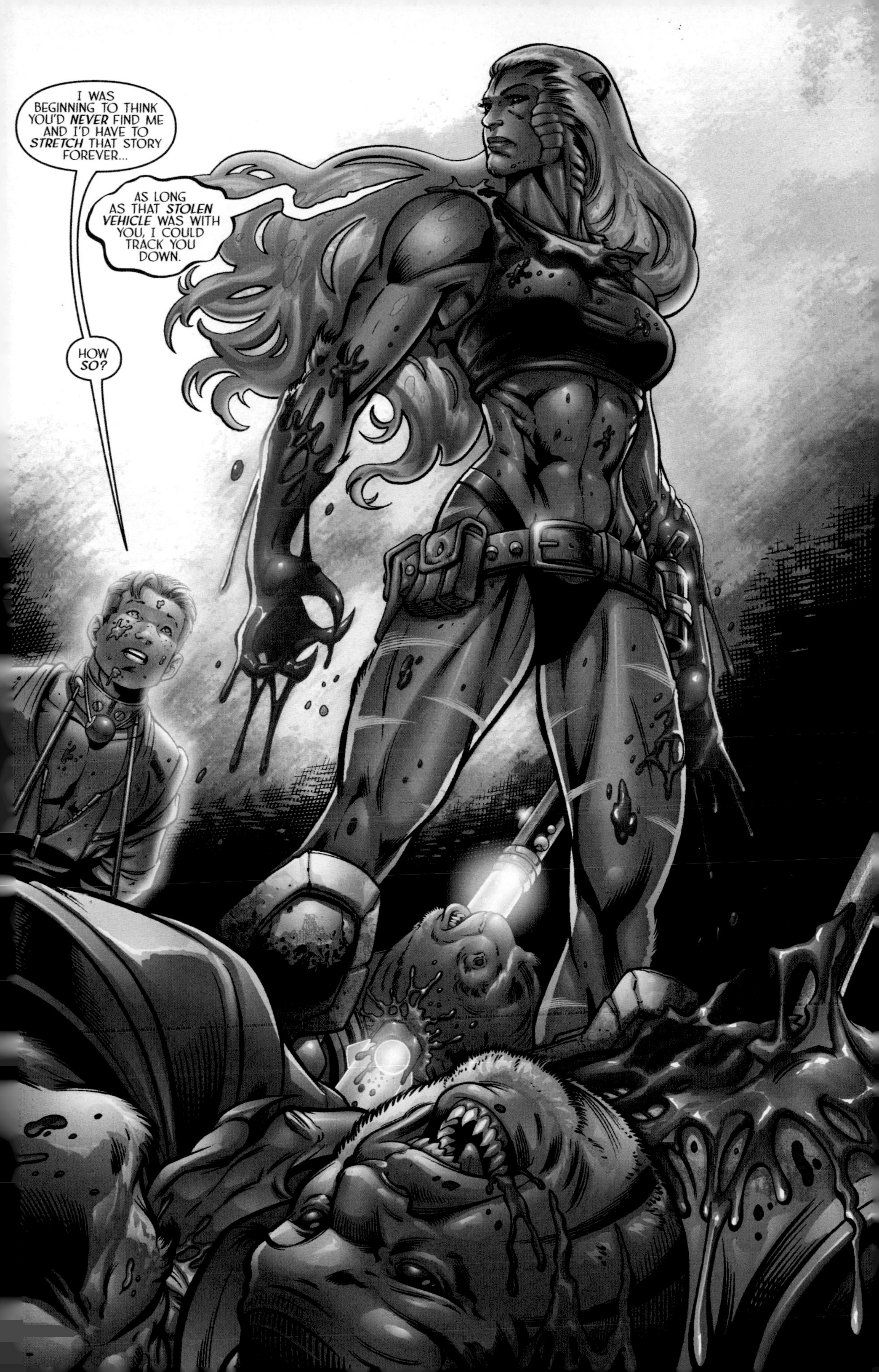
I WAS BEGINNING TO THINK YOU'D NEVER FIND ME AND I'D HAVE TO STRETCH THAT STORY FOREVER...
AS LONG AS THAT STOLEN VEHICLE WAS WITH YOU, I COULD TRACK YOU DOWN.
HOW SO?

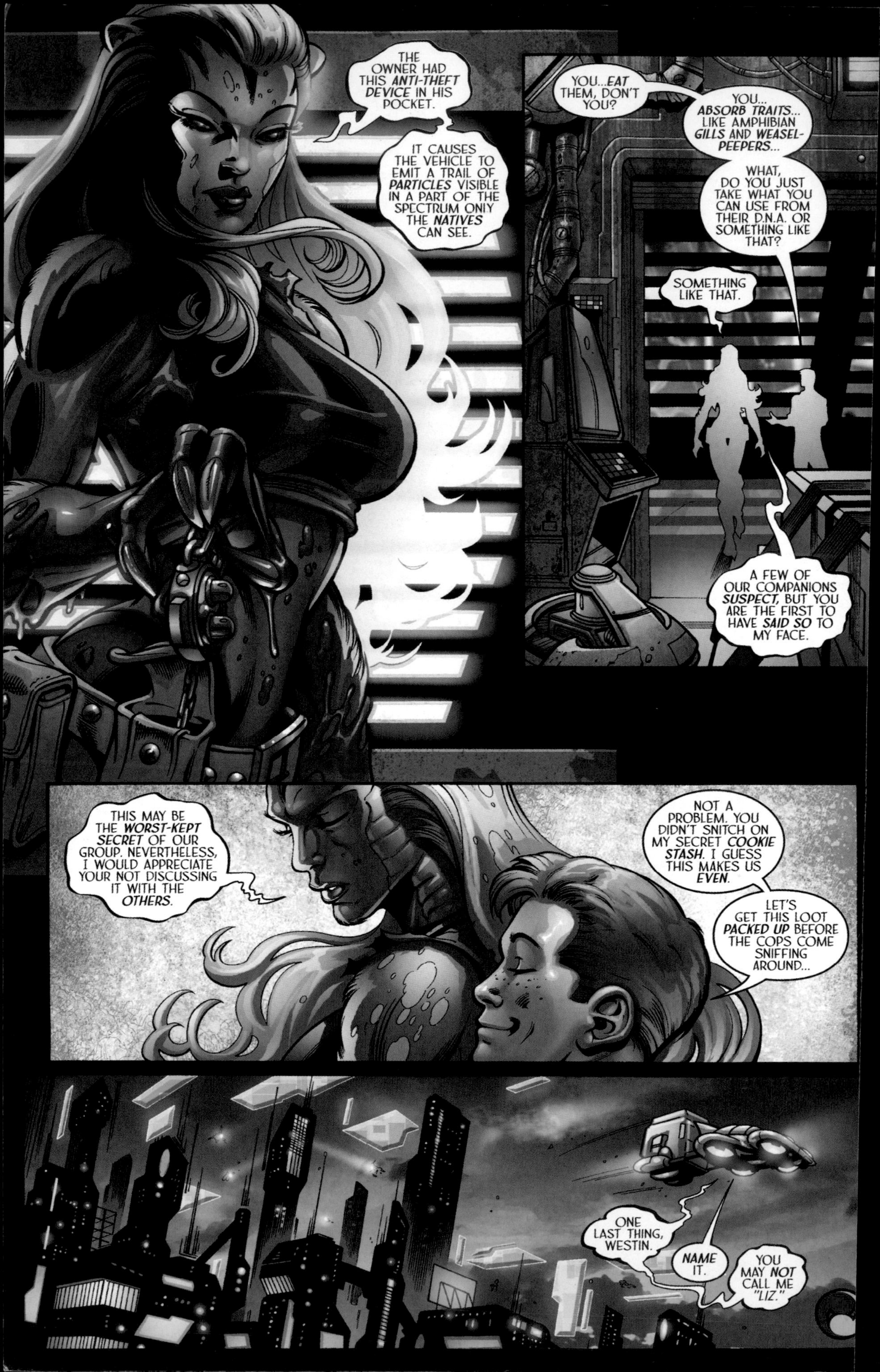
THE OWNER HAD THIS ANTI-THEFT DEVICE IN HIS POCKET.
IT CAUSES THE VEHICLE TO EMIT A TRAIL OF PARTICLES VISIBLE IN A PART OF THE SPECTRUM ONLY THE NATIVES CAN SEE.
YOU...EAT THEM, DON'T YOU?
YOU... ABSORB TRAITS... LIKE AMPHIBIAN GILLS AND WEASEL-PEEPERS...
WHAT, DO YOU JUST TAKE WHAT YOU CAN USE FROM THEIR D.N.A. OR SOMETHING LIKE THAT?
SOMETHING LIKE THAT.
A FEW OF OUR COMPANIONS SUSPECT, BUT YOU ARE THE FIRST TO HAVE SAID SO TO MY FACE.
THIS MAY BE THE WORST-KEPT SECRET OF OUR GROUP. NEVERTHELESS, I WOULD APPRECIATE YOUR NOT DISCUSSING IT WITH THE OTHERS.
NOT A PROBLEM. YOU DIDN'T SNITCH ON MY SECRET COOKIE STASH. I GUESS THIS MAKES US EVEN.
LET'S GET THIS LOOT PACKED UP BEFORE THE COPS COME SNIFFING AROUND...
ONE LAST THING, WESTIN.
NAME IT.
YOU MAY NOT CALL ME "LIZ."

STORYTELLERS

TONY BEDARD
WRITER

PAUL PELLETIER
PENCILER

DAVE MEIKIS
INKER

JAMES ROCHELLE
COLORIST

OSCAR GONGORA
LETTERER

The CrossGen Universe created by Mark Alessi & Gina M. Villa

CrossGen Entertainment, Inc.
CrossGen Intellectual Property, LLC
President Chief Executive Officer & Publisher · **Mark Alessi**
Executive Vice President Chief Operating Officer · **Joe Panfilio**
Director of Conventions & Facilities · **John Smith**
Director of Marketing & Communications · **Bill Rosemann**
Vice President Special Projects · **Brandon Peterson**
Vice President Sales · **Chris Oarr**
Director of Sales Book Trade · **Robert Boyd**
Director of Sales Direct & Foreign Markets · **James Breitbeil**
Senior Vice President Chief Financial Officer · **Michael A. Beattie**
Controller · **Brian Soltis**
Director of Human Relations · **Karla Barnett**
Office Manager · **Shirley Burdett**
Senior Vice President General Counsel · **Jennifer Hernandez**
Paralegal · **Tammy Jackson**
CrossGen Education, LLC
Vice President · **Beth Widera**
CrossGen Media, LLC; CrossGen Productions, LLC
Senior Vice President Product Development · **Tony Panaccio**

MegaCon, LLC
Director · **Beth Widera**
CrossGen Technologies. LLC; CrossGen Interactive, LLC; Comics on the Web, LLC
Senior Vice President Chief Technology Officer · **Jim Stikeleather**
Director of Information Technology · **Courtland Whited**
Internet Services Director · **Gabo Mendoza**
CrossGen Publishing, LLC; CrossGen Comics, LLC; Code 6 Comics, LLC
Senior Vice President Chief Creative Officer · **Gina M. Villa**
Director Ancillary Publishing · **Ian M. Feller**
Director of Production Control · **Charles Decker**
Vice President Writing Development · **Barbara Kesel**
Vice President Art Director · **Bart Sears**
Assistant Art Directors · **Michael Atiyeh, Butch Guice, Dave Lanphear,**
Rick Magyar, Laura Martin, Mark Pennington, Andy Smith
Freelance Coordinator · **Michelle Pugliese**
Vice President Production · **Pam Davies**
Production Supervisor Advertising/Web · **Sylvia Bretz**
Production Supervisor Books · **Janet Bechtle**
Production Designers · **Erin Flanagan & Randy Martin**
Production Assistants · **Marisol Quintana & Ron Domingue**

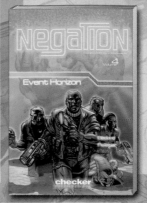